THE KNOW-IT-ALL BOOK

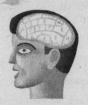

365 Steps To being Very Clever Indeed

DAVID S. KIDDER
AND NOAH D. OPPENHEIM

HODDER &
STOUGHTON

Copyright © 2007 by TID Volumes, LLC

Illustration credits on page 376

First published in Great Britain in 2007

The right of David S. Kidder and Noah D. Oppenheim to be identified as the Authors of the Work has been asserted by them in accordance with the Copyright, Designs and Patents Act 1988.

1

British Library Cataloguing in Publication Data
A record for this book is available from the British Library

ISBN 9780340954744

Offset by Avon DataSet Ltd, Bidford on Avon, Warwickshire
Printed and bound in Great Britain by Clays Ltd, St Ives plc

The paper and board used in this paperback are natural recyclable products made from wood grown in sustainable forests. The manufacturing processes conform to the environmental regulations of the country of origin.

Hodder & Stoughton
A Division of Hodder Headline Ltd
338 Euston Road, London NW1 3BH
www.madaboutbooks.com

For José and Jack—David

For Allison—Noah

Acknowledgments

This book was a collaboration. Our thanks extend to Rodale's Leigh Haber, who nurtured this project to completion. Joy Tutela of the David Black Agency was a passionate advocate and friend. Andy Carpenter and Tony Serge realized our vision. Nelson Kunkel and Vernon Steward offered critical contributions at the beginning.

Each entry was researched and composed by a writer with expertise in the relevant field of knowledge. All the entries were then reviewed for accuracy by scholars with advanced degrees.

CONTRIBUTING WRITERS

History—Alan Wirzbicki

Literature—Matt Blanchard

Visual Arts—Eric von Dorster

Science—Jennifer Drapkin

Music—Robbie Whelan

Philosophy—Frederick Stazz

Religion—Andrew Silver

CONTRIBUTING EDITORS

History—James Downs, PhD

Literature—Georgette Fleischer, PhD

Visual Arts—Irina Oryshkevich, PhD

Science—David Boyajian, MD

Music—Melissa Cox, PhD

Philosophy—Thomas Kelly, PhD

For a list of the research sources our writers employed, please visit www.theintellectualdevotional.com

Introduction

Wouldn't it be nice to know it all? Or, at least, to appear so? To wow friends, colleagues, and loved ones with your wit, wisdom, and erudition? We hope this volume is a useful tool toward that end. What follows is a compendium of 365 daily exercies in learning and reflection. Complete this one year course of study and you will find yourself the smartest in any room.

Like a fine meal, each daily reading is stimulating, refreshing, and easy to digest. Read one each day to exercise your mind, explore new fields, and reconstruct the education you've already fogot. Each entry is drawn from a different field of knowledge: History, Literature, Visual Arts, Science, Music, Philosophy, and Religion. You'll explore each subject once a week.

A brief summary of each:

MONDAY – HISTORY

A survey of people and events that shaped the development of Western civilization.

TUESDAY – LITERATURE

A look at great writers and a synopsis of their most important works – poems and novels that continue to inspire readers today.

WEDNESDAY – VISUAL ARTS

An introduction to the artists and artistic movements that yielded the world's most influential paintings, sculptures, and works of architecture.

THURSDAY – SCIENCE

From the origin of black holes to a description of how batteries work, the wonders of science are simplified and revealed.

FRIDAY – MUSIC

What inspired our greatest composers, how to read a sheet of notes, and why Mozart is so revered – a comprehensive review of our musical heritage.

SATURDAY – PHILOSOPHY

From ancient Greece to the twentieth century, the efforts of mankind's greatest thinkers to explain the meaning of life and the universe.

SUNDAY – RELIGION

An overview of the world's major religions and their beliefs.

We hope your progress through this collection of knowledge inspires your curiosity and opens new areas of exploration in your life. It might also help you win a large fortune on a quiz show.

—David S. Kidder and Noah D. Oppenheim

The Alphabet

In circa 2000 BC, the Egyptian pharaohs realized they had a problem. With each military victory over their neighbors, they captured and enslaved more prisoners of war. But the Egyptians could not pass down written orders to these slaves as they could not read hieroglyphs.

Early writing systems, such as Egyptian hieroglyphs, were extremely cumbersome and difficult to learn. These systems had thousands of characters, with each symbol representing an idea or word. Memorizing them could take years. Only a handful of Egyptians could actually read and write their complicated script.

Linguists believe that almost all modern alphabets are derived from the simplified version of hieroglyphs devised by the Egyptians four thousand years ago to communicate with their slaves. The development of an alphabet, the writing system used throughout the Western world, changed the way the ancients communicated.

In the simplified version, each character represented only a sound. This innovation cut back the number of characters from a few thousand to a few dozen, making it far easier to learn and use the characters. The complicated hieroglyphic language was eventually forgotten, and scholars were not able to translate the characters until the discovery of the Rosetta stone in 1799.

The alphabet was extremely successful. When the Egyptian slaves eventually migrated back to their home countries, they took the writing system with them. The alphabet spread across the Near East, becoming the foundation for many writing systems in the area, including Hebrew and Arabic. The Phoenicians, an ancient civilization of seaborne traders, spread the alphabet to the tribes they encountered along the Mediterranean coast. The Greek and Roman alphabets, in turn, were based on the ancient Phoenician script. Today most Western languages, including English, use the Roman alphabet.

ADDITIONAL FACTS

1. Several letters in modern-day English are direct descendents of ancient Egyptian characters. For instance, the letter B derives from the Egyptian character for the word house.

2. The most recent edition of the Oxford English Dictionary *contains 171,476 words in current usage, among the most of any language.*

Ulysses

James Joyce's *Ulysses* (1922) is widely regarded as the greatest novel written in English in the twentieth century. It retells Homer's *Odyssey* in the context of a single day—June 16, 1904—in Dublin, Ireland, recasting Homer's great hero Odysseus in the unlikely guise of Leopold Bloom, an aging, cuckolded ad salesman who spends the day running errands and making various business appointments before he returns home at long last.

Though Bloom seems unassuming and ordinary, he emerges as a heroic figure, displaying compassion, forgiveness, and generosity toward virtually everyone in the odd cast of characters he meets. In his mundane and often unnoticed deeds, he practices an everyday heroism that is perhaps the only heroism possible in the modern world. And despite the fact that he always feels like an outsider—he is a Jew in overwhelmingly Catholic Ireland—Bloom remains optimistic and dismisses his insecurities.

Ulysses is celebrated for its incredibly rich portraits of characters, its mind-boggling array of allusions to other literary and cultural works, and its many innovations with language. Throughout the course of the novel, Joyce flirts with literary genres and forms ranging from drama to advertising copy to Old English. The novel is perhaps most famous for its extensive use of stream-of-consciousness narrative—Joyce's attempt to render the inner thoughts of his characters exactly as they occur, with no effort to impose order or organization. This technique became a hallmark of modernist literature and influenced countless other writers, such as Virginia Woolf and William Faulkner, who also experimented with it in their works.

Not surprisingly, *Ulysses* poses a difficult journey for the reader, especially its famous last chapter, which recounts the thoughts of Bloom's wife, Molly. Molly's reverie goes on for more than 24,000 words yet is divided into only eight mammoth sentences. Despite the challenge it poses, the chapter shows Joyce at his most lyrical, especially in the final lines, which reaffirm Molly's love for her husband despite her infidelity:

> *and then he asked me would I yes to say yes my mountain flower and first I put my arms around him yes and drew him down to me so he could feel my breasts all perfume yes and his heart was going like mad and yes I said yes I will Yes.*

ADDITIONAL FACT
1. Ulysses *was banned for obscenity in the United States for nearly twelve years and in the United Kingdom for fourteen years, because of its (mostly indirect) sexual imagery.*

Lascaux Cave Paintings

The cave paintings at Lascaux are among the earliest known works of art. They were discovered in 1940 near the village of Montignac in central France when four boys stumbled into a cave. Inside they found a series of rooms with nearly 1,500 paintings of animals that were between 15,000 and 17,000 years old.

There are several theories regarding the function of the paintings. A natural feature of the cave may have suggested the shape of an animal to a prehistoric observer who then added highlights to relay his vision to others. Since many of the paintings are located in inaccessible parts of the cave, they may have been used for magical practices. Possibly, prehistoric people believed that the act of drawing animals, especially with a high degree of accuracy, would bring the beasts under their control or increase their numbers in times of scarcity.

The animals are outlined or portrayed in silhouette. They are often shown in what is called twisted perspective, that is, with their heads in profile but their horns facing front. Many of the images include dots, linear patterns, and other designs that may carry symbolic meaning.

The most magnificent chamber of the cave, known as the Great Hall of the Bulls, contains a painted narrative. From left to right, the pictures depict the chase and capture of a bison herd.

As soon as the paintings had been examined and identified as Paleolithic, the caves were opened to the public in 1948. By 1955, however, it became increasingly evident that exposure to as many as 1,200 visitors per day was taking its toll on the works inside. Although protective measures were taken, the site closed in 1963. In order to satisfy public demand, a life-sized replica of the cave was completed in 1983, only 200 meters from the original.

ADDITIONAL FACTS

1. *The cave painters were conscious of visual perspective; they painted figures high on the wall, styled so that they would not appear distorted to the viewer below.*

2. *The only human figure depicted in the cave appears in the* Shaft of the Dead Man. *The fact that it is drawn more crudely than the animals suggests that they did not think it was endowed with magical properties.*

Cloning

In 1997, a baby sheep named Dolly introduced the world to reproductive cloning. She was a clone because she and her mother shared the same nuclear DNA; in other words, their cells carried the same genetic material. They were like identical twins reared generations apart.

Scientists at the Roslin Institute in Scotland created Dolly by a process called *nuclear transfer.* Taking the genetic material from an adult donor cell, they transferred it into an unfertilized egg whose genetic material had been removed. In Dolly's case, the donor cell came from the mammary gland of a six-year-old Finn Dorset ewe. The researchers then gave the egg an electric shock, and it began dividing into an embryo.

One of the reasons Dolly's creation was so astounding was that it proved to the scientific community that a cell taken from a specialized part of the body could be used to create a whole new organism. Before Dolly, almost all scientists believed that once a cell became specialized it could only produce other specialized cells: A heart cell could only make heart cells, and a liver cell could only make liver cells. But Dolly was made entirely from a cell extracted from her mother's mammary gland, proving that specialized cells could be completely reprogrammed.

In many ways, Dolly was not like her mother. For example, her telomeres were too short. Telomeres are thin strands of protein that cap off the ends of chromosomes, the structures that carry genes. Although no one is sure exactly what telomeres do, they seem to help protect and repair our cells. As we age, our telomeres get shorter and shorter. Dolly received her mother's six-year-old telomeres, so from birth, Dolly's telomeres were shorter than the average lamb her age. Although Dolly appeared to be mostly normal, she was put to sleep in 2004 at the age of six, after suffering from lung cancer and crippling arthritis. The average Finn Dorset sheep lives to age eleven or twelve.

ADDITIONAL FACTS

1. Since 1997, cattle, mice, goats, and pigs have been successfully cloned using nuclear transfer.

2. The success rate for cloning is very low in all species. Published studies report that about 1 percent of reconstructed embryos survive birth. But since unsuccessful attempts largely go unreported, the actual number might be much lower.

3. Before she died, Dolly was the mother of six lambs, all bred the old-fashioned way.

4. A group of Korean researchers claimed to have cloned a human embryo in 1998, but their experiment was terminated at the 4-cell stage, so there was no evidence of their success.

The Basics

Music is organized sound that can be replicated through imitation or notation. Music is distinct from noise in that the sounds of a door creaking open or fingernails on a blackboard are irregular and disorganized. The sound waves that map these noises are complex and cannot be heard as identifiable pitches.

Some of the basic ways that we analyze musical sounds are:

PITCH: How high or how low a sound is to the ear. Pitch is measured technically by the frequency of a sound wave, or how often waves repeat themselves. In western music there are twelve unique pitches (C, C-sharp or D-flat, D, D-sharp or E-flat, E, F, F-sharp or G-flat, G, G-sharp or A-flat, A, A-sharp or B-flat, and B). The pitches followed by sharps or flats are called accidentals, and they are most easily described as the black keys on the piano keyboard. They are located musically, one half step between the two pitches on either side of them. For example, D-sharp and E-flat have the same pitch. When referring to pitches in the context of notated, or written music, they are called *notes*.

SCALE: A stepwise arrangement of pitches (for example, C, D, E, F, G, A, B, C) that often serves as the basis for a melody. A piece, or a portion of a piece, will often use only notes found in a particular scale. Western music primarily uses the major scale or the minor scale, in one form or another. To most people, the major scale, because of its particular arrangement of pitches, has the quality of sounding "bright," "happy," or "positive." A minor scale, likewise, is usually described as "dark," "sad," or "pessimistic."

KEY: An arrangement or system of pitches, usually based on one of the major or minor scales, that is meant to serve as a reference point and a guiding force of a melody. The tonic of a key is often the starting and ending point for a piece written in a particular key—so if a piece is in E major, then the pitch E will serve as the piece's tonal center.

ADDITIONAL FACTS

1. *All of these basic elements can be notated on the staff, which is a repeating set of five parallel horizontal lines. Often it is divided into measures to indicate metric divisions in the piece and marked at the beginning of each staff of the page with a clef to indicate reference points for identifying pitches.*

2. *When a piece strays from its basic key, this is called modulation. Keys are indicated in written music by a key signature at the beginning of each staff.*

3. *There are hundreds of scales used in the world's many different musical cultures. In India, music played on the sitar and other instruments chooses pitches from a collection of twenty-two possibilities, with the distances between scale steps sometimes larger and sometimes smaller than those used in Western music. This can make differences between pitches extremely subtle and demands a high virtuosity from Indian classical musicians.*

Appearance and Reality

Throughout its history, one of the great themes of philosophy has been the distinction between appearance and reality. This distinction was central to the thought of the earliest philosophers, called the *Presocratics*, because they lived before Socrates.

The Presocratics believed that the ultimate nature of reality was vastly different from the way it ordinarily appeared to them. For instance, one philosopher named Thales held that appearances notwithstanding, all reality was ultimately composed of water; Heraclitus thought the world was built from fire. Further, Heraclitus maintained that *everything* was constantly in motion. Another thinker, Parmenides, insisted that *nothing* actually moved and that all apparent motion was an illusion.

The Presocratics took seriously the possibility that all of reality was ultimately made up of some more fundamental substance. And they suspected that uncritical, everyday observation tends to present us with a misleading picture of the world. For these reasons, their thinking is often considered a precursor to modern science as well as philosophy.

Many later philosophers—including Plato, Spinoza, and Leibniz—followed in this tradition and presented alternative models of reality, which they claimed were closer to the truth than ordinary, commonsense views of the world.

ADDITIONAL FACTS

1. *The distinction between appearance and reality is also central to the venerable philosophical tradition known as* skepticism.

2. *Immanuel Kant also addressed the difference between appearance and reality. He distinguished between things we experience and what he called a "thing-in-itself."*

Torah

The Torah is the name generally given to the first five books of the Hebrew Bible, or the Five Books of Moses, and of the Old Testament of the Christian Bible. The word *Torah* can also refer to the entire breadth of Jewish law encompassing several texts as well as oral traditions.

The Five Books of Moses are the basis for the 613 laws that govern the Jewish faith, and they are the foundation for the world's three great monotheistic faiths—Judaism, Christianity, and Islam. They are as follows:

GENESIS: Tells the story of creation as well as the history of the Israelites, Abraham, Isaac, and Jacob and their families

EXODUS: Recounts the exodus from Egypt to Canaan, including Moses receiving the Ten Commandments

LEVITICUS: Contains the rules and practices of worship

NUMBERS: Relates the journey of the Israelites in the wilderness

DEUTERONOMY: Consists of speeches made by Moses at the end of his life that recount Israelite history and ethical teachings

The five books are traditionally believed to have been given to Moses on Mount Sinai. Alternative theories claim the beginning of the Torah was given on Mount Sinai but that the revelation continued throughout Moses's life.

Historically, archaeologists have argued that the Torah was written sometime between the tenth and sixth centuries BC. Proponents of the Documentary Hypothesis, which according to Orthodox Jews is heretical, claim that the original five books came from four sources, eventually compiled into one by a fifth author or redactor. The arguments in favor of this theory are the multiple names used for God, varying styles of writing, and the repetition of stories.

From the beginning, the Torah was accompanied by an oral tradition, which was necessary for its complete understanding. Although it was thought to be blasphemous to write the oral tradition down, the necessity for doing so eventually became apparent, leading to the creation of the Mishna. Later, as rabbis discussed and debated these two texts, the Talmud was written in order to compile their arguments.

The Jewish tradition uses the text of the Torah to derive innumerable laws and customs. Rabbinic scholars have spent entire lifetimes parsing every word for meaning.

ADDITIONAL FACT

1. *Torah scrolls, written in Hebrew by hand, contain 304,805 letters and may take more than a year to produce by hand. If a single mistake is made, the entire scroll becomes invalid.*

Hammurabi's Code of Laws

Hammurabi was a king of Babylonia, an ancient civilization in present-day Iraq. He ruled for forty-three years and conquered several rival nations, but he is most famous as history's first lawyer. Near the end of his reign, Hammurabi issued one of the first written codes of law in recorded history, which spelled out the rules for his citizens and the punishments for lawbreakers. The very concept of laws that applied to everyone was an unheard of novelty in Hammurabi's time, when most societies were governed only by the whims of their despotic rulers.

The code itself, however, was extremely cruel by modern standards. Hammurabi prescribed the death penalty for even minor infractions. Women who entered a tavern, men who harbored runaway slaves, and wives who left their husbands without good cause were all subject to capital punishment. The crude code reflected the superstitions of its ancient society. In disputes between Babylonian citizens, Hammurabi's code called for the accused to jump into a river. If he was guilty, he would drown. But if he was innocent, he would "escape unhurt," and the accuser would be put to death for making a false charge.

The king's scribes wrote the laws on a black stone pillar that was dedicated to the god of justice and displayed in public. In the inscription, Hammurabi called on "all coming generations" to observe the laws, and not to "alter the law of the land which I have given." Future kings, Hammurabi said, must uphold the rule of law rather than govern according to their own impulses. The notion that rulers could not arbitrarily change the laws governing their citizens was a revolutionary concept. Respect for the rule of law remains one of the fundamental hallmarks of successful governments.

ADDITIONAL FACTS

1. *The pillar that displayed Hammurabi's laws was unearthed in 1901 by a French archaeologist and now stands in the Louvre Museum in Paris.*

2. *Hammurabi's code was inscribed in cuneiform, a complex writing system used by most ancient civilizations in the Near East. Modern scholars were unable to decode cuneiform characters until 1835.*

3. *Babylonian scientists used a counting system based on the number sixty, which is why minutes have sixty seconds.*

Ernest Hemingway

Among the major American writers of the twentieth century, few have been as influential or imitated as Ernest Hemingway (1899–1961)—and few have had as many detractors. Renowned for his novels and short stories, Hemingway became such a public figure during his life—and constructed such an extensive mythology around himself—that it is sometimes difficult to separate the legend from the reality.

Born in Oak Park, Illinois, in 1899, Hemingway had writerly aspirations early on; by eighteen, he was employed as a reporter for the *Kansas City Star*. Within months, he landed a position as a Red Cross ambulance driver on the Italian front in World War I, where he was wounded. After the war, he spent several years in Paris in the company of Gertrude Stein and other expatriate American writers of the so-called Lost Generation, who were disillusioned by the war's brutality. In Paris Hemingway refined his trademark style—a repetitive, stripped-down, self-consciously masculine prose that is deceptive in its seeming simplicity.

After writing a number of short stories based on his boyhood summers in upper Michigan and his later travels through Europe, Hemingway penned his first major novel, *The Sun Also Rises* (1926). This book, about a disaffected young American whiling away time in Spain and France, brought Hemingway instant acclaim. He followed with *A Farewell to Arms* (1929), a tragic World War I romance between an American ambulance driver and an English nurse, and *For Whom the Bell Tolls* (1940), a tale of guerrillas in the Spanish Civil War that was inspired by Hemingway's own work as a journalist during the conflict. The protagonist of the latter novel epitomizes what many have termed the "Hemingway code hero"—a stoic, disillusioned male who exhibits grace and nobility in the face of violence and adversity.

As his fame increased, Hemingway earned—and cultivated—a reputation for writing only about war, bullfighting, hunting, big-game fishing, and other overtly masculine topics. Though some critics dismissed Hemingway's work as macho posturing, the undeniably masterful storytelling of his novella *The Old Man and the Sea* (1952) earned him the Nobel Prize for Literature in 1954. Even with this crowning achievement, Hemingway spent his last years mired in depression and declining health, ultimately taking his own life with a shotgun in 1961. His influence on the style of the modern novel, however, remains monumental.

ADDITIONAL FACT

1. *The annual Imitation Hemingway Contest draws hundreds of entries that pay mock homage to the author's unmistakable style. Past honorees include pieces entitled* The Old Man and the Flea *and* For Whom the Cash Flows.

Bust of Nefertiti

One of the most famous works of Egyptian art, the limestone bust of Nefertiti was discovered in 1912 by German archeologist Ludwig Borchardt near the modern Egyptian town of Tell el-Amârna. It was found in the workshop of the ancient sculptor Thutmose and smuggled out of the country disguised as pieces of broken pottery.

Nefertiti was the most important queen of Pharaoh Amenhotep IV, who ruled Egypt from 1353 to 1335 BC. During his rule, the pharaoh changed his name to Akhenaton—"one who serves Aten, the Sun God"—and embraced a new, monotheistic religion that emphasized ethics. Nefertiti was granted high status, equal nearly to that of her husband. Some scholars believe that she was the force behind the new religion and that she even ruled as co-regent for some time. After Akhenaton's death, nearly all traces of him and his powerful wife were wiped out, perhaps by the priests whose religion they had rejected.

Nefertiti's bust, which is nearly 3,400 years old and about twenty inches tall, was found in nearly perfect condition. Only the earlobes were chipped. The work was left unfinished, however, since the left eye socket seems never to have been filled. It is possible that Thutmose used the bust as a model for his pupils. Whether the bust captures the queen's likeness or portrays an ideal beauty is open to question.

A controversy erupted in 2003 when Joann Fletcher, a British archeologist funded by the Discovery Channel, identified a previously discovered mummy as Nefertiti. Although she offered substantial evidence, Egyptian authorities rejected her claims.

The bust can be seen today at the Altes Museum in Berlin. It remains not only one of the best known works of Egyptian art but also a model of feminine beauty, giving new significance to Nefertiti's name, which translates to "the beautiful one is come."

ADDITIONAL FACTS

1. In the last days of World War II, the bust of Nefertiti was moved out of the Soviet sector of Berlin, creating a dispute over its ownership. It was returned sixty-six years later, in 2005.

2. A Google search for Nefertiti turns up 1,820,000 hits, a testimony to the lasting power of her image in the twenty-first century.

3. A pair of Hungarian artists calling themselves Little Warsaw recently stirred a controversy by setting the bust of Nefertiti atop a headless sculpture of a woman in a transparent garment.

Eratosthenes

Many scientists in Ancient Greece believed the world was round. But none of them knew how big it was until the third century BC when Eratosthenes (276–194 BC), chief librarian of Alexandria, devised an ingenious way to measure the earth's size.

Eratosthenes knew of a special well near Syene, Egypt. At noon on June 21, the longest day of the year, the sun's rays penetrated all the way to the bottom of the well. This meant that the sun was directly overhead. Eratosthenes realized that if the sun was directly overhead in Syene, then its rays must be hitting at an angle in Alexandria, which was due north. If he could measure the angle by which the sun was off center, then he would have the clue he needed to extrapolate the size of the earth. So, at noon on June 21 in Alexandria, he took a measuring stick and captured the angle cast by its shadow.

Eratosthenes knew that the angle of the shadow was equivalent to the angle formed by the two cities and the center of the earth. So, he divided the size of that angle by 360, the number of degrees in a circle, to determine the fraction of the earth that separated the two cities. The answer was one-fiftieth. In other words, if you walked back and forth between Syene and Alexandria fifty times, then you would have walked the equivalent of the earth's circumference.

All that remained was to measure the precise distance between the two cities. Eratosthenes hired a pacer, a professional walker trained in taking perfectly equal steps. From the measurements of the pacer, Eratosthenes estimated the circumference of earth to be 24,700 miles. Today, using the exact same principles developed by Eratosthenes 2,000 years ago, modern instruments estimate the distance around the equator to be 24,902 miles.

In Eratosthenes's time, the known world extended from Spain to India. He believed that a vast ocean covered the rest of the world. If it weren't for the enormity of the ocean, Eratosthenes thought it would be possible to sail from Spain to India by heading west. It was this idea that inspired Chistopher Columbus to undertake his famous voyage in 1492.

ADDITIONAL FACTS

1. Eratosthenes was the first historian to seriously attempt to put historical events in chronological order. We use his dates for most of ancient history.

2. We also owe to Eratosthenes many modern concepts like longitude, latitude, musical scales, and prime numbers.

3. Other scientists in Eratosthenes's time nicknamed him Beta, and it wasn't because he was the coolest boy in his fraternity. Eratosthenes had so many interests that his contemporaries considered him a dabbler. To them, he was second-class, a beta.

Melody

Melody, often referred to in everyday speech as the *tune,* is perhaps the most immediately recognizable element of music. A melody can be played on one instrument or many and, along with harmony and rhythm, is considered one of the three basic elements of all music.

A melody is a succession of pitches arranged in a tuneful sequence. The pitches make some sort of coherent sense or seem to belong together. Melody is distinct from harmony in that melody refers to several notes played one after another, not sounded as in polyphony.

Over time, the definition of melody has grown to include sequences of notes that would have seemed adventurous or even harsh to the ears of older composers. Mozart, Schubert, and Sibelius are held up as melody-making geniuses. On the other hand, modernists like Stravinsky wrote melodies—for example, the haunting tune that starts his ballet, *Rite of Spring*—that many composers of the eighteenth and nineteenth centuries, and indeed, even some audiences today, would consider unmelodic noise.

Usually melodies are divided into shorter musical units called phrases. These phrases generally end at resting points that are called cadences. Often the phrases that usually comprise the overall structure of a melody give the impression of a question and answer. One part of the melody poses a musical idea, and another completes it. If a phrase ends on a note that indicates an unresolved, or incomplete-sounding cadence, the whole phrase is referred to as an antecedent. Likewise, the following phrase with its complete-sounding cadence is referred to as a consequent.

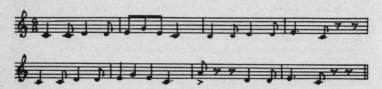

ADDITIONAL FACTS

1. In the Middle Ages, many composers would often share simple stock melodies such as the fifteenth-century French tune "L'homme armé" ("The Armed Man") as the central themes to their pieces.

2. More modern melodies, like "Twinkle, Twinkle, Little Star," have been shared in the same way, but in modern times a much higher premium has been placed on the talent that goes into writing an original melody.

3. The practice of arranging a melody or an entire piece for a large ensemble of different instruments is called orchestration. There are entire conservatory courses dedicated to this subject, and some composers are respected particularly for their ability to orchestrate.

Socrates

Widely considered the founder of Western philosophy, Socrates (469–399 BC) never wrote a single book. We know of him only secondhand, from what other people wrote about him.

Born in Athens, Greece, in the fifth century BC, Socrates distinguished himself as a soldier in one of Athens's many wars, and afterward became a curious figure in Athenian society. He would converse with whomever he could find, especially the young men of the city. Unlike the Sophists—paid teachers who traveled the country teaching young men rhetoric and other political skills—Socrates did not receive payment, and more important, *he claimed to have nothing to teach!* Socrates said he had no actual knowledge and that if he was wiser than others, it was only because he was aware of his own ignorance.

Most of what we know about Socrates comes from his greatest student, Plato (427-347 BC). Many scholars believe that Plato's earlier dialogues are the most accurate representation of the historical Socrates and the way he treated philosophy. In these dialogues, Socrates typically confronts a fellow Athenian who claims to know something—for instance, the nature of justice. Socrates then proceeds to prove his neighbor does not know what he claims at all.

In 399 BC, Socrates was put on trial for corrupting the youth of Athens with his teachings. At his trial—recorded by Plato in the dialogue *Apology*—Socrates made his famous claim that the unexamined life is not worth living. He pleaded his innocence, but was convicted. Socrates was put to death by being forced to drink hemlock, a poison. His last hours, spent discussing philosophy with his friends and admirers, are movingly documented in Plato's dialogue *Phaedo.*

ADDITIONAL FACTS

1. *The Socratic Method, still used by professors in many law schools, is based on Socrates's style of aggressively questioning his students.*

2. *Many of Socrates' contemporaries remarked on how ugly he was.*

3. *The comic poet Aristophanes (448–380 BC) pokes fun at Socrates in his play* The Clouds.

Noah

Noah is the remarkable figure in the Genesis flood story. According to this story, God surveyed creation and became angry at mankind's sins. He regretted creating humans and resolved to destroy them all. Before doing so, however, God noticed Noah.

Noah was blameless and God decided to save him from certain destruction. God told Noah that in seven days he would make it rain for forty days and forty nights, causing a great and terrible flood. Noah was instructed to build an ark large enough to hold himself, his wife, his three sons and their wives, and a pair (one male and one female) of every animal that existed. In this way, Noah would be able to replenish the earth.

Noah followed God's instructions, loading the animals and his family into the ark. After forty days, the rains ended, but the ground was still submerged. In order to determine when the waters had receded, Noah opened a window and sent out a dove.

Finally, after 150 days at sea and another 100 grounded on Mount Ararat, the land was dry enough for Noah to begin the replenishing process. Noah emptied his ark, allowing the animals to mate. God then told Noah that he, too, should "be fruitful and multiply" (Genesis 8:17). God also promised Noah that he would never again destroy humankind and symbolized this covenant with the appearance of a rainbow.

Christian and Jewish historians and theologians give slightly different interpretations to the Noah story. For Christians, Noah represents an ideal faith in God—marked by trust and obedience and for which Noah and his family were saved. For Jewish interpreters, Noah represents a reluctant faith marked by Noah being one of the last to enter the ark as a sign of reluctance. This suggests his faith may not have been so strong. Despite their differences, both traditions view Noah and the flood as critical expressions of the religious narratives.

ADDITIONAL FACTS

1. *The story of Noah includes the first appearance of wine in the Bible. After the flood, Noah gets drunk and his sons discover him uncovered.*

2. *God's command to Noah, "Be fruitful and multiply," is also given to Adam and Eve [Genesis 1:28] and Jacob [Genesis 35:11].*

Sparta vs. Athens:
The Battle for the Ancient World

Sparta, a small city in the rugged mountains of southern Greece, fielded the most feared military in the ancient world. Spartan soldiers, hardened by grueling training that began at birth, never lost a battle in the bloody conflicts that raged almost constantly between the small city-states of ancient Greece. To build this remarkable army, elders in Sparta tested every newborn for weakness and deformities. Babies deemed unlikely to become strong soldiers were tossed into a gorge. For those that passed the test, training was cruel and relentless. The Greek historian and essayist Plutarch wrote that for many of the Spartan soldiers marching to battle was a relief: "For the Spartans, actual war was a holiday compared to their tough training."

The rivalry between militaristic Sparta and its neighbor Athens dominated the history of ancient Greece. Athens, the birthplace of democracy, was a far less rigid society. Unlike Sparta, where there was little time for culture, Athens was home to some of the most extraordinary accomplishments of philosophy, art, and science in human history. The playwrights Aeschylus, Aristophanes, Euripides, and Sophocles, as well as philosophers Aristotle, Plato, and Socrates were born in Athens during the city's golden age in the fifth century BC.

While Athens and Sparta temporarily joined forces to defeat two attempted Persian invasions, they spent much of the classical period competing for the leadership of the Hellenic world. When the cities fought, as they did repeatedly between about 550 and 350 BC, it was a clash of civilizations in the fullest sense. While Sparta's famed soldiers held the advantage on land, Athens made up the difference with its sea power. The rivalry came to an abrupt end when Philip of Macedonia invaded from the north. The Greek city-states were swallowed up into the empire that Philip and his son, Alexander the Great, extended over much of Greece and Asia.

ADDITIONAL FACTS

1. Sparta was the capital of the Greek region of Laconia. The word laconic in modern English is derived from the taciturn attitude of hardened Spartan soldiers.

2. To prove their toughness, Spartan boys competed to see how much whipping they could endure.

3. Many of the buildings on the Acropolis in Athens, including the famous Parthenon, were constructed during the city's golden age in the fifth century BC.

The Harlem Renaissance

The Harlem Renaissance, or New Negro movement as it was originally christened, was a flourishing of African-American literature and art in the Harlem neighborhood of New York City in the 1920s and early 1930s. The stage for this rebirth was set when millions of newly freed southern blacks, after enduring the hardships of slavery and Reconstruction in the 1800s, moved to New York and other northern cities in an exodus known as the Great Migration. By the end of World War I, a poor but culturally vibrant black community had taken root in Harlem.

Much of the foundation of the Harlem Renaissance was set by the African-American historian and social theorist W. E. B. DuBois, famous for his sociological treatise *The Souls of Black Folk* (1903) and for his role in the founding of the NAACP in 1909. DuBois asserted a new sense of black cultural consciousness and pride, inspiring a generation of young writers and artists to create a distinctive African-American voice.

One of the leading writers of the Harlem Renaissance was James Weldon Johnson, who penned the novel *Autobiography of an Ex-Colored Man* (1912) and the celebrated collection of verse sermons entitled *God's Trombones* (1927). Johnson was followed by Nella Larsen and Zora Neale Hurston, whose respective novels *Passing* (1929) and *Their Eyes Were Watching God* (1937) were among the first critically acclaimed major literary works by African-American women.

The Harlem Renaissance produced an especially rich body of poetry. Whereas some of the movement's poets, such as Countee Cullen, relied on traditional forms, others, such as Langston Hughes, incorporated rhythms from the newly burgeoning genre of jazz music into their works. Such links between the music and literature of the Harlem Renaissance were inextricable, and major figures in the two fields inspired one another throughout the movement.

In the 1930s, the Harlem Renaissance waned as the Great Depression hit the black community in New York particularly hard. Nonetheless, the new styles and themes pioneered during the era endured, paving the way for Ralph Ellison, Richard Wright, Lorraine Hansberry, Toni Morrison, Alice Walker, and others among the new generations of African-American novelists, poets, and playwrights.

ADDITIONAL FACT

1. *The Harlem Renaissance era also saw the emergence of a number of notable black painters, including Palmer Hayden, Lois Mailou Jones, and William H. Johnson.*

The Parthenon

Commissioned by the famous statesman Pericles, the Parthenon was constructed between 447 and 432 BC to celebrate the victory of the Greeks over the Persians. Situated over the site of an earlier temple on the Acropolis in Athens, it was dedicated to Athena Parthenos, the patron deity of the city. The building is one of the most well-preserved Greek temples in existence.

According to the ancient author Plutarch, the Parthenon was built by the architects Ictinus and Callicrates. The thirty-eight-foot effigy inside was created by the classical sculptor Phidias, who also supervised the extensive sculpture of the structure's exterior.

Ancient Greek temples were generally rectangular and accessible from all sides by stairs. Many, like the Parthenon, had columns that extended around the periphery. When building temples, the Greeks tended to follow the rules of one of three architectural orders—Doric, Ionic, or Corinthian. The orders are easily recognizable by their differing proportions and their capitals—the carved tops of their columns. Unlike most Greek temples that were built according to the rules of one particular order, the Parthenon combined elements of two—the Doric and Ionic. Its architects also made use of optical refinements, that is, slight distortions that enhanced the appearance of the building. For example, the base of the building and the roofline gently bow upward because if they were perfectly straight, the naked eye would perceive them as sagging. Similarly the columns are thicker toward the bottom, a refinement that makes them appear taller to a viewer standing at their base.

Originally, the Parthenon had a wooden ceiling and a tiled roof, and it was painted in bright colors. Square reliefs or metopes ran around the temple above the columns and depicted mythological battles that served as metaphors for the Greek victory over the Persians. A continuous frieze illustrating the annual festival of Athena Parthenos appeared beneath and behind the columns on the four walls of the building itself.

The Parthenon was used as a house of worship for many centuries after the fall of Athens. It was converted into a church in the sixth century, then into a mosque by the Turks who conquered Greece in 1458. During a battle in 1687, a Venetian shell landed on a Turkish powder keg stored in the temple and destroyed much of the building.

In 1801, Lord Elgin, the British ambassador to the Ottoman Court in Istanbul, received permission to ship the most well-preserved of the Parthenon's sculptures to England, where he eventually sold them to the British government. Today they can be seen at the British Museum despite efforts on the part of the Greeks to have the works returned. The temple itself has been visited by countless tourists since the Greeks regained control of Athens in 1832.

The Solar System

At school, we were taught that the solar system consists of the sun, nine planets, and their moons. It's not that simple.

No one really knows how many planets there are because there is no settled scientific definition of a planet. All astronomers agree upon the validity of the four terrestrial planets—Mercury, Venus, Earth, and Mars—and the four gaseous giants—Jupiter, Saturn, Uranus, and Neptune—but arctic Pluto is a matter of great dispute.

Pluto is about two-thirds the size of our moon and takes 248 years to orbit the sun. The tiny ice planet travels in a strange elliptical orbit on a different plane than the other eight. Its coldness, distance from the other planets, and warped path around the sun has led many scientists to believe that it is really a comet in the Kuiper Belt, a region of icy debris on the outskirts of the solar system.

Pluto has a recently discovered rival on the Kuiper Belt, a hunk of frozen rock officially referred to as 2003 UB313 but informally called Xena. The object is three times farther from the sun than Pluto and has an even stranger 560-year orbit, tilted 45 degrees off the plane of the rest of the planets. But 2003 UB313 is larger than Pluto, and many scientists feel that if Pluto deserves to be called a planet, then it does, too.

ADDITIONAL FACTS

1. *Two other large frozen objects in the Kuiper Belt—Quaoar and Sedna—are almost as big as Pluto. They may become the eleventh and twelfth planets.*

2. *Astronomer Michael E. Brown discovered 2003 UB313 and nicknamed it Xena after the TV show starring Lucy Lawless as an ancient Greek warrior princess. He hopes to make Xena the official name.*

3. *Our solar system has 153 known moons, but that number is highly contested.*

4. *Seven moons in the solar system are larger than Pluto. This includes Jupiter's Io, which has an atmosphere and active volcanoes.*

Harmony

Music may start with a melody, but harmony is what gives it color. Harmony refers to the sounding of two or more different pitches in unison, but the mechanics of harmony are vast and complicated, and many theorists have spent the better part of their careers analyzing it.

The distance between two notes is referred to as an interval, and intervals are expressed numerically. For example, the distance from A to E is called a fifth. The earliest polyphonic music was written in the Middle Ages, and at that point composers favored the hollow-sounding intervals of the fourth (i.e., C to F or D to G) and the fifth. Therefore, melodies would be followed by a parallel harmonic line one fourth or one fifth below.

By the Renaissance, however, the triad had become the main unit of harmony, remained so for centuries, and still is in many types of music. Triads are chords, or a combination of three or more notes heard simultaneously or in close succession, based on the interval of the third (i.e., E to G or B to D). The precise intervals that make up chords are what give them the quality of being major (bright, happy-sounding) or minor (dark, sad-sounding). The notes that make up a triad can also be rearranged to create an inversion, which is another tool that is used to vary harmony.

Harmony has many functions: to "add clothing" to a piece of music, to give music more depth, to echo or complement a melody line, or just to provide a grounded accompaniment beneath a melody. Harmony that pleases the ear or seems stable or at rest is called consonance, while that which sounds harsh, unfamiliar, or unstable is called dissonance. Without the instability of temporary dissonance, tonal music would be boring; without the stability of consonance, it would be unsatisfying. The idea of what is consonant, or acceptable to our ears, has broadened over the course of music history. Even the question of whether consonance is essential has become debatable.

ADDITIONAL FACTS

1. *Johann Sebstian Bach was known to construct masterful harmonies in his choral works, and in the twentieth century, Claude Debussy's works were often driven by lush, shifting harmonies rather than by their melodies.*

2. *Sixth-century philosopher Pythagoras believed that the "purest" harmonies were based on mathematical ratios like 2:1, 3:2, and 4:3. He formulated this theory while listening to the sounds produced by blacksmiths hammering anvils of various sizes at the same time.*

3. *The word harmony comes from the Greek* harmonia, *which means " fastening" or "to join."*

Plato

Plato (429–347 BC) was born in fifth-century Athens to a wealthy family. A young Athenian of his station would have been expected to pursue politics, but instead Plato followed the path of his mentor, Socrates (470–399 BC), and became a philosopher.

Plato's philosophical writings are dialogues in which two or more characters discuss a philosophical issue. The main character in most of Plato's dialogues is Socrates. Since Plato never speaks in the dialogues, scholars face the question: How much of what Plato puts into Socrates' mouth is Plato's own philosophy, and how much is just a report of Socrates? Many scholars believe Plato's earlier dialogues are historically accurate accounts of Socrates' teachings. Later, they believe, Socates became a literary character for Plato's own purposes.

Plato is best known for his theory of forms—abstract, immaterial things imitated by the physical objects of this world.

Another famous Platonic view is that all knowledge is recollection. Plato believed the soul was immaterial and existed before it inhabited a body. Before it was embodied, the soul knew the forms, without being distracted and limited by sensory perception. When human beings come to know something, it is because our souls recollect what they knew before they were embodied.

Furthermore, Plato divided the soul into three parts: the appetitive part (which desires sensual pleasure like food, drink, and sex), the spirited part (which desires glory and honor), and the rational part (which desires to understand the forms). In the dialogue *The Republic,* Plato describes what it is for a soul to be just, by drawing an extended analogy between a just soul and a just city. Plato describes the perfectly just city as having groups of citizens that correspond to the three parts of the soul. He believed those groups must harmoniously interact in the same way that the three parts of the soul should. In both cases, the soul and the city, Plato believed that the rational should dominate.

ADDITIONAL FACTS

1. Plato appears only in one of his dialogues, Apology, *which describes the trial of Socrates, at which he is sentenced to death. Plato says nothing in the dialogue, but his inclusion indicates that he was present at the actual event.*

2. Plato was the teacher of Aristotle (384–322 BC).

Cain and Abel

Cain and Abel were the eldest sons of Adam and Eve, born after their expulsion from the Garden of Eden. Cain, the elder, was the first human being to be born—as opposed to being created—according to the Torah. Cain tilled the Earth while Abel was a shepherd, herding lambs.

One day, God asked Cain and Abel to each make a sacrifice to him. It is said that Abel thought very hard about what kind of sacrifice would make God happiest. He decided to sacrifice one of his precious lambs. Cain, on the other hand, thought only about what he needed least. He sacrificed some fruit and grain. God clearly preferred Abel's sacrifice.

Cain quickly became jealous of his younger brother and murdered him. When God came to look for Abel, he could not find him. He asked Cain where Abel was. Cain replied, "I don't know. Am I my brother's keeper?" (Genesis 4:9)

After God realized what Cain had done, he punished him with a curse; he could no longer farm and had to wander for the rest of his life. Cain worried he would be harmed by people he met, so God placed a protective marking on him.

Besides the religious and moral lessons, the Cain and Abel story illustrates the historical conflict between people who were using the sparse fertile land for growing crops and those who were using it to raise livestock. A similar tale appears in Sumerian culture about a beautiful goddess forced to choose between two suitors: a farmer god and a shepherd god.

ADDITIONAL FACTS

1. *The nature of the mark placed on Cain is not described. Some claim that it was a mark on his face or red hair. Still others argue that it was black skin, a theory later used to justify slavery.*

2. *In some Muslim versions of the story, Abel is claimed to have offered no resistance while his brother murdered him and is seen as a symbol of pacifism.*

Alexander the Great

Alexander the Great (356–323 BC) was born in Macedonia, a mountainous kingdom in northern Greece, and educated by the famous Athenian teacher Aristotle. His father, King Philip II, had expanded Macedonia's territory to include most of the ancient city-states of Greece, including Athens. Alexander inherited his father's crown at age twenty, following Philip's assassination at a theater.

As king, Alexander surpassed his father by engineering an amazing string of conquests, creating an empire that encompassed much of the Mediterranean world at the time. No other king had dominated such a wide swath of the ancient world. From his base in Macedonia, Alexander's armies conquered Greece, Syria, Egypt, Mesopotamia, and the Persian Empire. In 330 BC, six years after he became king, Alexander defeated Darius, the king of Persia. Alexander eventually extended his kingdom as far as India. His reign ended abruptly when he died in the ancient city of Babylon at age thirty-three.

The empire Alexander created was divided among his officers, but it continued on for hundreds of years until it was conquered by the Romans. In the conquered territories, Alexander and his troops had encountered new civilizations with different customs. Rather than simply destroy the cultures of defeated nations, the Greeks absorbed them. A new, hybrid culture known as Hellenism emerged. For the first time in history, a large part of southeastern Europe and the Near East spoke the same language and shared a cultural background. Greek remained the *lingua franca* of the ancient world for centuries; the books of the New Testament were originally written in Greek. The cultural ferment caused by the arrival of Alexander's armies remains perhaps his most meaningful legacy to the modern world.

Alexander remains of great interest today. Contemporary historians continue to examine his ruthless command of the army, his love for horses, his study of philosophy, and, more recently, they have questioned his sexual orientation.

ADDITIONAL FACTS

1. *When Alexander was a child, he was unhappy with his father's conquests. According to Plutarch, the young Alexander was sad that there would be less left for him to conquer when he became king.*

2. *After conquering Egypt, Alexander founded the city of Alexandria on the Mediterranean coast, one of a dozen cities he named after himself. In Alexandria, the Greeks built a gigantic library to house thousands of parchments. The library burned down a few centuries later, destroying a vast amount of knowledge about the ancient world.*

3. *Alexander was an avid hunter, who reportedly hunted 4,000 animals, including lions, during a single hunt in what is now known as Uzbekistan. Ancient Greeks hunted game with a spear, a net, and little else.*

Paradise Lost

John Milton's epic poem *Paradise Lost* (1667) is a vast, detailed rendition of mankind's fall from innocence told in the Biblical book of Genesis. Considered the finest epic poem in English, Milton's masterpiece is important not only as a landmark in Western literature but also as an influential work of the Protestant Reformation.

Paradise Lost is written in blank verse—unrhymed iambic pentameter, a structure with five two-syllable feet per line. Shakespeare used blank verse in many of his plays, but Milton significantly expanded its possibilities and applications. He also made extensive use of the epic simile, a type of long, complex comparison that Homer and other classical poets used frequently in their epics.

As *Paradise Lost* opens, Satan and the other fallen angels have just rebelled against God and lost the war in heaven. As punishment, God has cast them into hell. Desiring revenge, Satan and his followers decide to try to corrupt humankind, God's most prized creation. Satan sneaks out of hell and enters Eden. As Adam and Eve sleep, Satan disguises himself as a toad, whispers into Eve's ear, and sows the seeds of discontent. Aware of Satan's plot, God sends the angel Raphael to warn Adam. When Satan returns to Eden, he finds that Eve has persuaded Adam to let her work alone. In the guise of a serpent, he convinces her through flattery and cunning to disobey God and eat the fruit from the Tree of Knowledge. Adam despairs upon learning of Eve's deed but makes a conscious decision to eat the fruit as well, as he would rather join Eve in her fallen condition than continue to live in Eden without her. After a visit from the archangel Michael, who shows Adam a vision of the misfortunes that await humankind, Adam and Eve leave Eden "hand in hand," shedding tears, "wand'ring steps and slow."

Villains are often the most interesting characters in literary works, and *Paradise Lost* is no exception. Satan is the most complex, fully realized, and fascinating figure. He is an antihero, demonstrating vision, leadership, and eloquence but directing those qualities toward proud, selfish ends. Moreover, he is not blindly evil but rather very self-aware, tormented by the wretched knowledge that God has banished him. Ultimately, Satan comes across as a tragic figure—a theological twist that prompted some of Milton's detractors to accuse him, literally, of too much sympathy for the devil.

ADDITIONAL FACTS

1. Milton went blind (possibly from glaucoma) and by 1654 had to dictate his writings to an assistant.

2. Milton followed Paradise Lost *with* Paradise Regained *(1671), which retells the New Testament story of Jesus's confrontation with Satan during his forty days in the wilderness.*

Venus de Milo

One of the most famous sculptures of all time, the *Venus de Milo* received its name from the fact that it was discovered by a peasant on the Aegean island of Melos in 1820. The work was seized by Turkish officials and eventually sold to a French naval official. In 1821 it was presented to Louis XVIII, who donated it to the Louvre Museum in Paris, where it can be seen today.

The statue, which is six and a half feet tall, is sculpted out of Parian marble. Its subject is Aphrodite, the Greek goddess of love and beauty, known to the Romans as Venus. A sculpted arm holding an apple was found nearby. Many scholars believe that the arm was originally attached. According to myth, Paris of Troy had given Venus a golden apple to identify her as the most beautiful woman in the world.

The artist and date of the sculpture have given rise to much debate. Initially authorities at the Louvre declared it a classical (fifth- or fourth-century BC) work, possibly executed by Phidias or Praxiteles. However, the base on which the statue had been found identified the artist as Alexandros of Antioch of Menander, a colony that was not founded until later, in the Hellenistic period. Although museum officials eventually agreed that the sculpture was Hellenistic, it is still exhibited as the work of an anonymous artist.

The *Venus de Milo* has been admired throughout the world ever since its discovery. The British playwright Oscar Wilde recounted the story of a man who ordered a plaster copy of the statue and then sued the railroad company when it arrived from Paris without arms. What surprised Wilde even more was the fact that the man won his case.

ADDITIONAL FACTS

1. The statue was claimed by Ludwig I of Bavaria, who insisted that it had been found on territory that he had purchased in Melos in 1817.

2. In 1964, the statue was exhibited in Japan, where more than 1.5 million people viewed it from a moving sidewalk.

The Greenhouse Effect

The phrase *greenhouse effect* can be used to describe two different scientific phenomena. The first is the entirely natural process by which the atmosphere prevents heat from escaping back into space. It is the mechanism by which the average surface temperature on earth is maintained at a hospitable 60 degrees Fahrenheit.

When energy from the sun reaches the planet's surface, some of it is absorbed, warming the ground, and some of it is reflected into space. Water vapor, carbon dioxide, methane, and other gases in the atmosphere—known collectively as the greenhouse gases—trap some of the outgoing energy, like the glass panels of a greenhouse. Without the greenhouse effect, the earth would be so cold that life would be impossible.

The expression *greenhouse effect* also refers to an increase in the atmosphere concentration of greenhouse gases from human activities such as burning fossil fuels over the last century that scientists believe is contributing to global warming. The earth's surface temperature has risen one degree in the past hundred years, with a sharp increase in the past two decades, according to the National Academy of Sciences. The year 2005 was the hottest year on record. At the same time, greenhouse gases, proven to retain heat, have increased dramatically. Carbon dioxide in the atmosphere is up 30 percent since before the industrial revolution, and the levels of methane have more than doubled.

Perhaps most important, there is more water in the atmosphere. As polar ice caps have melted, the sea level has risen four to eight inches, increasing worldwide rainfall by 1 percent. This may spark a vicious cycle. More water in the atmosphere means more heat trapped at the surface. As the surface becomes hotter, the ice caps will melt faster, leading to more water in the oceans and still more water vapor in the atmosphere. Again, that will fuel the cycle, causing the surface to become hotter and the ice caps to melt faster.

ADDITIONAL FACTS

1. *Scientists from the Environmental Protection Agency estimate that the global surface temperature will rise 1 to 4.5 degrees Fahrenheit in the next fifty years and the sea level will rise two feet along the US coastline.*

2. *Recent reports from NASA estimate that at present melting rates during summers, the Arctic may be completely free of ice by the end of the century.*

3. *The carbon dioxide saturated atmosphere of Venus causes a runaway greenhouse effect, a positive feedback cycle of reheating that leaves Venus's surface hot enough to melt lead. Mars has almost no atmosphere, and hence no greenhouse effect, which is part of the reason it is so cold.*

4. *The greenhouse effect was discovered in 1824 by the french mathematician and physicist Joseph Fourier.*

Medieval/Early Church Music

The first known written music comes from the Middle Ages. It takes the form of plainchant—also known as Gregorian Chant—sung melodies used by monks during the Catholic Mass. The Mass is a ritual reenactment of Christ's Last Supper, intended to provide a spiritual connection between man and God. Part of this connection was established through music.

The Mass is divided into two sets of rituals: the ordinary and the proper. The ordinary consists of six Latin prayers (*Kyrie Eleison, Gloria in Excelsis, Credo, Sanctus, Agnus Dei,* and *Ite missa est*), which always contain the same text and occur at every Mass. The prayers of the proper, which include the *Introit, Gradual, Offertory,* and *Communion,* consist of texts that vary according to seasonal liturgy and local traditions. Medieval musicians passed Gregorian melodies along orally, creating new ones by combining melodic formulas.

Most medieval music is monophonic, consisting of a single melodic line. But around the tenth century, some musicians began to write in a style called organum—two parallel melody lines, usually a fourth or a fifth apart. Two centuries later, Léonin and Perotin (music directors at the cathedral of Notre Dame in Paris), composed organa with up to four independent, nonparallel musical lines.

In the thirteenth century, a complex polyphonic form known as the motet emerged. It was made up of a Latinate cantus firmus, or fixed melodic line, with several other complementary parts sung in French, Latin, or both. Guillaume de Machaut was an early master of the motet, and in the fourteenth century, he would compose the first complete polyphonic setting of the Mass ordinary.

ADDITIONAL FACTS

1. *During this period in southern France, aristocratic poets, called troubadours, composed secular songs about love and war. Wandering musicians called jongleurs would travel from one royal court to another, singing their own songs and those of the troubadours. Today a musician who travels from town to town is still sometimes referred to as a troubadour.*

2. *In the mid-1990s, the Benedictine Monks of Santo Domingo de Silos released a two-CD series called* Chant *that made plainchant popular (mostly to the new-age audience) for the first time since the Middle Ages.*

3. *Hildegard von Bingen (1098–1179) was the earliest known female composer. She was an abbess and a mystic, and she wrote many monophonic works for the Catholic Church, almost all of them written for female voices. She also wrote a Catholic mystery play called the* Ordo virtutum. *She has been beatified, but not yet canonized, by the Catholic Church.*

Forms

Consider all the beautiful things in the world. Do they have anything in common? What explains the fact that they are all beautiful? According to Plato (429–347 BC) the answer to both these questions is that there is a form or idea called beauty and each beautiful thing is beautiful because it has some relation to that form. Plato believed that there are many forms that function in this way, not just the form of beauty. There is a form of redness, that accounts for all red things in the world; a form of the good that accounts for all the good in the world; and so on.

Platonic forms, like beauty, are timeless and unchanging. Furthermore, the form beauty is itself beautiful. It has no features other than being beautiful, and it is beautiful in an unrestricted and unqualified way. Other beautiful things have additional features like size and shape, and they are only beautiful to a limited degree. Individual beautiful things are beautiful by virtue of participating in beauty. Plato thought of participation as imperfect imitation. Thus, individual beautiful things imitate beauty, but only up to a point.

For Plato, the forms are more real than the particular physical objects that imitate them. Where the forms are timeless and unchanging, physical things are in flux, constantly coming to be, and then going out of existence. Where the forms are unqualified perfection, physical things are qualified and conditioned.

Plato believed that long before our bodies ever existed, our souls existed and inhabited heaven, where they became directly acquainted with the forms themselves. Real knowledge is knowledge of the forms. But knowledge of the forms cannot be attained through sensory experience, because the forms, after all, are not in the physical world. Therefore, our knowledge of the forms, our *real* knowledge, must be the recollection of our initial acquaintance with the forms in heaven. Therefore, what appears to us as *learning* is in fact merely *remembering*.

ADDITIONAL FACTS

1. *Plato first presented his theory of forms in his dialogue* Phaedo, *which describes the last hours of his teacher Socrates. The theory is spoken by Socrates himself, but many scholars think that it expresses Plato's view, not Socrates's.*

2. *In the dialogue* Meno, *Socrates argues for the recollection theory of learning by showing that a young slave with no education can understand a proof of Euclid.*

Abraham, Isaac, and Jacob

Abraham is considered the patriarch of monotheism. His sons Isaac (with Sarah) and Ishmael (with Hagar) and their descendants are credited with the founding of Judaism and Islam, respectively.

When Abraham was a young man—then called Abram—living in Ur, God appeared and instructed him to travel to the land of Canaan. Late in life, Abram grew concerned that he had no children. His wife, Sarai—then called Sarah—appeared to be barren so she allowed him to sleep with her maidservant Hagar. Hagar subsequently gave birth to Abram's first son, Ishmael. Out of anger and jealousy, Sarai had Abram banish Hagar and Ishmael.

God then made a covenant with Abram. In exchange for Abram's service and devotion, God would grant him a son with Sarai, who would give rise to a great and numerous people. The land of Canaan would be theirs. As a sign of this covenant, at the age of ninety-nine, Abram changed his name to Abraham and Sarai to Sarah. Abraham was circumcised and promised his future sons would be as well.

Sarah gave birth to Isaac, who fulfilled the promise that Abraham made with God. When Isaac was a young man, God told Abraham to sacrifice him as an offering. Abraham, in his absolute devotion, agreed to do so. However, just before he was about to kill his own son, an angel stopped him. In the Torah, this is seen as one of the great examples of faith.

Isaac married Rebekah and had twins. The second-born, whom Rebekah favored, was Jacob, later called Israel. Jacob had twelve sons who went on to found the twelve tribes of Israel and thus the people known as Israelites. With his first wife, Leah, Jacob had Reuben, Simeon, Levi, Judah, Issachar, and Zebulun. With a handmaiden of Leah, he had Gad and Asher. With his favorite wife, Rachel, he had Joseph (who was his favorite son) and Benjamin. And with a handmaiden of Rachel he had Dan and Naphtali.

ADDITIONAL FACTS

1. *According to Islam, the Muslim people are descendents of Ishmael. Because Ishmael was actually Abraham's first-born son, Muslims claim to be the true heirs to the covenant with God. They believe that Abraham was an important prophet and that it was actually Ishmael whom he nearly sacrificed.*

2. *In Christian belief, parallels are drawn between Abraham's readiness to sacrifice Isaac and the sacrifice of God's own son, Jesus Christ.*

Julius Caesar

Julius Caesar (100–44 BC) was a Roman general who rose to prominence in the first century BC conquering what is now France, Belgium, and western Germany. The Roman Senate, led by Pompey, was threatened by Caesar's growing popularity and ordered him to disband his army. Caesar refused. He marched his legions on the Capitol, crossing the Rubicon River—the decisive moment from which he could not turn back—and started a civil war. He chased his enemies across Europe and ultimately to Egypt where Pompey was killed. Before leaving Egypt, Caesar fell in love with Cleopatra and installed her as queen. When Caesar returned to Rome, he ruled as dictator. Caesar was assassinated on the Ides (the fifteenth day) of March in 44 BC by a conspiracy that included his best friend, Brutus.

Innumerable legends surround Caesar. When he was still in his twenties, he was captured by pirates in the eastern Mediterranean. After being ransomed by his men, he raised a small army from the local leaders, located the pirates, and crucified them all.

Years later, in 62 BC, when Caesar was climbing through Rome's political ranks, a scandal erupted. A patrician named Publius Clodius was discovered at a religious ritual where men were prohibited. The ritual was held in Caesar's house, and a rumor soon spread that Clodius was there because he was having an affair with Caesar's wife, Pompeia. Caesar knew the rumors weren't true and said so. Nevertheless he divorced her, noting that Caesar's wife and family must be above suspicion.

Caesar was declared dictator by the Senate in the midst of his civil war against Pompey. It was a time of crisis, and the leader was thought to require decisive, emergency powers. But the emergency never passed. The Republic was not to be restored.

Caesar ruled as dictator, but he was largely careful to maintain the appearance of consulting the Senate—stacked with his supporters—and respecting the Republic's traditions. However, in the final years of his life, he grew careless, allowing his Asian subjects to worship him as a god, and coins with his image were minted, the first time a living Roman was so honored. They bore the inscription, "Perpetual Dictator." These gratuitous honors are thought to have fueled the resentment that culminated in his overthrow and murder.

ADDITIONAL FACT

1. *After a successful military campaign in Asia, Caesar famously declared, "Veni, vidi, vinci." (I came, I saw, I conquered.)*

Homer

The stories told in Homer's *Iliad* and *Odyssey* have been so long embedded in Western culture that they are inescapable even to this day. From the Trojan Horse to the Cyclops, from Achilles' heel to the Sirens' song, elements of both epics remain mainstays of our literature and everyday language nearly 3,000 years after they were written.

The *Iliad* and *Odyssey* are epic poems—lengthy verse works in Greek that were likely read or sung aloud and passed down orally for generations before they were committed to writing. Homer's exact role in this process remains a mystery, and there is debate over whether he actually existed at all. In any case, scholars believe that both works were composed in or around the eighth century BC in Ionia, an area of ancient Greece that is now part of the Mediterranean coast of Turkey.

The *Iliad* tells of the exploits of Achilles, Agamemnon, Hector, and other heroes during the Trojan War between Achaea (Greece) and Troy. According to myth, the war began when the Trojan prince Paris kidnapped Helen of Sparta, the most beautiful woman in the world, and took her back to Troy to be his wife. The *Iliad* begins nine years into the conflict, focusing on the rage of the Achaean warrior Achilles and exploring the combination of greatness and fatal flaws that the hero displays. Along the way, Homer incorporates the evocative imagery—"rosy-fingered Dawn," the "wine-dark sea"—for which the poem is justly renowned.

The *Iliad's* sequel, the *Odyssey*, recounts the trials of the Greek hero Odysseus as he attempts to sail home from the Trojan War to rejoin his wife, Penelope. The journey takes ten years to complete, largely because Odysseus angers the sea god, Poseidon, who does everything in his power to hinder Odysseus's voyage. Using his own cleverness and help from the goddess Athena, Odysseus eventually returns home to Ithaca and dispatches the numerous suitors who have advanced on his still-faithful wife.

Regardless of the specifics of their authorship, the *Iliad* and *Odyssey* had an enormous cultural and practical impact on everyday life in ancient Greece. It was common to memorize the epics from start to finish. Though Greece's golden age waned in the 100s BC, Homer's works endured, inspiring the epics of ancient Rome, such as Virgil's *Aeneid*.

ADDITIONAL FACTS

1. *Though the Trojan War was long believed to be merely legend, archaeological discoveries in Turkey in the late 1800s suggested that it may have had some historical basis.*

2. *The famous phrase describing Helen of Troy as the "face that launch'd a thousand ships" appears not in the* Iliad *but in Christopher Marlowe's play* Dr. Faustus *(1604).*

⌘

Hagia Sophia

The Hagia Sophia was built in Constantinople (present-day Istanbul) under the personal supervision of the Emperor Justinian. At the church's dedication, the Byzantine ruler purportedly claimed that he had surpassed Solomon, the Old Testament king responsible for the famous temple in Jerusalem.

It is often said that the Hagia Sophia unites the mysticism of the East with the ambitious scale of Roman imperial architecture, such as the Pantheon.

Isidore of Miletus and Anthemius of Tralles, mathematicians rather than architects, designed the masterpiece, which was built between 532 and 537. The dome of the church rises 180 feet and is supported by four pendentives or triangular sections that distribute the hemisphere's weight evenly on four piers. Forty windows at the dome's base allow light to flow in, making it seem weightless, as if floating above the worshippers below. At first, the church was decorated with gold mosaics and decorative patterns. Subsequent emperors added many images of holy figures.

Over the years, Hagia Sophia, which means "church of the holy wisdom" in Greek, has suffered considerable damage from earthquakes. Originally the Byzantine emperor's personal church, it was converted to a mosque after the capture of Constantinople by Ottoman Turks in 1453. Since images of the human form are prohibited by Islam, the figurative mosaics were plastered over. Four minarets (towers from which the faithful are called to worship) were added, along with Arabic calligraphy that can still be seen in the building today. In 1936, under the Turkish ruler Mustafa Kemal Atatürk, the building was secularized and converted into the Ayasofia Museum, one of the chief tourist attractions of modern Istanbul.

In 1993 UNESCO placed the Hagia Sophia on a list of the world's most endangered historic sites. Since then, the building's foundation has been reinforced and many more of the old mosaics have been uncovered.

ADDITIONAL FACTS

1. In the mid-sixth century, the Hagia Sophia was thoroughly described by Procopius in a Byzantine treatise entitled On Architecture.

2. Porphyry columns initially taken by the Romans from an Egyptian temple in Heliopolis were brought to Constantinople and used in the construction of the Hagia Sophia.

3. The church was sacked during the Fourth Crusade in 1204.

Black Holes

A black hole can result when a massive star dies out. The dying star collapses into itself, becoming smaller and smaller, denser and denser, until it compresses into a single point with no radius and infinite density. The point, called a singularity, is so dense that nearby light cannot escape its gravitational pull. Everything close to the star gets sucked into blackness.

When a rocket launches into space, it needs to travel fast enough to escape the gravitational pull of the Earth. If it fails to reach the appropriate escape speed, then it simply falls back down. The gravitational pull of a black hole is so strong, the escape speed is faster than the speed of light. Therefore, nothing can escape because nothing can travel faster than light. The boundary surrounding the singularity where the escape speed equals the speed of light is called the event horizon. Anything that falls inside the event horizon gets sucked into the singularity.

Of course, all of this is theoretical. We can't actually see black holes because they don't give off any light. We know of their existence only because other objects in space interact with their mass. A large number of stars orbiting around a black center indicates there might be a black hole in the middle. Also, black holes are so dense that they can bend light. As a result, scientists on Earth sometimes will see multiple images of the same star. When they do, they infer that somewhere between us and the star is a black hole.

Black holes pose a dilemma for physicists. They seem to defy the law of quantum mechanics that states that energy cannot be created or destroyed. The light sucked into the center of a black hole seems to be destroyed, as it is crushed into an infinitely small space. But if the light is somehow conserved, then can it escape someday? Is it possible for a black hole to reverse itself? These are unanswered questions of astrophysics.

ADDITIONAL FACTS

1. *There is no reason to believe that black holes will suck up all the energy in the universe. They pull in only objects that cross the event horizon.*

2. *Albert Einstein, rejecting the principles of quantum mechanics, once said, "God does not play dice with the universe." Stephen Hawking, referring to black holes, once said, "God not only plays dice. He sometimes throws them where they cannot be seen."*

3. *If you were to cross the event horizon of a black hole, to an outside observer it would look like you were moving slower and slower but never quite reaching the horizon. The illusion is caused by the black hole's immense gravity. It pulls on the light you emit, which means that light takes longer and longer to reach the outside observer. But from your point of view, you cross the event horizon and nothing special occurs until you are crushed to death at the singularity.*

Instruments and Ensembles

The combined sound of a particular assortment of musical instruments, more than any other technical aspect of music, is what makes much Western art music, or classical music, so distinct. The sonic color, or timbre, of a string quartet or an orchestra is a big part of what separates this type of music from contemporary rock or pop.

Not including the human voice, there are five categories of musical instruments: strings (plucked or played with a bow), winds (played by blowing air through a mouthpiece, a hole, or a reed), percussion (usually struck with drumsticks or mallets), keyboards, and in the twentieth century, electronic instruments.

By about 1750, the baroque orchestra had been established: a wind section including flutes, oboes, bassoons, horns, and trumpets; timpani (kettle drums); continuo (often a combination of a keyboard instrument playing chords, with the bass line reinforced by a cello); and a string section. The violin was the dominant voice of the baroque period's complex melodic lines. Predated by the medieval fiddle, it emerged in its current form during the first half of the sixteenth century in northern Italy.

With the advent of the classical period, the winds were increasingly used to round out the harmonic textures of the orchestra. The larger symphonies of Franz Joseph Haydn and Wolfgang Amadeus Mozart are generally written for two of each of the woodwind and brass instruments, plus timpani and strings.

By the mid-nineteenth century, composers such as Hector Berlioz were writing for larger orchestras that included harps, as well as newer instruments like the English horn, alto clarinet, and various percussion instruments.

By the late nineteenth and early twentieth centuries, Richard Wagner, Gustav Mahler, and Arnold Schoenberg were writing pieces for very large orchestras, sometimes with a hundred musicians. Later composers introduced instruments from popular music and jazz, such as the saxophone, synthesizers, and other electronic devices.

ADDITIONAL FACTS

1. *In early music, composers wrote whole pieces without specifying which instruments were to play them. It wasn't until Monteverdi's 1607 opera* Orfeo *that a musical score came with suggestions as to which instrument should play which written part.*

2. *The name* piano *comes from "pianoforte" because it plays both piano (soft) and* forte *(loud) music. It was developed by harpsichord maker Bartolomeo Cristofori around 1700 in northern Italy.*

◇∞◇

Plato's Cave Allegory

"See human beings as though they were in an underground cave-like dwelling with its entrance, a long one, open to the light across the whole width of the cave. They are in it from childhood with their legs and necks in bonds so that they are fixed, seeing only in front of them, unable because of the bond to turn their heads all the way around . . ."

—Plato, *The Republic*

In his writings, Plato uses the character of Socrates, his real-life teacher, to espouse his own philosophical views. *The Republic* is written in the form of a dialogue between Socrates and his students.

In this famous passage from *The Republic*, Socrates describes a scenario in which men, trapped in a cave, can see only the shadows of objects projected on the wall. They are forced to face forward while a fire burns behind them. Objects are held up in front of the fire, projecting images the men identify. For instance, the men in the cave may think they see a book, but what they see is only the book's shadow as it is held up behind them.

When a man escapes the cave to witness the true nature of things, he is at first pained by the brilliance of the sun and confused by the physical objects. But when he eventually understands the true nature of the world, he pities the masses who know only shadows. Of course, the men in Socrates' cave resist learning the truth and think their escaped friend is crazy when he tries to describe it.

In the allegory, the men trapped in the cave represent the world's ignorant masses. They see only representations of objects, the sights and sounds that can be discerned by our physical senses. The man who escapes the cave to witness the true nature of things is the philosopher. Using their intellect, philosophers are able to discern forms—abstract, immutable truths that are the real foundation of the universe. The philosopher who escapes the cave knows the real nature of things.

The Republic is ultimately concerned with the question of justice. Plato believed that in order to establish justice, one must know what is good. Therefore, philosophers who understood the form of the good should rule as kings. The rest of society should be organized to fulfill those rulers' demands.

ADDITIONAL FACTS

1. Plato was born in Athens in 428 BC.

2. Plato referred to his philosopher kings as "Guardians."

Sarah

Sarah was the wife of Abraham and the matriarch of the Jewish people.

Sarah was so beautiful that when she and Abraham fled to Egypt during a famine, her beauty caused Abraham to fear for their safety. Concerned that Pharaoh would kill him and take Sarah for himself, Abraham pretended that he and Sarah were siblings. Pharaoh did take Sarah, but spared Abraham and gave him many gifts in return. God then punished Pharaoh, allowing Sarah and Abraham to escape Egypt together.

Although she was beautiful, Sarah was barren for the majority of her life and could not bear Abraham's child. Thus, as was the custom, she gave her handmaiden, Hagar, to Abraham so that he could continue his lineage. Hagar then gave birth to Abraham's first son, Ishmael.

After the birth, Sarah's relationship with Hagar was strained. Hagar no longer respected Sarah, and Sarah became jealous. Finally, Sarah asked Abraham to banish Hagar and her son. According to Jewish tradition, Sarah had more prophetic insight than Abraham, and so Abraham deferred to her wishes.

When Sarah was ninety years old, God told Abraham that she would finally bear his child, causing Abraham to laugh. God insisted, and when Sarah overheard she laughed as well. But Sarah felt ashamed for doubting God and affirmed her faith. One year later, she gave birth to Isaac whose line would become the twelve tribes of Israel.

Nearly forty years later, Sarah died in Hebron, at the age of 127. According to some writings, Sarah's death was related to Abraham's near sacrifice of Isaac. In one story Satan told Sarah that Abraham had killed Isaac. When she discovered that Isaac had actually survived, she died of joy.

ADDITIONAL FACTS

1. *Sarah is buried with her husband, Abraham, in the Cave of the Patriarchs in Hebron. Their son Isaac and his wife, their grandson Jacob, and his first wife, Leah, are buried there as well.*

2. *The only one of Judaism's patriarchs and matriarchs not buried in Hebron is Jacob's second wife, Rachel, who is buried in Bethlehem.*

Rosetta Stone

In 1799, French soldiers in Napoleon's army discovered a mysterious black rock buried in the sands near the city of Alexandria, Egypt. The stone was inscribed in three ancient languages. The rock's first inscription was in Greek. Scholars determined it dated from about 196 BC, when Egypt was a province of the Greek empire created by Alexander the Great. The other two inscriptions on the black rock were in different versions of hieroglyphics, the traditional writing of the Egyptians.

For thousands of years, Egypt was one of the great empires of the ancient world. Ruled by kings known as pharaohs, the Egyptians built gigantic monuments such as the Great Pyramids and the Sphinx. Egyptian armies controlled lands from present-day Sudan to Syria. The pharaohs built thriving cities and splendid tombs for themselves.

But for centuries before the discovery of the Rosetta Stone, historians and archeologists were unable to read the vast number of written records left by Egypt's scribes. They wrote in a complicated script that was incomprehensible to even the most learned modern scholars.

The Rosetta Stone, which recorded an edict issued by the Greek authorities to the Egyptian population, unlocked the secrets of ancient Egypt. By lining up the Greek text with the hieroglyphics, a French scholar named Jean-Francois Champollion was able to decode the complex Egyptian language after years of study. Deciphering hieroglyphics allowed historians and archeologists in the nineteenth century to develop a much fuller understanding of ancient Egypt.

Translating the Rosetta Stone was a scholarly accomplishment in its own right. Champollion was a prodigious linguist who was fluent in dozens of languages. A British scholar, Thomas Young, also helped decode the inscriptions. The Rosetta Stone was seized by the British in 1801 and now resides in the British Museum in London.

ADDITIONAL FACTS

1. During World War I, the Rosetta Stone and other important exhibitions were moved from the British Museum to a subway station to protect them from the bombing of London.

2. The text on the Rosetta Stone outlined the good deeds of the thirteen-year-old Greek pharaoh, Ptolemy V, in an effort to convince his Egyptian subjects of his divinity.

3. Ancient Egyptians believed that bodies should be preserved after death and carefully embalmed the corpses of their kings in a process known as mummification. As late as the nineteenth century, charlatans in Europe sold mummies ground up into a powder, claiming it had medicinal value.

Heart of Darkness

Joseph Conrad's 1899 novella *Heart of Darkness* was a work far ahead of its time, in many ways the first truly twentieth-century novel. Though rooted in the realistic style of the late nineteenth century, it addressed numerous themes that would typify the modernist era that followed. It is also notable as one of the first literary works to look critically at the rampant abuses that European imperialism had wreaked in Africa and Asia during the 1800s.

Heart of Darkness is concise, only about eighty pages long. It is told in flashback by a man named Marlow, who has taken a job with a Belgian colonial trading business called only "the Company." He is sent to the Belgian Congo to captain a steamboat up the Congo River to the Company's remote Inner Station, which is run by an ivory trader named Kurtz. Upon arriving in Africa, Marlow is struck by the decaying Company facilities and the racist Europeans' unabashed exploitation of native Africans.

Conrad's Congo is a shadowy, intensely atmospheric world in which virtually every character remains ominously nameless—the Manager, the Accountant, and so on—and the jungle looms massive and impenetrable just beyond the edge of each isolated Belgian settlement. As Marlow makes his way up the river into increasingly remote territory, his journey becomes as much psychological as physical. The trappings of civilization fall further away at each outpost, and he begins to see himself as traveling into the primal, unknown reaches of the human mind itself. Meanwhile, as Marlow learns more about the enigmatic Kurtz, it becomes evident that Kurtz's intent to civilize the African natives has gone awry. He has succumbed to his own fascination with the darkness and savagery of Africa.

Heart of Darkness is particularly familiar today because of its unorthodox but spectacular film adaptation, *Apocalypse Now* (1979). The film resets the novel in 1970s Vietnam, with Marlon Brando in the Kurtz role as a US Army colonel gone dangerously insane in a remote part of Cambodia. The screenplay preserves many elements of Conrad's story while updating it with hallucinatory music and visuals influenced by the 1960s counterculture.

ADDITIONAL FACTS

1. *All of Conrad's major works are in English, despite the fact that he was of Polish descent (his birth name was Józef Teodor Konrad Korzeniowski), and English was his third language.*

2. *Conrad's exploration of the human unconscious in* Heart of Darkness *mirrors some of the ideas set forth by his contemporary, Sigmund Freud. To this day, critics often analyze the novel from a Freudian viewpoint.*

3. *T. S. Eliot reused one of the book's famous lines, "Mistah Kurtz—he dead," as the epigraph to his poem "The Hollow Men" (1925).*

Byzantine Art

The Byzantine Empire takes its name from the city of Byzantium, renamed Constantinople in the fourth century by the Emperor Constantine, who moved his court there from Rome. Today the city is known as Istanbul. After the decline of the Roman Empire in the west, the eastern half continued to be run by the Byzantine emperor in Constantinople.

The reign of Justinian (527–565) is known in art history as the First Golden Age of Byzantium. It witnessed the creation of such works as the Hagia Sophia in Constantinople and the church of San Vitale in Ravenna, Italy. A Second Golden Age, from the late ninth to the eleventh century, produced Saint Mark's Cathedral in Venice. Along with the Orthodox Faith, the Byzantine style spread to Russia and eastern Europe, eventually inspiring the spectacular Cathedral of Saint Basil in Moscow.

The subject of most Byzantine art is religious. Biblical narratives and idealized representations or icons of holy figures predominate. The goal was less to represent the actual likeness of Christ, the Virgin Mary, or some saint than to capture his or her spiritual essence. Nude figures and life-sized sculpture, so prevalent in Greco-Roman culture, were generally shunned.

Byzantine architecture is typified by the use of domes resting on pendentives. The internal walls of churches are often richly decorated with marble panels, patterns sculpted in low relief, and glass mosaics.

Traces of classical art surface occasionally. Although sculpture is rare in Byzantine art, small ivory carvings depicting mythological scenes exist, such as the famous Veroli Cabinet, with its panel of the Sacrifice of Iphigenia, based on Euripides' play *Iphigenia in Aulis*.

In Byzantium, religious images were worshipped with such passion that in 726 the Emperor placed a ban on icons, claiming that they led to idolatry. For nearly a century all images of Christ and Mary in human form were prohibited. The so-called iconoclasts (image-destroyers) obliterated such images wherever they could find them. Assisted by the support of the pope in Rome, the opposition party, the so-called iconophiles, had the ban repealed in 843.

ADDITIONAL FACTS

1. *The term* byzantine *often carries negative connotations, referring to something that is either scheming or devious—as were many of the Byzantine rulers—or excessively complex and intricate—as was their art.*

2. *The Byzantine style came to an end with the fall of Constantinople 1453. Nevertheless its influence continues to manifest itself in the Orthodox Church, where traditional icons are produced to this day.*

Supernova

Most stars die quietly, using up all their fuel through nuclear fusion. Then 99 percent fade away into dull celestial objects called white dwarves. But if a star is big enough and hot enough, it can, under the right conditions, explode. The explosion is called a supernova.

Before a star explodes, it fuses elements, producing energy. Its massive gravity leads to the formation of oxygen, silicon, phosphorus, and calcium, making all the heavy elements until it reaches iron, a cosmic dead end. Fusing iron into even heavier elements does not produce energy but requires energy. The star has nothing to burn, so its iron core continues to collapse into itself under the force of its own gravity. The most massive stars collapse into black holes. But slightly smaller stars, with masses five to eight times the size of our sun, simply explode.

A supernova takes less than fifteen seconds to complete. The explosion is so bright that a supernova from a single star can outshine an entire galaxy for months. It generates enough heat to create even heavier elements: mercury, gold, and silver.

According to the big bang theory, life on earth exists because of supernovae. The theory holds that all the elements heavier than oxygen were created in the past explosions of giant stars. The potassium in your banana did not have its beginnings on an island in the Caribbean. It may have been created a long time ago in a supernova.

ADDITIONAL FACTS

1. In 1006, an extremely bright supernova was observed in Egypt, Iraq, Italy, Switzerland, China, Japan, and possibly France and Syria.

2. Galileo Galilei used a supernova in 1604 to disprove Aristotle's theory that the universe never changes.

3. Even radioactive elements, such as uranium, are formed in supernovae.

Renaissance Music

Renaissance music was produced from the middle of the fifteenth century to about the end of the sixteenth—a period that saw the rise of Martin Luther, the Protestant Reformation, and the Catholic Counter-Reformation. It is characterized by several intermingling florid vocal or instrumental parts, all of relatively equal importance.

The music of this time shared the aesthetic of the period's art and literature. Renaissance artists, writers, and musicians saw themselves as pulling the world out of the dark, clerical, mystical world of the Middle Ages. They emphasized a return to the ideals of classical Greece and Rome: love, pleasure, intellect, and the beauty of the human body and emotion.

The Franco-Flemish region in particular flourished with composers. Guillaume Dufay (1400–1474), and Gilles Binchois (c.1400–1460) wrote some of the earliest polyphonic masses and secular songs in the new style. Binchois' pupil Johannes Ockeghem, court composer to the Duke of Bourbon, wrote motets featuring some of the earliest instances of canon-singing. Canon is a staggered imitation, as in the children's song "Row, Row, Row, Your Boat."

Josquin Desprez (c.1440–1521) was considered the greatest composer of the era, renowned for his highly emotional mass settings and sophisticated secular chansons, or love songs. In Italy, Giovanni Pierluigi da Palestrina (1525–1594) was an itinerant court composer who imitated and elaborated upon the mass settings of his predecessors and made the stylistic bridge between the Renaissance and the Baroque periods.

ADDITIONAL FACTS

1. *The idea of a church hymn began in the Renaissance, and many of them were composed by Martin Luther.*

2. *Most Renaissance music was composed for the courts, and some pieces are only identifiable by the seal of the nobleman who solicited them, rather than the composer's own signature.*

3. *The English madrigal song form was the first type of song to feature refrains of "fa-la-la" actually written in the music.*

Aristotle

"All men by nature desire to know."

—Aristotle, *Metaphysics*

The influence of Aristotle (384–322 BC) on philosophy and Western culture generally would be hard to exaggerate. Born in Macedonia, north of Greece, in 384 BC, Aristotle traveled to Athens where he studied at Plato's school, the Academy. After Plato's death, Aristotle founded his own school, the Lyceum.

In fifth-century Athens, the study of philosophy included rhetoric, natural science, biology, and other fields of inquiry. Consequently, Aristotle made major contributions to almost every branch of human learning.

Aristotle believed philosophy should be studied in a precise order. First, one should learn logic, because logic explains how facts about the world relate to one another. Aristotle developed the theory of syllogisms—arguments that are logically valid. He devised a list of basic syllogisms and rules for reducing more complicated arguments to one of those forms. The most famous Aristotelian syllogism is:

> *All men are mortal.*
> *Socrates is a man.*
> *Therefore, Socrates is mortal.*

After logic, Aristotle believed students should investigate concrete natural phenomena. He wrote many works on the subject—*Physics, Parts of Animals, Generation of Animals, Motions of Animals, Meterology, On Generation and Corruption*—and deduced several general principles to explain the physical world.

The final subject for study, according to Aristotle, is practical philosophy, which includes ethics and politics. He treated these topics, respectively, in *Nichomachean Ethics* and *Politics*. In Aristotle's conception, ethics is mostly a matter of good training. He believes that people usually know the proper way to behave, and they must simply be morally strong enough to behave in accordance with this knowledge. Being a good person amounts to having the inclination to do the right thing, and this inclination can be bred into us. Politically, Aristotle believed that the goal of the state is to provide the context for the happy and self-sufficient lives of its citizens. He was partial to democratic government, but he acknowledged that occasionally a monarchy is more appropriate.

ADDITIONAL FACTS

1. Aristotle is sometimes referred to as "the Stagirite," because he was born in the Macedonian city Stagira.

2. Between his time at Plato's Academy and the founding of his own school, Aristotle was tutor to Alexander the Great, also a Macedonian, who ruled much of the Mediterranean world.

Sodom and Gomorrah

The story of Sodom and Gomorrah appears in Chapter 19 of the Book of Genesis. Sodom and Gomorrah were two towns in the Jordan river valley. The inhabitants of these towns had sinned, and God wished to destroy them. Abraham protested that the innocent should not be killed with the wicked, and God agreed to spare the towns if Abraham could find ten worthy men. He sent a group of angels to investigate.

When the angels arrived, they came upon Lot, a nephew of Abraham. Lot invited the angels into his home and prepared a meal for them. Later, the citizens of Sodom appeared at Lot's house and demanded, "Where are the men that came in to thee this night? Bring them out unto us, that we may know them." (Genesis 19:5) Instead, Lot offered his virgin daughters to the men of Sodom, but they were not satisfied. At this point, seeing that the situation was dire, the angels told Lot to get himself and his family out of Sodom. The angels instructed Lot and his family not to look back as they fled. Lot was able to escape to a nearby town, but as Sodom and Gomorrah were being destroyed, his wife glanced back and was turned into a pillar of salt.

It is unclear *what* sins were actually committed by the citizens of Sodom and Gomorrah. Traditionally, Jews believe that they committed the sin of inhospitality. The story occurs just after the Torah tells how much God appreciated Abraham's hospitality. Abraham's good behavior can be starkly contrasted with how the citizens of Sodom reacted to their visitors. Taken together, these two stories seem to emphasize the importance of being a good host.

Conservative Christians, on the other hand, see the sins of Sodom quite differently. When the citizens of Sodom demanded to "know" the angels, it is believed by some that this "knowing" was really a euphemism for sex. According to this view, the men of Sodom were homosexuals, and God punished them for their sexual orientation.

ADDITIONAL FACTS

1. *The contemporary term* sodomy *is derived from the Biblical town of Sodom.*

2. *The actual existence of Sodom and Gomorrah is disputed, but some believe they may lie under the Dead Sea. Historians think the towns may have been near a fault line and that God's wrath was actually a terrible earthquake that flattened them.*

Emperor Constantine

In the early years of Christianity, this small sect faced ruthless persecution throughout the giant Roman Empire. In 64 AD, only a few decades after Christ's death in Jerusalem, Emperor Nero ordered the first official persecution of Christians in Rome. The Roman historian Tacitus recounted the particular cruelty of the executions ordered by the deranged tyrant Nero, some of which involved feeding believers to dogs. "In their very deaths they were made the subjects of sport," Tacitus wrote.

Roman authorities considered Christianity a threat to the empire's security. As they viewed it, Christians worshipped a criminal crucified by Rome and rejected the divinity of the emperor and the pagan gods. As the religion spread, the persecutions intensified sporadically for 200 years. Nevertheless, while the first Christians were often poor, the religion began to attract adherents from the mainstream of Roman life.

After seeing a vision and converting to Christianity, Emperor Constantine issued the Edict of Milan in 313 AD, legalizing Christianity throughout the empire. By that time, Christian worship was widespread. In fact, within a few generations of the edict, Christianity replaced paganism as the official creed of the Roman Empire. In the span of four centuries, Christianity had gone from an outlaw faith embraced by a few Jewish malcontents to an imperial religion. The Roman Empire collapsed in the fifth century AD, but Christianity continued to spread in Europe and became the unifying faith of the continent.

The Roman Catholic Church remains headquartered at Vatican City in Rome, a few blocks from the ruins of the colosseum where ancient Roman authorities once fed Christians to the lions.

ADDITIONAL FACTS:

1. *Constantine's conversion to Christianity didn't prevent him from killing off many of his political enemies, including several members of his own family. During his thirty-one-year reign, Constantine executed his brother-in-law, his second wife, and his eldest son.*

2. *Sick of Rome, which he considered an unsuitable capital for his empire, Constantine founded a city at the Hellespont, where Europe meets Asia. It was originally named New Rome, but soon came to be known as Constantinople in honor of the emperor. The city is now known as Istanbul, the largest city in modern-day Turkey.*

3. *As emperor, Constantine abolished the gladiatorial games that had amused the Roman masses for centuries, although they continued illegally for decades.*

Modernism

In the modernist movement in literature, which flourished from roughly 1900 to 1940, authors explored new ways to tell stories and rethought the question of how best to explore objective reality and truth. Major figures in literary modernism included the novelists Marcel Proust, Gertrude Stein, James Joyce, Virginia Woolf, and William Faulkner, and the poets T. S. Eliot and Ezra Pound.

During the late 1800s, Western literature had been dominated by realism. Gustave Flaubert, Theodore Dreiser, Émile Zola, and other novelists of that period had attempted to depict characters, situations, and social conditions accurately and with a meticulous eye for detail.

Around the turn of the twentieth century, however, revolutionary ideas in a number of fields called into question our ability to identify and describe reality—and even the existence of an objective reality in the first place. In psychology, Sigmund Freud explored the idea of the unconscious, asserting that the human mind and the self were knowable only through psychoanalysis. In linguistics, Ferdinand de Saussure contended that language was an arbitrary and unreliable cultural construct. In anthropology, Sir James Frazer brought new sophistication to the study of non-Western cultures and religions, exposing alternatives to the Western worldview. And in physics, Albert Einstein's theories of relativity undermined even the seemingly certain principles of space and time.

Collectively, these disparate ideas exerted enormous influence on the literary and artistic worlds. Whereas the realists of the 1800s had been obsessed with portraying the world accurately, new authors and artists of the 1900s—soon dubbed modernists—became preoccupied with the question of how reality could be accurately rendered if objective truth did not exist.

Modernist writers tackled this problem through experimentation. One of their major innovations was stream-of-consciousness narrative, the attempt to convey a character's inner thoughts verbatim, without authorial interference. This technique appears in Joyce's *Ulysses* (1922), Woolf's *Mrs. Dalloway* (1925), and Faulkner's *The Sound and the Fury* (1929). Some authors tried to depict the same event or image from multiple perspectives, stacking subjective accounts on top of one another—or pitting them against one another—in an attempt to approximate objective truth. Woolf's *To the Lighthouse* (1927) is a prime example of this approach. Still others, notably Stein, experimented radically with language, using extensive repetition, which she called "insistence," and other techniques to explore shades of words' meaning. And virtually all modernists played with the flow of time in their works, discarding linear chronology and jumping abruptly around past, present, and future—a characteristic that gives modernist fiction and poetry an often-deserved reputation for difficulty.

Gothic Art

The Gothic era began in the twelfth century with the development of a new type of architecture in the Île de France, an area that includes Paris and the surrounding countryside. By 1250 the style had spread to many parts of Europe, affecting both sculpture and painting.

The term *Gothic* was coined in Italy and originally carried a negative connotation, associating the architectural style with the 'Goths' or barbarians who had destroyed classical civilization. Gothic artists, on the other hand, referred to their own work as *opus modernum* or *opus francigenum*, modern or French work.

The reconstructed royal Abbey Church of Saint-Denis, just north of Paris, is usually considered the earliest example of Gothic architecture. Between 1137 and 1144, Abbot Suger commissioned a new choir for the church. It was built with larger windows and taller arches and thus seemed lofty and weightless, a strong contrast to the somber solidity of the earlier, Romanesque style.

Gothic architecture was more fully developed at Notre Dame in Paris (begun in 1163) and Chartres (rebuilt from 1194 to 1220). Flying buttresses and external arches were erected to support the weight of the building on the outside. These massive structures allowed more stained glass windows to be cut into the walls, thus making their interiors brighter and more resplendent with color.

The influence of Gothic architecture outside of France is visible at Salisbury Cathedral (begun in 1220) and the Duomo (Cathedral) of Orvieto, Italy (begun circa 1310).

In northern Europe, Gothic painting is most commonly seen in stained glass windows and book illustrations, such as the famous illuminated manuscript, *LesTrès Riches Heures du Duc de Berry*, painted by the three Limbourg brothers between 1413 and 1416. In Italy, on the other hand, the Gothic style manifests itself in the paintings of Giotto and Simone Martini.

Sculpture was used extensively to decorate both the interiors and exteriors of Gothic Cathedrals, as can be seen in the magnificent portals at Chartres or at Naumburg Cathedral in Germany.

The Gothic style flourished in France and much of Northern Europe until the early sixteenth century. In Italy, it faded earlier with the onset of the Renaissance.

ADDITIONAL FACT

1. *In the eighteenth century, the word* gothic *was associated with fiction that emphasized the grotesque and mysterious; today it often refers to a movement in music, dress, and culture that began in the 1980s with the work of music groups such as Siouxsie and the Banshees.*

Nociception: The Perception of Pain

The perception of pain, called nociception, is essential to human survival. Pain is a simple, effective way to learn about the dangers of the world. It signals us to react: to recoil from scalding water, to step away from broken glass, to ease off a twisted ankle.

All higher species, especially those related most closely to us, have nervous systems that seem to process pain. Although we can't ask them if they are hurt, birds and mammals writhe, moan, and yelp much the same way that humans do. Like us, they experience a rise of blood pressure, dilated pupils, perspiration, and an increased pulse rate in response to a harmful stimulus.

Nociception is a crucial survival tool for complex organisms. Children born with a rare condition—congenital insensitivity to pain and anhydrosis (CIPA)—seldom live past age twenty-five. Although these children appear normal at birth, the trouble begins when they grow teeth: They can bite off their fingers without feeling a thing. They break bones, burn hands, and scrape knees; but they don't know they are hurt until they see blood or bruises. They often die from massive infections caused by multiple injuries.

Clichéd as it may sound, pain is truly all in our heads. Different parts of the brain work together in a network to form what is sometimes called the pain matrix. Some areas of the matrix tell us about intensity, while others inform us about the location, duration, and type of pain—burning, throbbing, or sharp. The sensation of pain triggers the feeling of distress, thanks to a part of the brain called the anterior cingulate cortex. Interestingly, it does not distinguish between physical and emotional pain. It responds equally to a broken arm and to a broken heart.

ADDITIONAL FACTS

1. People who are good at empathizing with others have more active anterior cingulate cortices. They actually feel other people's pain.

2. Human fetuses develop the neural circuits to feel pain at twenty-nine weeks, well into the third trimester.

3. Newborns who are circumcised without anesthesia show greater responses to pain at four-month and six-month vaccinations.

4. Amputees often complain of phantom limb pain. They experience intense, shooting pain that seems to come from the limb that is no longer there. These cases were some of the first evidence that pain comes, in part, from the brain.

Baroque Period

The word *baroque* originates from a Portuguese word meaning "misshapen pearl." This symbol is an appropriate metaphor for the art, architecture, and music of the period, which lasted roughly from 1600 to 1750. It was an era of contrasts—in art, between light and dark colors, smooth and broken surfaces; and in music, between loud and soft, fast and slow. It was characterized at first by a simplification of complex Renaissance musical styles, and eventually by ornate new aesthetic structures that seemed a huge challenge to all previous currents of thought.

Claudio Monteverdi (1567–1643) was the most influential composer of the early baroque, and his *Orfeo* (1607) is generally regarded as the first dramatically and musically successful opera. Most baroque music was based on the dialogue between a supporting musical accompaniment called the basso continuo—usually played on a combination of a chord-playing instrument (like the organ, the guitar, or the harpsichord) and a bass-line instrument (like the cello, viola da gamba, or the bassoon)—and an extravagant concerto-like solo line—usually played on the violin or a wind instrument (such as the recorder, oboe, or flute).

Cadences, or harmonic stopping points, were emphasized, and many works were divided into sections that alternated between slow and fast tempos, and further into even, symmetrical musical phrases. Regional dance rhythms such as the minuet and the gigue were incorporated, and the violin gained prominence because of its versatility, volume, and ability to highlight strong rhythms. Later baroque music is characterized by steady rhythm, intense emotion, elaborate melodic lines, and virtuoso demands on performers.

In the baroque, leading male roles in operas were often performed by castrati, singers who had been castrated before puberty to maintain their high vocal ranges. Castrati were noted for their ranges, power, vocal flexibility, and breath control.

The early baroque emerged in the writing of Italian composers (Monteverdi, Cavalli), but the style eventually spread to England (Purcell), France (Couperin, Rameau), and Germany (Schütz, Buxtehude). In the Italian high baroque, Arcangelo Corelli (c.1653–1713) and Antonio Vivaldi (1678–1741) wrote beautiful, complex concertos, while in Germany, Georg Philipp Telemann (1681–1767) and Johann Sebastian Bach (1685–1750) competed to be the *Meister* of church music in parishes and royal courts all across northern Europe.

ADDITIONAL FACT
1. *The choirboys of St. Paul's Cathedral in London, the largest baroque cathedral in Europe, were often kidnapped by choirmasters from other groups and forced to sing for the competition.*

Metaphysics

Metaphysics is the most general study of reality—what there is, and what *it* is like.

The first question—What is there?—is explored by ontology, a subfield of metaphysics. Ontology asks: Is everything that exists material or are there immaterial things like souls? Are there abstract mathematical objects, like numbers and sets? Ontology also asks: What does it mean for something to exist? Is existence a property, like being red, which some things have, and other things lack? Or is existence just the collection of everything that is, so that there can't be anything that does not exist? If existence is a property like redness, what kind of property is it? When I say that horses exist, but unicorns do not, what am I saying about horses that I am denying about unicorns?

Metaphysics also asks a second type of question, about the features and relations of things. For example, if there are numbers, do they exist in space and time? Do they exist contingently; that is, could they have failed to exist, or could they cease to exist?

Many philosophers share one tenet of metaphysics that believes that there are two very general kinds of things: substances and properties. Substances are objects in the ordinary sense, while properties are ways those substances are. For instance, a sweater is a substance, while the color of a sweater is a property of the sweater. Many metaphysical questions arise from the notions of substance and property.

One question that philosophers have long asked is whether properties are individual or general. To say that properties are general means that for any two red things, say a sweater and a rose, there is literally a single property called redness had, or instantiated, by both things. *Instantiation* is a philosophical term that describes the relation between a substance and a property. To say that properties are individual means that there are literally two different properties—the redness instantiated by my sweater and the redness instantiated by the rose. And, those properties perfectly resemble one another.

ADDITIONAL FACTS

1. *Metaphysics gets its name from the early editors of Aristotle's writings. These topics are treated in the book that came after Aristotle's* Physics. *Because the book had no title of its own, the editors called it* Metaphysics—*in Greek, "after physics."*

2. *What we now call "metaphysics" Aristotle just called "first philosophy."*

Joseph

Joseph was Jacob's eleventh son and his first with Rachel. Within the Jewish faith, Joseph is widely recognized for his trust in God and cagey capacity to live as a Jew among Gentiles.

Genesis explains that Joseph was Jacob's favorite son—a fact exhibited by Jacob's gift to him of a multicolored coat—and that Joseph's uncanny abilities to interpret dreams only exacerbated fraternal jealousies. Famously, Joseph reported one dream in which his father, mother, and elder brothers would kneel down before Joseph as his servants. Angered by Joseph's dream, his brothers formed a plot to kill him. Joseph was only seventeen. They stopped only when the eldest brother, Reuben, intervened. Instead, they threw Joseph into a pit.

Joseph was eventually discovered and sold to the Egyptian, Potiphar, as a slave. He served Potiphar dutifully until Potiphar's wife tried to seduce him. When he refused her advances, she accused him of rape, and Potiphar had Joseph imprisoned.

Joseph was then sent to jail where he met an imprisoned servant of the pharaoh who interpreted his dream. The servant was later released, and when the pharaoh had a troubling dream, he sought Joseph's advice. Joseph interpreted the dream to mean Egypt would face seven years of plentiful harvests followed by seven years of extreme famine. The pharaoh trusted Joseph and stored excess food for seven years. When Joseph's prophecy came true, the gracious pharaoh gave him unprecedented power.

As the predicted famine spread throughout the region, Joseph's brothers fled to Egypt in search of food. In order to punish them for their sins against him, Joseph disguised himself and took his brother Benjamin as a slave, sending the others home. Another brother, Judah, begged to be taken in Benjamin's stead. Joseph saw this as a sign that his brothers had changed.

He allowed his family to move to Egypt. There, he and his eleven brothers founded the twelve tribes of Israel.

ADDITIONAL FACTS

1. *It is speculated that one of the reasons the pharaoh accepted Joseph in the first place was that the pharaoh may have been a Hyksos, an ethnicity with some ties to the Hebrews.*

2. *Joseph's story was adapted by Andrew Lloyd Webber and Tim Rice into the musical* Joseph and the Amazing Technicolor Dreamcoat, *which debuted on Broadway in 1982.*

The Spread of Islam

After the death of the Prophet Muhammad in 632 AD, the religion that he founded in Mecca spread with astonishing speed throughout the Middle East. Muslim armies carrying his banner conquered the Arabian Peninsula, Persia, Syria, Armenia, Egypt, North Africa, and Afghanistan. In 711 AD, less than a century after the prophet's death, his followers conquered modern-day Spain, bringing Islam to Europe.

Stretched over three continents, the Islamic empire, or caliphate, struggled to maintain its fragile unity. The capital moved from remote Mecca to Damascus, the oldest city on earth and the caliphs built splendid mosques to cement their rule.

But in the middle of the eighth century, the caliphate began to fragment. The largest of the rival caliphates, the Abbasid, moved their capital to Baghdad, while the Iberian provinces established their own caliphate. Still, during the medieval period, the Muslim world flourished. Scientists, poets, and mathematicians turned Baghdad into a fabled city of romance and learning.

To Christian Europe, still in the midst of its Dark Ages, the success of Islam was terrifying. Muslim armies reached France before finally being turned back by the Franks under their leader Charles Martel in 732. Some historians see that battle as a turning point in history, one that prevented the further spread of Islam in Europe. Later, the pope dispatched European armies to the Middle East to wage a holy war against the Muslims.

The destruction of the caliphate, however, came from the east. In 1258, Baghdad was captured by an invading Mongol army. The Mongols torched the city's great libraries and murdered as many as a million of its inhabitants. The Mongol leader, a grandson of Genghis Khan, executed the last caliph by rolling him up inside a carpet and letting his horses stomp him to death.

ADDITIONAL FACTS

1. *During the European Dark Ages, Islamic scholars were more scientifically advanced than their European counterparts, and many English words related to science and math, including "algebra" and "chemistry," are derived from Arabic.*

2. *During a war in Central Asia in the eighth century, the caliph's army discovered from a prisoner of war the Chinese secret of how to make paper.*

3. *One of the most famous books from the caliphate is* The Thousand and One Nights, *a collection of tales and fables that has enjoyed immense popularity in the West since it was first translated in the eighteenth century.*

Catch-22

Joseph Heller's *Catch-22* gave the English language one of its finest war novels and black comedies, and a now-common figure of speech. Upon publication in 1961, the unusual work met with mixed reviews: Some called it brilliant; others, shocking and offensive. In any case, *Catch-22* was a landmark protest novel that introduced absurdity and surrealism into mainstream American literature.

The protagonist of *Catch-22*, Yossarian, is a US Air Force bombardier based on the small Italian island of Pianosa during World War II. His squadron is run by comically inept generals who promise the airmen that they will be sent home after they complete a certain number of missions—but then keep increasing this required number of missions so no one can leave. The war's bureaucratic absurdity is embodied in the simple but insidious Air Force regulation that gives the novel its title. "Catch-22" states that a soldier can be exempted from combat missions if he is deemed insane, but if he actually puts in a request for this exemption, he is clearly sane enough to fly.

The novel is populated with an unforgettable cast of misfits and oddities. Squadron commander Major Major Major (so named because his father thought it would be funny) is promoted all the way to the rank of major by a computer glitch on the first day of his career. Mess officer Milo Minderbinder runs a ruthless black-market syndicate and will do anything for a profit, even signing a contract with the Germans to bomb his own squadron. And medic Doc Daneeka, after being "killed off" by a paperwork error, is unable to convince anyone that he is really still alive—least of all his own wife, who appreciates the monthly payouts from his life insurance policy.

Catch-22's narrative jumps forward and backward in time with no warning and few contextual clues, mimicking the chaos of the war and leaving the reader completely disoriented. Meanwhile, the squadron's carnival-house antics make the novel uproariously funny—until things start to turn sinister. A master of black comedy, Heller reveals plot details gradually and offhandedly until it becomes clear that what seemed hilarious at the outset is actually deadly serious once the full truth is known.

Heller said that *Catch-22* was not really about World War II in particular but about the absurdity of bureaucracy and authority in the modern world in general. Indeed, this message gave the novel a cult following among antiestablishment, countercultural movements of the 1960s.

ADDITIONAL FACTS

1. Catch-22 *was originally titled* Catch-18, *but after Leon Uris's novel* Mila 18 *appeared earlier in 1961, Heller decided to change the name at the last-minute.*

2. Heller flew dozens of bombing missions in American campaigns in Italy and North Africa during World War II.

The Cathedral of Notre Dame of Paris

The Gothic Cathedral of Notre Dame is located on the eastern side of the Île de la Cité, an island on the River Seine in the middle of Paris.

The cathedral was built on the site of an ancient Roman temple dedicated to Jupiter that was replaced in 528 by a Christian church. Inspired by the magnificence of the recently restored Abbey Church of Saint Denis, Bishop Maurice de Sully decided to tear down the old Parisian church and build a grander one. Construction on the new cathedral began in 1163 and continued until the beginning of the fourteenth century.

As in most Gothic cathedrals, the façade of Notre Dame has three levels. Above these rise two towers, connected by the gallery of gargoyles,—sculptures of hideous beasts that were believed to keep evil spirits away from the church. Below the gallery is the rose window, which is pieced together from hundreds of stained glass panes and measures over thirty feet in diameter.

Lower down is the Kings' Gallery, which originally contained statues of the twenty-eight kings of Judah and Israel. During the French Revolution, the figures were decapitated by angry mobs that thought they were portraits of French kings. The sculptures were replaced in 1845 by the notable French architect, Viollet-le-Duc.

On the façade are three entrances to the church. The central and largest portal is dedicated to Christ in Judgment. To its left stands the portal of the Virgin and to its right the portal of Saint Anne, the Virgin's mother.

The cathedral has a rich history. In 1185 it was the site from which Heraclius of Caesarea announced the Third Crusade. In 1431 it staged the coronation of Henry VI and in 1804, that of Napoleon. During the French Revolution, the church was initially renamed the Temple of Reason, then the Temple of the Supreme Being. In 1970, it was used for Charles de Gaulle's funeral.

ADDITIONAL FACTS

1. Victor Hugo wrote The Hunchback of Notre Dame *in order to raise public awareness of Notre Dame's history at a time when the building was in danger of being razed.*

2. Kilomètre zéro, which marks the starting point for all distances measured on French highways, is located on the square in front of the cathedral.

The Placebo Effect

The placebo effect is the beneficial influence of a treatment that has no medical value. Inject a sick person with salt water or give him a sugar pill, and for some reason, he often feels better. This is especially true for subjectively assessed disorders such as migraines, back pain, and depression. The placebo effect may account for a large part of the therapeutic value we ascribe to medications.

The placebo effect for pain medications has been at least partially explained by brain chemistry. When the brain experiences pain, it releases endorphins—chemicals that naturally act like morphine to relieve pain. Brain imaging studies have shown that when a person takes a placebo, it triggers the release of endorphins. Neurologically, it's as if he had taken a drug.

There is also the less understood but equally powerful nocebo effect. Often, when people are told that they are going to experience negative side effects from a drug, they do, even if there is no medical reason for it. In one study, people were given a sugar pill and told that it induced vomiting. Later, 80 percent of them started throwing up. Similarly, in another study, women who believed they were going to die of a heart attack were found to be four times more likely to die of a heart attack than women with the exact same medical profile who did not think they were at risk. Thinking sick may make you sick.

In some realms of medical treatment, the placebo effect actually seems to be getting bigger. In studies of antidepressants, the response rate to placebos has been increasing by 7 percent every ten years. In 1980, 30 percent of depressed people given a placebo improved without any other treatment; in 2000, it was 44 percent. This may be due to widespread advertising and heightened expectations for drugs. In general, the public has more faith in psychiatric medication than it did twenty years ago, which gives placebos more power.

ADDITIONAL FACTS

1. *The color of pills may also have an effect on some patients. In one Italian study, blue placebos made excellent sleeping pills for women but had the opposite effect on men.*

2. *Painful injections may have more therapeutic value than ones that hurt less.*

Form

The term *form*, when used in classical music, refers to the structures that guide the composition of a piece—a set of characteristics that are common to a substantial number of works. There are several important forms that determine how compositions are divided into movements and thematic sections. They serve as blueprints for each piece.

BINARY FORM (A-B): The first section of the piece (A) begins in the tonic key then modulates (changes key) to what is called the dominant key or the relative major key. The second section (B) begins in the dominant or the relative major key and then modulates back to the home key. So, if the piece is in A-major, the A section begins in A-major, then modulates to the key of E. The B section begins in E and then modulates back to A-major. If the piece is in A-minor, the A section begins in that key and modulates to C-major, and the B section reverses that process.

TERNARY FORM (A-B-A): The A section is in the tonic key, the B section is in the dominant key or relative major, and then the first section is repeated, making sure the piece ends where it started, in the tonic.

COMPOUND BINARY FORM: Also called sonata form, this is a three-part structure. The first part, called the exposition, establishes the home key; presents a main theme and additional, often contrasting themes; and creates tension by modulating away from the home key. In the second part, called the development, the composer presents thematic material in a variety of combinations and guises, often modulating extensively. The third part, the recapitulation, brings back the initial themes and ends the piece in the same key as it started.

RONDO FORM: This is a variant on ternary form, and it takes the form A-B-A-C-A-D-A, with each letter representing a thematic section. Each of the parts B-C-D is called an episode and acts as harmonic and melodic complements to the initial A theme.

THEME AND VARIATION: The composer presents a melody and then varies that melody through ornamentation, changes in harmony, changes in texture, changes from major to minor, and other techniques. This form can be represented by the letters A-A'-A''-A''', etc)

ADDITIONAL FACTS

1. Shades of sonata form first appeared in Bach's late baroque pieces, but the adoption of the form is one of the biggest stylistic changes to mark the transition between the baroque era and the classical era. Mozart was a master of sonata form.

2. Both Bach (Goldberg Variations) and Mozart (Variations on "Twinkle, Twinkle, Little Star") were interested in theme and variation.

Matter/Form

Aristotle's (384–322 BC) theory of matter and form is one of the most important and influential aspects of his philosophy. However, it is a subtle doctrine and not often well understood. At its core, it was an attempt to explain the natural world before the advances of modern science.

Aristotle saw that the world was populated by substances—concrete individual things, like plants and animals. You can think of substances as the sort of things that typically function as the subjects of sentences when we speak about them. For instance, Socrates is a substance because we say, "Socrates is pale." Aristotle called certain qualities of substances, such as the quality of being pale, accidents. Accidents are things said of substances; when we speak about them, they usually function in sentences as adjectives.

Another way of grasping this difference is through Aristotle's distinction between accidental change and substantial change. An example of an accidental change is when Socrates goes from being pale to being tan, after spending time in the sun. Socrates, the substance, persists, and what changes are mere accidents of Socrates, his paleness and his tan. An example of a substantial change is the death of Socrates. In this case, a genuine substance, Socrates, goes out of existence.

This idea of substantial change leads to Aristotle's matter/form theory. Even when Socrates dies, his corpse continues to exist. Something persists. Aristotle identifies matter as that which persists through substantial change. However, the matter of Socrates, which once contained various intricate biological processes, has ceased those processes. Now that he is dead, the matter remains but the matter's form has changed. Form is defined as the principle of organization and activity that determined how Socrates' many parts interacted.

Aristotle concluded that individual substances are combinations of matter and form. In his works on natural philosophy, Aristotle used the matter/form theory to explain a wide variety of natural phenomena.

ADDITIONAL FACTS

1. *Aristotle's theory of matter and form is called* hylomorphism.

2. *Aristotle's hylomorphism had a huge impact on Western Christianity, through St. Thomas Aquinas, who made it one of the pillars of his own metaphysics.*

3. *René Descartes (1596–1650) severely criticized the use of Aristotelian substantial forms in the physics of the seventeenth century.*

Moses

Moses is generally recognized as one of most important Biblical figures in Jewish history.

The Hebrew people, descendents of Abraham, left Israel during a drought and settled in Egypt, where one of Jacob's sons, Joseph, was well-liked by the pharaoh. As time passed, and the pharaoh's friendship with Joseph was forgotten, the Hebrew people became the slaves of the Egyptians.

Moses was born to Amram and Jochebed in Egypt during the reign of a particularly vicious pharaoh, Ramses II, who decreed that Hebrew slave children should be killed. At first, Jochebed succeeded in hiding Moses, but this eventually proved too difficult. When Moses was three months old, his mother put him in a basket and pushed him down the Nile River, hoping someone kind would find him. As it turned out, the pharaoh's daughter found Moses and raised him as her own son.

Moses grew up and finally learned his true heritage. Shortly thereafter, he saw an Egyptian beating an Israelite; and, in response, Moses killed the Egyptian. Having committed such a heinous crime, Moses was forced to flee Egypt and live in the Sinai Peninsula for forty years. One day, Moses saw a bush that was on fire but not burning. When Moses inspected it more closely, God commanded him to return to Egypt and lead the Israelites out of Egypt.

Moses then returned to Egypt and tried to persuade the pharaoh to free the Hebrews. The pharaoh refused, causing God to send ten plagues against the Egyptians. The tenth plague— the killing of the firstborn son in all Egyptian families—proved to be the breaking point, and pharaoh freed the Israelites. However, after allowing the Israelites to leave, pharaoh pursued them. By the time the Israelites reached the Sea of Reed (Red Sea), pharaoh's armies had caught up to them and trapped them. In order to save them, God parted the Red Sea for the Israelites, only to close it afterward, drowning the Egyptians. After passing the sea, Moses led the Hebrews through the desert to Mount Sinai, where he ascended the mountain alone and received the Ten Commandments directly from God.

Although the historical truth of Moses's existence is debatable, as a leader and lawgiver, he is the foremost icon of Jewish history.

ADDITIONAL FACTS

1. *Some theories claim that Moses was not Hebrew at all, but rather a renegade and sympathetic Egyptian priest.*

2. *The anti-Semitic stereotype that Jews have horns most likely stems from a mistranslation of Moses's description after he descended from Mount Sinai. Being so close to God allegedly changed his physical appearance, but it is said that "rays of light protruded from his face," and not, as some mistakenly believed that "horns protruded from his head."*

Charlemagne

After the collapse of the Roman Empire in 476 AD, Europe entered a period of war and anarchy that later historians would label the Dark Ages. Rival tribes fought constantly over the decaying remains of the empire. Progress in the arts and sciences stalled. Without the unity provided by Rome, there was little holding the continent together.

Charlemagne (742–814), the leader of a kingdom in modern-day Germany, created a large European empire in the eighth century that for the first time reunited many of the territories that once belonged to the Western Roman Empire. On Christmas Day in 800 AD, the pope crowned him the first Holy Roman Emperor, the leader of newly resurgent Christendom.

At the time of his coronation, Charlemagne's empire included modern-day France, Belgium, the Netherlands, Switzerland, and most of Germany. Charlemagne was a king of the Franks, a German tribe that had annexed many of its neighbors.

The Holy Roman Empire proclaimed in 800 AD never actually united Europe. As Voltaire joked in the eighteenth century, it was neither "holy," nor "Roman," nor an "empire." By one count, it comprised more than 300 semi-independent principalities, some of them no bigger than a few square miles. Still, it was a major force in central Europe for centuries to come. Charlemagne's forces spread Christianity and fought (unsuccessfully) to reclaim territory held by the Muslim caliphate in Spain.

Charlemagne's legacy is still seen across Europe—literally. Recent genetic studies show that a large percentage of Europeans descend from the Frankish king. He is considered one of the founding fathers of France and Germany. His empire, in reduced form, endured until the last Holy Roman Emperor abdicated in 1806.

ADDITIONAL FACTS

1. The sword Charlemagne carried into battle was named Joyeuse; a weapon thought to be the famous sword is now housed at the Louvre Museum in Paris.

2. In popular medieval legend, Charlemagne was one of the "nine worthies," the greatest knights of history. Other worthies included King Arthur and Alexander the Great.

3. During a battle in Spain in 778 AD, one of Charlemagne's noblemen, Roland, was killed by Basques. The story of Roland's courageous death became the foundation for the Song of Roland, one of the most famous pieces of medieval literature.

Gabriel García Márquez

Colombian author Gabriel García Márquez, more than probably any other figure, is responsible for drawing the world's attention to Latin American literature during the twentieth century. In his novels and short stories, he has explored the history and people of his home continent through a lens that combines real events with pervasive currents of fantasy and myth.

Born in the town of Aracataca in northern Colombia in 1928, García Márquez grew up immersed in family stories told and retold by his elders, particularly his grandparents. After college, he worked as a journalist for various foreign press agencies, living in France, Venezuela, the United States, and Mexico. He began writing fiction in the mid-1950s and published his first major work, the short story collection *No One Writes to the Colonel*, in 1961.

García Márquez's masterpiece is unquestionably the novel *One Hundred Years of Solitude* (1967), a sprawling tale of six generations in the fictional town of Macondo. The history of the town and its founders—the Buendía family—mirrors the historical trends of Latin America as a whole: As Macondo comes into increasing contact with the outside world, it passes from unspoiled pastoral isolation through civil war, dictatorship, labor unrest, and other hardships that accompany the transition to modernity. In the novel, history moves cyclically as both individuals and groups repeat the same mistakes over and over—a fact that García Márquez emphasizes by giving characters in different generations of the Buendía family the same names.

Many of García Márquez's works exemplify the genre that has been dubbed magic realism—a mix of highly realistic depiction with significant elements of the fantastic and supernatural. During *One Hundred Years of Solitude*, among other occurrences, Macondo sees a torrential rainstorm that lasts for five years, a cascade of yellow flowers from the sky upon news of a character's death, and the birth of an infant with a pig's tail. Within the context of magic realism, most of these events are accepted as commonplace, and the characters witness them without comment or wonder.

After two other major releases—the novel *The Autumn of the Patriarch* (1975) and the novella *Chronicle of a Death Foretold* (1981)—García Márquez was awarded the Nobel Prize for Literature in 1982. His works have sold tens of millions of copies in the original Spanish and in translation, counting him among the few contemporary novelists who have maintained both critical and popular success.

ADDITIONAL FACT
1. *Many of García Márquez's works take place in the same fictional universe, with some of the same characters and locations popping up in different stories and novels.*

Renaissance Art

The period known as the Renaissance followed the Middle Ages and led to the modern era. The word is derived from *renascere*, Latin for "to be born again," and it refers to the rebirth of Greek and Roman culture. Artists and intellectual figures of the Renaissance consciously rejected the ideas of the Middle Ages and sought inspiration in classical models.

The roots of the Renaissance can be traced as far back as the early fourteenth century when the Italian poet Francesco Petrarch developed a philosophy that placed great value on individualism and human achievement. This marked a change from medieval society's complete preoccupation with God's power.

In terms of the visual arts, the Renaissance began in Florence in the early fifteenth century. It was at this time that sculptors and architects began to seek ancient models to work from. At the same time, painters invented one-point perspective, a system to represent depth and volume on a two-dimensional surface.

Renowned Florentine artists of the Early Renaissance include the sculptor Donatello, whose *David* was the first freestanding nude since antiquity; Brunelleschi, the architect who designed the famous Dome of the Cathedral in Florence; and Masaccio, who was the first painter known to use one-point perspective.

The High Renaissance, which is usually dated 1495–1527, produced some of the greatest masters of European civilization, such as Leonardo da Vinci, Michelangelo, Raphael, and Titian. It was in this period, too, that work began on the reconstruction of St. Peter's Basilica. The architect Bramante initiated the process and designed the first version of the new church. Work on the project continued after his death under the supervision of many artists, including Michelangelo. The new basilica was not completed until the mid-seventeenth century.

ADDITIONAL FACTS

1. In northern Europe, the Renaissance was slower to arrive as the Gothic style continued to prevail until the sixteenth century.

2. The Late Renaissance generally refers to the period between 1527 and 1600. Works produced in this period are often referred to as "Mannerist," since they are highly complex in form and rich in esoteric intellectual conceits.

Mendelian Genetics

When Gregor Mendel, a Czech monk, began his pea experiments in the mid-1800s, there were two leading theories of inheritance. The first stated that the traits of parents blend together equally to create a child. The second proposed that the environment in which a child was conceived shaped his features. Mendel disproved them both.

On his frequent walks through the gardens of his monastery, Mendel noted the simple traits of a common pea plant (*Pisum sativum*). He noticed that the flowers of the plants were either purple or white—nothing in between—and that the pods were either yellow or green. The stem was either long or short, and the seeds were either round or wrinkled. In total, he found seven traits that never seemed to blend together, and so he began to experiment.

When Mendel bred green-podded peas with yellow-podded peas, their offspring all turned out green-podded. But when he bred this first generation with itself, one quarter of the next generation turned out yellow-podded. The same thing happened with height. When he bred long-stemmed peas with short-stemmed peas, the following generation was all tall, but one-quarter of the grandchildren's generation was short.

This pattern led Mendel to conceive of what would later be called alleles, genes, and dominant-recessive inheritance. Essentially, Mendel concluded that each plant received one hereditary unit, or allele, from each parent for each trait, or gene. Although only one of the alleles would be outwardly expressed—the dominant allele—both had an equal chance of being passed on to the next generation. So, after the long-stemmed peas were mated with short-stemmed peas, their offspring all had a dominant allele for tallness and a recessive allele for shortness. They all appeared tall but they all carried an unexpressed allele for shortness. So, when that generation was mated with itself, one quarter of their offspring had two alleles for tallness, half had a tall and a short allele (they appeared tall), and one quarter had two alleles for shortness. Those with two shortness alleles appeared short. This basic observation is the foundation of modern genetics and explains why certain traits appear to skip generations.

ADDITIONAL FACTS

1. Between 1856 and 1863, Mendel cultivated and tested approximately 28,000 pea plants.

2. Although Mendel kept excellent records, his results often struck later scientists as being too exact. They generally suspect him of falling prey to confirmation bias and smoothing his data.

3. Mendel's work was largely ignored in his lifetime, and he died in obscurity. Botanists rediscovered his work in 1900, and it changed the study of genetics forever.

Antonio Vivaldi

Born a sickly child to a Venetian violinist, Antonio Vivaldi (1678–1741) entered the priesthood in 1703. He quickly became a violin teacher, a conductor, and a composer-in-residence at the *Pio Ospedale della Pietà*, a Venetian conservatory for orphaned girls. The young women were trained rigorously in music, and their concerts, often comprised of Vivaldi's original works, were very popular with the city's music-loving audiences.

Vivaldi was stunningly prolific, producing more than 500 concertos in his lifetime, more than any other known composer. Although Vivaldi composed vocal works, most of his pieces are instrumental, and he is most famous in that area. His concertos are beautifully expressive, covering a range of emotions, from delicate sadness to majestic bombast.

Many of Vivaldi's works were programmatic—meant to tell a story, evoke an emotion, or give the impression of real-life events, usually in the cycle of nature. The concertos often took the form of three movements: an Allegro (brisk tempo) movement, a slow movement in the same or related key, and a concluding allegro movement, even more lively than the first.

Vivaldi's compositions have titles like *The Night*, *The Storm at Sea*, and *The Goldfinch*, but his most famous is *The Four Seasons*, a catchy set of four concertos that remains one of the most popular pieces of Western classical music today. With this and other pieces, Vivaldi revolutionized the role of the soloist, giving it unprecedented importance with his extraordinary sense of drama and flourish. Vivaldi also had a huge influence on Johann Sebastian Bach and on the composers of the classical era with his memorable themes, adventurous rhythmic motifs, and the overall clarity of his compositions.

ADDITIONAL FACTS

1. An abbreviation of the words Laus Deo Beataeque Mariae Deiparae Amen *appeared at the top of most of Vivaldi's manuscripts. It means, "Honor to God and to Blessed Mary [the mother of God]."*

2. Vivaldi is thought to have earned 50,000 ducats a year at one point in his life, one of the highest salaries paid for a musician at that time.

Logic

Logic is the study of formally valid arguments. An argument consists of several sentences that are premises, or assumptions, and a sentence that states a conclusion. Here is an example:

> *Socrates is a man.*
> *If Socrates is a man, then Socrates is mortal.*
> *Therefore, Socrates is mortal.*

This is an instance of a valid argument. A valid argument is an argument in which the truth of the conclusion follows from the truth of its premises. Notice, however, that the validity of this argument does not depend on anything about Socrates, manhood, or mortality. It is valid because its schema, or construction, is valid. The following is a schematic presentation of the same argument:

> *1. p*
> *2. If p then q*
> *3. Therefore, q*

No matter what sentences we fill in for p and q, this is a valid argument. The original argument (1)–(3) is the same argument, only with particular sentences filled-in for p and q. Words like "and, "or," "some," and "any" are called logical terms. The study of logic examines which schemas for arguments are valid. It examines the relation between different logical terms like "if-then" and "and" and the roles they play in building valid arguments

ADDITIONAL FACTS

1. Ever since Aristotle developed the first logical system, logic has often been considered the first subject one should learn in philosophy.

2. Gottlob Frege (1848–1925) invented modern logic in his 1879 work Begriffschrif. *Although Frege revolutionized logic, he is almost unknown outside the field.*

3. The principle that every truth is either true or false is denied by some philosophers. Other philosophers even deny that all contradictions are false!

King David

King David, who ruled after King Saul, was Israel's second and greatest king. He was the son of Jesse and was raised as a shepherd. His story is told in the Book of Samuel, and he is perhaps most well known for the story of David and Goliath.

Goliath was a Philistine and a giant, estimated by some to be nine and one-half feet tall. At the time of his encounter with David, the Philistines were at war with the Israelites. Before marching into battle, however, Goliath challenged the Israelites to send out a warrior who

could defeat him. Goliath made this challenge daily for forty days, but no Israelite accepted it. Finally, David, who was still a teenager and was only present at the battleground because he was bringing food to his older brothers, rose to the occasion.

King Saul was amused by David's bravery and offered him a weapon and armor, but David refused. He marched out to meet Goliath armed only with a sling and some stones. Before Goliath could strike, David slung a stone that hit Goliath in the head, knocking him down. David then seized Goliath's sword and decapitated him, completing the upset victory.

From this moment on, David's popularity soared throughout Israel. King Saul began to perceive him as a threat and tried to have him killed. Saul's own son and heir, Jonathan, befriended David and helped him survive. Eventually, David was chosen to succeed Saul as Israel's second king.

As king, David unified the Northern and Southern tribes of Israel and moved the capital to Jerusalem. He ruled for approximately forty years beginning around 1000 BC, but not without difficulty. While king, David fell in love with and impregnated a married woman named Bathsheba. In order to cover up his sin, he ordered that her husband, a soldier in his army, be sent to the frontlines where he was killed. In response, God dispatched a prophet, Nathan, to confront David with his crime.

Despite his imperfection, Jewish belief holds that God promised David his lineage would rule Israel forever. The Jewish messianic tradition therefore holds that when the Messiah arrives, he will be a descendant of David.

ADDITIONAL FACT

1. *It is speculated that Goliath's size may have been the result of a pituitary gland defect, causing abnormal growth. Another hypothetical symptom of this defect would be tunnel vision, perhaps explaining how David could have sneaked up on him without Goliath's knowledge.*

Magna Carta

In 1214, England's King John was defeated in a war with France's King Philip II. John returned home and attempted to rebuild his royal treasury by levying heavy taxes on the barons who had not supported his overseas campaign. The barons rebelled and by summer 1215 captured London.

With the fall of London, King John negotiated a settlement at Runnymede, a meadow by the River Thames. The settlement was a guarantee of basic liberties and a series of limits on the absolute power of the king, summarized in a proclamation called the Magna Carta. On June 19, the Magna Carta was affixed with the royal seal and ordered to be read throughout the land. It bound not only King John but his heirs, forever.

The first draft of the agreement applied to any baron, but the language was changed to any freeman in the final version. At the time freemen were a minority of the English population, but over the centuries, the term would come to include all citizens.

The first section of the Magna Carta promised that the Church in England "shall be free, and shall have its rights undiminished, and its liberties unimpaired."

Subsequent clauses codified the feudal relationship between the king and his nobles. There were also guarantees that no man could be imprisoned without due process, and there was a provision that no feudal taxes could be imposed without the kingdom's "general consent." The final clause established a council of barons and clergy that was authorized to use force against the crown to enforce the agreement.

The Magna Carta is considered the bedrock of freedom and rule of law in England and the earliest seed of constitutional monarchy. However, it was largely ignored for hundreds of years after it was issued. Pope Innocent II annulled the document that very September. It was reissued in 1217, but was considered legally irrelevant.

The Magna Carta's importance was revived by Sir Edward Coke, a parliamentary leader in the seventeenth century, who repeatedly cited its principles in his fight against the Stuart kings. And, it was later an inspiration to the American colonists in their fight for independence.

ADDITIONAL FACTS

1. *Magna Carta means "Great Charter" in Latin.*

2. *Four original copies of the Magna Carta survive. Two copies are stored at the British Library while the others can be seen in the cathedral archives at Lincoln and Salisbury.*

3. *In 1957 the American Bar Association acknowledged the debt American law had to the Magna Carta by erecting a monument at Runnymede.*

"Ozymandias"

I met a traveller from an antique land,
Who said—"Two vast and trunkless legs of stone
Stand in the desert. . . . Near them, on the sand,
Half sunk a shattered visage lies, whose frown,
And wrinkled lip, and sneer of cold command,
Tell that its sculptor well those passions read
Which yet survive, stamped on these lifeless things,
The hand that mocked them, and the heart that fed;
And on the pedestal, these words appear:
My name is Ozymandias, King of Kings,
Look on my Works, ye Mighty, and despair!
Nothing beside remains. Round the decay
Of that colossal Wreck, boundless and bare
The lone and level sands stretch far away."

Percy Bysshe Shelley (1792–1822) was one of the principal English Romantic poets of the early 1800s. These poets reacted against the rationalism that had dominated art and literature during the Enlightenment of the 1700s, celebrating instead the sublimity of nature and the power of human emotion, passion, and freedom.

Shelley's "Ozymandias" (1818) is a sonnet, the same strict fourteen-line verse form that Petrarch, Spenser, Shakespeare, and others had used during the Renaissance. Usually, a sonnet is written in iambic pentameter, with each line composed of five iambs (two-syllable units that follow an unstressed-stressed pattern). Moreover, a Petrarchan sonnet, like "Ozymandias," typically is divided into two parts: the opening eight lines, or octave, and the final six, or sestet. Often, the octave poses a question that the sestet answers; in "Ozymandias," the octave paints an image upon which the sestet comments ironically.

The speaker in "Ozymandias" relays a story he has heard of a once-great statue now lying broken and toppled in the desert. The statue's "frown" and "sneer of cold command" arrogantly convey the power that Ozymandias held. This arrogance reaches a height in the statue's boastful inscription—"Look on my Works, ye Mighty, and despair!"—which immediately is undercut by the image of the vast sands that long ago buried these "Works" and surrounded the statue with nothingness.

Shelley's critique of political power and its ability to endure in the face of time, nature, and history is typical of the Romantic outlook. Implicit in "Ozymandias" is the suggestion that there is more lasting value in art than in any temporal political authority. After all, the poem and the images contained within it, have endured far longer than the reign of any human ruler.

ADDITIONAL FACT
1. *"Ozymandias" was inspired by a fallen statue at the funerary temple of Ramses II near Luxor, Egypt. According to the ancient historian Diodorus, the statue was once inscribed with the words, "King of Kings am I, Ozymandias. If anyone would know how great I am and where I lie, let him surpass one of my works."*

The Birth of Venus

The Birth of Venus by the Italian painter Sandro Botticelli (1446–1510) captures the moment when Venus, the goddess of beauty, is being blown to shore after her birth from the sea. The work was painted in tempera on wood around 1482 for a villa in Castello owned by the wealthy Florentine banking family, the Medici.

In the Early Renaissance, many artists were influenced by neo-Platonist thinkers, such as Marsilio Ficino, who felt that Greek and Roman culture could be reconciled with Christian beliefs. In the 1480s Botticelli was commissioned by the Medici to execute a series of large-scale paintings that combined pagan mythology with Christian concepts. Among these were such masterpieces as his *Primavera, Pallas and the Centaur*, and *The Birth of Venus*.

According to Greek legend, Venus was born from the foam that appeared on the sea's surface when the Titan Chronos castrated his father Uranus and threw his genitals into the ocean. The goddess came ashore on the island of Cyprus, where her cult later flourished. According to Neo-Platonic thought, the legend of Venus's birth was an allegory for the creation of the human soul.

In Botticelli's painting, two wind gods, one of whom is Zephyrus, blow Venus to land. The goddess, who stands on a large scallop shell, is modeled on the ancient Venus *pudica* (modest Venus) type, such as the ones carved by the Greek sculptor Praxiteles. Roses float in the air around her as she is greeted by a woman, possibly the nymph Pomona, who prepares to drape a flower-covered garment over her newly born body. Both the roses and the leaves of the orange trees are painted with accents of gold.

Later in life, Botticelli fell under the influence of a charismatic Dominican monk named Girolamo Savonarola. Savonarola organized a "Bonfire of the Vanities" in 1497 to encourage people to destroy luxury objects. Repenting his interest in pagan culture, Botticelli supposedly burned some of his own works.

ADDITIONAL FACTS

1. Today The Birth of Venus *can be seen in the Uffizi Galleries in Florence.*

2. The orange grove on the right, with its dark green leaves accented with gold, may represent the Garden of Hespeides of Greek mythology.

3. The woman offering Venus a robe is wearing a dress adorned with daisies, primroses, and cornflowers—all spring flowers appropriate for celebrating a birth.

Surface Tension and Hydrogen Bonding

Water is the strangest, most ubiquitous substance on earth. Its solid form is less dense than its liquid form, which is why ice floats. It can absorb large amounts of heat without changing very much, which is why coastal towns have moderate temperatures. And, it has a "skin," a thin layer of molecules that try to stick together at the surface.

Water's unusual properties are the result of its shape. A water molecule consists of two hydrogen atoms and one oxygen atom (H_2O). It looks like Mickey Mouse: the two hydrogen atoms are the ears, and the oxygen atom is the head. Because electrons aren't distributed evenly in the water molecule, the ears are positively charged and the head is negatively charged. Since opposites attract, the ears of one water molecule are attracted to the chin of another water molecule, forming a hydrogen bond. In ice, water molecules bond together stably to form a tetrahedron, a four-sided pyramid. But in liquid the structure of water molecules is looser. Hydrogen bonds are constantly breaking up and getting back together. In fact, the average hydrogen bond lasts only a fraction of a second.

In the middle of a glass of water, any given molecule is being pulled equally in all directions, so there is no net effect. But at the surface, there is no force to pull water molecules up. Molecules are pulled more to the side and down, which is what creates water's sticky skin, or surface tension. Surface tension allows us to fill a glass above the brim. It makes water bead up and form drops and allows it to be stretched into bubbles.

ADDITIONAL FACTS

1. *Water-striders, light insects with pad-like feet, take advantage of water's surface tension. They literally walk on water.*

2. *Water's surface tension is strong enough to drown flying insects that accidentally fall into it. They can't flap their wings fast enough to escape the pull of the water molecules.*

3. *Detergents work by lowering surface tension, which allows water to more effectively soak into pores and dirt.*

The Four Seasons

Antonio Vivaldi wrote *The Four Seasons* in 1725, each of the four concertos representing a season of the year. Written for solo violin and a small orchestra, each concerto is further divided into three movements: the first, an allegro, or fast section; the second, a slow section called adagio or largo; and the third, a concluding allegro or presto finale. When Vivaldi published *The Four Seasons*, he included four sonnets with the manuscript laying out the impressions he was trying to give with each season.

The first concerto, "Spring," is in the key of E. Its pulsing pace and jubilant opening theme are immediately recognizable, spirited, and pleasant. In the second movement the solo violin is meant to represent a sleeping goat herd, and the viola part barks like an excited dog.

"Summer," in the key of G minor, has a sterner feel. We hear sounds from the orchestra that emulate distant thunder in the first movement, and the roar of the storm arrives in the second movement. The poem for "Summer" includes the lines "Blazing sun's relentless heat / Men and flocks are sweltering, / Pines are scorched..."

The program for "Autumn" begins with a peasants' dance to celebrate the gathering of the harvest, followed by a quiet resting period, and in the morning, a lively hunt. "The cup of Bacchus flows freely, and many find their relief in deep slumber," read the accompanying words.

"Winter" evokes "frosty snow in biting, stinging winds," and its slow movement—a tribute to the peace and quiet of the hearth—moves into a spirited final allegro that is meant to feel like a romp in the snow and the thrill of slipping along an icy path.

ADDITIONAL FACTS

1. The Four Seasons *was originally published under the name* Il Cimento dell' Armonia e dell' Inventione, *which means* The Contest Between Harmony and Invention.

2. *At one of Vivaldi's performances in 1715, the audience was wowed by his virtuosity on the violin. One account reads, "Everyone was astounded."*

3. *Vivaldi, like Mozart after him, died poor and was buried in an unmarked grave.*

Stoics

The Stoics were a philosophical school that flourished in the Greco-Roman world from the fourth century BC to the second century AD. Originating with Zeno of Citium in Cypress (344–262 BC), but eventually spreading to Athens, Rome, and the rest of the Empire, Stoicism had a major influence on ancient civilization.

Although they are best known for their ethical views, the Stoics also had views on logic, epistemology, metaphysics, and natural science. The Stoics believed living things were composed of passive matter and an active force they called *pneuma*. They identified God as the intelligent designer of the world who keeps it evolving and changing according to strict natural laws.

The most important question for the Stoics was how a person should live. Their answer was: One should seek happiness—in Greek, *eudaimonia*. But what is happiness? For the Stoics, happiness was an "excellent activity of the soul"—being virtuous, courageous, modest, and patient. They believed it was reasonable to desire things like wealth, fame, and health, but happiness had nothing to do with actually possessing them. Indeed, the Stoics believed that a person who was fully virtuous could be happy regardless of his physical well-being. He could be happy even while being tortured.

Further, the Stoics believed that emotions are not merely feelings, but always involve beliefs. For instance, they thought being afraid of disease required believing that disease was bad. However, since a truly virtuous person could be happy in the face of disease, it was wrong to believe that disease is bad. Therefore, the Stoics recommended purging emotion.

ADDITIONAL FACTS

1. *The Roman emperor Marcus Aurelius (121–180 AD) is a famous Stoic. His personal diary, known as the* Meditations, *is an important work of Stoic philosophy.*

2. *The Stoics got their name from the porch* (stoa poikilê) *in the Agora at Athens, where they gathered to discuss philosophy.*

King Solomon

King Solomon was King David's second son with Bathsheba and successor to the throne of Israel. During his reign, Solomon consolidated his power through political marriages and friendly relations with Egypt and Tyre, and he became known for his abiding wisdom and sense of justice.

Solomon's reign as king was a glorious one, at least initially. It was under his rule that the first temple in Jerusalem was built, in the tenth century BC. The temple was the center of Jewish worship, as well as the home of the Ark of the Covenant, which contained the original Ten Commandments. It stood for nearly 400 years until it was destroyed by the Babylonian ruler Nebuchadrezzar II in the sixth century BC. In addition to the temple, King Solomon brought great wealth to the kingdom of Israel, in the form of other ornate structures and stores of gold.

While the temple was perhaps Solomon's greatest accomplishment, it was also an early cause of his downfall, criticized by some as being pagan. It was known to have reflected Canaanite and Phoenician architecture and was seen by critics as an idolized monument, forbidden in Judaism.

Solomon established peace through alliances and political marriage. In 1 Kings 11:3, it is said that he had 700 wives and 300 concubines. For all of the political benefits, Solomon's polygamy led to significant internal strife as many of the women practiced idol worship and he did little to enforce Jewish traditions upon them. Tensions grew as many doubted his leadership, and after he died, the northern and southern parts of Israel split apart after nearly a century of unification.

Still, King Solomon is remembered for his great wisdom, epitomized by the following story. Two women went before Solomon claiming a baby was theirs. Solomon, in a surprising decision, ordered the baby cut in half. While the false mother was willing to allow this, the true mother—not wanting any harm to come to her child—asked Solomon to let the other woman take the baby. Thus, Solomon, knowing no woman would allow harm to her own child, was able to ascertain the identity of the true mother.

ADDITIONAL FACTS

1. Solomon's first temple, which was destroyed in 586 BC was replaced by the second temple, completed in 515 BC. The second temple was subsequently destroyed by the Romans in 70 AD It is believed that during the coming of the Messiah, a third temple will be built on the same spot as the first two.

2. After the Babylonians destroyed the temple, the Ark of the Covenant disappeared. While it is assumed that the Ark was stolen and destroyed, some people believe that it exists and is hidden.

Genghis Khan

Genghis Khan (1160–1227) was a Mongol warrior, who in the span of two decades led his ruthless army of nomadic tribesman to conquer vast stretches of Asia. When he died in 1227 AD, the Mongol Empire he founded was the largest contiguous empire in the history of the world. Although the empire quickly disintegrated under his heirs, the bloody Mongol invasions marked a turning point in the history of both Europe and Asia and earned the Mongol king a reputation for brutality that endures to the present.

Genghis Khan was born as Temujin, the son of a Mongol chieftain. The Mongols in eastern Asia traditionally lived a nomadic lifestyle, wandering from one region to the next. After the murder of his father, Temujin became chief of a Mongol tribe at age thirteen. He was a charismatic leader. Temujin was eventually able to unify the rest of the Mongol tribes, whose leaders then named him Genghis Khan—the "emperor of all emperors."

After unifying the Mongols, Genghis began a campaign of conquest that would last the rest of his life. His armies conquered portions of modern-day China, Russia, Mongolia, Iran, Afghanistan, Pakistan, India, Kazakstan, Turkmenistan, Uzbekistan, and Kyrgyztan. At its height, shortly after Genghis Khan's death, the Mongol empire stretched from Korea to Eastern Europe.

The Mongol armies were disciplined, effective, and notoriously vicious. Their usual strategy was to give an enemy city the opportunity to surrender peacefully but then kill every resident if the offer was refused. As a result of such terror, Genghis Khan was able to convince whole nations to surrender without a fight.

Before the Mongols, contact between Europe and Asia was minimal. But the Mongol empire founded by Genghis Khan opened the way for trade and the exchange of ideas between the two continents. The Mongols opened the Silk Road, a trade route between Asia and Europe, and Europeans, such as the Italian Marco Polo, traveled to the land of the Khans.

ADDITIONAL FACTS

1. *Mongol nomads lived in round tents known as yurts, which could be moved whenever the tribe migrated to a different region. About half of Mongolia's population still herds livestock, although many nomads settled in the cities during the last half of the twentieth century.*

2. *For centuries, the splendors of the Mongol Empire fascinated Western writers. A luxurious summer capital built by Kublai Khan, the grandson of Genghis, inspired the famous 1797 poem "Kubla Khan" by the British romantic poet Samuel Taylor Coleridge.*

3. *The Mongols repeatedly tried to invade the island of Japan, but their crude navy was destroyed by wind. In Japan, the legend of the kamikaze (divine wind) was passed down for centuries as evidence of Japan's invincibility. At the end of World War II, desperate Japanese pilots crashed their planes into American ships in suicide missions meant to recreate the divine wind that had saved Japan from the Mongols.*

William Faulkner

William Faulkner (1897–1962) is considered the greatest literary voice of the American South. In his novels and short stories, he broke new stylistic ground while confronting the South's considerable ghosts—the Civil War, Reconstruction, and the decline of the old aristocracy.

 Faulkner was born and raised in Mississippi, which is the setting for most of his works. His family was prominent and well established, with roots in the state going back generations; his great-grandfather had been a Confederate colonel in the Civil War and a local legend. As a young man, Faulkner bounced around between various jobs, including a stint in the Royal Canadian Air Force and a position as a clerk in his grandfather's bank. All the while he attempted to gain notoriety as a poet.

Faulkner's first major success was not a poem but a novel, *The Sound and the Fury* (1929), which is still considered his finest. It details the slow decline of the once-great Compson family, which reaches rock bottom in its dysfunctional final generation of children: suicidal Quentin, promiscuous Caddy, hateful Jason, and mentally retarded Benjy. Throughout, Faulkner writes in a stream-of-consciousness narrative and discards any notion of a chronological plot.

The Sound and the Fury is just one of many novels in which Faulkner explores the decline of the old South and the seeming irrelevance of its values in the modern world. Many of these works share the same setting—fictional Yoknapatawpha County, Mississippi—with many of the same places and family names popping up in different books. Foremost among Faulkner's other Yoknapatawpha novels are: *As I Lay Dying* (1930), describes a family's journey to bury its deceased matriarch; *Light in August* (1932), recounts the tribulations of man of uncertain racial heritage; and *Absalom, Absalom!* (1936), portrays a man obsessed with building his own southern dynasty.

Faulkner's works are notorious for their thematic and narrative difficulty. Absurdly long sentences overflowing with adjectives, stream-of-consciousness narration, twists and turns of time, and multiple (and often unreliable) narrators lay a thorny path for the reader. But the end result of these techniques is a body of work that explores the South with greater depth than any other author. For this achievement, Faulkner was awarded the Nobel Prize in Literature in 1950. He died in Byhalia, Mississippi, in 1962.

ADDITIONAL FACT

1. *Due to Faulkner's thick southern drawl, few in the audience at his Nobel Prize acceptance speech had any idea what he said until the text of his remarks was published in newspapers the next day. Since then, it has been acclaimed as one of the finest Nobel Prize acceptance speeches in history.*

Leonardo da Vinci

Leonardo da Vinci (1452–1519) is universally recognized as one of history's great creative geniuses. Excelling in a variety of disciplines—painting, sculpture, architecture, music, engineering, and the physical sciences—he is often deemed the quintessential Renaissance man.

Born in 1452 in Vinci, Italy, da Vinci was the illegitimate son of Ser Piero da Vinci. Throughout his life he referred to himself simply as Leonardo; *da Vinci* means "from Vinci." He began his artistic career in Florence as an apprentice to the sculptor and painter Verrocchio, for whom he worked from 1470 to 1477.

Da Vinci left Florence in 1481 in order to work for Ludovico Sforza, the Duke of Milan. During his years in Milan, he worked on a variety of projects. He designed fortifications, made models of equestrian statues, and painted *The Last Supper.* Although he never completed any of the equestrian statues, he did make a full-scale model of one that was later smashed to bits when French troops used it for target practice

Da Vinci returned to Florence in 1499, where he worked on a number of paintings, most notably the *Mona Lisa.* Between 1513 and 1516, he resided in Rome, lured there by the papal court. Next he moved to France, where he had been invited to live at the estate of the French king, Francis I, who had just recaptured Milan. He died at the Chateau of Cloux in 1519.

Although da Vinci is most famous for painting the *Mona Lisa* and *The Last Supper,* he is also known for his voluminous sketchbooks in which he compiled drawings and annotations on a wide range of subjects, from the physics of flight to human anatomy. Among these is even an illustration of a fetus in the womb. Da Vinci must have sketched it from his imagination since dissections of women were forbidden at the time.

Due to his genius and fame, da Vinci has served as a continual inspiration for other artists. His contemporary, Raphael, purportedly used his likeness for the figure of Plato in the famous Vatican fresco, *The School of Athens.* In more recent times, he has appeared as a character in a wide range of fiction, from the television series *Star Trek* to the best-selling novel *The Da Vinci Code.*

ADDITIONAL FACTS

1. *In 1999, two full-scale recreations of da Vinci's model for a huge equestrian statue were erected, one in Grand Rapids, Michigan, the other in Milan.*

2. *In January 2005, a series of sealed-off rooms were discovered in a monastery next to the church of the Santissima Annunziata in Florence. Some believe that these were the site of Leonardo's secret workshop.*

Earthquakes

The crust of the earth is made of several plates, fifty miles thick, which move slowly over the earth's molten core, like ice on a frozen pond. When two plates pull apart, collide, or rub against each other, the result is an earthquake. Earthquakes cause approximately 10,000 deaths every year.

The point from which an earthquake originates is called the hypocenter. The epicenter is the point on the earth's surface vertically above the hypocenter. If the hypocenter is deep within the earth, the quake isn't likely to cause much damage. But if the quake is shallow, it can be catastrophic. Earthquakes produce several types of waves that shake the ground. The first are called primary waves or P-waves. They flow longitudinally like sound waves, compressing and decompressing the ground. They move very quickly—they can travel from one side of the world to the other in twenty minutes—but cause little damage.

The next type of wave is called an S-wave. They travel slowly and transversely, displacing walls and fencing. The final type of wave, and by far the most dangerous, is the L-wave. L-waves cause the ground to move up and down like the waves in the ocean, causing landslides, fires, and tsunamis. As the earth readjusts from an earthquake, there are several aftershocks—small tremors caused by the ground settling into place. Buildings weakened by the original earthquake often collapse due to aftershocks.

The intensity of an earthquake is measured on the Richter Scale. Each number on the scale represents an increase of a factor of ten. A 3.0 is ten times stronger than a 2.0 and 100 times stronger than a 1.0. Earthquakes below 4.0 usually can't be felt on the surface. Earthquakes above 6.0 are considered strong, while quakes above 7.0 are severe. The worst earthquakes, caused when two plates collide with each other (which has happened in Alaska and Chile) can register above a 9.0.

ADDITIONAL FACTS

1. *The 1989 World Series between the Oakland Athletics and the San Francisco Giants was interrupted by a 7.1 earthquake that caused a ten-day delay in the games.*

2. *The explosion of volcanoes can also cause earthquakes. When Krakatoa erupted in Indonesia in 1883, the explosion was so loud it could be heard in Perth, Australia, 3,000 kilometers away.*

3. *According to a myth from India, four elephants hold up the earth. They stand on the back of a turtle, who balances on top of a cobra. The movement of any of these animals starts an earthquake.*

4. *The indigenous people of Mozambique believe that the earth is a living creature with the same problems as people. When it gets sick with fever and chills, we feel it shake.*

Henry Purcell

Born into the grand tradition of royal English court music, Henry Purcell (1659–1695) was the son of Thomas Purcell, one of the King's Musicians at Westminster Abbey. Henry started as a choirboy at the Chapel Royal, but he soon became a disciple of John Blow (1649–1708), who served two terms as the organist at Westminster Abbey, and was one of the leading English composers of the era. In 1677, Purcell became composer for the King's Violins, the royal string band, writing his simple but beautiful *Fantasias* for strings.

In 1679, at age twenty, Purcell succeeded his teacher as organist at the Chapel Royal and began composing incidental music for theater as well as church music. In 1689, he wrote his most famous work, the opera *Dido and Aeneas*. At the time, opera was not very popular in England—most composers favored the masque, a hybrid of Italian cantatas, French secular music, and English song.

Dido and Aeneas was much smaller in scale than most modern operas. The libretto, or text of the opera, dealt with Aeneas, a hero on his way home from the Trojan War, who falls in love with Dido, Queen of Carthage, and then abandons her. Purcell's version, which contrasted soloists, chorus, and instrumental dances, required a limited number of principal singers. Several of the best-known sections of the music were based on the idea of the ground bass—a simple, repeating theme in the lower-voiced string instruments that provides a familiar, recognizable accompaniment to the different melodies moving above it. Purcell's melodies are dramatic and captivating, despite the limitations of the ground bass, and the result was a groundbreaking work for English composers.

Purcell, like Wolfgang Amadeus Mozart and Franz Schubert after him, died very young, but he is regarded as one of the greatest English composers of any era, and his work was paid tribute by later English composers such as Ralph Vaughan Williams and Benjamin Britten.

ADDITIONAL FACTS

1. Purcell's Dido and Aeneas *was the first real opera written in the English language. Unlike previous works, it is all music, with no stoppages for the performers to perform a spoken part.*

2. Purcell published his first piece, a short song, at age eight.

3. Two anthems by Purcell, My Heart is Inditing *and* Thou Knowest, Lord, the Secrets of our Hearts, *were used at the coronation of James II and the funeral of Queen Mary, respectively.*

Epicureanism

The Epicureans were followers of a school of philosophy founded in the fourth century BC by Epicurus (341–271 BC). They lived communally and abstained from political activity.

The Epicureans believed all that exists are atoms and the void, or empty space. Consequently, the soul itself is composed of atoms; it is material and dies with the body. The Epicureans believed in gods, but they thought that the gods would be too occupied with their own pleasures to concern themselves with human affairs.

Like many philosophical schools in the Hellenistic world, the Epicureans focused on the question: What is the good life? Their answer: The good life was a life of happiness. Happiness was the presence of pleasure, and the absence of pain. However, their psychology of pleasures and pains was unique.

The Epicureans divided pleasures into static pleasures and kinetic pleasures. Enjoying a kinetic pleasure involves having a desire, satisfying the desire, and then experiencing the lack of that desire. For instance, the desire for food is a kinetic pleasure as one is hungry, eats, and then is sated. Enjoying a static pleasure, by contrast, does not diminish your desire. Engaging in philosophical discussion is an example of a static pleasure: The more you philosophize, the more you want to philosophize.

While recognizing that some kinetic pleasures are necessary and good, the Epicureans warned against those that created the desire for ever greater quantities and varieties of stimulation. For example, a habit of consuming delicious desserts makes it harder to take pleasure in simpler desserts, or to be satisfied with the absence of desserts altogether. The Epicureans therefore believed one should live mostly in an austere way, eating simple foods and enjoying only the occasional luxury.

ADDITIONAL FACTS

1. *Contrary to what the Epicureans advocated, the word* epicurean *has come to mean "devoted to the pursuit of sensual pleasure, especially to the enjoyment of good food and comfort."*

2. *The school Epicurus founded in Athens was known as the Garden.*

3. *The Roman philosopher Lucretius was an Epicurean. He wrote a long poem about Epicurean metaphysics and natural philosophy called "On Nature."*

༺∞༻

The Temple and the Holy Ark

King Solomon built the first Jewish temple in Jerusalem in the tenth century BC with three main purposes in mind: First, to be the center of the Jewish faith in Israel. Second, to be a place for the performance of animal sacrifices to God. And lastly, to be a permanent home for the Ark of the Covenant, which contained the original Ten Commandments given to Moses on Mount Sinai.

King Solomon's original temple, built during one of the wealthiest periods in Israel's history, lasted until 586 BC, when it was destroyed by the Babylonian ruler Nebuchadrezzar II. The Babylonians looted and destroyed the temple, including, presumably, the Holy Ark and the Ten Commandments. With the destruction of the temple, the Jews were exiled from the southern portion of Israel, known as the Land of Judah.

When the Jews returned from their exile, they rebuilt the temple. This second temple took thirty-one years to construct and was completed in 515 BC. It thrived for five centuries. Around 19 BC, King Herod the Great began an ambitious expansion project, which included a large retaining wall around the entire site. The temple remained in this state until the end of the first century AD.

As the first century drew to a close, Roman-Jewish tensions rose. At the time, one-tenth of the Roman Empire was Jewish. Moreover, many of those who were not Jewish supported the Jews, only refraining from joining the religion because of its circumcision requirement. Although Roman-Jewish relations were peaceful for the most part, a group of zealots revolted in 66 AD. and Roman leaders feared the spread of rebellion. In response, they destroyed Jerusalem and the second temple. This was the second destruction of the Jews' holiest site, and it began the Jewish Diaspora out of Israel.

ADDITIONAL FACTS

1. *The site of the first two temples, the Temple Mount, regarded as the holiest location in Judaism, is also an extremely important location for Christianity and Islam. Islam's Dome of the Rock and Al-Aqsa Mosque, both built in the sixth century, make it the third holiest site in the Muslim faith.*

2. *Part of King Herod's retaining wall survived the Roman's destruction and still exists today, known as the Western Wall or the Wailing Wall. This section of the wall is a holy site that many pilgrims go to visit.*

The Black Plague

The plague, or Black Death, killed one-third of Europe's population between 1347 and 1350. Originating in Asia, the disease spread with devastating speed. In the squalid cities of medieval Europe, victims typically lived only a few days after the symptoms—vomiting, diarrhea, and black tumors on the skin—first appeared.

In many cities, the plague not only killed huge numbers but also destroyed law and order, pushing an entire civilization to the brink of collapse. The writer Giovanni Boccaccio, in his famous work the *Decameron* written in 1370–71, described the effects of the plague in the prosperous Italian city of Florence:

"In this suffering and misery of our city, the authority of human and divine laws almost disappeared, for, like other men, the ministers and the executors of the laws were all dead or sick or shut up with their families, so that no duties were carried out. . . . Every man was therefore able to do as he pleased."

The consequences of the plague in European society were profound. Many enraged European Christians blamed Jews for the disease, and the pogroms that followed the Black Death were among the worst outbreaks of anti-Semitism in history.

Many Europeans also began to question the teachings of the Catholic Church and the existing political order. How could God permit such a cruel disease? Some disillusioned Europeans turned to fringe sects such as the flagellants, named for their practice of whipping themselves. Respect for the Church, as a result, declined. According to many historians, the plague destroyed the old feudal order of the Middle Ages and cleared the way for the Renaissance.

ADDITIONAL FACTS

1. *Scientists continue to debate the cause of the Black Death. The leading candidate, the bubonic plague, still exists but can be treated easily with antibiotics.*

2. *Although almost everyone who was exposed to the plague in the Middle Ages died, about 5 percent of victims survived the epidemic, and some people were able to avoid catching it entirely. Modern scientists believe they were protected by a rare genetic combination that gave them greater resistance to the germ.*

3. *After the Black Death, it took four centuries for Europe's population to rebound to its pre-1347 levels.*

The Great Gatsby

Critics and readers alike have long tried to single out one work as the Great American Novel, and thus far, most have settled on F. Scott Fitzgerald's (1896–1940) *The Great Gatsby* (1925). Indeed, virtually no other work has captured, and criticized, so brilliantly the essence of the American Dream.

The title character, Jay Gatsby, is a mysterious millionaire who owns a mansion in the nouveau-riche town of West Egg, Long Island, across the harbor from old-money East Egg. Each weekend, he throws opulent parties that draw hundreds of "casual moths" to his estate. At one of these soirées, Gatsby meets the story's narrator, his new neighbor Nick Carraway. Nick's immediate impression is that Gatsby has "one of those rare smiles with a quality of eternal reassurance in it, that you may come across four or five times in life."

But the more Nick learns, the more cracks appear in Gatsby's façade of perfection. Gatsby, it turns out, epitomizes the American ideal of the self-made man—in all the wrong ways. Born into poverty in the Midwest, he earned millions through dishonest business dealings, aided by organized crime. He changed his name, moved east, bought the mansion at West Egg, and constructed a fake personal history, all with the single goal of winning back his long-lost love, Daisy Buchanan, who has since married another man.

Gatsby is a paradox on nearly every level. He lives and breathes the American spirit of initiative, idealism, and upward mobility, but he does so entirely in pursuit of a woman who does not merit the effort. He sets forth an image of supreme confidence and self-assertion, but he is a lonely and lovesick man to the core. His library is filled with books, but their pages have not been cut, so not one of the books has even been opened.

The Great Gatsby is a scant 180 pages long, but Fitzgerald uses this brief space masterfully and meticulously, with scarcely a wasted word. The novel is at once a thriller, romance, mystery, and exposé of the decadence of the Jazz Age. But above all, it is Fitzgerald's prose—some of the most poetic the English language has ever seen—that makes this quintessentially American tale unforgettable.

ADDITIONAL FACTS

1. *Fitzgerald struggled for months to settle on a title for* The Great Gatsby. *In March 1925, he sent a frantic final telegram to his publisher requesting that the title be changed to* Under the Red, White, and Blue, *but it was too late.*

2. *Fitzgerald and his wife, Zelda, were infamous figures in Jazz Age society, their tumultuous life plagued by Zelda's notorious emotional instability and Fitzgerald's alcoholism.*

3. *In 1940, Fitzgerald died of a heart attack, leaving behind the unfinished novel* The Last Tycoon, *about a Hollywood movie mogul.*

The Last Supper

Leonardo da Vinci painted the *Last Supper* for his patron, Ludovico Sforza, from 1495 to 1498. Situated on the north wall of the monk's refectory at Santa Maria delle Grazie in Milan, it is one of the most famous paintings of a biblical subject in Western history.

The Last Supper depicts Christ celebrating the Passover meal with the twelve apostles just before Judas betrayed him to the Romans. According to Christian theology, this event marked the first celebration of the Eucharist, for it was at this meal that Christ transformed the bread and wine at the table into his body and blood.

All the figures are arranged on one side of the table, which acts as a sort of barrier separating the sacred event from the living monks who ate their meals in the refectory before the picture. From left to right appear the disciples Bartholomew, James the Minor, Andrew, Peter, Judas, and John. Jesus appears in the exact center. He is followed by Thomas, James the Major, Philip, Matthew, Thaddeus, and Simon.

According to the sixteenth-century author Giorgio Vasari, who wrote biographies of the most famous Italian artists of the Renaissance, Leonardo's fresco was meant to capture the precise moment of Christ's pronouncement, "One of you is about to betray me." (Matthew 26:21) The apostles are thus shown reacting to His words, each one expressing a different emotion— denial, doubt, rage, disbelief, or love.

Another relevant passage from the Gospels is Luke 22:21, in which Christ states, "the hand of him that betrayeth me is with me on the table." In Leonardo's painting, Judas is the only person besides Christ with his hand on the table. His face is in shadow, and his body physically recoils from Jesus. In older depictions of the scene by other artists, Judas had been depicted isolated from the rest of the group, either seated alone on the opposite side of the table or stripped of a halo. Leonardo distinguished him from the good apostles in a more subtle manner, focusing on his psychological state rather than on external attributes.

The mural began deteriorating not long after it was made. Leonardo, who worked with painstaking precision, had not used traditional fresco techniques because these required painters to work with great speed. Instead he experimented with an oil-and-tempera-based medium, which proved to be highly unstable; cracks and mildew appeared within a few years. Moreover, a doorway was cut through the wall in 1652, destroying the area where Christ's feet once appeared. Attempts at restoration in the eighteenth and nineteenth centuries had only partial success. During World War II, the refectory was struck by a bomb that caused further damage. In 1978, a major restoration campaign was undertaken by the Italian government and overseen for more than twenty years by Pinin Brambilla Barcilon. The newly restored fresco was reopened to the public in 1999 after the refectory was equipped with climate control.

∽∞∾

Sunspots and Solar Flares

The volatile surface of the sun burns at 6,000 degrees Celsius, heating the entire solar system. That's about 180 times hotter than a hot day on earth. But some parts of the sun's surface are cooler than others. Sunspots, which are roughly the size of our planet, appear dark in color because they are more than 2,000 degrees cooler than the surrounding surface. They have intense magnetic fields that choke off heat from the sun's blazing inner core.

Usually, sunspots appear in pairs, each having an opposite magnetic charge. The areas between oppositely charged sunspots are ripe for solar flares, explosions on the surface of the sun that release as much energy as a billion megatons of TNT. Solar flares bombard the earth with x-rays and magnetic radiation, causing geomagnetic storms. They intensify the Northern and Southern lights, disrupt power grids, and mangle radio transmissions.

Sunspots and solar flares wax and wane in an eleven year cycle, the latest of which peaked in 2000. On July 14, 2000—the so-called Bastille Day Event—an enormous solar flare sparked dazzling auroras as far south as Texas, triggered blackouts, and zapped satellites. Astronauts have to be wary of solar maximums because radiation storms can be lethal. The next lull in sunspot activity should be in 2006, when it will be safer to travel in outer space.

Sunspots may also affect the temperature on earth. Maximum sunspot activity is associated with a slight increase in energy release from the sun, including a dramatic rise in ultraviolet radiation. There has been an overall increase in sunspot activity in the last sixty years, which corresponds very closely with global warming. The mid-1600s to the early 1700s marked a low in sunspot activity, which coincided with a period of severe cold temperatures and long winters in Western Europe called the Little Ice Age.

ADDITIONAL FACTS

1. *Galileo Galilei used sunspots to track the rotation of the sun. Since the sun is mostly gas, different parts of it rotate at different rates. The equator takes roughly twenty-five days to rotate, whereas the poles take thirty-five days.*

2. *Chinese astronomers first observed sunspots in 30 AD.*

Johann Sebastian Bach

Bach (1685-1750) was the most important Baroque composer and perhaps the most important composer of all time. His religious vocal music—cantatas and chorales—his orchestral concertos, and his virtuoso organ works are filled with sublime harmonies and contrapuntal melodies, and his overall musical sensibilities amount to nothing short of genius. He influenced almost every composer to come after him, including the twentieth century's purveyors of jazz and pop.

Bach was born March 21, 1685, in the town of Eisenach, in a region called Thuringia. As a young man, he moved around between various appointments and sojourns in Lutheran churches in Arnstadt, Lübeck, Mülhausen, and Weimar. The constant theme of Bach's career was that people found his music mediocre, too complex, and unsatisfactory. Still, during his time as court organist at Weimar (1708–1717), he rose to the rank of Konzertmeister. In 1717, he moved to the court of Lutheran Prince Leopold at Cöthen.

In 1720, Bach's first wife died, and he married a court singer named Anna Magdalena, to whom he dedicated several books of etudes, which are now studied by most pianists in training. During his time at Cöthen, he produced some of his famous cantatas, as well as his legendary *Brandenburg Concertos* and the *St. Matthew Passion* oratorio. In 1722, he became director of music for the four churches and entire city of Leipzig, where he died in 1750 just a year after completing his monumental *Mass in B minor*.

ADDITIONAL FACTS

1. Bach had six children with his first wife and thirteen with his second wife.

2. Ten of Bach's children died in their infancies, but four—including Johann Christian Bach and Carl Philipp Emanuel Bach, became well-known composers.

3. Bach's early musical education was with his father and older brothers, but he was a largely self-taught composer.

Medieval Philosophy

The medieval period in Western philosophy is usually defined as lasting from the end of Classical Antiquity, in roughly the fifth century AD, until the beginning of the Renaissance, around the fifteenth century AD. In contrast to the bleak track record of other disciplines during the Middle Ages, the philosophy of this period was extremely rich, and it encompasses a number of outstanding figures.

The first major medieval philosopher was St. Augustine (354–430 AD), who attempted to synthesize Plato's philosophy with Christianity. Augustine had a major influence, not just on Church teachings, but upon Western philosophy and culture as a whole.

Another important medieval figure was Boethius (480–c.525 AD), best known now for his book *The Consolation of Philosophy*. However, his most important contributions to the field were his translations of Greek philosophy into Latin. Boethius was one of the last Western Europeans to know Greek, and after his death, knowledge of the language disappeared from European culture for centuries.

The early medieval period ended with two important figures: St. Anselm of Canterbury (1033–1109) and Peter Abelard (1079–1142). Anselm is best known for having offered the first analytic or "ontological" argument for the existence of God, in his book *Proslogion*. Abelard, in addition to being a major figure in the history of logic and semantics, is most famous for having fallen in love with his student Heloise, with whom he fathered a child and carried on a famous correspondence.

Later medieval philosophy has a very different character, in part due to the rediscovery of ancient Greek texts in the thirteenth century, especially those of Aristotle. The work of the major later medieval philosophers—St. Thomas Aquinas (c.1224–1274), John Duns Scotus (c.1265–1308), and William of Ockham (c.1287–1347)—was heavily influenced by Aristotle, and each of them produced influential commentaries on individual Aristotelian works. The most important of the three was Thomas Aquinas, who synthesized Aristotelian philosophy and Christian theology into a grand philosophical and theological system. Ever since, Aquinas has been a major, if not decisive, influence on Catholic thinking.

ADDITIONAL FACTS

1. Heloise's uncle was so outraged with his niece's affair that he had Abelard castrated. Both Abelarad and Heloise lived the rest of their lives in religious orders, but they carried on a correspondence, an early and moving example of ideal romantic love.

2. Ockham is best known for the principle that bears his name, "Ockham's razor," usually understood to mean the simplest theory should always be preferred, or that theories should be as simple as possible.

∽∾∾

Talmud

The Talmud compiles several hundred years of rabbinic commentary on the Torah and is regarded as a central text in the Jewish religion.

The Talmud consists of two parts. The first is the Mishna. When the Torah was originally revealed to Moses, it is believed that the written text was accompanied by a set of oral teachings. By around 200 AD., the Jewish temples had been destroyed and the community was the target of vicious persecution. It became necessary to record those secondary teachings.

The second part of the Talmud is the Gemara. The Gemara consists of rabbinic discussions of the Mishna. Whereas the Mishna contains absolute opinions, the Gemara is written as a dialogue of differing opinions.

The Talmud most commonly referred to and used is the Babylonian, or Talmud Bavli, compiled around 400–600 AD. A second Talmud exists, which came from Jerusalem, but the writings in this version are more fragmented and very difficult to understand.

The Talmud is used as a source of Halakhah, or Jewish law, and it was commonly employed to decide disputes that arose in society. As religious and secular laws were traditionally the same in Jewish communities, the Talmud had a wide range of applications.

ADDITIONAL FACTS

1. *One section of the Mishna called* Pirkei Avot, *"Sayings of the Fathers," contains famous rabbinic sayings and proverbs.*

2. *The Talmud is traditionally studied by the havruta method—in pairs, so students can review and discuss each line with a partner.*

Joan of Arc

Joan of Arc (1412–1431) was a young peasant woman who took command, at the astonishing age of seventeen, of the medieval French armies fighting the English. After a string of surprising victories, she was captured, convicted of heresy, and promptly burned at the stake. Inspired by Joan's courageous leadership, however, the French eventually drove the English off their territory. She remains a national hero and symbol of France.

War between the kings of Europe—and especially between the English and French—was a constant feature of medieval life. Indeed, at the time of Joan's exploits in 1429, the two countries were in the midst of the Hundred Year's War, a sporadic conflict that actually lasted 116 years. For the most part, war was simply a business proposition for the greedy feudal barons who ruled Europe in the Middle Ages. The nobles wanted land, and war was the way to get it. As a result, national borders during the medieval period changed constantly, and the common people of the continent, like Joan's family, felt little kinship with any particular ruler.

But by the time of Joan's birth, that was starting to change. Joan's campaign against the English marked one of the first examples of what would become European nationalism. For Joan, France was not just a line on a map or the possession of a monarch. It was her country, to which she felt a special, patriotic bond. In visions that she experienced as a teenager, Joan claimed that God wanted her to drive the English from France. What began as a territorial dispute among the inbred French and English aristocracies became a clash of nationalities. In the coming centuries, the different feudal kingdoms of Europe evolved into nation-states with distinct cultural identities, fueling both patriotism and its evil twin, xenophobia.

After Joan's capture in 1431, the English executed her on a trumped-up charge of heresy. The pope later overturned her conviction, and Joan was officially made a saint of the Catholic Church in 1920.

ADDITIONAL FACTS

1. During World War II, the underground fighters of the French Resistance adopted the cross of Lorraine, Joan's emblem, as their symbol.

2. Before allowing Joan to take charge of his armies, the French king had his mother-in-law examine Joan to ensure that she was a virgin. She was.

3. The nineteenth-century American author Mark Twain was fascinated by Joan and spent twelve years researching and writing a book about the woman he considered "easily and by far the most extraordinary person the human race has ever produced." Although the book is not among Twain's most well known, he considered it one of his best.

John Steinbeck

One of the best-loved American novelists of the twentieth century, John Steinbeck (1902–1968) infused his works with the local color of his native California. Though many critics dismissed his writing as less elegant and groundbreaking than that of his contemporaries, he has long been a favorite among readers. At any rate, Steinbeck's talent for crafting moving, richly symbolic, and socially relevant stories is indisputable.

Steinbeck was born in Salinas, California, the heart of the agricultural region between San Francisco and Monterey. After several years at Stanford University and various stints as a manual laborer, he began writing in earnest in the late 1920s. Steinbeck's first few efforts failed both critically and commercially, but he finally found success with his novel *Tortilla Flat* (1935), about Mexican *paisanos* in Monterey during the Great Depression. He followed with the novella *Of Mice and Men* (1937), the heartrending story of Lenny and George, two migrant workers on a California farm.

Steinbeck's masterpiece and most famous work is *The Grapes of Wrath* (1939), his novel about a family of Dust Bowl "Okies" who flee the drought-stricken Midwest to seek a better life in California. A desperately poor, salt-of-the-earth clan, the Joads endure great hardship during the journey but draw strength and hope from their mutual generosity and unbreakable family ties. The novel was a huge sensation and drew unprecedented attention to the plight of the Depression-era poor. It has remained both a popular favorite and a staple of English curricula ever since.

Later in his career, Steinbeck experimented ambitiously with different genres and forms, with varying degrees of success. Best known from this era are *Cannery Row* (1945), a picaresque tale of vagrants in the industrial neighborhood of Monterey, and the sprawling *East of Eden* (1952), a retelling of the book of Genesis in the setting of the Salinas Valley. Though Steinbeck considered *East of Eden* his best work—and it was an undeniable bestseller—critics saw it as preachy and heavy-handed. It does, however, offer a rich, detailed portrait of the people and history of the region, cementing Steinbeck's reputation as California's foremost literary interpreter.

In 1962, Steinbeck received the Nobel Prize in Literature for "realistic and imaginative writings, combining . . . sympathetic humor and keen social perception." This rather unique feat—the combination of a brutal, unflinching depiction of poverty with an ultimately optimistic outlook—has accorded Steinbeck an enduring place among American novelists.

ADDITIONAL FACT

1. *In his Nobel Prize acceptance speech, Steinbeck asserted that any writer "who does not passionately believe in the perfectibility of man has no dedication nor any membership in literature."*

Mona Lisa

Painted circa 1505 by Leonardo da Vinci, *Mona Lisa* is considered the prototype of the Renaissance female portrait. The work, which is painted in oil on a poplar panel, measures merely thirty-one by twenty-one inches. Despite its small size and relatively simple composition, it is one of the most famous paintings in the world.

The identity of the woman pictured in *Mona Lisa* remains a mystery. According to Giorgio Vasari, who wrote Leonardo's biography in 1550, the woman was Lisa di Antonio Maria Gherardini (Mona is a contraction of *ma donna*, Italian for "my lady"), wife of the Florentine merchant, Francesco del Giocondo. This identification is problematic, however, since Leonardo never delivered the painting to any patron, but kept it for himself until his death in 1519. More recently, Dr. Lillian Schwartz of Bell Labs performed a digital comparison of the *Mona Lisa* with a drawing purported to be a self-portrait of Leonardo. Based on similarities between the two likenesses, Schwartz claimed that the painting was a self-portrait of Leonardo in female form. This theory, too, is untenable since the attribution of the alleged self-portrait is dubious. What seems most probable is that the *Mona Lisa* is not a portrait at all, but Leonardo's image of the ideal woman.

Regardless of the subject, the painting demonstrates Leonardo's superb use of *sfumato*, that is, soft, hazy outlines that create a mysterious mood. Using this technique Leonardo succeeded in making the woman's expression ambiguous. Much ink has been spilled on the precise nature of Mona Lisa's smile; indeed her demeanor seems to change depending on the angle from which she is viewed.

The *Mona Lisa* has had a tortured history since da Vinci's death. It was purchased by Francis I for 4,000 gold pieces. Later it hung in Versailles and in Napoleon Bonaparte's bedroom before finding its way into the collection of the Louvre. In 1911, it was stolen from the Louvre only to reappear in a hotel room in Florence two years later. After someone sprayed acid and damaged the lower half of the *Mona Lisa* in 1956, the painting was hung behind a double layer of protective glass.

The Milgram Studies: Lessons in Obedience

In the 1960s, Stanley Milgram, a psychologist at Yale University, performed a frightening series of experiments on obedience. Milgram demonstrated how a situation can overpower an individual's conscience. His findings have been used to explain the great atrocities of our time: the Holocaust, the My Lai massacre, and the genocide in Rwanda.

Milgram drew his subjects from all walks of life, including lawyers, firemen, and construction workers. They all agreed to accept $4.50 per hour to participate in an experiment on learning and punishment. In the experiment, they were told by a doctor in a white coat to act as "teachers" by reading a list of associations to a "learner," who was out of sight but could hear in the next room. If the learner got an association wrong, then the teacher was instructed to give them an electric shock, increasing the voltage after each incorrect answer. The first shock was labeled, "slight shock–15 volts." The last was labeled, "danger: severe shock–450 volts."

Of course, the real experiment was on the teachers to see how much punishment they would administer. At 180 volts, the learner, who was an actor, would cry out that he could not stand the pain; at 300 volts, he refused to participate; at 330 volts, there was silence. To Stanley Milgram's surprise, 65 percent of the subjects pushed on to the end, 450 volts, even if they were told the learner had a mild heart condition. Many of the teachers were seriously disturbed—sweating profusely, biting their lips—but with the prodding of the white-coated experimenter, they continued in spite of their moral qualms.

Milgram's finding appalled the academic community of the 1960s, both because of his ethically questionable methods and his gruesome results. But, his research clearly demonstrated how ordinary people could be induced to perform inhumane acts simply by the presence of authority. Milgram also found that the more psychological distance the subject had from the victim, the more likely they were to follow orders to the bitter end. If the teacher read only the questions but did not administer the shocks, 90 percent finished the experiment. However, if the teacher had to touch the learner in order to administer the shocks, then only 30 percent went up to 450 volts.

ADDITIONAL FACTS

1. The Milgram studies have been replicated in Australia, Germany, Jordan, and other countries, all with similar results.

2. Milgram found identical rates of obedience for men and women.

Brandenburg Concertos by Johann Sebastian Bach

These six concertos, composed while Bach was living at Cöthen, were presented as a commission to the Margrave of Brandenburg in 1721. Five of them take the form of three movements, fast-slow-fast, and one—the first—has six movements, including two dances. The concertos are noted for Bach's ambitious combination of solo instruments and elegant counterpoint. The *Brandenburg Concertos* are also seen as the best blend of the German baroque's imperious style and the light-hearted gusto of composers like Antonio Vivaldi.

The first concerto—written for solo violin, three oboes, strings, bassoon, and two horns—is driven by a dynamic dialogue between the two horns and within the other woodwind sections. The second—for trumpet, recorder, oboe, solo violin, and strings—makes use of all the possible soloist permutations. The third concerto uses groups of three violins, violas, and cellos as soloists, along with the orchestral strings. It is unusual because the soloists often play the same parts as the orchestra behind them. The fifth concerto is for solo violin, flute, harpsichord, and strings, and the sixth for two solo violas, low orchestral strings (no violins), and cello. The sections in which the whole orchestra plays are called the tutti, or "all together," and they alternate with sections in which the solo instruments play, accompanied only by the continuo.

Brandenburg Concerto No. 4 is probably the most recognizable of the set, and it is a quintessentially baroque piece. Written for solo violin and two recorder solos, strings, and continuo, its fast first movement adheres very strictly to Vivaldi's ritornello form, with its recurring tuttis and strong cadences. Its second movement is a free-form andante, or walking-paced movement. The final presto, is fugal, meaning that Bach composes long themes and then imitates them in other parts, overlapping them successively.

ADDITIONAL FACTS

1. *Before composing the* Brandenburg Concertos, *Bach became deeply interested in Vivaldi and other Italian composers, and he wrote out keyboard reductions of their orchestral pieces as an exercise to better his own work.*

2. *The* Brandenburg Concertos *are referred to as* concerti grossi, *or concertos with more than one soloist.*

3. *Even though they were composed for Christian Ludwig, Margrave of Brandenburg, the concertos were never played for him.*

Arguments for the Existence of God

Although many people—believers and atheists alike—argue the existence of God. It cannot be proven. Philosophers since Aristotle have tried to do so.

There are three kinds of argument for the existence of God. The first is called ontological, and it goes back to the medieval philosopher St. Anselm of Canterbury (1033–1109). St. Anselm's own theory was more complicated, but the basic outline of the ontological argument is as follows:

> God is the most perfect possible being. (Definition)
> It is more perfect to exist, than not to exist.
> If God did not exist, then God would lack a perfect existence. (From ii)
> Therefore, God exists. (From i and ii)

The second kind of argument for God's existence is the cosmological. The basic form of the cosmological argument is to argue that there must be a first cause of everything that exists, a cause which is itself not caused. This first cause must be God, because nothing but God could exist without being caused. A variation on the cosmological argument is the argument that everything except God is contingent, in other words, it is possible for everything else not to exist. But every contingent thing requires a cause that is itself necessary. This necessary cause is God.

The third kind of argument is the argument from design. Not as logically strict as the other two, according to this argument the world has features that are best explained by the hypothesis that it was created by an intelligent designer. Features of the world often cited include the harmony among its physical laws that make life possible, the adaptation of organisms to their environments, and the fact that human beings are intelligent, self-conscious beings.

ADDITIONAL FACT
1. *Since Charles Darwin (1809–1882), many philosophers—but not all—have insisted the argument from design does not work, because every feature of the world is adequately explained by science, especially evolution.*

Kabbala

Kabbala, or Jewish mysticism, explains the many mysteries of Judaism. It seeks to answer questions from, "Why did God create the earth and humans?" to, "Why, if God is so good, is there evil in the world?" Kabbala tries to arrive at mystical discoveries through the hermeneutical interpretation of Torah and Talmud. Its purpose is to find mystical truth or ascension to God.

Central to Kabbalistic belief is the notion that God has two forms: the one in which God manifested himself in order to create the earth and another that is wholly unknowable. Between these two aspects of God are ten Sefirot, or creative forces, which mediate between the unknowable God and the manifested God. Practitioners of Kabbala believe these forces can be influenced to draw divine powers like compassion or judgment into the world. Kabbalism also holds that each letter in the Torah has a powerful meaning that can be deciphered.

The most important Kabbalistic text is the Sefer ha-zohar, or simply Zohar. This work was "discovered"—more likely written—by Moses ben Shem Tov de León in Spain during the thirteenth century. De León attributed the work to a second century rabbi. This text was, as are other Kabbalistic texts, nearly incomprehensible unless the reader already had a very strong knowledge of the Hebrew Bible

Although Kabbala grew during the Middle Ages, its wide reach today stems from its spread during the eighteenth century, beginning with the Hasidic movement. Today, Kabbala has made headlines as various celebrities have adopted its practice. However, most Kabbalistic experts, insist this version of Kabbala, consisting of spiritual charms, stones, and necklaces, is a corruption of the tradition's true practice.

ADDITIONAL FACTS

1. *Critics of Kabbala dislike that it identifies two aspects of God, a notion difficult to reconcile with monotheism.*

2. *The red strings worn by celebrity adherents to Kabbala supposedly ward off evil spirits.*

The Italian Renaissance

The Italian Renaissance, which began in the city of Florence in the late fourteenth century and peaked during the reign of a local ruler named Lorenzo the Magnificent, was a period of tremendous political, religious, and artistic change. The term comes from an Italian word for rebirth, and for intellectuals, the Renaissance, indeed, felt like a rediscovery of the arts. It followed what some regarded as a thousand-year period of cultural stagnation in Europe after the fall of the Roman Empire.

Artists and intellectuals flocked to Lorenzo's court at the city on the Arno. Famous painters, including Leonardo da Vinci, Botticelli, and Michelangelo, worked in Florence. Lorenzo himself wrote poetry and hunted game.

The Renaissance marked a historical turning point, when the Middle Ages ended and the modern era began. The Renaissance spread from the Florence of the Medicis to other parts of Italy, and then northward to the rest of Europe. Aided by the invention in Germany of a new kind of mass-production printing press, the ideas of the Renaissance changed the culture of Europe profoundly.

The basic creed of the Renaissance was humanism, an intellectual movement that replaced blind obedience to religious teachings with a return to classical thinking. The willingness to cast aside tradition led to new forms of architecture, painting, and scholarship. The Renaissance was, above all else, a shift in mentality away from hidebound medieval traditions to a more inquisitive, modern outlook on the world.

ADDITIONAL FACTS

1. *Occasionally, visitors to Florence are so overwhelmed by the magnificence of Renaissance art and architecture in the city that they faint—a condition Florentines refer to as* Stendhalismo, *after the nineteenth-century French writer who was reportedly unable to walk after arriving in the city.*

2. *Movable type, which enabled the mass production of books in Europe, was invented by Johann Gutenberg in 1448. Prior to the invention, books had to be hand-copied. Completing a single volume could take years or even decades.*

3. *The political theorist Niccolò Machiavelli, who learned about politics and governance firsthand as an adviser to the Medicis, dedicated his landmark treatise on power* The Prince *to Lorenzo di Pero's son.*

4. *Perhaps the most famous building in Florence is the city's cathedral, which is spacious enough to hold 30,000 worshippers. The famous eight-sided dome, completed in 1436, was the first of its kind ever built and is considered one of the first and finest examples of Renaissance architecture.*

Don Quixote

Miguel de Cervantes' *Don Quixote* (Part I, 1605; Part II, 1615) is arguably the most prominent cultural landmark of the Spanish-speaking world. It is celebrated as the preeminent work of Spanish literature and widely considered the first modern novel in any language.

The title character is a fifty-year-old man from the region of La Mancha in central Spain. Influenced by books about chivalry, he announces one day to his bemused family that he has changed his name to Don Quixote and that he is going out into the world on his noble steed—really his skin-and-bones barn horse, Rocinante—to do great deeds and right all wrongs. He enlists a "squire," an illiterate peasant named Sancho Panza, who thinks Don Quixote is crazy but plays along, half-believing his new master's promise that he will give Sancho an island to govern.

The pair sets off on a long string of misadventures. Don Quixote continually misinterprets the world around him, mistaking innkeepers for knights, prostitutes for maidens, monks for enchanters, and windmills for giants. Often, his exploits harm their intended beneficiaries more than they help. He dedicates all his deeds to a "princess," Lady Dulcinea del Toboso—really a peasant girl who is completely indifferent to the actions being performed in her name.

Don Quixote both parodies and pays homage to the chivalric romance—a genre that was a staple of secular literature during the Middle Ages. These epic poems told loosely connected tales of heroic knights, typically featuring themes of courtly love. Some were based on true events, but others were purely legend. In *Don Quixote*, Cervantes tackled the same subject matter, but with a more cohesive narrative, unprecedented psychological depth, and ironic self-awareness. He also added surprisingly postmodern twists: After another writer published a fake sequel to the first part of *Don Quixote* in 1614, Cervantes decided to write the fake sequel into the real second part of the novel. He makes Don Quixote and Sancho aware of this false account, enabling them to comment on it with derision.

Though we take such characteristics for granted in today's literature—and indeed take the novel form itself for granted—they were enormous innovations at the time. The character of Don Quixote himself is a great achievement, a figure whom different eras and groups have variously interpreted as a buffoon, a tragic hero, and a courageous figure refusing to conform. His embodiment of so many qualities is precisely what has made Cervantes' protagonist one of the most timeless characters in fiction.

ADDITIONAL FACT

1. *Of all the books published throughout history,* Don Quixote *is second only to the Bible in terms of total number of copies printed.*

Albrecht Dürer

Albrecht Dürer (1471–1528) is one of the best-known Renaissance artists from northern Europe. His father was a Hungarian goldsmith who settled in Nuremberg, Germany, and taught his sons the skills to create the exquisite engravings and wood cuts of his later career.

Dürer was one of the first northern artists to travel to Italy in order to study art. After spending time in Venice in 1494, he returned to Nuremberg, where he combined Renaissance theory with the technique he learned in Germany.

In 1498, Dürer published a cycle of fifteen woodcuts illustrating the Apocalypse—the end of the world as described in the Book of Revelations. Particularly famous is his portrayal of the Four Horsemen of the Apocalypse: Death, Famine, War and Pestilence.

Between 1513 and 1514, he printed his three "Master Engravings." The best known of these is *Knight, Death and the Devil*, depicting a medieval Christian knight riding fearlessly through temptation and peril.

Soon after Martin Luther posted his Ninety-Five Theses in 1517, Dürer became an ardent follower of the Reformation. His great late masterpiece, the *Four Apostles* (1523–1526), includes lengthy inscriptions of Luther's German translation of the Gospels, in which the apostles decry human error and pride. Dürer presented the painting to the city fathers of Nuremberg, a city which by this point had embraced Lutheranism.

In his later years, Dürer became increasingly interested in the theory of art. He published a study on perspective based on the work of Piero della Francesca in 1525. Two years later, he wrote a book on the science of fortifications. He was working on a major treatise on proportions when he died in 1528.

Known as the "Leonardo of the North," Dürer dedicated his life to harmonizing the classical ideals of the Italian Renaissance with the naturalism of his native Germany.

ADDITIONAL FACTS

1. *Although best known for his engravings, Dürer also excelled in watercolors as is manifest in his* Great Piece of Turf, *admired today for its scientific accuracy.*

2. *Dürer experimented with an optical device for replicating reality on a two-dimensional surface.*

3. *In his engraving* The Fall of Man *(or* Adam and Eve*), Dürer included four animals to represent the four humors or temperaments: the sanguine, the melancholic, the phlegmatic, and the irate.*

Galileo Galilei

Galileo Galilei (1565–1642), born outside of Pisa in Italy, has been called the father of modern physics, the father of modern of astronomy, and the father of modern science. A short list of his accomplishments includes the invention of the compound microscope, the discovery of moons around Jupiter, designs for the first pendulum clock, and the invention of a telescope that could see deeply into space. His scientific experiments laid the groundwork for modern scientific method, and his concept of inertia directly inspired Newton's laws of motion.

But probably Galileo's greatest accomplishment was the stand he took against the Roman Catholic Church of the Renaissance. At the time, it was considered an act of rebellion to teach that the sun was the center of the solar system, a theory that had originated with Copernicus. In keeping with a literal interpretation of the Bible, the theory condoned by the church was that the sun and planets revolved around the earth. In his treatise *Dialogue Concerning the Two Chief World Systems*, Galileo used the observations he made with his new telescope to defend Copernicus. During the Inquisition, the sixty-nine-year-old Galileo's book was banned, and he was ordered to appear before the court in Rome. He was found guilty of defying church doctrine and sentenced to life in prison. His sentence was commuted to house arrest, and he died eight years later in his home near Florence, under the watch of Inquisition guards.

In 1992, 359 years after Galileo's trial, Pope John Paul II formed a commission that recognized Galileo's bravery and formally apologized for his punishment.

ADDITIONAL FACTS

1. Galileo's father discouraged him from studying mathematics. He wanted him to be a doctor.

2. Galileo was also the first person to report seeing mountains and valleys on the surface of the moon.

3. Both of Galileo's daughters were born out of wedlock and became nuns.

George Frideric Handel

Incorrigibly social and cosmopolitan, George Frideric Handel (1685–1759) was the best composer, besides Johann Sebastian Bach, of the late baroque. He was born in 1685 in the small German town of Halle to a Catholic family, and he wrote his first two operas before the age of twenty. He then began to compose brilliant choral pieces in Latin for the Catholic liturgy.

Between 1707 and 1711, Handel spent time in northern Italy, hobnobbing with the great Italian composers Antonio/Arcangelo Vivaldi, Corelli, and Domenico and Alessandro Scarlatti, whose sense of melody would have a great influence on him. After leaving Italy to accept a post in the court of the Elector of Hanover—who happened to be heir to the British crown—Handel convinced his new employer to let him take a year off to travel to London. Once there, Handel began popularizing opera to the English public. *Rinaldo* (1711) was the first opera he wrote specifically for London, and though it was in Italian, it enjoyed immense success. Many others followed, including *Acis and Galatea* (1718), *Radamisto* (1720), and *Giulio Cesare* (1724). These works made him the king of the newly opened Royal Academy of Music, where the finest operas in England were being staged.

When the Elector of Hanover finally arrived in London in 1717 to take the crown as George I, Handel was concerned the new monarch would be angry that he had spent more time in London than back in Hanover. According to one legend, Handel composed the famous *Water Music* suite to win back the king's favor; when the king heard how brilliant Handel's music had become, he doubled his salary.

During Handel's later years in England, he shifted his focus from opera to oratorio, a dramatic but unstaged genre for soloists, chorus, and orchestra, usually religious in content. He completed more than thirty before he died. He wrote his beloved *Messiah* (1742), followed by *Samson* (1743), *Semele* (1744), *Solomon* (1749), and others. He died in London in 1759.

ADDITIONAL FACTS

1. Handel's father originally wanted him to be a lawyer, not a musician.

2. Handel's Messiah *oratorio is performed each year at Christmas at countless churches worldwide.*

3. Handel's first opera in England, Rinaldo, *featured live sparrows being released during a scene that took place in the woods.*

Skepticism

"Have you ever had a dream, Neo, that you were so sure was real? What if you were unable to wake from that dream? How would you know the difference between the dream world and the real world?"

—Morpheus, *The Matrix*

Are you living in a computer simulation? How do you know? It seems like you are holding a real book, made of real paper. But how do you know that isn't because a computer is telling your brain to have the experience of holding a book, made of real paper? How do you know that any of your experiences about the world are worth trusting?

This dilemma is known as the problem of skepticism about the external world. Skepticism, more generally, is any set of philosophical arguments or claims intended to undermine our belief in some alleged body of knowledge. A skeptic is someone who uses skeptical arguments to undermine our ordinary claims of knowledge.

Here's another form of skepticism: How do you know that other people have thoughts, feelings, and experiences? They act as though they have thoughts. And if you ask them, they will say they have experiences. But how do you know they are telling the truth? Any evidence that tries to support the claim that other people are thinking beings can be reinterpreted to suggest that they are very elaborately programmed robots.

Many philosophers have claimed to have resolved the problem of skepticism about the external world and other minds. Still others have admitted defeat.

ADDITIONAL FACTS

1. *René Descartes (1596–1650) wrote the most famous and influential presentation of skepticism in his* Meditations on First Philosophy, *in which he considers the possibility that a very powerful, but malevolent, demon has created him and is systematically deceiving him. Descartes asked his reader, how do I know that I am not being deceived by such a demon?*

2. *While Immanuel Kant (1724–1804) regarded it as a great "scandal" that philosophy had not yet solved the problem of skepticism, Martin Heidegger wrote that the great scandal was not that the problem was not solved, but that philosophers thought that it stood in need of a solution.*

Hasidism

The Hasidic movement was founded by Rabbi Israel ben Eliezer, known as the Besht, or Baal Shem Tov, in the mid-eighteenth century.

The core beliefs of Hasidism are pantheism and devekut. Pantheism holds that God is present in all natural physical objects. This caused great unrest among Jews as it conflicted with the widely held belief that God did not have any physical presence. Devukot is a state of ecstatic communion with God, open to every Hasid.

Traveling through Poland and the Ukraine, the Besht emphasized that emotional communion with God and love of fellow Jews was more important than technical Torah scholarship. He placed a great stress on heartfelt prayer, as opposed to study.

In the eighteenth century, Hasidism quickly spread throughout Eastern Europe, encountering opposition to its beliefs wherever it went. Still, various sects were formed, as groups adhered to the specific teachings of certain rebbes, or spiritual leaders. The movement thrived until World War II and the Holocaust. With much of their population executed, and their homes and towns destroyed, Hasidic Jews mostly emigrated to either Israel or the United States.

Today Hasids are often most strongly identified with their manner of dress. While specific attire differs from sect to sect, most Hasidic men wear a long black coat, prayer belt, black hat, and a set of white threads, called tzitzit, hanging outside their clothes at the waist. Additionally, men are not allowed to shave the sides of their faces, which is why many Hasidic Jews wear curls, called payot, and beards. The requirements for Hasidic women are less uniform but quite severe. They are required to wear conservative skirts and long sleeves, and married women must cover their hair.

Hasidic Jews chose this manner of dress to preserve as many of their customs as they could from the eighteenth century. They also believe it is important to stand out from secular society and look Jewish. Thus, a group that was once radical, is today seen as quite conservative.

ADDITIONAL FACTS

1. *The word* Hasidism *can also be used to refer to a group of Jews during the third century BC. These Hasidic Jews were conservative and opposed Hellenistic Jews who advocated assimilation.*

2. *Not all Hasidic sects get along. The Satmer sect is anti-Zionist while the Chabad sect supports the State of Israel.*

The Reconquista

Almost as soon as the Muslim caliphate conquered Spain in 718 AD, Christian Europe began plotting to win the peninsula back. It took almost 800 years of sporadic war but the *reconquista* was ultimately successful in 1492, when the last stronghold of Moorish control on the peninsula, the great fortress of Granada, fell to the Spanish monarchs Ferdinand and Isabella. But the Moors, as Spain's Muslims were called, left a strong cultural legacy to the modern nations of Spain and Portugal.

During the eight centuries of Moorish rule, the Iberian Peninsula was known as al-Andalus. The caliphate was the only extended period of Islamic rule in otherwise Christian Western Europe. Muslim Spain was, by many measures, a stunning success. The architectural marvels built by the caliphs rivaled their Christian counterparts at the time.

Christian Europe was both fascinated and terrified by the Moors in their backyard. Retaking Iberia became a key goal for medieval Christians and a rallying cry for the Church. Charlemagne, among other European kings, sent his troops to fight the Moors. The Crusades, though aimed at Muslim-held territories in the Middle East, were influenced by the friction between Christians and Muslims generated by Moorish control of Spain.

The cities under Moorish control began to fall to Christian armies after 1100 AD. Christians captured Zaragossa in 1118. Lisbon, the capital of modern-day Portugal, fell in 1147. The great Moorish capital, Córdoba, was captured in 1236. The fall of Granada in 1492 completed the reconquista. The conquering Christians were not nearly as tolerant as the Moors. A few months after the fall of Granada, Jews were expelled from Spain. A few years later, the remaining Muslims on the peninsula were ordered either to convert or leave Iberia. The once-thriving caliphate had vanished, but Spain and Portugal, two countries that were soon to become major players on the world stage, had emerged from the ruins.

ADDITIONAL FACTS

1. *In 1294, with the boundaries between Portugal and Spain still unsettled, Portugal signed a treaty of alliance with England. It is the oldest treaty in the world still in force.*

2. *One of the most famous warriors of the reconquista period was a Christian general named El Cid, who actually fought for both Christians and Muslims.*

3. *The Koran forbade depicting human figures in mosques, which lead to a reliance on geometric forms and patterns. This distinctive architectural style remains visible in many Spanish towns where mosques were converted into Catholic churches after the reconquista.*

The Canterbury Tales

Though details about Geoffrey Chaucer's life are elusive, the legacy of his magnum opus, *The Canterbury Tales* (c. 1390s), is clear. It played a central role in establishing English as a literary language, a real alternative to the French and Latin that were standard—even in England—at the time. By upending the notion that English was inherently inferior to classical languages, Chaucer paved the way for Edmund Spenser, Sir Philip Sidney, Christopher Marlowe, William Shakespeare, and other subsequent giants of English literature.

The Canterbury Tales is a set of twenty-four stories told by various pilgrims who are journeying in a group from the London area to Canterbury to visit the shrine of St. Thomas à Becket. The prologue suggests that Chaucer originally intended to include 120 tales, but it is uncertain whether the work is incomplete or whether Chaucer simply changed his mind and chose to stop at twenty-four.

Chaucer's pilgrims are a hodgepodge of people from different walks of life: the Knight, the Miller, the Pardoner, the Prioress, the Wife of Bath, and so on. Their tales cover a range of literary genres, from sermon to allegory, from hagiography to chivalric romance. The subject matter of the tales also varies widely, from courtly love to religious hypocrisy to episodes of bawdy humor.

The language of *The Canterbury Tales* is Middle English, the bridge between the Old English of *Beowulf* and the modern English in use today. Though spelling, pronunciation, and word order have changed significantly since Chaucer's time, much of his language is accessible to present-day readers. For instance, the Wife of Bath's tale opens with this description of the supernatural beings who allegedly populated Arthurian England:

> In th'olde dayes of the king Arthour,
> Of which that Britons speken greet honour,
> Al was this land fulfild of fayerye.

All but two of the tales are in verse. Chaucer chose to depart from prevailing French verse forms and use iambic pentameter—a ten-syllable-per-line form that has since become a staple of English poetry. This momentous decision on Chaucer's part set the stage for Shakespeare and others to apply iambic pentameter brilliantly in plays and sonnets during the centuries that followed.

ADDITIONAL FACT
1. *After the Black Death ravaged England in the late 1340s, Chaucer's family inherited a fortune from relatives who died in the epidemic. This financial windfall enabled Chaucer to obtain an education rather than become a tradesman or merchant.*

Michelangelo

Michelangelo (1475–1564) is often regarded as the greatest artist of the Italian High Renaissance. A gifted painter, architect, poet, and engineer, he considered himself first and foremost a sculptor. Giorgio Vasari, who knew Michelangelo personally and wrote his biography, claimed that he could breathe life into inanimate marble.

Michelangelo was born in 1475 in the town of Caprese in Tuscany. An exceptionally talented youth, he was invited to join the intellectual and artistic circle surrounding the wealthy scion of the Medici family, Lorenzo the Magnificent. From Florence he went to Rome, where he received a commission to sculpt a *Pietà* (an image of the Virgin lamenting the dead body of her son), which he completed in 1499.

By 1501, Michelangelo had returned to Florence where he worked on his famous sculpture of David. Called back to Rome several years later, he was asked to design and execute an elaborate monument with forty larger than life-sized figures for the tomb of Pope Julius II. This project was soon interrupted by another request from the pope, who wished Michelangelo to paint the entire ceiling of the Sistine Chapel. The young artist, who had little experience working in fresco, completed the task in a mere four years.

Once the ceiling was done, Michelangelo returned to the pope's tomb for which he carved the figure of Moses and The Dying Slave between 1513 and 1516. Since Julius II died before his tomb was ready and his family was reluctant to pay for such an extravagant monument, Michelangelo was unable to finish the commission to his own design. Disappointed, he spent much of the next twenty years working on various projects for the powerful Medici family, most notably their funerary chapel in the basilica of San Lorenzo.

In 1534, Michelangelo returned to Rome to paint a fresco of the *Last Judgment* on the altar wall of the Sistine. He signed the work by painting his own likeness onto the flayed skin of the martyr Bartholomew. Several years after Michelangelo completed the painting, Pope Paul IV had the nudes in the *Last Judgment* covered with drapery, as he considered them offensive. Most of the drapery was left intact in the recent restoration of the chapel.

Michelangelo also made his mark on the urban planning of Renaissance Rome. In 1537, he was asked to redesign the space atop the Capitoline Hill, the ancient center of the city. Nine years later, he was appointed chief architect of new Saint Peter's, for which he designed the famous dome. Unfortunately he did not live to see its completion. He died in Rome at the age of eighty-four.

ADDITIONAL FACT

1. In the Creation of Adam *in the Sistine Chapel, Michelangelo portrayed God within an oval created by airborne angels. Two Brazilian doctors, Gilson Barreto and Marcelo de Oliviera, recently suggested that the artist consciously based the composition on the oval cross section of the human brain.*

∽∾∾

Static Electricity

Why does your hair sometimes stand up after you comb it? Why do door handles sometimes shock your hand after you put on your coat in winter? The answer is static electricity.

All matter consists of atoms. Each atom is made of neutrons, protons, and electrons. Neutrons have no charge; protons are positively charged; and electrons are negatively charged. Protons and neutrons are tightly bound together in the center of the atom, called the nucleus, while the electrons orbit around them, like planets orbiting around the sun. When there are just as many protons as electrons, the atom has no charge. But sometimes, electrons rub off onto other atoms. The atoms that gain electrons become negatively charged; the atoms that lose electrons become positively charged. Atoms with opposite charges are attracted to each other or a neutrally charged object. Atoms with the same charge are repulsed by each other.

This is why your hair stands up on end. The electrons from your hair rub off onto your brush. Your hair becomes positively charged. Each positive strand of hair wants to move as far away from the other strands as possible, so you get "fly-away" hair.

Some materials, like metals, grab electrons and let them flow freely through them. These are called conductors. Other materials, like plastic and fabric, are more rigid and stop electrons from moving. These are called insulators. When you put on your coat in winter, electrons from your coat rub off onto you. You become negatively charged. When you touch a metal door handle, the electrons jump from your hand to the metal knob, a good conductor. This heats the air, creating a spark. This is more likely to happen in winter because the air is dry. Moisture in the air absorbs electrons (water is a good conductor), deadening the spark.

ADDITIONAL FACTS

1. *Lightning is static electricity on a larger scale. During a storm, the movement of electrons creates positive charges at the tops of clouds and negative charges at the bottoms. Usually, electrons will jump from one cloud to another to equalize the charge, but sometimes they jump to the neutrally charged ground in a lightning bolt.*

2. *Benjamin Franklin discovered that lightning is static electricity in his famous kite experiment.*

3. *Franklin also invented the lightning rod, a device that arguably has saved more lives than any other in history.*

Handel's *Messiah*

In 1741, George Frideric Handel received a commission from the Viceroy of Ireland to compose a piece for a Dublin charity concert. For twenty-four days starting on August 22, Handel worked at a furious pace on what would become his most famous piece, the oratorio *Messiah*. Although Handel was already famous in London, his composition of *Messiah* ensured that the composer would be a household name for generations to come. Even today, choirs across the world perform the piece to celebrate the Christmas season.

The oratorio genre originated in the seventeenth century, and its name comes from the prayer halls that were attached to sixteenth and seventeenth-century Catholic churches, halls in which these pieces were originally performed, theaters being closed during penitential seasons. Oratorios are choral/orchestral works that alternate between solo parts and choruses and are almost always set to narrative texts with characters and plot lines. They are like operas without the theatrical staging—performed in halls without costumes or on-stage action.

Unlike most oratorios, *Messiah* does not have a linear plotline. It is a disconnected series of meditations on Christ and recitations of biblical prophecies. The content was unusual for Handel, a largely secular composer. The famous *Hallelujah* chorus is one of the best known Baroque pieces, as are the choruses titled "O we, like sheep, have gone astray," and "For unto us a child is born." After its triumphant premiere in Dublin in 1742, Handel's fame skyrocketed, solidifying his career as a commercial composer. He never quite equaled *Messiah*, the most famous oratorio ever written, but he finished his career in London assured his name would go down in history.

ADDITIONAL FACT
1. *The speed with which Handel completed* Messiah *has led some to believe that he was truly divinely inspired. Other accounts say that Handel always worked faster than the average composer, and that* Messiah *was no exception.*

René Descartes

Born in 1596 in La Haye, France, René Descartes (1596–1650) worked for several years as a military engineer before writing revolutionary works in philosophy, mathematics, and science. He died in 1650.

Descartes' philosophical project was to replace the Aristotelian system of science that was then the basis of university education in France and throughout Europe. His most famous work was his *Meditations on First Philosophy*. The book recounted his thoughts over six days spent in a small room during his travels. Descartes attempted to question all of his beliefs and retain only those whose truth he could not doubt. It was during this effort that Descartes made his famous observation that because he could not doubt he thinks, he could not doubt he exists—"I think therefore I am" or, in the original Latin, "*Cogito ergo sum.*"

While Descartes concluded his fundamental existence was not in doubt, he believed he could doubt the nature of his body. Because his ability to think was irrefutable but the existence of his physical body was not, Descartes argued mind and body are distinct.

Descartes believed bodies were described by physics. They are geometrical things in motion with size, shape, and velocity. Minds, on the other hand, are immaterial thinking things. Hence, for Descartes, animals were mere machines. Because they do not think (he assumed), they do not have minds, and they must simply be complex arrangements of moving parts.

ADDITIONAL FACTS

1. Descartes called bodies "res extensa"—extended things—and minds "res intelligens"—thinking things.

2. Descartes invented coordinate geometry.

Jesus Christ

Jesus of Nazareth was born and raised a Jew during the period of the Roman Empire. Christians believe he was the son of God and the long-awaited Messiah. The Four Canonical Gospels tell the story of his life.

Jesus was born in Bethlehem to Mary, who Christians believe was a virgin impregnated by the Holy Ghost. Mary's husband, Joseph, is rarely mentioned in the Gospels and therefore is believed to have died before Jesus reached his middle-teen years. Jesus adopted Joseph's trade, carpentry, before beginning to teach when he reached his thirties.

Jesus taught through short stories, parables, paradoxes, and metaphors. Some of his most famous teachings are the Sermon on the Mount and the parable of the Good Samaritan. Additionally, he performed miracles, healing the sick and even resurrecting the dead. He befriended and taught women, which was condemned by the religious establishment of the time.

Throughout his teachings, Jesus emphasized the coming of the Kingdom of Heaven, as well as the forgiveness of sin. The meaning of this has been interpreted in several ways. Some, because Israel was occupied by the Romans, believed that Jesus was speaking of political freedom. More common, however, was the belief that Jesus was preaching about the end of the world. This apocalyptic end was thought to be the coming of the Messianic age described in the Torah. Jesus was believed to be the Messiah, or savior, promised by the Old Testament, who would usher in an era of redemption and harmony.

Although Jesus had many followers, he regularly challenged the status quo. In order to demonstrate his displeasure with the Jewish elders of Israel, he created a disturbance at the Temple during Passover. The Sanhedrin, the Jewish high court, convicted him of blasphemy and handed him to the Romans on the charge of sedition against the State. The Roman leader in Israel, prefect Pontius Pilate, sentenced Jesus to be executed by crucifixion. Three days after his burial, however, Christians believe Jesus was resurrected from his tomb, proving his godliness before ascending to Heaven.

ADDITIONAL FACTS

1. *In 532, then known as the 248th year of the Diocletian Era, Dionysius Exiguus attempted to determine the date of Jesus's birth. After much study, he determined the exact year and re-dated it December 25, 1 AD, establishing the western calendar still in use today. However, that calendar is based on a miscalculation. It is now believed Jesus was born four to eight years before year 1.*

2. Christ *is the Greek term for "messiah."*

The Inquisition

In the century after 1492, Spain became the most powerful country in the world. Spanish *conquistadors* captured vast territories in the New World, from Peru to Cuba. Galleons laden with gold and other riches returned to Spanish ports, instantly making the crown wealthy almost beyond comprehension. Spanish armies also controlled other parts of Western Europe, including modern-day Belgium and the Netherlands.

Within Spain's borders, a domestic campaign for religious purity gained steam. After expelling the Jews in 1492 and ordering Muslims to convert to Christianity, the authorities in Madrid were determined to turn their newly powerful country into a pious Christian kingdom. Many Spanish churchmen feared that Jewish and Muslim converts to Christianity still practiced their old faith in secret, threatening the religious unity of Spain.

The Spanish Inquisition aimed to root out heresy and punish the so-called "false converts," often with a grisly execution. Other countries in Catholic Europe conducted inquisitions, but Spain's was notorious for its length and severity; the last execution for heresy carried out by the Inquisition—by strangulation—was in 1826.

Today, the Spanish Inquisition is synonymous with the overzealous religious persecutions and bigotry of the medieval period. It particularly targeted Jews, fueling European anti-Semitism. However, Spain was not alone. Religiously inspired violence was a constant feature of the Middle Ages, across the continent. In Britain, thousands were executed as witches, a practice that only ended gradually with the Enlightenment, when progressive thinkers began to reject a literal interpretation of the Bible.

ADDITIONAL FACTS

1. *Jews were not officially allowed to return to Spain until 1858.*

2. *The Roman Inquisition also murdered and imprisoned scientists, like Galileo, whose findings contradicted Church belief.*

The Divine Comedy

The Divine Comedy is the masterpiece of the Italian poet and philosopher Dante Alighieri (1265–1321). A detailed account of a man's journey through the afterlife, it has influenced Christian cosmology for centuries and formed the basis of the modern Italian language.

Born in Florence, Dante was active in the city's public life. In 1302, he fled into exile after his political stances earned him a death sentence from the Florentine government. It was in this exile that he wrote *La Commedia*, as he himself titled the poem. The moniker *La Divina Commedia* came into use only after Dante's death.

La Commedia is structured in threes, mirroring the Christian concept of the Holy Trinity. It includes three sections—*Inferno*, *Purgatorio*, and *Paradiso*—each comprised of thirty-three divisions, or cantos. One additional canto, a prologue, brings the total to 100. Even the poem's internal structure is based on threes: Dante wrote the entire work in terza rima, a form in which sets of three lines are joined in an interlocking rhyme scheme (ABA, BCB, CDC, etc.).

The protagonist of *La Commedia* is Dante himself. Lamenting his loss of direction in life, he encounters the spirit of the Roman poet Virgil in a forest. Virgil guides him to the gates of hell, which bear the legendary inscription *Lasciate ogne speranza, voi ch'intrate*—"Abandon all hope, ye who enter." Passing through the nine circles of hell, Dante sees damned souls suffering a host of eternal punishments. These terrifying images in *Inferno* culminate in the appearance of Satan himself, trapped in a lake of ice at the very bottom of hell.

In *Purgatorio*, Dante visits purgatory, the holding ground for souls not yet pure enough to meet God. After this stage, Virgil can go no further, for as a pagan he cannot enter heaven. Dante receives a new guide, Beatrice, who embodies divine grace in a figure of romantic love. After ascending the nine levels of heaven in *Paradiso*, Dante briefly sees God, culminating a journey that has mirrored that of the human soul on the path to God—from sin through repentance into salvation.

La Commedia had an enormous effect on the development of the Italian language. Virtually all Italian literature until the 1200s had been written in Latin, so Dante's decision to use vernacular Italian was a significant change. When the Italian city-states became a unified nation in 1861, the Tuscan dialect used in the works of Dante was established as the standard for written Italian, still in use today.

ADDITIONAL FACTS

1. The poet T. S. Eliot wrote, "Dante and Shakespeare divide the modern world between them; there is no third."

2. The motif of a hero journeying into the underworld also figures prominently in two major texts that inspired Dante—Homer's Odyssey and Virgil's Aeneid.

David

In 1501 the republic of Florence hired Michelangelo to sculpt a figure of David for the façade of its cathedral. The Old Testament king—a heroic warrior who had vanquished the giant Goliath in his youth—was commonly regarded as the protector of the Tuscan city. The commission had initially been granted to another artist who died shortly after blocking out a huge piece of expensive marble. According to legend, Michelangelo received the job because he was the only one willing to work with the "spoiled" stone. When Michelangelo completed the figure in 1504, it was considered too extraordinary to be placed high up on the church. Instead, it was placed before the Palazzo Vecchio on the Piazza della Signoria in the very center of Florence.

The scupture, one of the superb masterpieces of the High Renaissance, captures a tense David right before he attacks Goliath. This is not the victorious youth of Donatello's famous rendering, but an adolescent poised for action. Inspired by classical models, Michelangelo carved a beautiful, athletic body standing with his weight on one leg and his noble head turned to the left. David's muscles bulge with gathering power as he prepares to slay the giant. His over-sized hands and feet suggest both the distorted proportions typical of adolescents and the promise of future strength.

According to an anecdote published by Michelangelo's biographer Giorgio Vasari, a Florentine citizen, Pietro Soderini, complained that David's nose was too large. Responding to the critique, Michelangelo pretended to chip away at the nose. When the sculptor was done, Soderini exclaimed, "Now you have given it life!"

The sculpture was pelted with stones when it was first erected on the Piazza della Signoria, probably by supporters of the exiled Medici clan who saw the figure as a symbol of the republic. In 1527, its left arm was broken during a riot. The statue was removed from the Piazza in 1873 in order to rescue it from damage caused by the elements and pollution. Once it was safely enclosed in the Academy of Fine Arts, a copy was installed in its place. In 1991, a deranged Italian painter attacked the original with a hammer, smashing one of its toes.

The statue was cleaned with distilled water in anticipation of its 500th birthday, Plans for installing a permanent jet stream to prevent further dirt buildup are currently being discussed.

Today the David can be seen in the Galleria dell'Accademia along with other sculptures by Michelangelo, such as the four unfinished slaves that he designed for the tomb of Julius II.

The Ozone Layer

The earth's atmosphere is divided into several layers. Humans live in the troposphere, an oxygen-rich environment that extends just above the peak of Mount Everest. The next layer, ten to fifty kilometers above the surface of the earth, is called the stratosphere. It contains 90 percent of the world's ozone (O_3), an important molecule that makes human life on the surface possible. The *ozone layer* refers to the part of the stratosphere with the highest concentration of ozone, an area approximately twenty-five kilometers above sea level.

Ozone is a rare molecule. It contains three oxygen atoms, whereas normal oxygen molecules (O_2) contain only two. For every two million oxygen molecules, there are only three ozone molecules. But the ozone layer absorbs 97 to 99 percent of the harmful ultraviolet (UV) light that comes from the sun. UV radiation causes cataracts, sunburns, and skin cancer. It also damages crops and marine life.

Ozone absorbs UV radiation in a self-perpetuating cycle. When ultraviolet radiation hits an ozone molecule, it splits into an oxygen molecule (O_2) and an unstable single oxygen atom. The single oxygen atom quickly binds to an oxygen molecule, forming another ozone molecule. Unfortunately, certain man-made organohalogen compounds can interfere with this highly efficient process when they are released into the atmosphere. Chlorofluorocarbons (CFCs) are the most famous.

When CFCs were invented half a century ago, they were thought to be miracle compounds. They were stable, cheap, nontoxic substances that could be used as refrigerants, propellants in sprays, cleaners for electronics, and sterilizers in hospitals. By 1988, more than 320,000 metric tons of CFCs had been used worldwide. In fact, CFCs are so stable that they can survive for over 200 years in the atmosphere. When CFCs reach the stratosphere, ultraviolet radiation breaks down the molecules. This releases chlorine, which binds to ozone, destroying it. A single chlorine atom can destroy 100,000 ozone molecules. The depletion of the ozone layer in the last half of the twentieth century lead to the 1987 Montreal Protocol, which officially banned the use of CFCs in developed countries.

ADDITIONAL FACTS

1. A *"hole"* in the ozone layer has appeared over Antarctica every spring since the early 1980s. It's not literally a hole but rather a thinning of up to 60 percent during the worst years.

2. Although the ozone layer is still markedly thinner than it was fifty years ago, recent scientific reports suggest that it is on the mend and could be restored by the end of the century.

3. The chlorine from swimming pools, sea salt, and volcanoes cannot reach the stratosphere.

Musical Genres

Historically, music has been written and performed to fit particular social occasions. Before the 1700s, music served one of three functions: chamber music (played by small ensembles in the salons and drawing rooms of the aristocracy), church music (masses, motets, anthems, and hymns), or theater music (incidental music played between acts of a play, or opera).

Over the years, several standard genres, used by many composers, have developed. There are, of course, more musical genres, but these are the ones in which composers have established themselves as great talents:

BALLET: *Ballet d'action*, a style of public dance performance that was dominant in Paris by the eighteenth century, was an outgrowth of the north Italian courtly dances of the fourteenth century.

CHAMBER MUSIC: During and after the classical era, Viennese masters like Franz Joseph Haydn, Wolfgang Amadeus Mozart, and Ludwig van Beethoven set the standard for how chamber music should sound, its structure, and the ensembles it should utilize—string quartet, piano trio, small wind ensembles, etc.

CONCERTO: From the Italian *concertare*, or "coming together," concerto literally refers to a group of instruments playing in unison, but in the baroque period, this came to mean an orchestra accompanying one or many solo instruments, trading the main themes of the composition back and forth.

OPERA: This genre is a combination of theatrical staging, passionate singing, orchestral music, and oft-poetic librettos (scripts) put together to tell a story. It is distinct from oratorio in that it is actually acted out on a stage, but different from theater because the lines and the narrative are delivered entirely in song.

SUITE: Multi-movement works that incorporate dances or other short instrumental types or that are arranged to tell a programmatic story.

SYMPHONY: A multi-movement piece for full orchestra, the symphony has its roots in the *concerto ripieno*, a late baroque style of concerto-writing that used the entire ensemble, rather than just one or a few soloists, as the main melodic voice.

ADDITIONAL FACTS
1. *Some of the most famous concertos are Bach's* Brandenburg Concertos, *Mozart's concertos for French horn, and Sergey Rachmaninoff's complex* Concerto No. 3 *for piano.*

2. *Other genres include the multiple forms of church music (liturgical music, anthems, hymns, and chorales) and salon music, such as Frédéric Chopin's* Nocturnes *or Franz Schubert's* Lieder, *both of which were written to be performed as entertainments at social gatherings or at the piano in a private residence.*

Cogito, Ergo Sum

Possibly the most famous sentence in philosophy, René Descartes's "cogito, ergo sum"—I think therefore I am—appears in his work *Discourse on Method*.

Descartes's famous conclusion came at the end of a project to subject all of his beliefs to radical doubt. In other words, Descartes set out to reject any belief he could not know for certain to be true. For instance, he rejected his belief in the world of sensory experience because he believed his senses could be deceived. However, he found one belief he could not doubt—that he was thinking. Descartes claimed it was impossible for him to doubt that he was thinking, because in doubting this, he would be thinking. Then Descartes declared, if he knew for certain that he was thinking, he knew for certain that he existed. Thus, Descartes had found one unquestionable belief—belief in his own existence.

Descartes's cogito argument is a common jumping-off point for what philosophers call the problem of self-knowledge: What is unique about our awareness of ourselves from the inside? That is, in what ways is it different to think about our own thoughts, feelings, and desires as opposed to anything else? Some people think one difference is that we cannot be mistaken when we honestly report what we are thinking or feeling. This idea seems plausible if you consider the case of pain. If you feel that you are in pain, it seems impossible that you could be *wrong* in believing that you are in pain.

ADDITIONAL FACT

1. *Descartes believed that he had given a proof for the existence of God that was so strong it could not possibly be doubted.*

Sermon on the Mount

This famous sermon, delivered on a mountainside in Galilee by Jesus around 30 AD, and recounted in the Gospel of Matthew, is the central expression of his teachings.

During this sermon, Jesus called upon his followers to be even more righteous than the Ten Commandments demanded. He explained that obeying the Ten Commandments alone was not good enough for salvation. Not only can one not kill, but one cannot have angry thoughts; not only can one not commit adultery, but one cannot have lustful thoughts; not only can one not steal, but one cannot have thoughts about one's material needs. Jesus called for his followers to obey only the teachings of God and not the teachings of rabbis, as God was the only one perfect enough to enlighten.

Moreover, it is in this sermon that Jesus asked his audience to "turn the other cheek" and submit to more punishment, instead of following the retaliatory, Old Testament concept of "an eye for an eye and a tooth for a tooth." Similarly, Jesus also asked that they peacefully "resist not evil."

Interpreting this sermon has proven very difficult. It seems that Jesus has set the bar for salvation too high for even his most devout followers to achieve. Nevertheless, some absolutists suggest that in order to reach salvation, the sermon must be followed line by line. Others suggest Jesus was speaking in hyperbole and that, in real-world application, these doctrines were guidelines that would have to be modified.

Albert Schweitzer claimed that because Jesus believed the end of the world was imminent, survival—which would be difficult to achieve if doctrines such as "resist not evil" were followed to the letter—was unimportant. Another approach holds that Jesus's followers were expected to fail in obeying his guidelines, but therefore they would learn to repent.

Despite these varied interpretations, the sermon remains a major source of Christian belief.

ADDITIONAL FACTS

1. It is widely debated whether the Sermon on the Mount as depicted in the Gospel of Matthew is actually one sermon or a series of Jesus's beliefs taken from other, shorter sermons, that Matthew compiled into one.

2. The sermon also includes the Golden Rule, the Lord's Prayer, and famous sayings such as, "Judge not, that ye not be judged."

Martin Luther

"I cannot and I will not recant anything, for to go against conscience is neither right nor safe."

—Martin Luther

By 1500 AD, nearly all of Europe embraced Christianity. While the individual kingdoms of medieval Europe often bickered and fought, they all worshipped the same God. After the collapse of the Roman Empire in the fifth century, the spread of Christianity accelerated, eventually reaching France, England, Germany, Russia, and Scandinavia. Medieval Christendom—the community of believers—stretched from the olive groves of Italy to the fjords of Iceland.

But this unity masked growing unhappiness with the church during the Middle Ages. The horrors of the plague left many Europeans disillusioned, as many could not understand why God would allow so many to die. The Renaissance challenged traditional Christian teachings. And the venality and corruption of the Roman Catholic Church itself dismayed many of its most ardent believers.

In 1517, a frustrated German clergyman named Martin Luther tacked a document to the doors of the cathedral in Wittenberg. The document contained Luther's Ninety-Five Theses, a scathing indictment of the pope's leadership and the general state of the Roman Catholic Church.

Luther's main accusation was that the church leadership in Rome had become too greedy and decadent. At the time, the pope was selling indulgences to rich laymen to fund the construction of new cathedrals. An indulgence officially forgave its buyer for his sins. The practice of selling forgiveness to the highest bidder deeply offended Luther.

Almost immediately, Luther's theses provoked a major schism within European Christianity. In many corners of Europe, his criticisms of the church found a receptive audience. Luther's followers became Protestants, rejecting the traditional authority of the pope in a religious movement known as the Reformation. Within a few years, England and many other pockets of northern Europe had rejected the pope's leadership, leaving the continent divided along religious lines.

Back in Rome, the pope condemned Luther as a heretic, and a series of religious wars ensued between Catholics and Luther's followers. Those wars continued intermittently for a century, until the Peace of Westphalia in 1648. With Luther's revolt against Rome, the religious unity of Western Europe had been shattered forever.

ADDITIONAL FACTS

1. *England's King Henry VIII initially opposed Luther, but he rejected Catholicism in 1534 after the pope refused to allow him to divorce his wife, Catherine of Aragon.*

2. *In 1522, Luther produced a German translation of the New Testament in only eleven weeks, giving Germans the first chance to read the holy book in their own language.*

Beowulf

The eighth-century poem *Beowulf*, whose author remains unknown, is the great heroic epic of Old English. From its pages, scholars have learned volumes about the development of the English language. It also reflects the mix of pagan traditions and Christianity that characterized northern Europe during the early Middle Ages.

Beowulf opens at the mead hall of the Danish king, Hrothgar, in the sixth century. For years, a monster called Grendel has terrorized Hrothgar's court, breaking in at night and devouring his warriors. Beowulf, a young prince from Geatland (a region in the south of Sweden), arrives out of the blue with a band of men and dispatches the monster quickly. Grendel's equally fearsome mother, however, returns to avenge her son, so Beowulf tracks her down to her lair and slays her as well. Upon returning to his kingdom a hero, Beowulf rules as king for fifty years and eventually dies defending his people from a dragon.

Thematically, the poem mixes tenets of the old Germanic warrior code with elements of Christianity, which at the time was still relatively new to northern Europe. The original Beowulf legend, as told and retold orally for generations, had glorified strength, valor, loyalty, and vengeance. The *Beowulf* poet occasionally tries to incorporate Christian themes of humility and forgiveness into the original Germanic story, and the tension between the two is at times jarring.

Beowulf is written in Old English, the heavily Germanic forerunner to Middle English and modern English. As evidenced in the poem's opening verse, Old English is virtually unreadable today without translation:

Hwæt we Gar-Dena in geardagum,	Lo, praise of the prowess of people-kings
þeod-cyninga þrym gefrunon,	of spear-armed Danes, in days long sped,
hu ða æþelingas ellen fremedon.	we have heard, and what honor the athelings won.

Like much Old English poetry, *Beowulf* uses complicated rules of alliteration that helped bards recite the thousands of lines of verse from memory. It also makes heavy use of kennings—short, descriptive metaphors that add color to the poet's descriptions. For instance, the *Beowulf* poet refers to the sea as the "whale-road" and a king as a "ring-giver."

Though *Beowulf's* influence on the development of English literature is often overstated—as the poem was largely forgotten until the 1800s—it is nonetheless a priceless literary and historical document. Since its renewed rise to prominence in the twentieth century, it has inspired the works of poets and novelists from W. H. Auden to J. R. R. Tolkien.

ADDITIONAL FACT

1. Only one manuscript copy of *Beowulf* exists. Likely created around 1000 AD, it was damaged badly in a fire in 1731 and is now kept at the British Library in London.

The Sistine Chapel

The Sistine Chapel in the Vatican Palace is best known for the ceiling painted by Michelangelo between 1508 and 1512. Covering the walls of the room are frescoes by Sandro Botticelli, Pietro Perugino, Luca Signorelli, and other early Renaissance masters. The area beneath these paintings was once covered by a set of tapestries designed by Raphael.

The word *Sistine* stems from the name of the original patron of the chapel, Pope Sixtus IV. The building itself was built between 1475 and 1483, according to the dimensions of Solomon's Temple as described in the Old Testament. In 1507, Pope Julius II commissioned Michelangelo to redo the ceiling, the vaults of which had originally been covered with a painting of a starry sky by Pier Matteo d'Amelia. Michelangelo was initially reluctant to take on the task since he had little experience painting. All the same, he succeeded in creating a vast pictorial program with more than 300 figures depicting the creation, fall, and redemption of mankind. Although he claimed to have designed and painted the ceiling entirely by himself, it is more than likely that he was provided with a theological advisor and assistants. His poems describe how difficult it was to paint in a reclining position on top of a scaffold.

Nine scenes from Genesis run down the center of the ceiling. The first three are devoted to the Creation, the next three to the story of Adam and Eve, and the final three to the story of Noah. Michelangelo painted them in reverse order, hesitating to represent God until he had gained more experience with the brush. Seated on the architectural framework dividing the scenes are male nudes known as *ignudi*. Smaller nudes carrying biblical texts appear in the painted bronze medallions arranged regularly over the entire ceiling. The four vaults at the corners of the room show scenes of the Israelites' salvation. Seven huge Old Testament prophets and five pagan sibyls (female seers from Roman mythology later absorbed into Christian tradition) are seated along the base of the ceiling. Beneath them are sixteen lunettes portraying Christ's ancestors.

Michelangelo was careful to depict God over the part of the chapel reserved for the cardinals.

A complete restoration of the frescoes, funded by Fuji Film, was carried out between 1981 and 1994. The cleaning disclosed that Michelangelo had used extremely vibrant colors, a revelation that shocked many modern art historians.

Eighteenth-century German scholar Johann Wolfang von Goethe, admiring the ceiling on his tour of Italy, noted that, "Without having seen the Sistine Chapel, one can form no appreciable idea of what one man is capable of achieving."

Radiocarbon Dating

Scientists use radiocarbon dating to determine the age of once-living organisms. The method can accurately date anything from bone and cloth to wood and straw. Scientists look for levels of carbon-14, a rare form of carbon that begins to decay and disappear as soon as an organism dies. The older the object, the less carbon-14 it will contain.

All living organisms on earth are based on carbon. Normal carbon atoms (carbon-12) have six protons and six neutrons. However, sometimes cosmic rays entering the earth's atmosphere will bombard nitrogen atoms, changing them into a special type of radioactive carbon called carbon-14. Carbon-14 has two more neutrons than normal carbon. Over the course of 5,730 years, half of any given sample of carbon-14 will decay back into nitrogen. In other words, carbon-14 has a half-life of 5,730 years.

Plants and animals can't distinguish between carbon-12 and carbon-14. They consume them both until they die. However, when a plant or animal dies, the levels of carbon-14 in the organism start to decline. (The carbon-14 begins to decay and, because the organism is no longer consuming carbon, it is not being replenished.) At the same time, the amount of carbon-12 in the sample remains constant, as it is a stable molecule that does not decay. To determine the age of a dead object, scientists compare its ratio of carbon-14 to carbon-12 to the ratio in an equivalent living object.

If a dead object has half the ratio of a living object, then it is approximately 5,730 years old, because carbon-14 has a half-life of 5,730 years. If the ratio is one-quarter the living comparison, then the object is 11,460 years old. If the ratio is one-eighth, then the object is 17,190 years old, and so forth. If an object is much older than 60,000 years, there isn't enough carbon-14 left to be used scientifically.

ADDITIONAL FACTS

1. *Radioactive uranium has a half-life of 704 million years and can be used to date objects on a geologic scale.*

2. *Potassium-40, which is naturally found in the human body, has a half-life of 1.3 billion years. It has been used to date the beginning of life on the planet.*

3. *Willard F. Libby developed radiocarbon dating at the University of Chicago in the 1950s. He won the Nobel Prize in Chemistry in 1960.*

4. *Anything that has died since 1940 will be harder to test using carbon dating because nuclear activity has changed what had been roughly constant levels of radioactive material on the planet.*

Classical Period

The classical period of music, which immediately followed the baroque period and directly preceded the romantic period, lasted from about 1750 (the death of Johann Sebastian Bach) to about 1827 (Ludwig van Beethoven's death). It coincided with the intellectual epoch known as the Age of Enlightenment, whose disciples, philosophers like René Descartes, Voltaire, and Henri Rousseau, emphasized individual rights and freedoms, human worth, and rationality. Many endeavors in art, politics, and philosophy were celebrations of the human mind's ability to reason.

In art and music, this spirit translated into a devotion to Greco-Roman culture and aesthetic ideas: proportion, balance, poise, and simplicity. Apollo, the god of reason, thought, and music was exalted. The classical composers—Johann Christian Bach, and later Franz Joseph Haydn, Wolfgang Amadeus Mozart, and the early Beethoven—shared a remarkable unity of style. Their emphasis was not on experimental effects or unpredictability. Rather, they were formalists who strove toward perfection. Like the Renaissance sculptors, they tried to make art that would last for centuries, as near as possible to a flawless representation of human ideals.

During the classical period, composers perfected and standardized the concerto, sonata, and symphony forms. The precedents they set were adhered to as the ultimate standard in art music for decades that followed. At the same time, they did not sacrifice the emotional quality of their work. Mozart's symphonies and operas, Haydn's string trios, and Beethoven's violin sonatas are rich in expressive textures. They are admired for their originality and their lyrical, moving melodies as much as for their mastery of form.

ADDITIONAL FACTS

1. *The term* classical *music is often used to distinguish between European art music and rock, pop, or folk music. This distinction first came into use sometime in the 1790s.*

2. *Classical composers, like the baroque composers before them, depended on patronage to make a living. They worked generally in the royal courts, but within that context had a relatively low standing as servants to the monarch or lord. Many of them, such as Mozart, died paupers and were buried in unmarked graves.*

The Mind/Body Problem

Stubbing your toe causes you to feel pain. Your toe hitting an object is a physical event, and it causes your nerves to fire in a certain pattern, which sends a signal to your brain. But what exactly is the pain you feel?

There are two questions philosophers ask about the relation between states of your body—like stubbing your toe—and states of your mind—like feeling pain. First, are mental states identical with physical states? Is pain just the firing of those neurons in the brain? If so, then it would seem that your mind is nothing more than your brain. But, if pain is something more than firing neurons, then there is room to think that your mind is something extra, something you have in addition to a body and brain. This position is called dualism.

The second question is: If the mind is distinct from the brain, how do events in the body, especially events in the brain, cause events in the mind, and vice versa? After all, if the mind is distinct from the brain and the rest of the body, it seems that it must be immaterial, in other words, not made up of matter. So how does it interact with the matter that makes up your brain and body? Some philosophers believe that the mind and the body can interact in the same way that matter can interact with matter. Other philosophers, called epiphenomenalists, believe that the body can cause effects in the mind, but the mind cannot cause effects in the body.

The mind/body problem remains a live debate in philosophy because it raises important questions about psychology and neuroscience. Further, it poses serious obstacles in the effort to develop artificial intelligence. We may be able to recreate the brain with a computer, but can we recreate the mind?

ADDITIONAL FACTS

1. *Descartes was a substance dualist. He believed that the mind and the body are distinct things, and that they could exist without one another.*

2. *Thought experiment: Is it possible for someone to have a brain that is exactly like yours, with all the neurons firing exactly the same way, but who doesn't experience or feel anything? If you believe that a zombie like this is possible, then you think that dualism is true.*

3. *Descartes believed that the mind and body interact, and he thought he knew where: in the pineal gland (also known as the epiphysis), a part of the brain!*

The Good Samaritan

The Good Samaritan is one of the most famous parables told by Jesus. It is recounted in the Gospel of Luke and defines a standard of love toward which Jesus wished his followers to aspire.

A lawyer asked Jesus how to be saved. Jesus asked in reply, "What is written in the Torah?" The lawyer recounted the Torah sayings of "Love God" and "Love thy neighbor." Jesus said that following these doctrines leads to salvation. So the lawyer asked, in essence, "How can I identify who is my neighbor?" Jesus then began the parable.

Jesus told of a traveler who is attacked, robbed, and left on the side of a road. A priest passes by, but he avoids the man due to his disheveled appearance. Next, a Levite, a member of another revered sect, passes and ignores the stricken man as well. Finally, a Samaritan passes by. Samaritans were an ostracized and hated ethnicity at the time. According to the story, though, the Samaritan is the only one who decides to help by clothing, sheltering, and feeding the victim.

Turning to the lawyer who was questioning him, Jesus explained that it was the Samaritan, least likely to help the traveler and with nothing to gain, who was actually the traveler's neighbor.

This is an excellent example of how Jesus often shocked his audience to get his point across. The celebration of a Samaritan, though hardly controversial today, would have caused astonishment at the time, thus emphasizing the importance of aiding people in need and the closeness of all humankind.

Although this is a relatively small passage in Luke, the concept of the Good Samaritan has become accepted into the mainstream by Christians and non-Christians alike.

ADDITIONAL FACTS

1. *Ethnic Samaritans, now numbered in the hundreds and mostly living in northern Israel, became so scarce that the effect of choosing a Samaritan as the hero of the story has been lost. Over time, however, some re-tellers have attempted to insert more relevant ethnicities.*

2. *A* Good Samaritan *now refers to a person who unselfishly helps a person in need, regardless of other circumstances.*

3. *Good Samaritan Laws exist in many countries today. They protect people who help others from being sued.*

Spain in the New World

When Columbus set sail in 1492, he wasn't looking for a new world. Rather, he was trying to find a new sea passage to Asia for King Ferdinand and Queen Isabella. But the opportunity to conquer the vast areas Columbus found was irresistible. Spanish soldiers spent the next fifty years conquering huge territories in Central and South America, killing thousands of Native Americans in the process. Extracting fabulous riches from the New World, Spain was at its height as a world superpower.

In 1550, Ferdinand and Isabella's grandson, King Charles V, summoned two prominent scholars to the country's main university at Valladolid for a far-reaching debate about his foreign policy. The bloodshed in the Americas worried the king. Was it right to continue expanding Spain's empire at such a cost in human lives?

On one side of the debate at Valladolid was a Dominican monk named Bartolome de las Casas. As a child in 1493, las Casas had attended the victory parade in Seville that greeted Christopher Columbus after his discovery of the Americas. In 1502, las Casas moved to America with several relatives, part of the initial wave of Spanish settlement. In the New World, las Casas was appalled by the cruelty of the Spanish conquistadors that he witnessed firsthand. In front of the king, las Casas pleaded for a more humane Spanish policy in the Americas.

On the other side of the debate was Juan Ginés de Sepúlveda, a humanist scholar who believed that the Spanish had a duty to "Christianize" the American Indians by whatever means necessary. To Sepúlveda, native tribes like the Aztecs were barbarians who practiced human sacrifice and cannibalism. Not only did the Spanish have a right to subjugate the natives, Sepúlveda said they had a positive obligation to spread Western civilization. "The perfect should command and rule over the imperfect," he wrote in 1547, citing Aristotle to defend what he called the "just war" against the Indians.

Within two generations, the Spanish had destroyed the great Aztec and Inca empires. The king was sympathetic to the pleadings of las Casas, but it was too late. For better or worse, the European colonization of the Americas was underway.

ADDITIONAL FACTS

1. *Large parts of South America remained Spanish possessions for the next three centuries until the Napoleonic wars in Europe weakened Spain's grasp on its colonies. Mexico gained independence in 1821, and Peru followed in 1824. Spain did not lose its last colonial possessions until the Spanish-American War in 1898.*

2. *Far more Native Americans died from the diseases introduced by European explorers than perished in war. Smallpox was one of the many "virgin soil epidemics" that killed millions of Indians.*

3. *Spanish explorers founded the city of St. Augustine, Florida, in 1565, making it the oldest continually occupied European settlement in the United States.*

◦◦◦

Salman Rushdie

Born in Bombay to Muslim parents, raised among Hindus and Sikhs, educated in England, and now living in New York, novelist Salman Rushdie (1947–)is a walking embodiment of post-modernism and post-colonialism. His devilishly clever and quirky novels, steeped in both realism and fantasy, are for many the literary voice of modern India. Rushdie's novels address a host of political and religious issues, especially the tense relationship between Hinduism and Islam in India and Pakistan.

Ironically, much of Rushdie's fame is due not to his remarkable writing but to the furor that erupted in response to his novel *The Satanic Verses* (1988). The novel contains passages that many Muslims perceived as blasphemous slights against the Prophet Muhammad. The novel was banned in India, Pakistan, Egypt, Saudi Arabia, and elsewhere, and violent public protests and book burnings were widespread, from the Middle East to Great Britain. In early 1989, the Ayatollah Khomeini of Iran issued a fatwa, or edict, calling for Rushdie's death and exhorting Muslims worldwide to track him down. Rushdie spent the better part of a decade in hiding, protected by agents from Scotland Yard.

The notoriety of *The Satanic Verses* often eclipses Rushdie's greatest achievement, *Midnight's Children* (1981). The novel's protagonist, Saleem Sinai, is born at the stroke of midnight on August 15, 1947, the day India won independence from Great Britain and Pakistan was partitioned off as a separate nation. Like the hundreds of other "midnight's children" born during the same hour, Saleem has supernatural powers, and events in his life mirror developments in the young nation of India as a whole. Elements of the story are autobiographical—Rushdie himself was born in Bombay in 1947—but much of *Midnight's Children* takes place in a fantastical landscape, following in the footsteps of Günter Grass, Gabriel García Márquez, and other pioneers of magic realism. The novel earned Rushdie the Booker Prize in 1981.

Though Rushdie will forever be associated with the ayatollah's death sentence against him, his novels are actually quite light-hearted, celebrated for their inventive use of language. His prose is like a verbal jungle gym, full of allusions and playful tricks. His characters, like Rushdie himself, represent the modern immigrant experience and the intermingling of cultures in today's world. Rushdie has continued to write in this vein despite the threats against his life, producing the novels *Haroun and the Sea of Stories* (1990) and *The Moor's Last Sigh* (1995), among others.

ADDITIONAL FACT
1. *Rushdie's highly unflattering depiction of Indian prime minister Indira Gandhi in* Midnight's Children *prompted her to file a successful libel lawsuit against him. The issue was dropped only upon Gandhi's assassination in 1984.*

Raphael

Along with Leonardo da Vinci and Michelangelo, Raphael (1483–1520) is considered one of the three greatest artists of the High Renaissance in Italy.

Born near Urbino in 1483, Raphael was trained by his father, Giovanni Santi. Recognizing the boy's genius, Giovanni sent him to the workshop of Pietro Perugino, a leading painter in the region of Umbria at the time. In 1504, Raphael moved to Florence, the artistic hub of Italy in the early sixteenth century. Studying the works of Michelangelo and Leonardo, Raphael combined elements from both to come up with a style entirely his own.

In 1508, Raphael was summoned to Rome by Pope Julius II to work on a suite of papal rooms. In the first room, probably the pope's library, Raphael painted frescoes of what were considered the four major disciplines: theology, philosophy, law, and poetry. The most famous of these, philosophy, later entitled the *School of Athens*, presents Plato and Aristotle set in a vast architectural space and surrounded by all the great thinkers of ancient Greece.

Raphael remained in Rome for the rest of his short but prolific life. In addition to many altarpieces and devotional paintings, he also painted mythological scenes, such as the *Galatea*, which was commissioned for the Villa Farnesina in 1512, and which depicts the nymph pursued by the giant Polyphemus. Raphael likewise earned a reputation as an architect and was appointed to supervise the construction of new Saint Peter's Basilica when Bramante, its initial designer, died in 1514. He was also a gifted portraitist, as can be seen in his painting of Baldassare Castiglione, a prominent diplomat and author, who mentioned Raphael in his famous Renaissance treatise, *The Book of the Courtier*.

One of Raphael's most famous images of the Virgin and child, the *Sistine Madonna* (1512–1514) has provoked much discussion due to the unusually startled expression on the faces of both figures. Recent research has shown that the work's original location in the church was such that the figures would have been looking at a crucifix.

Raphael is generally said to be the most classical of the three great Renaissance masters. Johann Wolfgang von Goethe, in fact, claimed that Raphael did not have to imitate the Greeks since it was natural for him to think and feel as they did.

ADDITIONAL FACTS

1. *The earliest biography of Raphael appears in Giorgio Vasari's* Lives of the Artists *(1550).*

2. *In the* School of Athens, *Plato points his finger up to indicate his interest in abstract, ethereal concepts, while Aristotle gestures down to the ground to show his preference for concrete subjects and worldly affairs.*

3. *Raphael also explored Roman ruins, most notably the buried remains of the Golden House of Nero, the* Domus Aurea.

Albert Einstein

We tend to picture Albert Einstein as an old professor with a black moustache and tufts of white hair, but actually, he produced his greatest contributions to math and physics when he was only twenty-six years old. In 1905, while working as a patent office clerk in Bern, Switzerland, Einstein wrote four papers that are each regarded as works of genius. The year 1905 is known as *annus mirabilis*, Einstein's "year of miracles."

Einstein's first paper, "On a Heuristic Viewpoint Concerning the Production and Transformation of Light," proposed that light was made up of small packets of energy called energy quanta. We refer to them today as photons. This was the theory that won Einstein the Nobel Prize.

Einstein's second paper provided some of the first empirical evidence for the existence of atoms. Before 1905, the idea of an atom as the smallest unit of matter was regarded as a useful theoretical concept. Einstein described the movement of particles suspended in liquid, called Brownian motion, and proved that matter must have an underlying structure. That structure is explained by the modern concept of the atom.

Einstein's third and fourth papers treated the topic that most made him famous—his special theory of relativity. The theory explained the relationship between energy and mass, with the famous equation $E=mc^2$—the energy of an object equals its mass times the speed of light squared. Grossly simplified, this means that mass is another form of energy.

ADDITIONAL FACTS

1. *Einstein's papers on the theory of relativity were a continuation of work he began when he was sixteen years old.*

2. *Although Einstein encouraged President Franklin Roosevelt to build the nuclear bomb during World War II, he actively supported nuclear disarmament. He once said, "I know not with what weapons World War III will be fought, but I know World War IV will be fought with sticks and stones."*

3. *Einstein was asked to be the second president of Israel, but he declined saying he lacked the people skills.*

Franz Joseph Haydn

In the Viennese tradition of ingenious court composers, Franz Joseph Haydn (1732–1809) was the first real darling of the classical era. He was born in 1732 and grew up poor in the Austrian town of Rohrau to a laborer father. His aptitude for music was apparent even as a young boy, and at age eight he became a choirboy at the Cathedral of St. Stephen in Vienna.

From 1759 to 1761, Haydn worked in the court of Count Morzin, a low-level nobleman who went bankrupt and had to fire all his musicians. By that time, however, Haydn had attracted enough attention to be hired by a Hungarian Prince named Paul Anton Esterházy. He spent most of his life at the house of Esterház, composing for eight hours a day and managing all of the estate's musical activities, which included multiple opera and symphonic performances each week.

If Haydn's schedule sounds arduous, his career output is equally amazing: he wrote 104 symphonies, 68 string quartets, 47 piano sonatas, 26 operas, 4 oratorios, and hundreds of other pieces that have since been lost. He is credited with establishing the standard structure for a symphony—three or four movements of varied tempos, scored for strings, four or five wind parts and timpani—which he developed from the ideas of several Italian, Rococo composers. He is also credited with modernizing the string quartet format. Instead of making his quartets solo exercises for the first violinist, he moved his melodies and important themes around between the violin, viola, and cello parts.

Haydn spent the latter part of his life traveling between London and Vienna, while composing his most mature and lasting symphonies and string quartets. He met with, and provided inspiration for, the young Mozart, his most talented contemporary. He retired and eventually died in 1809 in Vienna at the age of seventy-seven.

ADDITIONAL FACTS

1. *In most baroque compositions, each movement is limited to one mood or emotional texture (sad, wintry, joyful, etc.). Haydn was one of the first composers to write pieces, namely his symphonies, that shifted through multiple expressive settings. He also eliminated the baroque continuo part and replaced it with more complex orchestrations using the many instruments in an orchestra.*

2. *While staying at Esterház, Haydn lived for two decades in servant's quarters, wearing a footman's uniform and having to deal with the humiliation of being chastised for not powdering his servant's wig properly.*

3. *When Haydn's voice changed in 1749, he was kicked out of St. Stephen's boys's choir to the streets with nothing but the clothes on his back, another indication of a musician's station in life. He survived by giving lessons, composing diversion music for the wealthy of the city, and working as a servant and apprentice to the Italian composer Nicola Porpora.*

Baruch Spinoza

Baruch Spinoza (1632–1677) was born in 1632 into Amsterdam's community of Marranos, Jews who had once secretly practiced their religion in Spain before being expelled. In 1656, he was excommunicated from the Jewish community and later changed his name to the more Latin-sounding Benedict, by which he is usually referred.

During his life and after, Spinoza's philosophical ideas were deeply controversial. In 1670, he published the *Theological-Political Treatise*, in which he argued that the Bible, like all scriptures, should be interpreted as a document produced by human beings, and not by God. Spinoza contended the real content of religion did not concern the nature of God, but rather with guiding people to do what is morally right through stories and precepts. Thus, religion is a system of moral and political control, and all religions are equally valid, insofar as they perform this task effectively. These views were so controversial in seventeenth-century Europe that Spinoza published the book anonymously.

Much of Spinoza's philosophical labors were devoted to his magnum opus, *Ethics*, which was published after his death. In this book, Spinoza presented a systematic account of God, nature, the mind, and the attainment of happiness. For Spinoza, everything in nature was governed by strict, and necessary, causal laws. Therefore, everything is a necessary consequence of necessary laws, and nothing could have been different than how it is. Spinoza believed God was simply the totality of nature, not an independent creator. He concluded there is no meaning, or purpose, to the world. In the final book of *Ethics*, Spinoza considered how, given this, we can still be happy.

Working for much of his life as a lens-grinder, Spinoza died at The Hague in 1677.

ADDITIONAL FACTS

1. Although we do not know for certain, Spinoza was probably excommunicated for denying that the soul is immortal and that God created the world for a purpose.

2. Spinoza called the state of happiness beatitude.

Apostles

Among Jesus's followers were his disciples, who traveled with and learned from him; and his apostles, whom he chose to continue his teachings after he died.

The twelve apostles were, in effect, the first missionaries. They were the twelve men Jesus dined with on the night before he was crucified. Additionally, they were among those Jesus revealed himself to after he had been resurrected.

The number twelve reflected the original twelve tribes of Israel. Some of Jesus's followers believed the restoration of ancient Israel would coincide with the coming Kingdom of Heaven.

Some of the more notable Apostles are:

SIMON: Simon was called Peter by Jesus. He was given a rare leadership role by Jesus and eventually became the first pope. Jesus told him, "You are Peter, and on this rock I will build my church." (Matthew 16:13–20) It is debated whether the "rock" was Peter himself, as the Catholics believe, establishing the papacy, or simply Peter's faith.

ANDREW: Andrew, Simon's brother, was one of Jesus's first followers and convinced Simon to become a disciple as well.

JOHN: John was purportedly the author of the Gospel of John and perhaps four additional New Testament books.

MATTHEW: Matthew, called Levi in some textual references, is believed to be the author of the Gospel of Matthew.

THOMAS: Thomas was very skeptical of Jesus's resurrection from the dead and demanded to feel his wounds before believing in the miracle.

JUDAS ISCARIOT: Judas was the man who betrayed Jesus by kissing him. This kiss allowed the authorities to identify him. By some accounts, Judas committed suicide out of guilt during the three days between Jesus's crucifixion and resurrection.

ADDITIONAL FACTS

1. According to Mormon beliefs, after Jesus was resurrected, he went to South America and chose a set of twelve apostles there. Among these were the Three Nephites, who did not die, but rather remain on Earth today awaiting the second coming of Jesus.

2. Apart from the twelve original apostles, several other successful missionaries have received the title of apostle over the centuries of Christian history. The honor is bestowed on people who bring Christianity to a particular country, area, or population for the first time.

British Settlement in North America

British settlers arrived on the shores of North America in two groups. First, in the early 1600s, English entrepreneurs built a colony at Jamestown in Virginia to look for riches in the New World, following the example of the early Spanish settlers in South America. After many setbacks, the Virginia colony grew into a prosperous commercial venture. At about the same time, another group of pious British settlers arrived in Massachusetts. This group was looking for religious freedom that had been denied them in England.

Many historians have identified the two groups of British settlers as the source of an enduring tension in the American identity. Driven by a religious fervor, the New England settlers wanted to build a community in the rocky soil of Massachusetts that would set an example for the whole world. John Winthrop, the leader of the Puritans who settled in Boston, described their mission in a famous sermon, "We shall be as a city upon a hill. The eyes of all people are upon us." The Massachusetts Bay Colony enforced a rigid code of laws based on the Bible, harshly punishing adulterers and suspected unbelievers.

The Virginia colonists, in contrast, were much more concerned with turning a profit. While the dour clergymen of Boston tried to enforce public virtue, the first act of the Virginia legislature in 1619 was to regulate tobacco prices.

The rest of the thirteen colonies reflected the mixed motives of the British. Pennsylvania became a haven for persecuted Quakers. New York started as a short-lived Dutch trading colony conquered by the British in 1664. The separate groups of British colonists initially felt little kinship with one another, but a common resentment of heavy-handed British rule helped bring the thirteen colonies together.

ADDITIONAL FACTS

1. *The colony of Maryland was founded in 1634 as a safe haven for British Catholics, whose religion had fallen out of favor in England after the reformation in the sixteenth century.*

2. *Several other European powers established short-lived colonies in North America. Swedish settlers founded Delaware in 1638, but their colony lasted only a few years. The state of Vermont was first settled by the French, briefly became an independent country in the eighteenth century, and in 1791 became the fourteenth state to join the Union.*

3. *The religious persecution suffered in Europe by many American colonists didn't stop them from mistreating religious dissidents in the New World. The Massachusetts Puritans, who had fled from England, hanged several Quakers in Boston for defying orders to leave the commonwealth.*

Pride and Prejudice

Pride and Prejudice (1813) is arguably the most popular work of British novelist Jane Austen. Along with Austen's other novels, it was groundbreaking for its focus on middle-class life. The aristocratic realm had largely been the focus of earlier British literature. Its surprisingly modern plot, replete with comedy and irony, has kept it a favorite for generations.

Born in 1775, Austen was the seventh of eight children. Her middle-class parents impressed upon her the value of reading and scholarship. She was enrolled briefly at a ladies' boarding school, which was more education than most Englishwomen of her station received at the time. Encouraged by her parents, she began writing, finishing a first draft of *Pride and Prejudice* as early as 1796. After the manuscript was rejected by a publisher, Austen set it aside and worked on other projects for more than ten years before returning to it.

Pride and Prejudice recounts the romantic anxieties of a young woman, Elizabeth Bennet, and her four sisters. Like Austen herself, Elizabeth is of middle-class upbringing. Although Mr. and Mrs. Bennet originally stood to inherit an estate, the fact that they have five daughters and no son means that the estate has been entailed, or forfeited, to a relative, the obnoxious brownnoser Mr. Collins. This unfortunate situation leaves Mrs. Bennet constantly fretting about her daughters' marital prospects.

At a ball one evening, Elizabeth meets a wealthy young man named Mr. Darcy. Though the two are intrigued by each other, Elizabeth is turned off by Darcy's arrogance, and he by the unsophisticated antics of her middle-class family. After a long string of awkward confrontations, mutual misunderstandings, and self-recriminations, Elizabeth and Darcy realize their love for each other and ultimately become engaged.

Pride and Prejudice is beloved for its wit, insight, and richly drawn characters. The feisty, independent Elizabeth is one of literature's great heroines. Mrs. Bennet is a clucking hen of a mother, prone to constant dramatics that the devoted Mr. Bennet bears with resignation. Perhaps most memorable is Darcy's venomously snobby aunt, Lady Catherine, who is aghast at the prospect of her nephew buying into the "upstart pretensions of a young woman without family, connections, or fortune." The combination of these affectionately rendered portraits with incisive humor and a satisfying ending makes *Pride and Prejudice* one of the most entertaining classics of English literature.

ADDITIONAL FACT

1. *Austen's untimely death in 1817 cut short her productive career. Her novels* Northanger Abbey *and* Persuasion *were published posthumously in 1818.*

Baroque Art

The age of the baroque is generally dated by historians as lasting from 1600 to 1750. The artistic style spread throughout western Europe, taking on different characteristics as it developed against the backdrop of the Protestant Reformation and the Catholic Counter-Reformation. Baroque art is usually described as theatrical, emotionally appealing, dynamic, and awe-inspiring.

Much baroque art in Italy and other Catholic countries was a direct response to Protestantism. Luther and his followers had criticized the Roman church for excess pageantry and for propagating the veneration of images. Catholic authorities responded by defending the use of devotional images, but decreed that artists should be forced to follow stricter guidelines and create pictures that related biblical events clearly, vividly, and realistically. Such images, they felt, would help nurture piety in believers. Architecture, on the other hand, should celebrate the power of the papacy and its victory over rebellious Protestant sects.

In Italy, the greatest baroque project was the completion of the new St. Peter's Basilica. This was very much a collaborative project. The famous sculptor and architect Gian Lorenzo Bernini oversaw the sculptural program of the entire basilica, and he designed the oval colonnaded piazza in front. Carlo Maderno built the façade. A wide variety of baroque painters executed altarpieces for the interior.

Baroque took a somewhat different direction in Protestant countries such as Holland. There it was used to glorify the young republic, rather than the papacy or ruling monarch. It also led to greater interest in atmospheric effects and human emotion in painting, as can be seen in the work of the two most famous Dutch artists of the seventeenth century, Rembrandt van Rijn and Jan Vermeer. In Protestant England, the Baroque made its mark in the architecture of Sir Christopher Wren, especially in his design for new St. Paul's Cathedral, built between 1675 and 1710.

In the eighteenth century, the baroque gradually gave way to the more ornate style of the rococo.

ADDITIONAL FACTS

1. The term baroque *was first used pejoratively in the nineteenth century to criticize the period. Today it is used colloquially to mean "extravagant," "complex," or "bizarre."*

2. *The Italian baroque painter Caravaggio's* The Death of the Virgin *caused a scandal when it was first exhibited because the artist depicted Mary with a bloated stomach, something that was considered indecorous for a saint. According to legend, Caravaggio used a local prostitute as his model.*

Charles Darwin and Natural Selection

In 1842, Charles Darwin began to write *The Origin of Species*. He was not the first person to propose that populations evolve over time, but he was the first to propose a theory for why it happened.

Born into the affluent gentry of Shropshire, England, Darwin enjoyed a privileged childhood. His father was a wealthy doctor, and his mother was the daughter of the famous potter Josiah Wedgwood. Naturally squeamish, Darwin could not follow in his father's footsteps as a physician. Still, his father wanted him to have a profession, so he was sent to the clergy. Darwin had an affinity for natural observation, anatomy, geology, and botany, but not much interest in religion. After three years of studying divinity at Christ's Church, Cambridge, Darwin seized the opportunity to leave the Church. At twenty-two years old, he climbed aboard the HMS *Beagle*, mostly to serve as a genteel traveling companion for the patrician captain, Robert FitzRoy, who feared the loneliness of command at sea.

For the next five years, Darwin sailed around the islands of the South Pacific, South America, and Australia. His observations of plants and animals, most notably the rare creatures of the Galápagos Islands, were the basis for his theory of evolution. He noticed how animals seemed to fit their environments. A bird with a long, narrow beak sipped nectar from a plant with long narrow flowers. He concluded that this did not happen by chance. The birds with the longest, most narrow beaks would have the best chance of survival, and therefore of passing on their physical characteristics to the next generation. Thus, the birds evolved over time to fit the flowers. Birds with short, fat beaks would have simply died out. This process of natural selection could be used to explain the characteristics of all creatures on earth. From seaweed to blue whales, all populations, he concluded, evolved through "survival of the fittest."

ADDITIONAL FACTS

1. Darwin did not reveal his findings to the public for more than twenty years. He had serious qualms about the impact they might have on religion.

2. The Origin of Species was a bestseller when it was finally published in 1859.

3. Darwin suffered from many debilitating illnesses after the release of the book. Although he was an adamant believer in science, he still tried quack remedies, such as soaking his neck in vinegar and tying a chain around his neck.

Haydn's *London Symphonies*

When Franz Joseph Haydn made his two longest visits to London in 1791–1792 and 1794–1795, he was greeted by fame and a frenzied media attention that had not been bestowed upon a foreign composer since Handel arrived eighty years earlier.

Haydn had just left Vienna and his young friend Wolfgang Amadeus Mozart, and the works he wrote while in England bear the stamp of the mutually influential musical relationship that the two composers shared. In fact, Haydn was the only composer whom the arrogant Mozart would recognize as his superior, though Haydn deferred modestly to his young colleague.

The *London Symphonies* were composed on commission for J. P. Salomon, an impresario who was organizing a series of concerts at London's Hanover Square Rooms. The first six were performed during the 1791–1792 season, and the second six during the 1794–1795 season. Among Haydn's most famous works, they were harmonically challenging pieces that owed a lot to Mozart's symphonic innovations.

Symphony No. 94, the "Surprise Symphony," is so-called because in the middle of the second movement, a loud bang from the full orchestra completely changes the feel of the piece. Some critics argued, presumably in jest, that it was to wake up any listeners who had dozed off.

Symphony No. 103 possessed the first symphony movement to begin with a drum roll (thus, it is sometimes called the "Drum Roll Symphony"), and *Symphony No. 104*, "The London," is possibly the finest example of mature classical symphony composition.

ADDITIONAL FACTS
1. *It is rumored that, on Haydn's departure for London, Mozart prophetically told him, "We shall never meet again." Mozart died before Haydn returned.*

2. Symphony No. 100 *is called "The Military" because of its clanging kettle drums and cymbals.*

3. *While writing the* London Symphonies, *Haydn was having a love affair with a woman named Widow Schroeter. He wrote that she was "still handsome," despite being older than sixty.*

A Priori Knowledge

Much of our knowledge of the world comes from experiencing it. We know there is a tree outside a window, for instance, because we see it. We know the tree requires sunlight and water to thrive, because scientists have carefully observed these facts. In general, we know about our immediate environment by perceiving it, and we gain scientific knowledge about the world by observing it and conducting experiments on it.

However, some of our knowledge does not depend upon experience in this way. For instance, we know that all bachelors are unmarried men. What is our justification for believing this? It does not depend upon any experience. If it were, then each of us would have to go out and investigate bachelors and determine that they are unmarried men in order to know this. But we don't. Just by knowing the meaning of the words *bachelor* and *unmarried men*, we know that all bachelors are unmarried men. (Admittedly, we need to experience the world in order to learn what those words mean. But the issue is whether, having understood what those words mean, we need further experience in order to justify believing that all bachelors are unmarried men. It appears that we do not.) Even more tellingly, what experience would lead us to deny that all bachelors are unmarried men? If no such experience is possible, it seems that our justification for believing it is independent of our experience.

Knowledge that does not depend upon experience is called a priori knowledge, because it is justified *prior* to experience. Other examples of a priori knowledge are mathematical expressions. We know that 1+1=2. But we do not know this through experience. A good test of whether some claim is justified a priori is: Would we be willing to give up this claim in the face of experience? To say that 1+1=2 is known a priori is to say we don't need to give up that claim, no matter how our experience turns out.

ADDITIONAL FACTS

1. *Philosophers disagree about whether we can have a priori knowledge of anything other than logic and the meanings of our words.*

2. *Some philosophers believe that we have no a priori knowledge whatsoever. Even our knowledge of mathematics and logic, they insist, ultimately depends upon experience.*

Mary Magdalene

Mary Magdalene, or Mary of Magdala, was one of Jesus's most prominent disciples and certainly his most discussed female disciple. The canonical Gospels recount that Mary Magdalene became a follower of Jesus when he exorcised seven demons from her.

Perhaps most important, Mary Magdalene was present at Jesus's crucifixion and was the first witness to his resurrection. On the third morning after Jesus's death, she went to his tomb and found it empty. Jesus then appeared before her. At first she did not recognize him, but he called out her name. Jesus instructed her to tell the other disciples of the miracle.

The details of Mary's life are the subject of much debate. Some scholars claim that Mary Magdalene is actually the same person as other women mentioned in the Gospels. For instance, at one point a female sinner is mentioned who lived in the house of Pharisee. This woman, whose sin may very well have been prostitution, did not have a name, but beginning in the third and fourth centuries, scholars began to allege that she was actually Mary Magdalene.

Another theoretical storyline of Mary's life is that she was Jesus's wife. Although there is little evidence on either side of this debate, supporters claim that Jesus is never explicitly said to be unmarried. Mary was closer to him than any other disciple, and it would have been very rare for a Jewish man of the time to be traveling and teaching while single. On the other hand, there is little evidence to suggest she was his wife and that being an unmarried teacher would not be too outlandish, considering Jesus's revolutionary worldview.

ADDITIONAL FACTS

1. *The tradition of giving painted Easter eggs on Easter may come from an interaction between Mary Magdalene and the Roman Emperor Tiberius Caesar Augustus. Due to Mary's presence at Jesus's crucifixion and resurrection, she was given an audience with the emperor; and, declaring that Jesus had risen from the dead, presented the emperor with an egg. The emperor responded that Jesus's rising was as likely as the egg turning red, which it promptly did.*

2. *Mary has been canonized a saint in the Roman Catholic, Eastern Orthodox, and Anglican churches.*

The Peace of Westphalia

In the winter of 1648, exhausted by thirty years of war and devastation, the major European powers met in the German province of Westphalia to hammer out a peace treaty. The Thirty Year's War had started out as a religious dispute between Catholics and Protestants in Germany. At Westphalia, the European powers decided that religion simply wasn't worth fighting about anymore. Each state, they agreed, should be allowed to choose its own religion and determine its own foreign affairs. No longer would rival European princes try to impose their own version of Christianity on their neighbors.

More important, the treaty enshrined the principle of national sovereignty that has guided foreign affairs until the present. Prior to 1648, the rulers of Germany's various regions reported to the Holy Roman Emperor. But it was never clear—especially in matters of religion—who really had the final say, the individual princes or the emperor. The treaty made it clear that individual German states, not the far-off emperor, were sovereign. Stripped of most of its power, the ancient Holy Roman Empire finally expired in 1806, just over a thousand years after Charlemagne's coronation as the first emperor in 800 AD.

The concept of national sovereignty ended religious bickering and helped stabilize Europe, but it did not end war. European princes simply found other reasons, besides God, to fight. Indeed, some critics have argued that by giving states total say over what happens within their borders, the treaty only lead to more rivalry between European countries and contributed to the disunity of Europe. The notion of sovereignty, they claim, has also given world leaders an excuse to ignore horrible human rights abuses in other countries. For better and for worse, the concept of national sovereignty remains central to international affairs today.

ADDITIONAL FACTS

1. Treaty negotiations were actually held in two separate towns, one for Protestants and another for Catholics, because the two camps refused to meet with each other directly.

2. Adolph Hitler famously referred to the Nazi regime as the German "Third Reich." In his reckoning, the first Reich was the Holy Roman Empire and the second was the short-lived monarchy headed by the Kaiser from 1871 until 1918.

Candide

The short novel *Candide* (1759) is the great satirical work of the Enlightenment, the intellectual and rational movement that swept Europe from roughly 1650 to 1800. Written by François-Marie Arouet, better known by the snappier pen name Voltaire, *Candide* skewers organized religion, the aristocracy, and the ideas of several Enlightenment philosophers.

The Enlightenment produced a mind-boggling array of illustrious writers and thinkers, but none had as incisive a wit or as keen an eye for satire as Voltaire. Born in 1694 in Paris, he demonstrated his gift for parody from a young age. Frequenting the Parisian salons with other intellectuals, known as philosophes, he espoused rationalism and attacked long-standing religious and political institutions. Voltaire's audacity got him into trouble in his early twenties, when he angered the duke of Orléans. He was exiled and then imprisoned upon his return to Paris. After his release, he was imprisoned yet again before leaving for another exile in England in 1726.

After a prolific three decades of plays, novels, and essays, Voltaire penned the now-famous farce *Candide*. The title character is an extraordinarily naive young man who grows up in the household of a German baron. He is schooled by the tutor Dr. Pangloss, who believes firmly that the world in which they live is *le meilleur des mondes possibles*—"the best of all possible worlds." After the baron banishes Candide from his home for falling in love with his daughter, Cunégonde, Candide travels throughout Europe. A ludicrous string of hardships and suffering ensues: Cunégonde sees her family killed by Bulgar hordes and then is sold into sex slavery, Pangloss contracts syphilis and is later hanged, an earthquake flattens the city of Lisbon, and Candide himself is repeatedly flogged. Nonetheless, both he and his tutor remain faithful to their blindly optimistic worldview, believing that *tout est au mieux*—"everything is for the best."

Candide is a merciless jibe at the philosophies of Voltaire's contemporary Gottfried Wilhelm Leibniz, who was renowned for his thorough optimism. Though Voltaire was not necessarily pessimistic, he saw Leibniz's beliefs as so optimistic as to be foolish—idle philosophical speculation that ignored the reality of the world. Accordingly, at the end of Voltaire's novel, Candide has a revelation of sorts and rejects Pangloss's teachings. He decides instead that the way to achieve fulfillment is to "cultivate one's garden"—in other words, to engage in practical pursuits that create tangible benefit.

ADDITIONAL FACTS

1. *Voltaire counted among his friends and acquaintances a wide range of European luminaries, from Frederick the Great to Jonathan Swift, from Catherine the Great to Casanova.*

2. *American composer Leonard Bernstein adapted* Candide *into a comic operetta in 1956. It has remained popular and is performed frequently to this day.*

Rembrandt

Rembrandt van Rijn, the most important artist of the Dutch School, is best known for his excellent and innovative portraits. Born in the Dutch town of Leiden in 1606, he studied with Pieter Lastman in Amsterdam. After returning home and setting up a productive workshop for several years, he moved back to the capital in 1631 and remained there for the rest of his life.

In the early years of Rembrandt's career, he tried to work in the dramatic Baroque style so popular at the time. He did not succeed in competing with other baroque masters, such as Peter Paul Rubens. His paintings were not as idealized as those of his Italian and Flemish contemporaries. In *The Blinding of Samson* of 1636, for example, he depicted the biblical hero as defeated and pathetic, something that so displeased the recipient of the painting, he returned it to the artist.

In portraiture, especially of multiple figures, however, Rembrandt enjoyed immediate success. In the *Anatomy Lesson of Dr. Tulp* (1632), for example, he captured the expressions of various physicians reacting to the dissection being performed in their midst. Previous group portraits of surgeons had shown the men in a formal lineup. In 1642, Rembrandt received his most important commission: a group portrait of a civic militia company. The painting, *The Company of Captain Frans Banning Cocq and Lieutenant Willem van Ruytenburch*, depicts the company preparing for a festive pageant rather than a genuine battle. The work is more commonly known as *The Night Watch*, a title stemming from a layer of dark varnish, since removed, that misled viewers into thinking the picture depicted a night scene. Today the more than fourteen-foot wide portrait can be seen in the Rijksmuseum in Amsterdam.

Rembrandt's style changed considerably over time. His representation of emotion grew increasingly subtle and suggestive as he abandoned the theatricality of his early days. His numerous self-portraits—more than sixty in all—likewise reflected his development both as an artist and as an individual. His early self-conscious poses and fancy attire gradually gave way to the weary dignity and wisdom of an experienced master.

After a series of financial crises, Rembrandt withdrew somewhat from the public realm. Nevertheless he continued to receive important commissions, such as *The Syndics of the Cloth Guild* (1662) in which five fabric inspectors look up as if their conference has been interrupted by the viewer.

Rembrandt was also a skilled printmaker. He experimented with a variety of techniques, papers and inks, and reworked his copper plates so that many of his prints are actually one of a kind.

Since Rembrandt had a large studio and many assistants who worked in his style, many works were erroneously attributed to him after his death. In 1968, a team of Dutch art historians formed the Rembrandt Research Project, the goal of which was to weed out the false attributions. The project concluded that only about 350 of Rembrandt's paintings have survived.

☙❧

Gravity

Gravity is a great mystery of the universe. The theory behind gravity is that every mass in the universe pulls on every other mass, and the strength of that pull is affected by distance. The greater the mass, the greater the pull. The greater the distance, the less the pull. But why does every object in the universe pull on every other object? No one knows.

In everyday speech, mass and weight are used interchangeably, but they are really quite different. Mass measures the amount of material in an object. A pillow and a paperweight might have the same mass, although they are different sizes. The paperweight is simply more dense than the pillow; the material inside the paperweight is packed more tightly.

Weight measures the force exerted on an object in a gravitational field. Mass does not change due to location, but weight can change depending on the environment. A mass on the surface of the earth experiences a pull from the planet of 9.8 meters per square second. If the same mass were taken to the surface of the moon, the object would actually weigh less because the moon is less massive than earth. The moon has one-sixth the gravitational pull, so the object would weigh one-sixth as much. In other words, a 150-pound man would weigh only 25 pounds on the moon.

Our bodies are designed to exist under the force of gravity from the earth. When astronauts experience weightlessness in space—more correctly called microgravity—they experience nausea, disorientation, headaches, loss of appetite, and congestion. They become spacesick. Normally, the blood that flows into your legs has to resist gravity to flow back up to your heart. In microgravity, the blood rushes back up to your brain because there is no resistance. It's like hanging upside down for a long time.

ADDITIONAL FACTS

1. Astronauts have to exercise for several hours a day in space to prevent their muscles from atrophying.

2. Sir Isaac Newton wrote the first mathematical formation of gravity in 1687.

3. The story that Newton conceived of gravity after seeing an apple fall from a tree is not true.

Wolfgang Amadeus Mozart

No composer's life or music is surrounded with more legend than that of Wolfgang Amadeus Mozart (1756–1791). Born in Salzburg, Austria, to Leopold Mozart, a low-level court composer and teacher, Mozart spent most of his childhood as a traveling prodigy, journeying to foreign courts and kingdoms in Munich, Vienna, London, Paris, and Rome. He performed for kings, queens, dukes, and popes, doing little tricks of musical memory and technical skill.

After a stint in Salzburg, Mozart spent much of his career in the court of Holy Roman Emperor Franz Joseph II in Vienna. His breakthrough composition was *Abduction from the Seraglio* (1781), an opera buffa, or comedic opera, the genre in which Mozart would find himself most comfortable. He collaborated with famed Viennese librettist Lorenzo Da Ponte on three successive operas, *The Marriage of Figaro* (1786), *Don Giovanni* (1787), and *Così fan tutte* (1790). He ended his career having written around forty symphonies, thirty piano concertos, five violin concertos, and literally hundreds of overtures, quartets, and works for flute, oboe, clarinet, chorus, and various other ensembles.

Mozart was a passionate man; he was utterly devoted to music, parties, good food, good wine, billiards, sex, and gambling. He also had a seemingly unending well of talent. Unfortunately, he and his capricious wife, Constanze, were very irresponsible with their money. Despite producing almost all of his best works in the last ten years of his life, Mozart had to beg money from his already overextended creditors. He died, probably of rheumatic fever, after overworking himself and not eating properly, at the age of thirty-five.

Today, Mozart's reputation endures as both an arrogant, immature genius and also undoubtedly the greatest composer of the Classical era, if not of all time.

ADDITIONAL FACTS

1. *In the nineteenth century, the romantics claimed Mozart's legacy as their own, making up myths about how he never got his due and starved for his music. In reality, he was recognized as a genius during his lifetime, and he was one of the highest paid composers of the era.*

2. *Mozart composed his first symphony when he was eight and his first opera when he was twelve.*

3. *Mozart's sister Nannerl was a child prodigy pianist, but she was probably never able to develop her own talents because she was a girl.*

4. *When Mozart died, his widow, Constanze, married a Danish diplomat whose tombstone reads, "Here Rests Mozart's Widow's Second Spouse."*

Gottfried Wilhelm Leibniz

Born in Leipzig, Germany, Gottfried Wilhelm Leibniz (1646–1716) began his university studies at the age of fourteen, and he completed his doctorate at the remarkably early age of twenty-two. Rather than become an academic, Leibniz entered the service of various German nobles, working at different times as a librarian, diplomat, engineer, and courtier. This variety of occupations mirrored the variety of Leibniz's intellectual interests. In addition to major and lasting work in philosophy, theology, and mathematics, Leibniz made significant contributions to chemistry, physics, logic, medicine, botany, optics, history, linguistics, jurisprudence, philology, and diplomacy. Not since Aristotle has a major philosopher contributed to so many different branches of knowledge.

In the realm of philosophy, Leibniz was a rationalist. His overarching project was to defend the principle of sufficient reason: that for every true proposition, there is a reason why it is true, rather than false.

Because Leibniz believed there was a reason for everything, he believed there must be a reason why God chose to create the world this way, rather than some other way. The reason, Leibniz argued, is that this world is the best of all possible worlds. That is the argument Leibniz made in the only book he ever published, *Theodicy*.

In a shorter work called *Monadology*, Leibniz put forth an unusual theory. He suggested that the world consists of an infinite number of point-sized immaterial things called monads. Our minds are monads, but not all monads are self-conscious, as we are. Physical things, like tables and chairs, are not monads, nor are they made up of monads. They exist because the monads perceive them; they are the mutual dream of the monads The monad theory has few followers today.

ADDITIONAL FACTS

1. Although Sir Isaac Newton (1642–1727) is widely credited with the discovery, Leibniz also developed differential calculus.

2. Leibniz invented a mechanical calculator that could do simple arithmetic.

The Last Supper

The Last Supper was the meal that Jesus had the night before he died. It is believed by many, and suggested in the Gospels of Mark, Matthew, and Luke, that this meal was a Passover Seder.

If it was a Seder, the Last Supper occurred on a Thursday, commemorated by Holy Thursday, and Jesus was crucified on a Friday, commemorated by Good Friday. The Gospel of John, however, indicates the meal was actually held a few days before Passover, and the Eastern Orthodoxy accepts John's account.

Jesus shared this meal with his twelve apostles. He had foreseen the events that would occur between the meal and his imminent death. He announced to his apostles that one of them would betray him. One by one they each said, "It won't be me." Finally, Judas Iscariot, having already agreed to hand Jesus over to the Sanhedrin, said this as well, and Jesus told him, "Yes, it will be you."

While eating bread and drinking wine, Jesus told his disciples, "This is my body" and, "This is my blood." He said he would not be able to consume these things again until the Kingdom of Heaven arose, and he instructed the apostles to similarly consume bread and wine in remembrance of him—the origin of the Eucharist. The chalice that Jesus used to drink wine during the Last Supper is believed by some to be the Holy Grail, said to hold miraculous powers. This same chalice was used by Joseph of Arimathea to catch Jesus's blood as it dripped from his crucified body.

Finally Jesus predicted at the meal that Peter would deny, on three separate occasions, ever having associated with him. Peter exclaimed that he would rather die than disown Jesus. However, after Jesus was convicted of blasphemy before the Sanhedrin, three people approached Peter as he tried to flee the town. Each accused him of knowing Jesus, and he denied it three times. After realizing what he had done, Peter wept from shame.

Louis XIV of France

King Louis XIV inherited the crown in 1643 when he was only four years old and ruled France for a staggering seventy-two years. During his long reign, the monarch, nicknamed the Sun King, expanded France's power in Europe and consolidated his own power at home. Ruling from his magnificent palace at Versailles, Louis XIV built a centralized, absolute monarchy that wielded power unparalleled in French history.

During his reign, Louis scattered new palaces across France and expanded Versailles into the most opulent home in Europe. Arts and sciences flourished during his reign and France's borders expanded.

Louis was said to have declared: *"l'état, c'est moi"*—"I am the state." The traditional checks on royal dominance in France—the clergy and the nobility—ceded much of their authority to the ambitious king in Paris. Louis broke the power of France's squabbling nobles by inviting them to Versailles. There, they became so preoccupied with court intrigue and politics, they didn't have time to organize any trouble. Louis also forced the pope to give him more control over the Catholic Church in France. He ordered the persecution of Protestants and Jews to foster religious unity.

During the seventeenth century, other European countries, particularly Sweden, followed France's example by creating absolute monarchies. This form of government swept away many of the last vestiges of feudalism, but it also lead to tyrannical behavior. This behavior led to the bloody Revolution in 1789.

ADDITIONAL FACTS

1. *The US state of Louisiana, a former French possession, is named after Louis XIV.*

2. *Louis associated himself with Apollo, the Greek god of the sun. His bedroom at Versailles was called the Apollo chamber.*

Postmodernism

The term *postmodernism* is notoriously difficult to define, whether in reference to literature, art, or anything else. This is partly because postmodernism is not so much a coherent style itself, but a reaction against an existing movement— modernism. In general, postmodern literature features the self-conscious blurring of different genres and styles, exploration of new or neglected perspectives, and mixing of high and low art forms, often marked by irony and humor. The timeframe of the movement is vague, but it is generally seen as beginning around the 1940s.

During the first half of the twentieth century, modernist authors had investigated questions of perspective and subjectivity. Many concluded that secure truths did not exist and that the world was therefore hopelessly fragmented. Most authors viewed this condition as the tragic result of human alienation in post-Industrial society. But many writers of the younger generation—the postmodern generation—believed otherwise, contending that this fragmentation presented an opportunity for exploration and new insight.

Postmodern writers addressed this opportunity in many ways. Some utilized comedy and irony: Thomas Pynchon's *The Crying of Lot 49* (1966) revels in self-consciously empty symbolism and false meaning, making it a source of humor rather than tragedy. Other writers blurred or broke down traditional barriers between genres: Truman Capote's *In Cold Blood* (1965) interprets a real news story about two murderers using novelistic dialogue and themes, effectively creating the new genre of journalistic fiction. And many writers focused on the disaffection of the individual in modern society: Don DeLillo's *White Noise* (1985) examines the absurd information overload and material excess of contemporary America.

Likewise, different writers took different tacks in exploring questions of perspective. Some, such as Toni Morrison and Maxine Hong Kingston, gave voice to minority viewpoints they believed the modernists had ignored. Others applied new perspectives to the retelling of existing stories. Jean Rhys's *Wide Sargasso Sea* (1966), for instance, tells the backstory of a character from *Jane Eyre*. Italo Calvino's *Invisible Cities* (1972) revisits the legend of Marco Polo through the lens of modern urban theory. And Tom Stoppard's *Rosencrantz and Guildenstern Are Dead* (1966) goes so far as to reinterpret *Hamlet*. Fascinating and often audacious experimentation of this sort has continued throughout the past decades, leading many people to claim that the era of postmodern literature is not yet over.

ADDITIONAL FACT

1. *There is no one typical postmodern author. Among many others, Umberto Eco, Paul Auster, Salman Rushdie, John Barth, William Gaddis, Jeannette Winterson, Vladimir Nabokov, Gabriel García Márquez, Philip K. Dick, and Michael Ondaatje have all been labeled postmodern.*

Girl with a Pearl Earring

The Dutch art historian Ludwig Goldscheider referred to Jan Vermeer's *Girl with a Pearl Earring* as the "the *Mona Lisa* of the North."

Set against a dark background, the girl turns her head, and with lips slightly parted she glances out of the painting. Her eyes and mouth are delicately accented with flecks of white and pink. The light reflecting off her teardrop pearl earring is rendered with a thick flake of impasto. Her simple golden dress betrays no indication of time or place but the turban-like sash around her head grants her a touch of the exotic. Both reveal Vermeer's skill at rendering folds of drapery.

The Girl with a Pearl Earring is one of only three or four bust-length figures that Vermeer painted. Most likely it was conceived as a *tronie*, a type of painting also done by Rembrandt, in which character or expression take precedence over the exact likeness of an identified individual. It may also have been designed as a pendant, or companion piece, to Vermeer's *Study of a Young Woman*, the so-called *Wrightsman Girl* at the Metropolitan Museum of Art in New York.

Some people have conjectured that the model for the picture was Vermeer's eldest daughter, Maria; others have speculated that it was Magdalena, the daughter of Vermeer's patron Pieter van Ruijven. Tracy Chevalier, author of the best selling novel, *Girl with a Pearl Earring*, imagined the girl as Griet, a maid with whom Vermeer fell in love.

The mysterious identity of the woman has contributed a great deal to the aura of the work, which was publicized only in 1881, when art collector Arnoldus Andries des Tombes bought it at auction for two guilders. In his will, he bequeathed the work to the Mauritshuis, in The Hague, where it has been on display since des Tombes's death in 1902.

As art critic Jan Veth poignantly stated, the painting of the *Girl with the Pearl Earring* looks as though it were "blended from the dust of crushed pearls."

ADDITIONAL FACTS

1. In Quiet Light, *a collection of poems based on the paintings of Vermeer by Marilyn Chandler McEntyre, includes a poem entitled "Girl with a Pearl Earring."*

2. In 1994, the painting underwent extensive restoration before being sent to Washington for a major retrospective of Vermeer's work.

Vaccines

Vaccines prepare the body to fight against a disease. They usually consist of either weakened or dead germs, lesser forms of the disease itself. When the immune system encounters the weakened germ, it makes specialized antibodies that easily vanquish the disease. Later, if the body encounters the real disease, it "remembers" the antibodies that it made earlier and easily fights off the illness.

Vaccines were invented during the height of the European smallpox epidemic in 1796. An English country doctor named Edward Jenner noticed that milkmaids would sometimes get cowpox, a lesser form of smallpox, from handling cows. These same milkmaids seemed resistant to smallpox. On a hunch, Jenner took infected fluid from the hand of a milkmaid and injected it into an eight-year-old farm boy. The boy came down with cowpox but quickly recovered. Jenner then injected the boy with smallpox, and he did not become sick. He concluded that cowpox could protect us from smallpox, and the first vaccine was, in fact, the cowpox virus. The word vaccine comes from the Latin *vacca*, or cow.

Vaccines have protected humans from some of the world's most deadly diseases—measles, mumps, rubella, tuberculosis, whooping cough, and smallpox. Interestingly, not everyone has to receive an injection to be protected from a disease. The principle of herd immunity holds that if enough people in a population receive a vaccine, they will act as barriers to the spread of the disease. Although the specific number varies from disease to disease, vaccinating 90 percent of a population is, in most cases, tantamount to vaccinating the whole population.

Certain groups are more likely to spread disease than others. In the United States, school-age children are the most likely to spread disease because they have such close proximity to each other. A study from Emory University found that inoculating just 30 percent of schoolchildren reduced the chances of a community-wide flu epidemic from 90 percent to 65 percent. If 70 percent of the children were inoculated, the chance of an epidemic dropped to 4 percent.

ADDITIONAL FACTS

1. *Both the Protestant and Catholic churches initially objected to vaccines. Timothy Dwight, a former president of Yale University once said, "If God had decreed from all eternity that a certain person should die of smallpox, it would be a frightful sin to avoid and annul the decree by the trick of vaccination."*

2. *Herd immunity applies only to diseases that are passed from person to person. For example, herd immunity does not protect from tetanus, which is contracted when an open wound comes in contact with contaminated materials.*

Mozart's *Requiem* Mass

During the last ten years of his life, starting around 1782, Wolfgang Amadeus Mozart became deeply interested in the contrapuntal composition styles of Johann Sebastian Bach and George Frederic Handel. He studied manuscripts of Bach's *Well-Tempered Clavier* and *The Art of the Fugue*, both didactic pieces meant to explore the possibilities of instruments and musical forms.

With Bach's composition techniques in Mozart's ears, he began work on his *Requiem* (1791), a setting of the Mass designed especially for a funeral. Its opening chorus, along with the full choral settings of the *Lachrymosa* and *Confutatis*, contain dark, powerful passages with intertwining, vaguely fugal arrangements that strongly recall Bach. The textured complexity of the *Requiem* demonstrates Mozart's deep emotional investment in the piece and suggests he explored the darker side of his own nature to produce it. The circumstances under which it was written are appropriately macabre.

The piece was solicited by a stranger dressed in gray who came to Mozart's Vienna home in July 1791. After Mozart's death, it was revealed that this stranger was actually an amateur musician named Count Franz von Walsegg, who wanted Mozart to write the piece so that he could put his name on it and pass it off as his own. Unaware of this fraud, Mozart wrote in his letters that he was haunted by this strange patron and spent far too much time on the *Requiem* than he should have. Mozart was in very poor health to begin with, probably because of his poor eating habits and restless lifestyle. After a trip to Prague to conduct the premiere of his final opera, *The Clemency of Titus*, Mozart died after one last day's work on the *Requiem*, a piece that would, profoundly, be his own death Mass.

ADDITIONAL FACTS

1. A pupil of Mozart's named Franz Süssmayr vowed to finish the piece, and he did, based on sketches of bass lines that Mozart had laid out at the start of the final Lachrymosa *section.*

2. In Peter Shaffer's film version of Mozart's life, Amadeus, *Mozart's colleague Antonio Salieri, an Italian composer who was in constant competition with Mozart for commissions, is depicted as being the masked stranger who requested the piece. This is a brilliant dramatic idea, but it's historical fiction.*

3. On December 4, 1791, the night before Mozart's death, the composer summoned his singer friends to his bedside to rehearse the individual parts of the Requiem.

Time

Since Aristotle, philosophers have tried to understand the nature of time. After the work of Sir Isaac Newton (1643–1727), many believed time is a thing with many parts. In other words, there are individual "times." For these philosophers, to say an event happened at a particular time is to mean that the event filled that part, or unit, of time.

Gottfried Willhelm Leibniz (1646–1716) argued against the Newtonian outlook. For Leibniz, there were events, which happen before, after, or simultaneously with one another. Time is merely the way we organize these relations in our minds. It is not an additional thing distinct from the things that stand in these relations.

Against Leibniz, Immanuel Kant argued that time was neither a thing that exists in itself, nor an order of relations among things that exist in themselves. Kant insisted time is merely a way in which our minds organize the experiences we have. For Kant, things that exist in themselves, outside of our minds and independently of us, are not in time.

Another realm of philosophical investigation is how human beings experience time. According to ordinary idiom, time flows. But does it? Whenever you say, "Now is the present," no matter when you say it, you say something true. In other words, the present is simply *when* you are. Some philosophers believe this is because you and I are special; we live at the present. According to these philosophers, time does flow: First, some time is the past, then it is the present, and later it is the future.

Other philosophers believe that "now" is like "here"; "here" does not refer to any particular place, just the place you happen to be when you say it. These philosophers believe you and I are not special. Time does not flow. It just has many parts, like space. We live in one part of time, which to us is the present, just like our physical location is our "here."

ADDITIONAL FACT
1. *Some philosophers believe that all times—past, present, and future—exist simultaneously. According to these philosophers, there are dinosaurs, cavemen, and dodo birds—just not where we exist.*

The Crucifixion

Around 30 BC, Jesus of Nazareth was angry at what he felt was impurity within the Jewish religious establishment. At the Temple in Jerusalem, moneychangers and merchants had set up shop in what was supposed to be the holiest of places.

 Leading his followers to the Temple during Passover, Jesus overturned tables, causing a visible disturbance.

In response, Joseph Caiaphas, the high priest of the Sanhedrin, the Jewish high court, arrested Jesus on charges of blasphemy. It is believed that Caiaphas was able to arrest Jesus because Jesus was identified, and betrayed, by one of his apostles, Judas Iscariot. When Jesus refused to cooperate, the Sanhedrin turned him over to the Roman prefect Pontius Pilate.

At this point, Pontius Pilate sentenced Jesus Christ to death by crucifixion. The reason for that harsh sentence is a matter of enormous debate. The most widely accepted view is that Pilate made the decision himself, either for fear that Jesus might foment a political rebellion, or simply out of mere brutality.

Regardless of how the decision was made, Pilate gave the order to execute Jesus, labeling him "King of the Jews." Jesus was forced to carry his cross (likely weighing more than 100 pounds) during his journey between the prison and Calvary, the site of his execution. Although Jesus is often depicted as carrying the entire cross, he probably carried only the horizontal piece, while the vertical stake was permanently fixed in the ground at the execution site. The site of Calvary was located somewhere outside of Jerusalem and was most likely a cemetery that the Romans used to quickly bury their victims.

While Jesus was hanging from the cross, Joseph of Arimathea approached and, using the same chalice that Jesus drank from during the Last Supper, caught some of Jesus's dripping blood. This chalice is known as the Holy Grail. After Jesus died, Joseph removed Jesus's body and buried it in his own tomb.

ADDITIONAL FACTS

1. In the years following the crucifixion, Pontius Pilate was removed from his post for excessive brutality.

2. The Catholic Church did not officially condemn the belief that the Jews killed Jesus until the Vatican II accords in 1965.

3. Despite claims that thousands of people were crucified during the Roman Empire, only one crucified body has ever been discovered. Most victims were simply left on their crosses to decay.

Peter the Great

Tsar Peter the Great (1682–1725) ruled Russia from 1696 to 1725 transforming the nation into a major world power during his forty-three-year reign. He governed as an absolute monarch, patterning himself after Louis XIV of France. He even built a glittering new palace at his capital of Saint Petersburg, intended to surpass even Versailles.

Prior to Peter's accession, Russia was not quite European and not quite Asian. Russians were Christians. But their sprawling country, larger than all of Europe combined, bordered the ancient Asian empires of China and Persia. Much of Russia had been a part of the old Mongol Empire.

Peter moved Russia squarely into the European camp. He moved the Russian capital from Moscow to Saint Petersburg, a city he founded on the Baltic Sea. He sought closer ties with European countries, adopted European customs in dress, and was the first Russian leader to visit the West. Peter reorganized the Russian military and government to copy European standards.

The tsar himself was ruthless, hot-tempered, and hard-drinking. "A want of judgment, with an instability of temper, appear in him too often and too evidently," an English observer wrote in 1698. Peter was also a physical giant, standing almost seven feet tall.

For the two centuries after Peter's death in 1725, the Russian Empire was a major European power. However, the autocracy of the tsars and the continued existence of serfdom, which was not abolished in Russia until 1861, prevented the development of a strong Russian middle class. Peter's ancestors ruled Russia until the revolution in 1917.

ADDITIONAL FACTS

1. *To discourage facial hair, Peter imposed a tax of 100 rubles on nobles who wanted to wear traditional Russian beards and a tax of one kopek on commoners.*

2. *After the communist Revolution in 1917, the Russian capital returned to its ancient home of Moscow. Saint Petersburg was renamed Leningrad in honor of Vladimir Lenin, but the name reverted to Saint Petersburg after the collapse of the Soviet Union in 1991.*

3. *The palace built by Peter is now the Hermitage museum in Saint Petersburg, one of the largest art museums in the world.*

Brave New World

The genre of dystopian literature—fiction depicting a nightmarish, anti-utopian future—was one of the major innovations of twentieth-century writing. The best known novel in this category is George Orwell's *1984*, which terrified Cold War–era readers with its vision of a totalitarian political state. But today, the most troubling and relevant work of dystopian literature is undoubtedly Aldous Huxley's *Brave New World*, which envisions a nightmare society arising not from political tyranny but from science and technology.

Published in 1932, *Brave New World* is shockingly prescient. The novel is set in a futuristic England in which production of human embryos is tightly controlled in government-run hatcheries. Each developing embryo is either coddled or subjected to brutal chemical treatments so that it will grow—or be deliberately stunted—to take its proper place in the rigid caste system that dictates a person's status and role in society. At the highest rung of the social ladder are Alphas, who are groomed for leadership and academia; at the lowest are Epsilons, who perform only manual labor. All children are conditioned rigorously after they are born, via schooling, hypnosis, and other psychological indoctrination. As always, they remain segregated by class.

Although this system produces great social stability, it does so at the cost of individual humanity and free will. This dehumanization has tragic consequences when a "savage" from a remote part of the American Southwest—one of the few human beings raised outside the system—is brought to London. He is fascinated to be part of this "brave new world" he has heard so much about, but his transition to his new surroundings goes less than smoothly.

Brave New World is one of the few science-themed novels that also has enduring literary relevance. Long a staple of English classrooms and book clubs, it has attracted especially close attention in recent years because of the growing attention paid to bioethics and cloning. Indeed, Huxley's predictions about the fearsome potential of science, which seemed unthinkably remote in his own day, appear ominously imminent just decades after he wrote them.

ADDITIONAL FACTS

1. *The novel's title comes from Shakespeare's* The Tempest, *in which the sheltered Miranda, upon first seeing humans from the outside world, exclaims, "O brave new world / That has such people in't!"*

2. *Huxley's grandfather, a prominent biologist, had been one of the foremost proponents of Charles Darwin's theories of evolution and natural selection.*

3. *In 1958, Huxley published the essay* Brave New World Revisited, *arguing that the world was indeed moving closer toward the dystopian future he predicted in* Brave New World.

The Taj Mahal

The Taj Mahal in Agra is considered by many people to be the most beautiful building in the world. The white marble mausoleum was built between 1631 and 1648 to house the tomb of Mumtaz Mahal, the wife of the Mughal ruler, Shah Jahan, who died while giving birth to her fourteenth child.

The complex consists of five parts: a formal gateway, a garden, the mausoleum itself, a mosque on the west, and an assembly hall on the east, which was erected for the sake of symmetry. A long reflecting pool divides the area in half and mirrors the tomb from the ideal viewing point at the front gate.

The identity of the architect responsible for the Taj Mahal is not entirely clear. Some attribute the design to Geronimo Veroneo, an Italian working in the Mughal court. More conclusive evidence points to the Persian architect Ustad Isa Khan Effendi, who apparently assigned the details of the building to his pupil Ustad Ahmad. The model for the design was Sultan Hasan's mausoleum in Cairo.

Construction of the complex took more than seventeen years and required 20,000 workers. The tomb purportedly cost thirty million rupees at a time when the price of gold was fifteen rupees per tola (11.66 grams). Material, which included twenty-eight types of precious and semi-precious stones, was brought from all over Asia. The white marble was quarried in Makrana in Rajasthan.

The tomb rests on a white marble plinth, 100 meters square. The entire building (minus the minarets) is as wide as it is tall. The dome rises 44.4 meters and is exactly the same height as the façade. A second smaller dome is placed on the inside of the balloon external dome. The only asymmetrical element is the tomb of Shah Jahan, placed at the side of his wife. Inlaid in stone at the main entrance are quotations from the Koran, inviting the "pure in heart" to enter the "gardens of Paradise."

According to legend, Shah Jahan—who spent his old age imprisoned by his son—planned to build a second, black marble tomb for himself on the other side of the river.

Time has taken its toll on the building. At one point, Lord William Bentinck, a British governor in India, proposed selling it off for its materials. In 1983, it was named a UNESCO World Heritage Site.

ADDITIONAL FACTS

1. Indian author Rabinadrinath Tagore called the Taj Mahal "a tear on the face of eternity."

2. The name Taj Mahal means "Crown Palace."

Marie Curie

When people talk about women in science, the first name that always comes up is Marie Curie (1867–1934). And with good reason. She was not only the first woman to win a Nobel Prize, she was the first person to ever earn two Nobel Prizes.

Marie Curie won her first Nobel Prize in Physics in 1903 for her research into radioactivity. Ten years earlier in Paris, Curie and others had been researching the properties of uranium. She noticed uranium emitted rays that could travel through wood and flesh. But curiously, no matter what she did to the uranium—heating it, cooling it, or combining it with other elements—the amount of emitted rays remained constant in relation to the mass of the uranium. Curie concluded that the emission of rays, or radioactivity—a term she coined—was a property of atoms, not the product of a chemical reaction.

Curie next began to examine pitchblende, a material rich in uranium. The pitchblende gave off more radiation than could be accounted for by uranium alone. She and her husband Pierre succeeded in finding two new elements in the pitchblende, both highly radioactive. One of them they named polonium, after Marie's home country of Poland. The other they named radium, after the Latin word for ray.

Curie won her second Nobel Prize in Chemistry in 1911 for the discovery of radium and polonium. To this day, she remains the only person other than Linus Pauling to have won two Nobel Prizes in two different fields.

ADDITIONAL FACTS

1. Marie Curie died from leukemia in 1934 after years of massive exposure to radiation.

2. The following year her daughter Irene won the Nobel Prize for her discovery of artificial radioactivity.

3. Until her granddaughter had them decontaminated, Marie Curie's notes were radioactive.

4. Marie Curie was the first woman ever to become a professor at the Sorbonne in Paris.

Mozart's *Don Giovanni*

With the international success of Mozart's *Marriage of Figaro* (1784), the composer received another commission from the Prague Opera House. He teamed up with librettist Lorenzo Da Ponte for a second effort, this time choosing the legend of Don Juan, as told in Giovanni Bertati's 1775 play *Don Giovanni ossia Il convitato di pietra*, as his subject.

The story is of an incorrigible rake and philanderer, Don Juan, whom Mozart and his librettist turned into something of a sympathetic character. In doing so, they mixed the genres of opera seria and opera buffa, so that in the end, *Don Giovanni* is neither a morality play, a tragedy, nor a comedy—but rather, something in between. It is for this reason that some historians think *Don Giovanni* (1787) was poorly received in Vienna, a city whose audiences were notoriously conservative and bound to musical conventions.

The music starts with Mozart's imperious, bombastic, minor-chord theme—a hauntingly appropriate accompaniment to the first scene, in which Don Giovanni kills a man. The opera alternates between the antihero's touching serenades, absurd and farcical seductions, and the moralistic tragedies that befall him. In the terrifying final sequence, the ghost of the murdered man drags Giovanni off to hell because he refuses to repent. In terms of emotional impact, *Don Giovanni* is probably Mozart's greatest work, and his unique stamp of brilliance is unmistakable on the piece.

The new genre of opera represented by *Don Giovanni* was dubbed *dramma giocoso*, and it enjoyed great success in every city but Mozart's own. By the time the composer died, *Don Giovanni* was one of the most widely staged operas in all of Europe.

ADDITIONAL FACTS

1. *It is rumored that after seeing* Don Giovanni, *Emperor Franz Joseph told Mozart that it had "too many notes," to which the composer replied, "Just as many as needed, Your Majesty."*

2. *While writing the libretto for* Don Giovanni, *Da Ponte holed up by himself in a room in his patron's house. In the next room there was a constantly stocked table of food and wine; and in a third room, a prostitute who was available for inspiration at the ring of a bell.*

3. *The opera premiered in Prague in 1787, Vienna in 1788, London in 1817, and New York in 1826.*

Epistemology

Epistemology is the branch of philosophy that deals with knowledge. One major project in epistemology that goes back to Plato is the attempt to define just what knowledge is. Traditionally, philosophers have defined knowledge as true, justified belief.

First, to say that knowledge is belief means that to know something, you must believe it.

Second, knowledge must be true because you cannot really know anything that is false. If something is false, you may very well believe it, and even believe you know it. But, according to the philosophical definition, you don't really *know* it.

Third, real knowledge is justified, because your belief must have reasons. If you pick a number from 1 to 1,000, for example 463, and a friend correctly guesses 463, did that friend *know* you had picked 463? Since he or she was merely right by accident, it seems wrong to say he or she knew it. Knowledge cannot be accidental—you must have reasons for forming some true belief in order for that belief to count as knowledge.

Recently philosophers have questioned whether all true, justified beliefs count as knowledge. Consider the following case: You are driving through the countryside, and you see a barn. You form the belief, "This is a barn." It is clearly a justified belief. It is also a true belief. You have, in fact, just seen a real barn. However, unbeknownst to you, you are in Fake Barn County, where most of the farmers don't build barns. They build the façades of barns. Therefore, the argument continues, it was not knowledge because had you seen a fake barn, you would have formed a false belief. Therefore, not all true justified beliefs are knowledge

ADDITIONAL FACTS

1. Examples like the fake barn story were first suggested by Edward Gettier in a classic 1963 essay entitled "Is Justified True Belief Knowledge?"

2. Philosophers still debate what further condition must be added to truth and justification for a belief to count as knowledge.

3. Other problems in epistemology include the problem of skepticism and the problem of induction.

4. Gettier's original paper, which revolutionized epistemology, is only a few pages long!

The Resurrection

Three days after Jesus had been crucified and buried in the tomb of Joseph of Arimathea, several women, including Mary and Mary Magdalene, went to his grave to perform burial rites. When they arrived at the tomb, however, they found it empty. The next day, Jesus began to appear before a number of his disciples in order to show them that he had been resurrected. Approximately forty days after he had arisen, Jesus ascended to heaven and left the terrestrial world forever. Today, the ressurection is celebrated on Easter, and its story is retold in the Gospels of Matthew, Mark, Luke, and John.

The resurrection of Christ is a central pillar of Christianity for the majority of Christians. Most members of the faith believe that Jesus's resurrection was an actual event and that he did, in fact, rise from the dead.

Among many interpretations of the event is the one most commonly held, known as the judicial view. It is believed that God was required to punish all of mankind for their sins. However, to avoid doing so, God sent Jesus, who was pure, to bear the burden of the sins committed by those people who accepted his teachings. In exchange for their devotion, Jesus took all of those sins with him when he ascended to heaven.

Although this view is widely held within Christianity, some Christians and many non-Christians believe that the story of resurrection is actually an allegory. They note that although the resurrection is retold in all four of the canonical Gospels, none of them claim to have seen it firsthand. In fact, nowhere in the Bible does anyone claim to have borne witness to the event. For liberal Christians who do not believe Jesus actually rose from the dead, the story is still central to their faith. It exemplifies hope.

ADDITIONAL FACTS

1. *It should be noted that while all four canonical Gospels describe various aspects of the resurrection, there are several contradictions among the four works. While some argue this is evidence that the event never happened, others believe it proves its truth. After all, it would be rare for four eyewitness accounts to line up perfectly.*

2. *Several alleged non-Christian accounts of the resurrection exist, including that of the Jewish historian Flavius Josephus. Josephus wrote in 98 AD that Jesus had arisen. However, the authenticity of this passage is questionable because it was edited by Christians at some point.*

3. *Alternative explanations for Jesus's absence from his tomb include: Jesus was buried in a shallow grave and his corpse was eaten by animals, his disciples stole his body or, even less widely believed, Jesus did not die on the cross, but merely fainted. He was later resuscitated in his tomb and went on to live again.*

Benjamin Franklin

Benjamin Franklin (1706–1790), the most famous and influential American of the eighteenth century, was an inventor, diplomat, journalist, and statesman. He was a signer of both the Declaration of Independence and the United States Constitution. In Franklin's long lifetime—he was born in Boston in  1706 when the city was still ruled by the Puritans and died in Philadelphia in 1790 on the eve of the industrial revolution—Franklin probably contributed more to the cultural and political life of the young United States than any of his contemporaries. Franklin helped discover electricity, published a successful newspaper, and invented the Franklin stove. His reputation in his time, wrote John Adams, was "greater than that of Newton, Frederick the Great, or Voltaire, his character more revered than all of them." Some historians have coined him as the "first American."

Franklin was the fifteenth child of Josiah Franklin, a candle maker who immigrated to Boston in the late seventeenth century. At the age of twelve, Franklin went to work for one of his brothers, a newspaper publisher. His job was to work with the presses, but soon he was writing articles for the newspaper itself. Tired of working for his ungrateful brother, Franklin moved south to Philadelphia at age seventeen. In Philadelphia, Franklin published newspapers and humorous books, eventually becoming one of the city's most prominent citizens. A man of infinite talent and curiosity, he started a hospital, an insurance company, a philosophical society, and a university (currently the University of Pennsylvania)—all still in existence today. He eventually retired from the printing business and turned to science. Franklin helped explore the properties of electricity and invented bifocals and the energy-efficient Franklin stove.

In the 1750s and 1760s, when the colonies began to tire of British rule, Franklin was living in England. He helped represent the views of the Americans before Parliament. Franklin returned from London convinced that the colonies had to break free from England. In 1776, he signed the Declaration of Independence in his hometown of Philadelphia. Franklin returned to Europe, representing the fledgling United States in France, where he was a celebrity because of his scientific discoveries. In the eyes of many Europeans, the young nation gained credibility simply through its association with the great scientist. Franklin returned to Pennsylvania and continued working almost until the day he died in 1790.

ADDITIONAL FACT

1. *Among Franklin's inventions was a musical instrument made of glass and known as the armonica. Before its popularity faded in the nineteenth century, the great Austrian composer Wolfgang Amadeus Mozart wrote two compositions for Franklin's invention.*

Postcolonialism

Postcolonial literature refers to the body of works written by authors from formerly colonized areas of the world, as well as works written about people from those areas. The bulk of this literature has been written since the 1950s and 1960s, when the last major European colonies in Africa, Asia, Latin America, and the Caribbean gained independence.

During the height of European imperialism in the late 1800s, European authors tended to celebrate their countries' world dominance, extolling the alleged "white man's burden" of civilizing the uncivilized. British writer Rudyard Kipling led this charge with often overtly racist poems and novels. Gradually, however, works such as Joseph Conrad's *Heart of Darkness* (1899) and E. M. Forster's *A Passage to India* (1924) cast a more critical eye on Europe's colonial involvement.

After decolonization swept through Asia and Africa following World War II, authors in newly independent areas began to chronicle the cultural, social, and psychological fallout. Many dwelled on questions of race, ethnicity, and national identity. They also examined the political and religious tensions created when Europe imposed artificial national boundaries on native peoples. Critics have noted that postcolonial works often focus on the concept of otherness—an idea that theorist Edward Said famously articulated in *Orientalism* (1978) his landmark treatise about the Western tendency to exoticize the East.

Postcolonialism is a sprawling movement, encompassing many regions and authors. Notable works from Africa include Alan Paton's *Cry, the Beloved Country* (1948) and Chinua Achebe's *Things Fall Apart* (1958); from Asia, Graham Greene's *The Quiet American* (1955), Anita Desai's *Games at Twilight* (1978), and Salman Rushdie's *Midnight's Children* (1981); and from the Caribbean, V. S. Naipaul's *A House for Mr. Biswas* (1961), Jean Rhys's *Wide Sargasso Sea* (1966), and Jamaica Kincaid's *Annie John* (1985).

Since the late 1980s, a new generation of postcolonial writers has taken the reins, applying a fresh perspective to many of the same themes. A significant number of these works, such as Hanif Kureishi's *The Buddha of Suburbia* (1990) and Zadie Smith's *White Teeth* (2000), focus on non-Western immigrants living in Britain or the United States. In general, they are more optimistic than their often anguished postcolonial predecessors, accepting the uprooted migrant condition as a reality of the modern world and exploring its positive and even comic aspects.

ADDITIONAL FACTS

1. Postcolonialism has been fruitful ground for women authors, many of whom have explored feminist themes and the advancement of women in the context of former colonies.

2. Although the bulk of postcolonial authors has come from minority backgrounds, Caucasian writers, such as Athol Fugard and J. M. Coetzee of South Africa, have also played an important role.

Hokusai

Katsushika Hokusai (1760–1849) is perhaps the most famous Japanese artist in the West.

Born into a poor family, Hokusai was adopted by a mirror-maker who taught him how to engrave. At the age of eighteen, Hokusai joined the workshop of Katsukawa Shunsho, an artist renowned for his portraits of actors. Restless by nature, Hokusai left Shunsho's shop in 1778 and began a wandering life. He changed his name more than fifty times, and he did not call himself Hokusai until the age of forty-six. At seventy-five, he referred to himself as Gakyo Rojin, "Old Man Mad about Painting." In the course of Hokusai's life, he lived in more than ninety houses. When one of his homes was destroyed by fire, he wrote in a hokka (a traditional type of poem): "It has burned down: how serene the flowers in their falling."

Seldom financially stable, Hokusai often resorted to publicity schemes. In one instance, he challenged Tani Buncho to a contest determining who was the better artist. As his entry, Hokusai first painted a broad sweep of blue on a huge piece of paper, then dipped a chicken's feet in red paint and set it loose on the paper. He called the result *Maple Leaves on a River*.

Over the years, Hokusai made more than of 30,000 drawings in 500 sketchbooks. Between 1814 and 1878, he published fifteen volumes of *mangas* (rough sketches) depicting a broad range of real and imaginary subjects rendered in a wide variety of styles. The last of the series appeared only in 1878, twenty-nine years after his death.

Hokusai is best known, however, for his *ukiyo-e*, a technique that originated in Tokyo. *Ukiyo-e*, which means "pictures of the floating world," are colored prints in which different wood blocks are used in succession to apply different colors. The most famous ukiyo-e by Hokusai is *The Great Wave off Kanagawa* from his *36 Views of Mount Fuji*. The print, which depicts fishermen fighting the forces of nature—not a traditional Japanese subject—was most likely influenced by Dutch engravings that made their way into Japan.

When Hokusai's work was first seen in Europe, it made an enormous impact on painters such as Paul Gauguin and Vincent van Gogh. James Whistler claimed that Hokusai was the greatest artist since Vélazquez. The exhibit *Rembrandt, Van Gogh and Hokusai*, held in Amsterdam in 1951, did much to enhance the Japanese master's reputation in the twentieth century.

ADDITIONAL FACTS

1. Hokusai was one of the principal shunga *(erotic print) masters of the Edo period, as can be seen in his series* Fukojuso.

2. In Fugaku Hyakkei (One Hundred Views of Mount Fuji, *1834–35) Hokusai captured the famous peak in composite views from multiple perspectives, a clear demonstration of his familiarity with the site.*

3. Hokusai's largest work measures more than 200 square meters.

Hypnosis

For more than 200 years, people have been trying to define hypnosis. Most of us picture a man with a sinister handlebar moustache and a black top hat, swinging a pocket watch in front of our eyes like a pendulum, telling us in an eerily calm voice, "You are getting sleepy . . . " After a few moments, we imagine, he can control our actions, our thoughts, and our memories.

Psychiatrists today understand hypnosis as a trancelike state of extreme receptivity to suggestion. But it is more like guided daydreaming than mind control. Although subjects of hypnosis often feel uninhibited, they will not do anything that is against their will. Electroencephalograph (EEG) studies of brainwaves during hypnosis show a boost of the low frequency waves associated with sleep and dreaming. EEG studies also show a reduction in the high frequency waves associated with full wakefulness, but they are not eliminated entirely. This may explain the dreamy quality of hypnosis, but it does not indicate that the subjects have become human puppets. They are still thinking for themselves.

There are three basic ways to hypnotize someone. The first is called fixed-gaze induction, which asks that the subject focus intently on an object (like a pocket watch) in order to tune out the outside world. Although common practice in the early days of hypnotism, this method is rarely used today. It simply doesn't work on a large percentage of the population. The second method involves bombarding the mind with rapid commands, "Stand up, sit down, blink, stand up." It is the method of choice for stage performers and interrogators. Psychiatrists use a third method, progressive relaxation, to focus and ease the subject into a state of hypnosis. By talking in a soothing voice and suggesting peaceful images, the psychiatrist creates an environment in which the subject can learn to undo harmful habits, such as overeating and smoking.

ADDITIONAL FACTS

1. *Franz Anton Mesmer, an eighteenth-century physician from Austria, is considered the father of modern hypnotism. He believed it to be a mystical force that he called "animal magnetism."*

2. *The words* mesmerism *and* mesmerize *come from Mesmer's name.*

3. *Many experts consider driving and watching television to be states of hypnosis.*

4. *People with active imaginations are the most likely to be susceptible to hypnosis.*

Sonata Form

In terms of music theory, the classical period's most important legacy is the establishment of sonata form as the most important compositional structure. It remained the standard model for hundreds of short pieces and symphonic movements for almost 200 years, extending its influence all the way to twentieth century composers such as Béla Bartók.

Sonata form is a musical construction used in individual movements within longer pieces, or just for shorter stand-alone compositions. It developed from the two-part, or binary, forms used in the baroque.

Baroque composers usually limited themselves to one emotion per piece or movement, and they also usually developed only one main theme or motivic complex per piece. Classical composers, on the other hand, liked to provide contrasting themes and emotions in a given piece, and sonata form provided a framework for them to do this. The form is as follows:

EXPOSITION: Sometimes preceded by a cursory introduction, this is the first section of a movement or piece in sonata form. It presents the main thematic material, usually in two parts: the primary theme, which is in the tonic, or home key, and the secondary theme, usually in the dominant or a related key. These two sections are often connected by a bridge that eases the modulation.

DEVELOPMENT: Harmonically unstable and with lots of modulation, this section is where the composer can show off his or her versatility and talent by taking the themes apart, reconstructing them, and recasting them in new harmonic environments.

RECAPITULATION: Here, the expository themes come back and are restated conclusively in the home key. It is often followed by a short coda, or ending section.

In some ways, sonata form resembles the structure of an expository essay, which is one of the reasons why many people see it as an outgrowth of the reason- and logic-based spirit of the time. Whatever its origins, sonata form is one of the most lasting contributions of the Classical composers.

ADDITIONAL FACTS

1. Despite its prevalence, the term sonata form was not used by the composers who invented it. Its first appearance was in the writings of music theorist Joseph Riepel, sometime around 1755.

2. Beethoven was famous for expanding the coda of his symphonies into another long, explorative, development section. His true genius emerges in some of these codas.

3. Also called compound binary form, sonata form is used in countless genres, including symphonies, concertos, string quartets, and choral works, not just in pieces that are actually called sonatas.

⊙◑⊙

John Locke

John Locke (1632–1704), the first major British Empiricist and one of the most important political philosophers of modern times, was born in 1632 in Wrington, England. Educated at Oxford, Locke was engaged in many of the major philosophical, scientific, and political movements of his day. He was a founding member of the English Royal Society—a scientific group whose most famous member was Sir Isaac Newton—and played a significant role in the Protestant opposition to King Charles II and his Catholic brother James.

Locke's major philosophical work is his *Essay Concerning Human Understanding*. Locke argued that when human beings are born, our minds are tabula rasa—blank slates. All of our knowledge subsequently comes from experience. In Locke's psychology, ideas come from our sensory experience of the world. We can compare ideas, we can combine them to make complex ideas, and we can extrapolate general ideas from more specific ones. However, our physical senses are the only place we can start, and this puts important limits on what we can expect to know. For instance, Locke was skeptical about our ability to know the underlying, real nature of things.

In political philosophy, Locke played an important role in the development of social contract theory. According to Locke, human beings were originally in a "state of nature," where there were no laws, and physical strength was the only basis of authority. However, we created a social contract, whereby we ceded certain natural rights to a government or other authority, in return for security and other guarantees. Locke's important contribution was his argument that any fair social contract must have certain qualities: It must respect its citizen's rights to life, liberty, and property. If these rights are violated, Locke argued, we are entitled to rebel against the governing authority, even the king.

ADDITIONAL FACTS

1. *For Locke's involvement in a Protestant plot against the king and his brother, Locke fled England for Holland. He returned to England in 1688, during the Glorious Revolution.*

2. *Locke's ideas were the foundation of the American colonists's Declaration of Independence.*

3. *Ideas like Locke's social contract theory of government influenced the leaders of the American Revolution.*

The Gospels

Gospel, meaning "good news," is most commonly used in reference to the four Canonical Gospels of the New Testament. These four Gospels—the Gospel of Matthew, the Gospel of Mark, the Gospel of Luke, and the Gospel of John—are the main sources for Jesus's teachings as Jesus himself is not known to have left anything in writing. The Gospels were each written between about 60 and 110 AD, most likely in Greek, though some people claim that Matthew was originally written in Aramaic.

The order of authorship and the interplay between the four Gospels is very complex. Matthew, Mark, and Luke all describe the story and teachings of Jesus's life, covering many of the same events, while John focuses more on Jesus's philosophical and theological ideas. Because Matthew, Mark, and Luke each depict Jesus's life, it is thought that they may have used each other as sources.

Today, it is most widely believed that Mark was written first and that Matthew and Luke used Mark as a blueprint. It is also speculated that Matthew and Luke used a second source, known simply as Q, which has never been discovered.

Mark does not begin with Jesus's birth, but rather picks up his life when he begins teaching. Matthew and Luke tell the stories of Jesus's birth, John the Baptist's teachings, Jesus's teachings, and Jesus's resurrection. John contains many of the same stories, but often out of chronological order.

In addition to these four Gospels, many other noncanonical, or apocryphal, Gospels exist. For the most part, these were written later than the first four and therefore have been accepted only sporadically throughout the Christian world. Many of these are criticized for making Jesus appear too magical. For instance, one story tells of Jesus making a bird out of clay, then waving his hand bringing the bird to life. Roman Catholics consider such accounts to be heretical.

ADDITIONAL FACTS

1. *Irenaeus of Lyons is credited with insisting that the New Testament contain only four Gospels and no more. His reasoning? Four was the number of winds as well as the corners of the earth.*

2. *The Gospel of John is the major source for suggesting that the Jews were to blame for Jesus's death. Although the author of the Gospel was most likely Jewish and his focus of blame was on specific Jewish leaders at the time, these passages of the Gospel have been used against Jews in times of persecution.*

3. *Although the Gospels are a major part of the New Testament, they make up only four of the work's twenty-seven books.*

George Washington

"First in war, first in peace, and first in the hearts of his countrymen."

—a eulogy at the funeral of George Washington

George Washington (1732–1799) was the military leader of the American Revolution and the first president of the United States. Prior to the outbreak of the Revolution in 1775, Washington was a prosperous Virginia plantation owner. He had fought alongside the British in wars against the French and various Indian tribes, but he soured on the crown's rule in the 1760s and early 1770s. By the time the Revolution started, Washington was a committed patriot. The Continental Congress unanimously chose Washington to lead the rebel army, and he took command in Cambridge, Massachusetts, on July 3, 1775.

On paper, Washington's task seemed virtually impossible. In 1775, Great Britain was the most powerful country in the world. Its well-trained troops and paid mercenaries were among Europe's finest. Against such a foe, Washington could hope only for few outright victories. Instead, Washington reckoned correctly that he could wear the British down by avoiding outright defeats. No matter how many troops Britain sent to its rebellious colonies, the colonists fought back. Washington's persistence convinced France, Spain, and the Netherlands to ally with the colonists. Eventually the British gave up. The Revolution was notable for its relatively small toll in lives. Through the entire war against England, the patriot army lost 6,824 men—a fraction of the casualties the United States would suffer in later wars.

Washington's canny leadership made him immensely popular in the newly independent country. But instead of seizing power, he retired to Mount Vernon, his Virginia plantation. Washington finally agreed to run for president in 1789, and he was elected without opposition.

As president, Washington's greatest legacy was what *didn't* do. In office, he purposefully set precedents to guide future presidents. He refused ostentatious titles, instead insisting that in a republican country he should be called simply "Mr. President." He refused to run for a third term in 1796, establishing an unwritten rule that was observed by presidents until 1940, when Franklin D. Roosevelt sought a third term. When Washington died in 1799, Americans mourned the loss of "the father of his country."

ADDITIONAL FACTS

1. Twelve US presidents held the rank of general. World War II commander Dwight D. Eisenhower was the last, serving from 1953 to 1961.

2. As president, Washington signed legislation establishing many of the basic building blocks of American government. Laws signed by Washington in his first term made the dollar the official US currency, established a site for the nation's capital, and created a cabinet to give him advice.

3. Washington considered slavery immoral, but he owned slaves and rebuffed suggestions during his lifetime that he free them as an example to others. In Washington's will, however, he finally did so.

Anton Chekhov

Anton Chekhov (1860–1904) was one of literature's great masters of the short story and one of its finest dramatists. In several landmark plays and countless miniature prose masterpieces, he mined remarkable stories from everyday life. Although his works are by and large serious, they consistently walk the tightrope between comedy and tragedy.

Chekhov was born into a debt-ridden family from southern Russia that had purchased its freedom from serfdom just a generation earlier. As a medical student in Moscow, Chekhov wrote short comic pieces to support his parents, selling hundreds of them under a variety of pen names. He continued writing after finishing his medical degree in 1884 and developed a large popular following by his late twenties. As Chekhov gradually tackled weightier subject matters and made his first forays into dramatic writing, he began to attract the attention of literary critics.

The now-legendary Saint Petersburg premiere of Chekhov's *The Seagull* (1896) was an unmitigated disaster. The play was falsely advertised as a comedy, and when the audience started hissing, Chekhov fled the theater in humiliation—an experience that nearly led him to abandon dramatic writing altogether. Later productions of *The Seagull*, however, were well received, and Chekhov scored another triumph when he revised one of his mediocre early plays into the extraordinary *Uncle Vanya* (1897). He followed with *The Three Sisters* (1901) and *The Cherry Orchard* (1904), also considered tragicomic masterpieces. These plays feature generational conflicts and other family troubles, with onstage dramatics kept to a minimum. The most important events happened offstage, conveyed through dialogue rather than action.

Though Chekhov is most renowned for his plays, his short stories are brilliant and arguably without equal. They unfold in a melancholy landscape of keenly observed reality, populated by characters who are mired in self-pity over the dullness and triviality of their everyday lives. The stories' plots usually are minimal and misleadingly simple, with the most important elements hidden under the surface and little or no resolution provided at the end. More than 200 in number, Chekhov's short stories were integral in establishing the short story as the major literary form it is today.

ADDITIONAL FACTS

1. *Chekhov continued practicing medicine even at the height of his writing career. In one well-known quip, he wrote, "Medicine is my lawful wife and literature my mistress; when I get tired of one, I spend the night with the other."*

2. *Chekhov's plays became canonical in both British and American theater almost immediately upon their translation into English in the 1920s. They are still widely performed.*

3. *Russian critics and intellectuals often pressured Chekhov to make his works more political. He always refused, believing that politicizing his work would reduce its universality.*

Romanticism

The movement known as romanticism (1750–1850) arose largely in response to neoclassicism. Whereas neoclassical artists placed great emphasis on the enlightenment values of reason, objectivity, order, and science, romantic artists were drawn to the realm of fantasy, intuition, subjectivity, and emotion. Inspired by the ardor that had spawned the American and French revolutions, romantics celebrated rebellion and personal freedom over social convention. Dismayed by the rapid growth of industrialization, they marveled at the wonders of nature and the purity of simpler, more primitive cultures. In contrast to neoclassicists, who preferred the clear lines and elegance of Greco-Roman art, romantics were fascinated by the complexity of Gothic architecture as well as the mystique of exotic cultures.

In England, romanticism appeared as early as 1749, when the novelist Horace Walpole decided to renovate Strawberry Hill, his villa at Twickenham, with Gothic motifs. Representative Romantic works of English painting include George Stubbs's *Horse Being Devoured by a Lion* (1763), Henry Fuseli's *The Nightmare* (1781), and William Blake's illustrations for his own books of poetry. English Romanticism reached its height in the paintings of John Constable and Joseph Mallard William Turner. In terms of architecture, the movement is best reflected in the neo-Gothic Houses of Parliament, which were begun in 1836.

French romanticism owed a great deal to both the writings of Jean-Jacques Rousseau and the French Revolution. Remarkable French painters of the period include Jean-Auguste-Dominique Ingres, Théodore Géricault, and Eugène Delacroix. The best example of French romantic architecture is Pierre Vignon's church, Le Madeleine; within its neoclassical shell are three Byzantine domes. Such conflation of historical styles characterizes much architecture of the period.

In Germany, the movement owed much to the struggling hero of Johann Wolfgang von Goethe's *Sorrows of Young Werther*, published in 1774. Caspar David Friedrich's *Cloister Graveyard in the Snow* (1817–19) and Philipp Otto Runge's Times of the Day (1809) are typical of German Romanticism.

The style is best represented in America by the works of John Singleton Copley, whose dramatic masterpiece *Watson and the Shark* (1778) was commissioned by the survivor of the attack.

The greatest Spanish artist of the romantic era was Francisco de Goya.

Cognitive Dissonance

In 1957, Leon Festinger, a social psychologist at Stanford University, published *Theory of Cognitive Dissonance*, one of the most influential papers on human behavior ever written. The theory is very simple. We all hold a variety of beliefs, ideas, and thoughts, which scientists call cognitions. For the most part our cognitions are unrelated to each other. For example, a love of opera has nothing to do with who was elected president in 1980. But when our thoughts or actions are related to each other, we feel a deep need for them to be consistent. Contradictions result in a state of dissonance that the mind cannot tolerate. The conflicting cognition or behavior must change to bring the brain back into a state of equilibrium. Since thoughts are usually easier to change than behavior, we are likely to alter our mindset.

Festinger gave the example of smoking. A man who smokes experiences cognitive dissonance when he hears about the health risks. One solution is to stop smoking. But since behavior is difficult to change, the smoker is more likely to change his beliefs about smoking in order to reduce the stress of dissonance. For example, he might choose to focus on the positive health aspects of smoking such as tension relief and weight loss. He might say to himself, "If I stop smoking, I'll gain weight, which is also bad for me." Alternatively, he could compare the dangers of smoking to other everyday risks, like the risk of being in a car accident. The smoker might think, "If people get on the road every day without hesitating, why should I worry about lighting a cigarette?" Such rationalizations allow people to keep their behaviors consistent with their beliefs, reducing cognitive dissonance.

ADDITIONAL FACTS

1. *Fraternity hazing works on the principle of cognitive dissonance. Researchers have found that the more humiliating the initiation ritual, the more freshmen are likely to say that they enjoy being part of the group. Social psychologists refer to this as the effort-justification paradigm.*

2. *Economists attribute buyer's remorse to cognitive dissonance.*

3. *Festinger also found that if people are paid to lie, they do not believe the lies. But, if they volunteer to lie for free, they often believe what they are saying. If they lie without the justification that they're being paid, they experience cognitive dissonance. So they attempt to believe what they're saying.*

Mozart's *Concerto No. 21* and *Symphony No. 41*

Mozart composed seventeen piano concertos in the latter half of his career. They are considered to be the best examples of classical concerto literature. Many of them utilize an adaptation of sonata form called sonata-ritornello form—a combination of regular sonata form and the concerto-writing style of Vivaldi. In this structure, the orchestra restates the themes played by the solo parts.

Sonata-ritornello form may have developed specifically for piano concertos as a means of making sure the audience heard and understood the melodies. Those melodies may have been difficult to hear because pianos did not have the volume they do today.

Mozart's *Concerto No. 21* is among the most brilliant of the seventeen. It has sunny, pleasant motifs in the first movement, while the middle slow movement is placid, beautiful, and often interpreted in a romantic or sentimental way. The final movement has lots of flashy technical passages.

Mozart's *Symphony No. 41*, written in a regal C-Major, is often called the "Jupiter Symphony" because of its grandiose first movement. It exemplifies Mozart's ability to write within sonata form without sacrificing his immense expressive talents. Loud trumpet and drums in the opening movement give the piece a sense of triumph, and the final movement, which mounts a massive, Bach-inspired fugue, manages at least six different themes that come together in an explosive finale, all the while still maintaining the requirements of the sonata structure.

Both of these pieces highlight the Classical style and sonata form at their most mature and impressive. Pieces like these two lead many musicologists and historians to insist that Mozart was the greatest composer who ever lived.

ADDITIONAL FACTS

1. *The K catalog (i.e., K467, K551) was established in 1861 by German musicologist Ludwig von Köchel as a way of keeping track of Mozart's works and their dates of composition. Nowadays, a Mozart composition is rarely mentioned without its accompanying Köchel number. Concerto No. 21 is K467, 1785.*

2. *No one knows exactly where the name "Jupiter" came from, but Mozart did not name his forty-first symphony as such. Mozart's son insisted that the name came from Peter Salomon, the same impresario who commissioned Haydn's London symphonies.*

3. *The lyric slow movement of Mozart's Piano Concerto No. 21 was used as the soundtrack to a soppy 1967 romance film called Elvira Madigan. As a result, it is often called "The Elvira Madigan" concerto, which is quite an unfortunate label for such a powerful work.*

Personal Identity

Recall yourself as a child. Despite many qualitative differences—now you are older, bigger, and, presumably, wiser—you are still the same individual as you were as child. The child you and the adult you are the same person. The problem of personal identity asks: Under what conditions is an individual at one time the same person as an individual at another time? In other words, what kinds of changes can a person undergo and continue to exist?

One possible answer is that a person is just a human organism, and so as long as he or she remains the same human organism, he or she remains the same person. But consider this thought-experiment: A scientist is going to remove your brain and put it into his head. He is then going to remove his brain and put it in your head. Finally, he is going to torture one of the resulting people. Before the operation occurs, you are a given a choice: Based only on self-interest, who would you rather be tortured: The person who has your body and the scientist's brain (A), or the person who has the scientist's body and your brain (B)?

If you believe you are just an organism, after this operation, you will still be A. After all, the brain is just an organ, and an organism does not cease to exist just because it undergoes an organ transplant. Therefore, if you opted to torture B, you are implicitly assuming that you are not an organism, and that your identity is determined some other way.

The importance of this thought-experiment is twofold. First, it shows that the nature of identity over time is not obvious. At first we are tempted to assume that we are just organisms, but thought-experiments lead us to question this assumption. Second, the question about personal identity is linked to a larger question about the self. What exactly do we care about when we say we are acting out of self-interest? The thought-experiment suggests that self-interest is connected to concern for our experiences and our memories, rather than our bodies.

ADDITIONAL FACTS

1. John Locke argued that person A and person B are identical when they are psychologically connected, most important, by memory.

2. Imagine a teleporter that disintegrated you, and then beamed information to a spacestation on Mars, where a person qualitatively indistinguishable from you is constructed. Would you use this as a means of long-distance travel? Is the person who emerges the same person as the one who entered?

3. What if the teleporter created two duplicates, rather than one? Would you survive in that case? Which one would be you? Is it better for there to be two, or just one, person who is connected to you in this way?

Catholicism

The Roman Catholic Church is the world's largest Christian sect, with more than 1.2 billion members. Countries as diverse as Italy, Ireland, Spain, the Philipines, Mexico, and Argentina are all almost completely Catholic.

The Catholic world is governed from Vatican City, the small independent state within the confines of Rome. There, the Pope, who is also the Bishop of Rome and thought to be the successor of Peter, leads the faith, with the aid of his Cardinals. The Catholic world is divided into more than, 2500 dioceses, each headed by a bishop. Within each diocese, each church is led by a priest or deacon, completing the Catholic hierarchy.

Central to the Catholic faith is the practice of the Seven Sacraments. These are:

BAPTISM: Signifying the forgiveness of original sin, done by submerging or splashing water on the believer.

CONFIRMATION: Signifying a second statement of faith for those who have been baptized.

THE EUCHARIST: Eating the body and drinking the blood of Christ. Catholics believe the bread and wine used in the ritual literally become flesh and blood.

PENANCE: Asking for the forgiveness of sins.

ANOINTING THE SICK: Blessing people who are in danger of dying with special oil.

HOLY ORDERS: Acknowledges people who become ordained priests.

MATRIMONY: Acknowledges people who are being married.

These seven sacraments are believed to be a gift from Christ to the church, and performing them is seen as a path to salvation. Catholics believe that salvation comes from both faith in Christ and doing good works, and not, as Protestants believe, faith alone. Thus, after being purified through baptism, in order to best achieve salvation, Catholics must ask forgiveness for each successive sin that they commit.

Throughout history, the Catholic Church has played an enormous role in the politics of Europe and the rest of the world. It has been involved in conflicts such as the Crusades, and it also has been a safe repository of knowledge during chaotic times such as the Middle Ages. Its popes and bishops have been major players on the world stage in every era.

ADDITIONAL FACTS

1. The Eastern Orthodox Church also believes in the seven sacraments. However, they and other sects do not believe the Eucharist is a literal consumption of Christ's body.

2. Pope Benedict XVI, elected in 2005, is expected to be a hard-line conservative pope, who will not waver from the church's conservative stances.

3. The concepts of purgatory and hell, often conflated, have distinct meanings in Catholicism. Whereas hell is a permanent state of damnation, purgatory, on the other hand, is a place where the deceased may become purified on their way to heaven, if they have not yet received forgiveness for their sins.

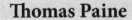

Thomas Paine

Thomas Paine (1737–1809) was a radical pamphlet writer and political philosopher whose famous 1776 book *Common Sense* convinced many Americans to join the Revolution against British rule. Paine despised the British monarchy and believed republicanism was the best form of government. Paine himself was a lifelong rabble-rouser and propagandist who was attracted to revolutionary causes against despotic governments. Truly a man of the world, Paine also participated in the French Revolution and wrote another fiery book, *Rights of Man*, defending the revolution that toppled Louis XVI.

Paine had a habit of alienating his own supporters and received little thanks for his efforts during his lifetime. After moving to France, he unexpectedly opposed the execution of the deposed king. Paine was soon arrested and sentenced to death by the revolutionary government that he himself supported. Paine escaped the guillotine by sheer luck, when the executioner failed to notice the chalk mark on his cell door that meant he was to be beheaded. Paine eventually returned to the United States, where his unconventional religious beliefs (he called the Bible a fabulous invention) made him an outcast. Destitute, he died in 1809.

Paine's writing style was uncompromising, inflammatory, and inspiring. In *Common Sense*, he referred to George III as a "royal brute" and monarchy as an "evil." Establishing a republican form of government in America, Paine believed, would inspire other suffering peoples across the world. "The cause of America is in a great measure the cause of all mankind," he wrote. Paine's tireless propaganda efforts won respect even from his critics. John Adams, the second president of the United States, who called Paine a "mongrel between pig and puppy," conceded that "without the pen of Paine, the sword of Washington would have been wielded in vain."

ADDITIONAL FACTS

1. Ten years after his death, Paine's skeleton was exhumed by an English admirer who wanted to rebury him in England. The reburial never occurred, though, and what became of Paine's bones remains a mystery.

2. Paine wrote the Rights of Man in response to Edmund Burke, a conservative British lawmaker who was aghast at the French Revolution. Paine argued that the miserable conditions of French peasants made revolution justified and scorned Burke's call for modest, incremental reforms instead of armed revolt.

3. Paine is generally credited with inventing the name "United States of America" for the thirteen colonies.

Virginia Woolf

British novelist and critic Virginia Woolf (1882–1941) was one of the most influential writers of the modernist movement. Along with Joyce, Faulkner, and others, she revolutionized the novel with radically new narrative techniques and thematic concerns. Woolf's involvement in the intellectual high society of England, meanwhile, made her a major cultural figure herself.

Woolf came from a privileged London background, and she largely educated herself by reading in the library of her father, a Cambridge-educated author and editor. After Woolf's mother's death in 1895, she began to experience nervous breakdowns and depression, which haunted her for the rest of her life. She wrote prolifically, however, and in 1912 married Leonard Woolf. In 1917, the couple started a small publishing house to produce and distribute Virginia's works and the writings of other authors.

Together, the Woolfs were active in the liberal London intellectual scene. For decades, they met on Thursday evenings at the home of Woolf's sister, Vanessa, in the Bloomsbury neighborhood of central London. Guests frequently included E. M. Forster, Lytton Strachey, John Maynard Keynes, T. S. Eliot, Aldous Huxley, and others. This Bloomsbury group, as it came to be called, discussed questions of philosophy, religion, politics, aesthetics, sexuality, and literature.

Like many writers of the time, Woolf and the Bloomsbury group were horrified by the pointless brutality of World War I. They grew to believe that the principles of nineteenth-century realist literature were inadequate to describe the world that confronted them after the war. They resolved to develop an entirely new frame of reference to interpret this changed world.

Woolf led the charge herself, experimenting with stream-of-consciousness narration—depicting the uninterrupted current of a character's thoughts—in *Mrs. Dalloway* (1925). The novel's simple plot, which follows a woman as she makes preparations for a party, is far less important than the inner workings of the characters' psyches. Though the narrative darts in and out of the minds of different people, only rarely do these characters connect on a significant level or find their thoughts on the same page.

Woolf was also fascinated by how people perceive the flow of time, from fleeting moments to sweeping decades. The lengthy first section of her novel *To the Lighthouse* (1927) focuses in great detail on a single day; the far shorter second section shows the passage of many years in just a few pages. Woolf advanced this exploration of both time and stream of consciousness in *The Waves* (1931), an experimental work that follows the voices of six friends from youth to old age.

ADDITIONAL FACT

1. Ultimately, Woolf was unable to bear the burden of her mental illness. In March 1941, after leaving a note for her husband, she drowned herself in the Ouse River near their Sussex home, Monk's House.

Francisco de Goya

Francisco José de Goya y Lucientes (1746–1828) was born the son of a goldsmith in Fuendetodós, Spain. Court painter to Charles IV, Goya became not only Spain's chief Romantic artist, but a harbinger of modern Expressionism.

Legends abound about Goya's early life as a bullfighter, guitar player, and ladies' man. In 1775, he moved to Madrid, where he became a designer for the Royal Tapestry Factory of Santa Bárbara. Between 1800 and 1808, he painted two of his most famous works, the *Maja Desnuda* and the *Maja Vestita*, which captured the same *maja*, or courtesan, first nude, then clothed.

In 1798, Goya published a series of eighty-three etchings and aquatints entitled *Los Caprichos*. The best known of these is number forty-three, *The Sleep of Reason Produces Monsters*, in which monsters representing nightmares surround the head of a man who has fallen asleep at his desk. In that same year the Spanish king, Charles IV, appointed Goya his official court painter. In 1799, Goya completed *The Family of Charles IV*, a group portrait that some critics believe was done in mockery of the royal family. (The family appears somewhat grotesque and vulgar despite their fine garments.) Goya's model for the composition was Diego Velázquez's *Las Meninas*. Like his predecessor, also court painter to a Spanish monarch, Goya included a portrait of himself before an easel in the background of the painting.

Another two of Goya's well known paintings are his *Second of May, 1808* and *Third of May, 1808*, which were based on Napoleon's invasion of Spain in 1808. On May 2nd, after the emperor had proclaimed his brother king, Spanish crowds attempted to fight off French soldiers. The next day, a French firing squad shot thirty Spanish civilians as a retaliatory measure. Goya presented the two works to Ferdinand VII six years later, after the Spanish king had regained the throne. While *The Second of May, 1808* shows the skirmish between the Spaniards and the French soldiers, *Third of May, 1808* depicts the firing squad about to execute a defiant yet fearful man, awaiting his death with outstretched hands.

Disillusioned with the political situation in Spain, Goya retired to his country home, the so-called *Quinta del Sordo* or "House of the Deaf Man." (Goya went deaf in 1792.) He covered the walls of his residence with a series of nightmarish "Black Paintings" that revealed his despair and feverish imagination. Perhaps the most horrifying of the murals is *Saturn Devouring His Children*, which portrays the frenzied primordial giant tearing into the bloody corpse of a child.

After 1824, Goya produced no more paintings. He went into voluntary exile in France, where he died in Bordeaux in 1828. His remains were returned to Madrid in 1899.

ADDITIONAL FACT

1. *In* The Third of May, 1808, *the French soldiers stand with their backs to the viewer, creating a faceless wall, while each of the Spaniards waiting to die responds with a different emotion. Goya made the victims appear vulnerable and human, and the members of the firing squad cold and insensible to the pain they are causing.*

Reproduction

In the plant and animal kingdoms, there are two main ways to reproduce: asexually and sexually. One is more risky, the other more costly.

Asexual reproduction requires only one parent. There is no time or energy wasted in finding a mate, courting, or the physical act of sex itself. Budding is a common form of asexual reproduction found in strawberries, aspen trees, and coral. In budding, the offspring grows from a part of the parent. Sometimes they break apart, but other times they remain connected for life. Fields of strawberries and forests of aspen trees are often thought of as one large organism, connected through a budding system of vines and roots. In fragmentation, another common form of asexual reproduction, the parent breaks itself into small pieces that each grows into separate individuals. In other words, the death of the parent leads to new life. Flatworms are known for fragmenting.

The offspring of asexual reproduction are always genetically identical to their parents. This is often a disadvantage, as without genetic variety, the population has a more difficult time evolving to changes in the environment. Asexual organisms tend to thrive in stable environments.

Sexual reproduction allows for more flexibility. In sexual reproduction, two separate parents contribute their genes to their offspring. Typically, the male and the female contribute half of their genetic endowment in a vessel called a gamete. The male gamete is usually a sperm, and the female gamete is usually an egg. When the sperm and the egg combine, they create a new organism that is genetically different from either parent. Sexual reproduction can therefore introduce a greater variety of traits into a population, at a faster rate than asexual reproduction. This is a great advantage in changing environments. As a rule, higher organisms all reproduce sexually. But they also have to expend a great deal of energy creating gametes and finding mates.

ADDITIONAL FACTS

1. *Starfish reproduce asexually through regeneration. If a starfish arm breaks off, it can grow into an entirely new organism.*

2. *Sometimes the cost of sex becomes too great, and the organism reverts to asexual reproduction. This may have happened to dandelions.*

3. *Some aphids and lizards reproduce through parthenogenesis, sexual reproduction without fertilization by a male.*

Ludwig van Beethoven

History has made Ludwig van Beethoven (1770–1827) into many things: the bridge between the Classical and Romantic periods; a tortured, suffering genius; and sometimes even the greatest composer of all time. But unlike Bach and Mozart, upon whom that same accolade has been heaped, Beethoven made bold steps to escape the conventions under which his talents developed. His truest legacy in the end is that he was Western music's first great musical personality. He forced himself into every piece he wrote and into the heart and mind of every listener who heard his music for the first time.

In his adult life, Beethoven was plagued by a painful intestinal condition, a swollen pancreas, and cirrhosis of the liver. Around 1800, he began to face a composer's worst nightmare: He was losing his hearing. Instead of despairing, Beethoven worked doubly hard and refused to put the whims of his patrons before his own burning creative desire. "What is in my heart must come out," he wrote in a letter, "and I so write it down."

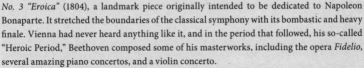

Beethoven's career went through three stages. In the first, much of his work, including his first two very classically Viennese symphonies, sounds similar to that of Haydn. That first stage ended with his *Symphony No. 3 "Eroica"* (1804), a landmark piece originally intended to be dedicated to Napoleon Bonaparte. It stretched the boundaries of the classical symphony with its bombastic and heavy finale. Vienna had never heard anything like it, and in the period that followed, his so-called "Heroic Period," Beethoven composed some of his masterworks, including the opera *Fidelio*, several amazing piano concertos, and a violin concerto.

In the final stage of his life, starting around 1810, Beethoven became more and more isolated from the outside world. He was lonely, constantly in love, and drifting into despair over his increasingly painful physical condition and growing deafness. He died in Vienna, among friends, in 1827.

ADDITIONAL FACTS

1. *Beethoven's father was an abusive, alcoholic court singer in the German town of Bonn. When Ludwig was a boy, his father tried to make his son into a Mozart-style prodigy by locking him in his room for hours to practice harpsichord.*

2. *In 1802 Beethoven wrote a famous letter to his brother known as the "Heiligenstadt Manifesto," named for the town where he wrote it, explaining in florid, sometimes abstruse language that he lived in a state of constant despair, and that if it weren't for his love of music and his passion for life, he would surely kill himself.*

Liberalism

Liberalism is a tradition in political philosophy that emphasizes individualism, equality, and freedom. It is a normative theory—it describes how things *ought* to be, rather than how they in fact are—about what kind of government or political system is justified.

A political system is justifiable only on liberal grounds to the extent that it secures some good for individuals. Liberals believe that individuals have desires and wants that precede political systems, and the purpose of political systems is to attain these goods for individuals.

Another requirement of the liberal theory is that all citizens be treated equally in the eyes of the government. There is significant disagreement within liberalism whether political equality of this kind is compatible with vast differences in wealth. Thinkers like John Locke and Robert Nozick believed people have a natural right to property—in other words, the right to property existed before any government. Therefore, they concluded that only very limited infringements on the pre-political rights of ownership are justified. Other thinkers, like the theorist John Rawls, argued that true equality cannot exist when there are great disparities in wealth.

The third important requirement in liberal political theory is that the government should preserve the freedom of its citizens. Liberals view the value of government as instrumental to secure goods for individual people. With this idea comes the idea that people have freedoms independent of the political system and that the system cannot unreasonably infringe upon these freedoms. However, there is significant disagreement among liberals about what would constitute an unreasonable infringement of freedom.

ADDITIONAL FACTS

1. Political philosophers outside the liberal tradition believe that the group or nation has rights of its own that must be taken into account. These theorists would say that, in the right circumstances, the good of individuals must be sacrificed for the good of the group.

2. Liberal political philosophy is not the same as political Liberalism in the United States and elsewhere. All mainstream political thinking in the United States is liberal, in the philosophical sense.

Eastern Orthodox

The Eastern Orthodox Church separated from the Roman Catholic Church during the Great Schism of 1054.

The Christian Church had long recognized the special status of the bishops in Alexandria, Antioch, Constantinople, Jerusalem, and of course, Rome. The Bishop of Rome, the heir to St. Peter, was elevated above all the rest. Still, over time, those in the Eastern regions of Christendom began to drift apart over differences in language, politics, and liturgical custom.

In the mid-eleventh century, the relationship had disintegrated to a breaking point. While both sides were in the midst of not particularly promising negotiations, Pope Leo IX died, creating a power struggle. The emissaries of the Western Church excommunicated the leader of the Eastern Church, the Patriarch Cerularius, initiating the separation that would prove to be irreparable.

As the Eastern Church established itself, it took the name Orthodox to signify its strict adherence to the original traditions of Christianity. The church had a stronger oral tradition than did the Catholics, allowing the Eastern Church to rely less heavily on the written text of the Bible.

The Eastern Orthodox believe that man was initially good, but fell prey to temptation and turned evil. Thus, every human who died before Jesus Christ was born went to hell. Christ's appearance on earth, however, by embodying both man and God, paved the way for humans' ascension to heaven. This retroactively brought all those who had been damned in the past to heaven as well. The Eastern Orthodox believe that God alone will choose who is saved and who is not. Therefore, the best thing to do to win God's favor is to follow the Eastern Orthodox traditions, which can be traced back to Christ.

Eastern Orthodox priests, unlike Catholics, are allowed to marry, as long as they do so before ordination. In fact, it is thought that priests who lead congregations should be married because they will have to regularly counsel married couples.

Today, the Eastern Orthodox Church is somewhat decentralized; each national church (the largest being Greek) has a Patriarch, and each of these Patriarchs has equal power. Thus, while both the Roman Catholics and the Eastern Orthodox can trace their lineage directly back to Christ, for the second millennium of Christianity, the Eastern Church has differed significantly from its Western cousin.

ADDITIONAL FACTS

1. *The term* Greek Orthodox *is sometimes used to refer to the entire Eastern Orthodoxy and not just the Greek National Church.*

2. *In the Eastern Orthodox tradition, fasting is often required to emulate the perfection of Adam and Eve who, before they succumbed to temptation, subsisted on merely the fruits available in the Garden of Eden. Fasting is looked upon as a privilege.*

The French Revolution

Before it was toppled in 1798, the French monarchy had grown corrupt and greedy, fueling the resentment of the lower and middle classes. While French peasants starved, the nobles lived a life of luxury. When Queen Marie Antoinette was informed that her subjects had no bread to eat, she is famously believed to have suggested, "Let them eat cake." At that time, political prisoners were sent to the Bastille, a feared prison in the heart of Paris.

The Revolution began July 14, 1789, with the storming of the Bastille to free the prisoners. The revolutionaries wanted to radically change French society, and they were willing to resort to great violence. Fired by the ideals of Enlightenment—liberty, equality, fraternity—the revolutionists sought to overthrow the hereditary monarchy and also to break the power of the church. They even sought to remake the calendar into a more rational system.

But the revolution was mired in violence and even anarchy. In just a few years, thousands of men and women were put to death on the guillotine, which the enlightened leaders of the revolution believed was a less painful, more modern way of beheading criminals. Painted blood red, the machine stood four meters tall and occupied a central square in the heart of Paris. A harpsichord-maker in the French capital hastily constructed the gruesome device for 960 francs.

Of course, most of the people who died on the guillotine were not criminals but merely political opponents of the new regime. Thousands died in the Reign of Terror that followed the overthrow of King Louis XVI, including eventually the king himself and Queen Marie Antoinette in 1793.

The defeat of continental Europe's most powerful and admired monarchy by a radical rabble was a profound shock to the continent. The age of absolute monarchy was over.

ADDITIONAL FACTS

1. *Prior to the revolution, only noblemen had the privilege of execution by beheading. Mere commoners were hanged.*

2. *The British thinker Edmund Burke believed that however corrupt the monarchy, the French Revolution was too bloody to be justified. His treatise,* Reflections on the Revolution in France, *is one of the founding documents of modern conservatism.*

3. *The French national anthem, "La Marseillaise," was written by a revolutionary officer from the city of Marseille in 1792. The bloodthirsty lyrics call for Frenchmen to "drench our fields / With their tainted blood," but that didn't stop the Beatles from using a recording of the anthem in the first few bars of their 1967 song "All You Need is Love."*

Moby-Dick

Herman Melville's *Moby-Dick* (1851) is the undisputed giant of American literature. The novel still looms large in Western culture, and few people are unfamiliar with its story—though probably just as few have actually read the book start to finish. Ironically, despite *Moby-Dick*'s major role in putting American literature on the map, the novel was poorly received, viewed as a step below Melville's other works.

The novel's narrator, Ishmael, decides to seek relief from a midlife crisis by joining the crew of a whaling ship. He travels to the whaling hub of New Bedford, Massachusetts, and finds work on a ship called the *Pequod*. Ishmael learns that the vessel's enigmatic and reclusive captain, Ahab, is missing a leg, which he lost to the jaws of an infamously ferocious white sperm whale called Moby-Dick. Only when the *Pequod* is well out to sea does Ahab emerge on deck and announce that the sole goal of the expedition is to hunt down and destroy Moby Dick, wherever he is in the vastness of the ocean.

Ahab's obsessive search takes the *Pequod* thousands of miles, around the southern tip of Africa and toward Southeast Asia. Despite numerous bad omens, Ahab focuses unwaveringly and maniacally on his quest for vengeance, all the while making near-biblical pronouncements:

> "Towards thee I roll, thou all-destroying but unconquering whale; to the last
> I grapple with thee; from hell's heart I stab at thee; for hate's sake I spit my last
> breath at thee."

Ultimately, the *Pequod* finds Moby-Dick in the waters of the Pacific. In the monumental battle that ensues, the whale destroys the ship, Ahab is killed, and the entire crew—save Ishmael—is sucked down into the depths.

Moby-Dick contains philosophical musings on countless topics, from the Bible to fate to the solitude of the ocean. The white whale itself is one of the great enigmatic symbols of literature, and theories about what it signifies vary greatly. Ahab views it as an embodiment of all the evil in the world and believes it his existential duty to confront and defeat this evil.

Ishmael tries to understand the whale by considering it piece by piece; individual chapters of *Moby-Dick* discuss the whale's head, spout, tail, and so on. But despite these efforts, Ishmael finds that the creature's gargantuan, unfathomable quality can be captured neither by the human mind nor by the written word. Some critics have therefore taken the whale as a representation of God, a reminder of the inevitable doom that befalls any man prideful enough to try to control the uncontrollable or comprehend the incomprehensible.

ADDITIONAL FACT

1. *An albino sperm whale dubbed Mocha Dick was seen for decades off the Chilean coast before it was finally captured in the 1830s. Melville clearly drew from the story, but it is unclear why he altered the whale's name.*

Joseph Mallard William Turner

The greatest English painter of the romantic movement, Joseph Mallard William Turner (1775–1851), is best known for his dramatic landscapes and depictions of nature's power.

Turner was born in Chelsea, now part of London. His father, a barber, was quick to recognize his son's artistic inclinations. In 1789, at the age of fourteen, Turner entered the prestigious Royal Academy of Arts. His first work was exhibited there the following year. Throughout the 1790s, he painted primarily in watercolor. In 1796, he exhibited his first oil painting, *Fishermen at Sea.*

Turner opened his own gallery on Harley Street in 1804 but continued to show in the Academy. For nearly thirty years—from 1808 to 1837—he also taught a course on perspective.

Throughout his life, Turner traveled a great deal, both in Britain and abroad. After visiting Wales, Yorkshire, and the Lake District, he went to Switzerland, then to France in 1802–3, where he studied paintings at the Louvre. During his travels, Turner learned to paint in the styles of various old masters, such as Titian, Canaletto, and Claude Lorrain. A subsequent trip to Italy in 1819 had a profound effect on his use of light and color. By 1822, Turner had established his reputation at home. The English King, George IV, commissioned him to paint *The Battle of Trafalgar.*

Inspired by descriptions of natural phenomena in English romantic poetry, Turner portrayed nature with reverence and trepidation. In many cases, he included lines of poetry, often from his own writings, in his paintings. He also prepared illustrations for the works of Lord Byron, Sir Walter Scott, and Samuel Rogers.

Although he taught at the Royal Academy, Turner was not universally admired during his lifetime. Criticized for expanding the boundaries of what was acceptable in art, he found a staunch ally in the art critic John Ruskin, who came to his defense in his famous book on landscape painting, *Modern Painters*, first published in 1843.

Today Turner is viewed as an important forerunner of modern movements such as impressionism and abstract expressionism. A special wing of the Tate museum in London is devoted to his works. In 1984, the Turner Prize was established to recognize the achievements of outstanding modern artists.

ADDITIONAL FACT

1. *In 1840, Turner painted what many consider his best work,* The Slave Ship *(or* Slavers Throwing Overboard the Dead and Dying. Typhoon Coming.*) The painting was based on an actual event reported in Thomas Clarkson's* The History of the Abolition of the Slave Trade. *A ship captain had cast sick and dying slaves into the ocean when he realized that he would be reimbursed only for slaves lost at sea, not those who died aboard his ship.*

❧

Stem Cells

Stems cells may be the key to unlocking the mystery behind some of the world's most perplexing diseases—Parkinson's, Alzheimer's, diabetes, and cancer. All of these diseases involve damaged tissues that need to be repaired or replaced. Stem cells have the unique ability to differentiate themselves into other specialized cells. They can also divide and renew themselves over long periods of time. For example, if stem cells could be introduced into a section of the brain that had been ravaged by Parkinson's disease, they might be able to replace the neurons damaged by the disorder.

There are two basic types of stems cells: embryonic stem cells and adult stem cells. Embryonic stem cells are pluripotent; they can grow into any type of cell in the body. They usually come from fertilized eggs that have been discarded after a fertility treatment. When an egg becomes fertilized, it begins to divide. After about five days, it is a collection of about 150 cells called a blastocyst. The inner cells of the blastocyst are pluripotent stem cells.

Little is known about the uses of human embryonic stem cells. Scientists only learned how to cultivate them in a laboratory in 1998, and other restrictions on research have been legislated. Still scientists have been using adult stem cells for therapeutic purposes for more than thirty years.

Adult stem cells are found in many places in the body—the skin, brain, and bone marrow—but they are not as versatile as embryonic stem cells. Adult stem cells are multipotent, meaning that they can only form a closely related family of cells. Thus, bone marrow stem cells can form only bone cells, cartilage cells, and fat cells. However, unlike embryonic stem cells that have to come from an outside source, adult stem cells often come from within the infirmed individual's body, making it less likely they will be rejected by the individual's immune system.

ADDITIONAL FACTS

1. Hair follicles also contain stem cells, and some researchers believe that those stem cells may lead to a cure for baldness as early as 2007.

2. Adult stem cells from bone marrow have been used to treat leukemia and lymphoma since the 1970s.

3. Using stem cells, scientists have been able to regenerate missing teeth in mice.

Beethoven's *Symphony No. 9* "Choral"

In 1792, Beethoven began studying with Haydn, and later with Antonio Salieri. Beethoven was a brash, arrogant student, famous in the region for his passionate keyboard improvisations. Many critics say that Beethoven finally became a mature composer when he learned to combine his zeal and love for music with the logic of classical forms.

Beethoven's strict adherence to classical convention ended in 1810, when he entered a stage of deep despair and alienation brought on by the hardships of his physical health, his loss of hearing, and his loneliness. He performed on piano for the last time in 1814, and after 1819, all conversation with the great composer was conducted through written notes.

It was in this frame of mind, toward the very end of his life, that Beethoven wrote his *Symphony No. 9* (1824). An admirable expression of his creative flame, it was written while the composer was completely deaf—a final expression of his love for music and his passionate artistry.

Lasting more than an hour, the four-movement symphony starts with a dramatic opening movement, loosely adhering to the classical formula. That leads into a light, but smoldering scherzo movement (a dance form.) The slow adagio section follows—a long, delicate, barely sane moment of quiet before the storm of the finale.

The final movement of the Choral Symphony is one of the greatest finales of all time and is almost universally recognizable. It is the first time a symphony made use of a full chorus alongside a full orchestra. When that chorus takes up the refrain of the *Ode to Joy*, an ecstatic hymn to life, the music builds slowly to the movement's booming, euphoric climax.

ADDITIONAL FACTS

1. *The text for the* Ode to Joy, *which contains the lines, "Joy, bright spark of divinity, Daughter of Elysium / Fire-inspired we tread Thy sanctuary . . ." comes from a 1785 poem by German poet Friedrich Schiller.*

2. *Legend has it that when Beethoven died, shortly after completing his ninth symphony, there was a rainstorm in Vienna. He was lying unconscious on his bed, and at the moment of a lightning strike, he suddenly sat up, shook his fist at the heavens, and fell back dead.*

Social Contract

The social contract is a concept in political philosophy used to understand the origin and legitimacy of political systems.

The idea behind the social contract is that at some hypothetical point in the past, human beings had no government and no laws. In order to safeguard their physical safety and provide the conditions for prosperity, these original humans made an agreement. In exchange for the stability and security of laws, everyone ceded some of his or her original freedoms to a government.

The first modern social contract theorist was Thomas Hobbes (1588–1679). In his book *Leviathan*, Hobbes describes life before government—as he called it, the "state of nature"—as "solitary, nasty, poor, brutish and short." Therefore, the only rational option for people was to form a social contract in which they gave up authority to a ruler. According to Hobbes, the state of nature was so bad that no matter how tyrannical or arbitrary the ruler is, his reign is preferable. Therefore, we have no right to revolt. Hobbes argued further that the sovereign must be granted absolute, unconditional power, with no checks or balances.

English philosopher John Locke (1634–1704) thought that the social contract had to do more than just protect people's physical safety. It also had to respect individuals' rights to life, liberty, and property. If the political authority constituted by the social contract violated these rights, Locke believed citizens had the right to nullify contract and rebel. Another important theorist of the social contract was Jean-Jacques Rousseau (1712–1718).

ADDITIONAL FACTS

1. Immanuel Kant (1724–1804) believed the highest accomplishments of human nature are impossible without living in a civil condition. Therefore, Kant held that we are obligated to leave the state of nature and form a social contract.

2. Rousseau's political ideas were influential in the French Revolution.

Protestant Reformation

In the early sixteenth century, after much of Europe had become displeased with the Roman Catholic Church, Martin Luther instigated the Protestant Reformation.

Martin Luther, a professor and preacher in Germany, studied religious texts at great length. His first disagreement with the Catholic Church concerned the church's practice of indulgences for sins. Indulgence was the Catholic tradition of forgiving sin. At the time, such absolution was for sale. In exchange for money, the donor's sentence in purgatory was reduced. Luther objected to the notion of buying salvation, arguing it was horribly detrimental to the faith.

In 1517, Luther nailed Ninety-Five Theses to the church door at Wittenburg, challenging the Catholic Church and the legitimacy of the pope, as well as the practice of indulgences. Luther believed that the church had lost sight of its original doctrines, namely those coming directly from the text of the Bible, and had created an unnecessary wedge between the clergy and churchgoers.

By posting the Ninety-Five Theses, Luther sparked a great debate that quickly spread to the rest of Germany, Switzerland, Austria, England, and Scotland. As discussion traveled, the writings of John Calvin, among others, further fueled the dissent among the European populace.

As the many reformers' beliefs began to coincide over time, the Protestant religion took shape. At the heart of this reformist faith was the belief that the only religious authority was the Bible itself, and not the pope. This revolutionized the structure of the church and emphasized that individuals could relate more directly to God, without priests as intermediaries.

The Protestants eventually fractured into many sects, such as the Lutherans, Calvinists, and Anabaptists; and the Catholics launched a Counter-Reformation, becoming more conservative.

ADDITIONAL FACTS

1. At age twenty-two, Martin Luther was returning to school during a lightning storm. After a lightning bolt struck near him, he exclaimed "Help, Saint Anne! I'll become a monk!" He survived and kept his promise, leaving law school for a monastery.

2. The Protestant Reformation was further strengthened by King Henry VIII of England's split with the Roman Catholic Church in 1529. The king appointed himself head of England's Church, enabling him to divorce his wife, Queen Catherine, which the pope would not allow.

3. Although no evidence of the original Ninety-Five Theses exists, many experts believe the legendary church-door posting is not very far-fetched: At the time, university's church doors were used to post notices much as bulletin boards are used today.

Thomas Jefferson

"Force cannot change right."   —*Thomas Jefferson*

Thomas Jefferson (1743–1826) was the third president of the United States and one of the most influential men in Revolutionary America. In his writings, including the Declaration of Independence in 1776, Jefferson articulated the ideals of the young republic with rare eloquence. Later, as president, Jefferson put aside his own doubts and approved the purchase of the Louisiana territory from France for three cents an acre, doubling the size of the United States.

Jefferson was born in 1743 in Shadwell, Virginia. Before the Revolution, he practiced law. Jefferson's interests were not confined to politics. He was also an architect and inventor. His education at the College of William and Mary, where he read philosophical works by John Locke, strongly influenced his political views.

In 1776, Jefferson attended the Continental Congress in Philadelphia that brought together the leading citizens of the thirteen restive colonies. High taxes and repression had convinced the delegates to support independence from the British crown. The leaders of the convention asked the thirty-three-year-old Jefferson to join John Adams and Benjamin Franklin in writing a formal statement to send to London. The result was the Declaration of Independence, a powerful denunciation of British rule, which borrowed from Locke and other philosophical influences.

What sort of government would replace British rule? Jefferson, a southern farmer and slaveholder, envisioned a republic of yeoman farmers with a weak central government and a strong separation of church from state. Jefferson's vision remained a potent influence on generations of politicians, especially in the south, who opposed a strong federal government. Despite Jefferson's declared opposition to a strong federal government, as president he approved the purchase of Louisiana from France, a decision that many constitutional scholars believe exceeded his executive powers.

After Jefferson's presidency, he retired to his hilltop mansion at Monticello, where he died on July 4, 1826, fifty years to the day after his Declaration of Independence sounded the clarion call against British rule.

ADDITIONAL FACTS

1. *A bust of Jefferson—along with Theodore Roosevelt, George Washington, and Abraham Lincoln—is carved onto the side of Mount Rushmore in South Dakota.*

2. *Jefferson and Adams were political opponents who twice ran against each other for the presidency but became friends after retiring from politics. Adams died on the same day as Jefferson.*

3. *Although Jefferson frequently argued that slavery was a moral evil, like many other Founding Fathers he owned slaves. According to a recent DNA study by one historian, Jefferson fathered a number of children with one of them, Sally Hemings.*

"The Road Not Taken"

Two roads diverged in a yellow wood,
And sorry I could not travel both
And be one traveler, long I stood
And looked down one as far as I could
To where it bent in the undergrowth.

Then took the other, as just as fair,
And having perhaps the better claim,
Because it was grassy and wanted wear;
Though as for that the passing there
Had worn them really about the same.

And both that morning equally lay
In leaves no step had trodden black.
Oh, I kept the first for another day!
Yet knowing how way leads on to way,
I doubted if I should ever come back.

I shall be telling this with a sigh
Somewhere ages and ages hence:
Two roads diverged in a wood, and I—
I took the one less traveled by,
And that has made all the difference.

There exists probably no American poem so frequently quoted yet so widely misinterpreted as Robert Frost's "The Road Not Taken" (1916). Almost without fail, readers miss the meaning of the poem by miles, seeing it as a rosy testament to the speaker's faith in free will and an inspiring call to defy convention and take the road "less traveled by." But close reading reveals that the poem actually is laden with the ironic resignation for which Frost was renowned.

The point most overlooked in the poem is the utter arbitrariness of the speaker's decision about which road to take. In describing his choice between the two paths, he emphasizes repeatedly that they are essentially identical. One path looks "as just as fair" as the other, and despite the speaker's desire to differentiate them, he acknowledges that "the passing there / Had worn them really about the same." On a whim, he chooses one over the other.

In the last stanza, Frost injects his trademark wry humor. The speaker admits that "ages and ages hence," as a reminiscing old man, he will probably retell this story "with a sigh" and claim that he courageously chose the unorthodox route, the one "less traveled by." But such a claim would be false. The speaker just finished telling us that his choice was totally arbitrary, as there was no "less traveled" path to begin with: they both "equally lay / In leaves no step had trodden black." Frost recognizes the human tendency to self-aggrandize, to sugarcoat the uncertainty of life, to take comfort in viewing life as a series of conscious, knowable choices between good and bad alternatives. But his ultimate point is that in reality, we have no way of knowing which path in life is best, and our decisions are just as often random, uneducated guesses.

ADDITIONAL FACTS

1. Frost was well aware that most readers misinterpreted "The Road Not Taken." During one famous lecture, he warned the audience, "You have to be careful of that one. It's a tricky poem, very tricky."

2. Frost's career started remarkably late for a poet. His first published collection, A Boy's Will *(1913), did not appear until he was almost forty.*

3. President John F. Kennedy greatly admired the works of Frost, who read his poem "The Gift Outright" at his inauguration ceremony in 1961.

Impressionism

Impressionism began in France in the 1870s. The aim of impressionist painters was to replicate the visual impression made by an object on the human eye. More than anything else, they were interested in the changing nature of light and the way it affected vision.

Unlike previous artists who chose subjects from history or mythology, impressionists painted the everyday world around them. They were, in fact, the first artists to consistently work outside. Since they had to paint quickly to capture the effect of light on an object, they did not sketch or plan their paintings in advance, but worked immediately from nature. Realizing that the eye rarely sees anything that is perfectly still, they did not give hard outlines to their subjects, but instead painted them with loose, large brushstrokes, creating the illusion of movement. Rather than mixing colors on their palettes, they dabbed pure colors side by side, directly on the canvas. From close up, the colors appear disparate; from a distance, however, they blend together.

The invention of photography was a major influence on the development of impressionism. Like photographers, the impressionists were interested in optics, light, and color; and they were concerned with capturing the world exactly as it appeared to the eye.

Although earlier artists such as Turner had already shown great interest in the qualities of light, the origins of impressionism are usually traced to the realist movement and one of its chief representatives in France, Édouard Manet. Like his impressionist friends (with whom he never, in fact, exhibited), Manet gravitated toward everyday subjects and loose brushwork. Like them, too, he was a rebel, who dared to scorn the conventions of the official, state-sponsored Académic des beaux-arts.

In 1874, when the impressionists were rejected from the exhibition held annually at the Salon des Artistes, they organized their own show. The group included luminaries such as Claude Monet, Auguste Renoir, Edgar Degas, and Alfered Sisley. A painting by Monet entitled *Impression: Sunrise*, provided Louis Leroy—a hostile critic—with the initially pejorative term *impressionists* for the artists.

All in all, the group staged eight shows, the final one in 1886. By that time, many of its members were working in new styles that would eventually be termed *postimpressionist*. Nevertheless, most major art movements of the modern era have been inspired by the impressionists' independence and courage to break with established tradition.

ADDITIONAL FACT

1. *Since impressionists worked quickly, often completing a painting in one day, they were much more prolific than earlier artists, who often spent weeks preparing one composition. Today hundreds of impressionist paintings can be seen throughout the world both in museums and in private collections. Particularly well known for their holdings are the Musée d'Orsay in Paris, the Art Institute of Chicago, and the Barnes Foundation in Philadelphia.*

Electromagnetic Spectrum

The electromagnetic spectrum describes the full range of electromagnetic radiation in the universe. *Electromagnetic radiation* is simply another term for light. All light is made of photons, tiny massless packets of energy that move in waves through the vacuum of space. Photons always travel at the same speed, 299,792,458 meters per second. But some of their wavelengths are longer than others. If a photon has a longer wavelength and wiggles less frequently, it has lower energy. If a photon has a short wavelength and wiggles more frequently, it has high energy. In this way, a photon is like a football player running down a field to catch a ball. No matter what, he has to be in the end zone in time to catch the ball. If he can run in a fairly straight line, he can get there with relatively little energy. But if he has to zigzag a lot, he expends more energy.

Radio waves are long wavelength, low frequency, and low energy forms of light. Their wavelength varies from about 1 to 100 meters. Because they are so low energy, they rarely interact with matter in any palpable way.

Visible light has a shorter wavelength and higher frequency than radio waves. Visible light is a small slice of the electromagnetic spectrum, but it is in this range that the sun and stars emit most of their radiation. It is probably no coincidence that our eyes are like two antennae finely tuned to this range of light. The colors of the rainbow—red, orange, yellow, green, blue, indigo, and violet—are in this tiny spectrum of light. Ultraviolet light comes directly after violet on the electromagnetic spectrum. Higher energy and higher frequency than visible light, ultraviolet light can damage eyes and skin with prolonged exposure.

ADDITIONAL FACTS

1. *Gamma rays are the most energetic form of light. They are released from the nucleus of an atom as part of a radioactive process. In theory, they can have an infinitely short wavelength.*

2. *In addition to heating food, microwave radiation, which falls between radio waves and visible light on the electromagnetic spectrum, is used for wireless Internet networks.*

3. *Although sound also travels in waves, it differs from light in that it cannot travel through a vacuum. That is why there is no sound in space.*

4. *Most substances on the surface of the earth absorb ultraviolet light, but snow reflects it. This is what causes snow-blindness.*

Romantic Period

The fiery passion of the 19th century romantic-era music, like the literature, art, and thought of the time, was a reaction to the preceding classical period, dominated by cool logic and reason. Where the music of Mozart and Haydn was meant to be pleasant, inspiring, balanced, and lasting, romantics like Hector Berlioz, Johannes Brahms, and Gustav Mahler put a higher premium on personal emotional expression. The romantics also had a devoted respect for history, mythology, magic, mysticism, and heroism. They created cults of genius around their great composers Beethoven, Schubert, and Wagner.

Melody was extremely important to romantic music—so much so that formal structures were often sacrificed in favor of letting those melodies develop naturally. The symphony was the greatest of genres, and many composers produced very little work of note besides their symphonic works. These symphonies became much longer, larger in instrumentation, gaudy, bombastic, and decadent in feel.

Wagner's operas were obsessed with Norse and medieval mythology, full of music that demanded impressive range, stamina, and power from its singers. Composers began demanding almost unreasonable virtuosity from their instrumentalists, to the point that only a few soloists in the world—sometimes only the composer himself—were able to play the pieces they wrote.

The main criticism leveled at romantic music is that its composers lacked taste, taking their music too far. However, a huge number of lasting works were produced in the nineteenth century, and it also saw the blooming of the great Italian and German opera styles.

ADDITIONAL FACTS

1. *The number of pieces written by each composer went down in the Romantic period, as compared to the Classical, but the length of the pieces went up. Wagner's* Ring Cycle *(a four-part opera series) lasts more than fifteen hours.*

2. *The size of ensembles also grew. Gustav Mahler's eighth symphony, the* Symphony of a Thousand, *was scored for extended orchestra, double choir, boys choir, three solo sopranos, two altos, and one tenor, baritone, and bass.*

3. *Romantic-era composers were less likely to come from the professional backgrounds and formal training that molded the Classical geniuses. Hector Berlioz, for example, was hardly a competent player on any instrument, but he still wrote some highly respected pieces.*

⌒◯⌒

George Berkeley

George Berkeley (1685–1753) was born in Kilkenny, Ireland, in 1685. He became a priest in the Church of England and spent three years in Newport, Rhode Island, trying to organize a college for Native Americans in the Bermudas. When this venture failed, he returned to England, where he was appointed Bishop of Cloyne, Ireland.

Berkeley's philosophical position was marked by strong commitments to idealism and theism. For Berkeley, idealism was the view that there are no material bodies, only spirits, minds, or souls, and the ideas or thoughts in those spirits. Thus, when we perceive something, we perceive not an independent object, but only our own ideas. Nothing can exist without either being a spirit, or being perceived by a spirit. Berkeley's principal argument for idealism was the following: Try to imagine a material body, for example, a tree, that is not perceived or thought about by anyone. You cannot, because in the very act of imagining it you are thinking about it, and therefore, it is thought about by someone.

God played an important role in Berkeley's idealism. Idealists face a dilemma: If our experiences are all a product of our perception, and not just our reaction to independent objects in the world, why are they all so consistent? Berkeley argued that God causes us to have experiences that are highly harmonious. God explains why our perceptions and experiences are so regular and law-governed.

Although Berkeley was an avid defender of God's existence, he did not appeal to authority, to scripture, or to simple faith. He sought to demonstrate that belief in God was justified on purely philosophical grounds.

ADDITIONAL FACT
1. *Berkeley advocated the curative powers of tar-water, a combination of water and pine tar. He composed a poem in its honor, which includes the lines:*

> *"Hail vulgar juice of never-fading pine!*
> *Cheap as thou art, thy virtues are divine.*
> *To shew them and explain (such is thy store)*
> *There needs much modern and much ancient lore."*

Constantine I

Constantine I, later called Constantine the Great by Christian historians, is credited with providing the spark that enabled Christianity to spread freely throughout Europe.

Christianity was an unsanctioned religion when Constantine was proclaimed emperor in 306 AD. As was Roman custom, Constantine believed that appeasing the gods was the only way to avoid suffering. He feared that the Christian refusal to make and worship idols tempted the wrath of Roman deities. Consequently, Christians were kept out of government and suppressed by the Roman armies.

However, in 312, Constantine had a change of heart after unifying the Latin-speaking Western Roman Empire by winning the Battle of Milvian Bridge. As Constantine prepared to go into the battle, he reportedly saw the Greek initials of Jesus Christ in the sky, followed by the inscription "Conquer by This." After emerging victorious, Contantine immediately began to recognize Christianity.

First, Constantine adopted a symbol combining Jesus's Greek initials as his personal emblem. More important, he joined with Licinius, Emperor of the Greek-speaking Eastern Roman Empire, and decreed the Edict of Milan.

The Edict of Milan recognized the right of Christians to practice their religion, returned confiscated Christian property, and allowed Christians to begin preaching in public, increasing the religion's spread. It also designated Sunday as a day of worship. The Edict of Milan opened avenues for increasing social and political participation by Christians.

During this period, the Church of the Nativity in Bethlehem and the Church of the Holy Sepulchre in Jerusalem were built. It is believed that on his deathbed, Emperor Constantine himself converted to the faith.

ADDITIONAL FACTS

1. The Edict of Milan was not officially an edict, nor did it originate from Milan. The source of the name is unknown.

2. Christianity was not made the official, and only legal, religion of the Roman Empire until the late fourth century under Emperor Theodosius I.

3. Constantine sponsored and encouraged the Council of Nicaea from which the Nicene Creed was issued in 325: "We believe in one God the Father, the Almighty, maker of heaven and earth, of all that is seen and unseen. We believe in one Lord, Jesus Christ, the Son of God."

∽∞∾

Napoleon Bonaparte

After the revolution in 1789, France endured a decade of war and instability before Napoleon Bonaparte (1769–1821) took power in 1799. Only thirty years old, Napoleon established a firm grip over the unruly and chaotic country, eventually crowning himself emperor in 1804. He was, from the beginning, an unlikely figure to lead France. Born on the Mediterranean island of Corsica, Napoleon could not even speak French until he was nine. But the young army officer sided with the revolutionaries and won the confidence of those who took power after the king's beheading. A series of military victories in Italy and Austria in the 1790s made Napoleon popular among the French public, and his eventual seizure of power was virtually unopposed in France.

Under Napoleon, the French pursued an aggressive foreign policy, exporting their revolution to the rest of the continent. One by one, Napoleon's armies toppled the ancient monarchies of Europe. The French believed the great ideals of their Republic—liberty, equality, and fraternity—were universal and should, if necessary, be imposed by force. Indeed, many European commoners greeted Napoleon's troops as liberators from the tyranny of their kings and queens. The composer Ludwig van Beethoven, an early admirer of Napoleon, dedicated his *Third Symphony* to the young emperor as his troops arrived in the composer's native Germany.

Napoleon remade the legal code in France and proceeded to impose it on conquered territories in Europe. The Napoleonic Code, which set forth laws governing property and other civil matters, remains the basis for the legal system in much of Western Europe to this day.

The French empire envisioned by Napoleon began to collapse after his failed invasion of Russia in 1812. In 1813, Napoleon was defeated and forced to resign by an international coalition that included Britain, Russia, Spain, Austria, and many other states. Napoleon made a brief comeback but was defeated for good at the Battle of Waterloo in 1815. By that time, however, most of the idealism surrounding Napoleon had faded. Napoleon's France had looted much of Europe. In fact, many of the treasures in the Louvre Museum in Paris, including art from the Vatican and Germany, were pillaged by Napoleon's forces. Across the continent, he left a trail of disillusioned followers.

ADDITIONAL FACTS

1. *After Napoleon's defeat at Waterloo, he was exiled to Saint Helena, a tiny island in the South Atlantic controlled by the British.*

2. *Contrary to myth, Napoleon was not exceptionally short. He stood five feet, six inches, slightly taller than the average Frenchman of his day. It was the English who alleged he was only five feet, two inches.*

The Scarlet Letter

The Scarlet Letter (1850) is the best known work of the nineteenth-century American novelist and short story writer Nathaniel Hawthorne. Like much of Hawthorne's writing, it explores social and moral questions through the context of colonial New England. The novel's extensive use of symbolism makes it an excellent example of allegorical literature.

The heroine of The Scarlet Letter is Hester Prynne, a young woman living in the Puritan town of Boston in the 1600s. Although in England she was married to a man many years her senior, he never followed her to the New World as promised, and she assumes his ship was lost during the voyage. In Boston, Hester becomes pregnant as the result of an adulterous relationship and gives birth to a daughter named Pearl.

Hester refuses to name the child's father, despite intense pressure from the strict Puritan town leaders. Consequently, they ostracize her and force her to wear a shameful symbol of her adultery—a scarlet letter A embroidered prominently on a piece of gold cloth. Despite the enormous social isolation and hardship she endures, Hester raises Pearl lovingly, never gives into despair, and holds no resentment against the rest of the community. Ultimately, the situation comes to a head as the identities of both Hester's still-living husband and the father of her child are revealed.

As a descendant of one of the original Puritan families of Salem, Massachusetts, Hawthorne was painfully aware that the Puritans' austere way of life and intolerant moral code often did more harm than good. Among his direct ancestors was John Hathorne, one of the judges who condemned nearly twenty people to death in the notorious Salem witch trials of 1692. Not surprisingly, throughout The Scarlet Letter, Hawthorne unfavorably contrasts the Puritan leaders' unfeeling severity with Hester's grace and selflessness.

The Scarlet Letter is richly symbolic and allegorical. Much of this symbolism is overt and easily understood, making the novel popular among English teachers who want to give their students an introduction to literary analysis. Hawthorne had a knack for adding meaning and atmosphere through the names of his characters, such as the guilt-ridden minister Arthur Dimmesdale and the mysterious old doctor Roger Chillingworth. And the scarlet letter itself acts as the novel's most complex symbol, initially a sign of Hester's shame and alienation but ultimately a mark of her strength and integrity.

ADDITIONAL FACTS

1. *Hawthorne was born Nathaniel Hathorne but added a "w" to his name when he first started publishing his writings.*

2. *One of Hawthorne's closest friends at Bowdoin College was Franklin Pierce, who went on to become the fourteenth US president.*

Whistler's Mother

James McNeill Whistler's famous portrait—known simply as *Whistler's Mother*—has become an iconic image of motherhood.

Whistler was born in Lowell, Massachusetts, in 1834. As a child, he lived abroad, spending six years in Saint Petersburg, Russia, where his father worked as a railroad engineer, and three in England. Upon his return to the States, he enrolled at West Point. However, after failing a chemistry exam in his third year, he was asked to leave. In 1854, Whistler moved to Washington DC and was employed by the US Coast and Geodetic Survey, where he learned to etch. In 1855, he sailed for Europe and eventually settled in London.

Whistler's mother, Anna Matilda McNeill Whistler, came to live with him in 1863. He painted her portrait when his usual model fell ill. The work, which he had entitled *Arrangement in Grey and Black: Portrait of the Artist's Mother*, was exhibited at the Royal Academy in London in 1872. As the title of the work suggests, Whistler considered the identity of his mother less important than the formal elements of the composition. As he himself noted, "To me it is interesting as a picture of my mother; but what can or ought the public to care about the identity of the portrait? . . . As music is the poetry of sound, so is painting the poetry of sight, and subject matter has nothing to do with harmony of sound or colour."

In the portrait, Anna wears a plain black dress and a white cap with translucent lappets hanging down like the ears of a spaniel. Whistler used different types of brushwork to convey different textures within the composition. He had originally intended to portray his mother standing but changed his mind when she was unable to pose for long enough periods of time. Anna's somber outfit was a sign of mourning; she had worn black since her husband's death in Russia in 1849.

The painting was exhibited again in Paris in 1883 and bought by the French government in 1890. It was initially displayed in the Musée du Luxembourg, then, following museum policy, moved to the Louvre Museum ten years after Whistler's death. Today it hangs in the Musée d'Orsay in Paris.

ADDITIONAL FACTS

1. The painting was featured on a 1934 United States postage stamp honoring the mothers of America.

2. The painting has given rise to many caricatures with figures such as Bullwinkle, Barbie, and Ronald Reagan posing as the mother.

3. Whistler preferred using coarse linen canvas, allowing excess paint to drip freely.

Circadian Rhythms

All living creatures have a built-in biological clock that controls wakefulness and sleep, metabolism, heart rate, blood pressure, and body temperature. The pattern of our daily biological functions is set to a circadian rhythm, a 24-hour cycle. If we disrupt our built-in tempo by even a few hours, we feel the effects immediately. Travelers who fly across the country often feel hot flashes, chills, stomachaches, headaches, grogginess, irritability, and sudden bursts of energy followed by fatigue. Jet lag has nothing to do with jets; it's the result of tampering with the body's natural rhythm.

In mammals, the internal clock is located in the suprachiasmatic nucleus (SCN), a collection of neurons in the hypothalamus, a part of the brain that regulates body temperature, fluids and electrolytes, hunger, and hormone production. The SCN is connected to the retina of the eye, where is takes in information about light. If it is dark outside, the SCN tells the body to secrete melatonin, a hormone that makes the body sleepy. If it is light outside, it inhibits melatonin production. But the brain is slow to adjust to new environments. Although it can handle the gradual change of the seasons, it didn't evolve to cope with changing time zones. Hence, jet lag.

In the winter, the SCN responds to the prolonged darkness by producing melatonin in two phases, one at the beginning of the night and one at the end of the night. This causes many people to wake up in the middle of the night during the winter, although they rarely feel a need to get out of bed. The net effect is that, for many people, it takes more time to get a full night's sleep in winter. This may be nature's way of getting us to stay under the covers longer when it's cold outside.

If the SCN is destroyed by accident or disease, human beings cease to have sleep/wake cycles completely. But if the SCN is healthy, even in the absence of light, the body continues functioning in a free-running rhythm. Animals and humans continue to sleep and to be awake for uninterrupted blocks of times, but the body phases into a 25-hour cycle. This indicates to scientists that the SCN does not depend entirely on cues from the outside world to keep time.

ADDITIONAL FACTS

1. The word circadian *comes from the Latin for "about one day."*

2. We sleep best when our body temperatures are the lowest, in the wee hours of the morning. Our temperatures begin to rise between 6 a.m. and 8 a.m.

3. Body strength and pain tolerance peak in the afternoon.

4. Heart attacks are most likely to occur in the morning.

Franz Schubert

At Beethoven's funeral in 1827, Franz Schubert (1797–1828) carried a torch in mourning, a gesture laden with more symbolism than he would know. He died a year later, carrying on the tradition of the tortured, devoted romantic composer whose flame burned out early.

Born in Lichtenthal, a suburb of Vienna, Schubert studied violin, singing, and piano as a young boy with Antonio Salieri, Mozart's main competition and one of Beethoven's teachers. Schubert was obsessed with composition and spent long hours every day sitting alone and writing. His father was a music teacher and urged Franz to become one as well. Franz gave in to his father's pressure and became a teacher in 1813 but spent most of his time composing, stopping only to discipline any student who dared interrupt him.

Schubert was not a master of the symphony like so many romantics. Instead, he started the German tradition of the romantic art song, or the lied. Schubert composed over six hundred lieder in his lifetime, including *Der Erlkönig* (1820), a dark and frightening song about an elf-king whose appearance foretells the death of a little boy, based on a poem by Goethe. The song cycle *Winterreise* (1827) is considered Schubert's finest work.

Schubert was a typical romantic-era bohemian. Poor his whole life, but utterly devoted to his music, he sold dozens of his songs for far less than they were worth. Schubert would compose every morning for several hours and then spend his evenings with a group of close friends who called themselves Schubertians. They would perform Schubert's latest works, recite poetry, and drink heavily in the beer gardens and cafés of Vienna.

Schubert was neither handsome nor particularly interested in women, but in 1822 he contracted syphilis, which was rampant among the prostitutes of central Europe. He died at age thirty-one, far before his creative energies were expended.

ADDITIONAL FACTS

1. *In 1823 Schubert started work on his famous* Unfinished Symphony. *When he died, a friend, Anselm Hüttenbrenner, kept the manuscript hidden for thirty-seven years. It premiered, to great acclaim, in Vienna in 1865.*

2. *Schubert often borrowed money from his friends and lived in their homes. He almost never had his own lodgings.*

3. *Schubert used texts from Goethe and other contemporary German poets, including Wilhelm Müller as the basis of his art songs.*

Idealism

In philosophy, an idealist is someone who believes that reality depends upon the mind.

When idealists claim that something depends upon the mind, they are claiming that the thing would not exist if there were not minds that thought of it. This is a radical position. In ordinary life, we take it for granted that there is a world of objects, and there is a way those objects are, independent of what we think about them.

Idealists, such as the philosopher George Berkeley (1685–1753), rejected the simple idea that there is a world of objects independent of human perception. He argued that objects exist only when we aren't thinking about them because God is thinking about them. Another form of idealism is transcendental idealism, the position adopted by Immanuel Kant (1724–1804) and Arthur Schopenhauer (1788–1860).

Kant acknowledged there are things that do not depend on the human mind for their existence. Kant called them "things in themselves." However, he insisted that the objects we actually experience are not the things in themselves, but the mere appearance of those things in themselves. And that appearance exists only in our minds. Schopenhauer accepted this Kantian distinction, but he denied that there are multiple things in themselves. For Schopenhauer, the ultimate nature of reality is a single, undifferentiated Will—a blind, striving force—which appears to us as a world of individual things in space and time.

In contemporary philosophy, idealism is more often adopted with respect to certain features of objects, rather than the existence of those objects. Thus, many contemporary philosophers argue that values—like moral goodness and beauty, etc.—are mind-dependent, that things in the world have values only because we believe them to have values. Other philosophers are realists about value: They hold that there is real moral goodness, moral badness, beauty, ugliness, etc., in the world, whether we experience it or not.

ADDITIONAL FACTS

1. *Scholars used to think of the history of philosophy as a long debate between realists and idealists. According to this line of thought, Aristotle (384–322 BC) was the first realist and Plato (427–347 BC) was the first idealist. However, few historians of philosophy would accept this today.*

2. *Schopenhauer claimed the origins of his transcendental idealism can be found in the philosophy and literature of Hinduism.*

Joseph Smith and Mormonism

Joseph Smith was born into a Vermont farming family in 1805. In his early teens, he claimed to have had his first vision, during which he saw Jesus Christ and God the Father. Three years later, Smith was visited by the Angel Moroni who told him that golden plates were hidden on his farm.

After years of being denied access to the plates, Moroni finally allowed Smith to see and translate them beginning in 1827. It is believed that Smith translated the plates, which were written in a form of ancient Egyptian, through divine intervention. While dictating the translation to relatives, Smith rarely paused or corrected himself.

The result of the translation was the Book of Mormon which, along with the Bible, is accepted by Mormons as the word of God. The Book of Mormon tells of an ancient prophet, Lehi, who was told by God to go to North America in 600 BC. In the Americas, the book recounts, God continued to choose prophets.

After translating the book and founding his new faith in 1830, Smith immediately began spreading his religion, causing great unrest wherever he went. He slowly but steadily moved west, from Vermont to New York and Pennsylvania, to Missouri, and finally to Illinois. In 1844, Smith was imprisoned on charges of suppressing a rival newspaper. He was subsequently killed by an angry mob. After Smith's death, Brigham Young took over and moved the Church farther west to Salt Lake City, Utah.

The Church of Jesus Christ of Latter-day Saints holds that it is not Orthodox, Catholic, or Protestant, but rather the restoration of the original church that Jesus Christ founded on earth. The Church believes that Smith was the first in a line of recent prophets, followed by Young and continuing today with the current president, prophet and seer of the church. This present-day prophet is believed to have the power to receive direct messages from God.

Among the church's many doctrines are beliefs in the importance of chastity, modest dress, and family prayer lessons. According to a diet code, known as the Word of Wisdom, Mormons cannot consume alcohol, tobacco, coffee, or tea. What they are perhaps most notorious for, though, is a form of polygamy known as plural marriage. Ironically, polygamy was actually banned by the church in 1890.

ADDITIONAL FACTS

1. In Illinois, Smith founded the city of Nauvoo, which in 1845 rivaled the population of Chicago.

2. The Mormons have the world's largest missionary program with 51,000 full-time missionaries worldwide.

Irish Potato Famine

In a single ten-year period from 1841 to 1851, hundreds of thousands of impoverished farmers in Ireland starved to death in one of the worst famines in modern European history. By some estimates, the population of the Emerald Isle fell by 20 percent. The famine was a human catastrophe of tragic proportions and had profound implications far beyond Ireland's shores. It prompted a huge exodus of starving farmers from the island, many of whom migrated to the United States to seek a better life, forming one of first major waves of immigration into the States.

For generations, potatoes thrived in Ireland's soil and were the country's main crop. In the 1840s, however, a potato fungus destroyed the potato plant and sparked a widespread famine, as many Irish farmers had no other supply of food.

At the time the famine occurred, Ireland was a part of the United Kingdom, the most powerful empire in the world, and many contemporaries and historians believe that the British government was criminally negligent in allowing the disaster to occur. One of Britain's most well-known satirists at the time, Jonathan Swift, wrote a famous article called "A Modest Proposal," criticizing the government's inadequate response to the crisis. He facetiously suggested that since the government wasn't sending food, the Irish should eat their babies to survive.

Ireland had been invaded by the English in 1169 AD. It remained a British possession until finally winning independence in 1922, except for the six counties of Northern Ireland that remain part of Great Britain. Disagreement over whether Northern Ireland should remain British or become a part of the rest of Ireland continues, although violence in the region has abated since the Good Friday agreement in 1998.

ADDITIONAL FACTS

1. *Potatoes are not native to Ireland, or even to Europe. Spanish explorers encountered Native American farmers growing the plant in South America and brought the crop back to the Old World, where it quickly became popular.*

2. *The arrival of Irish Catholic refugees in American cities during and after the famine provoked an angry reaction from some Americans who feared the United States would lose its Protestant religious character. Opponents of immigration from Catholic countries formed a political party, the Know-Nothings, which briefly flourished in the 1850s.*

3. *Irish immigration to the United States continued well into the twentieth century. Today, according to the Census Bureau, thirty-four million Americans claim Irish ancestry, nearly ten times the total population of Ireland.*

Walt Whitman

Walt Whitman (1819–1892) was the first great American poet and a significant contributor to the country's emerging literary voice. His works were especially influential in their pioneering of free verse, a poetic form that abandoned strict meter and rhyme schemes in favor of more irregular, variable structures. Free verse became a favorite of twentieth-century poets and is still in wide use today.

Whitman grew up in Brooklyn, where he worked as a teacher and journalist, taking advantage of New York City's cultural offerings, especially the theater. In his late twenties, he traveled through the Mississippi River region for several months, getting a feel for the American heartland. When he returned to Brooklyn, he wrote a large body of poems, publishing the first edition of his collection, *Leaves of Grass* (1855), on his own dime.

Leaves of Grass is an exuberant work, filled with poems celebrating democracy, brotherhood, the American landscape, and the human body. Due to its occasionally racy physical descriptions and its undercurrent of ambiguous or even overtly gay sexuality, many decried the work as obscene. The collection's most famous poem is its first, "Song of Myself," which sets the tone of the entire work from its opening lines:

> I celebrate myself, and sing myself,
> And what I assume you shall assume,
> For every atom belonging to me as good belongs to you.
>
> I loafe and invite my soul,
> I lean and loafe at my ease observing a spear of summer grass.
>
> My tongue, every atom of my blood, formed from this soil, this air,
> Born here of parents born here from parents the same, and their parents the same,
> I, now thirty-seven years old in perfect health begin,
> Hoping to cease not till death.

Leaves of Grass displays many hallmarks of transcendentalism, which thanks to Ralph Waldo Emerson and Henry David Thoreau was sweeping American artistic circles at the time. Originating in New England, transcendentalism was an optimistic intellectual philosophy that emphasized individuality, self-reliance, and the pursuit of a spiritual purity that transcended the concerns of the everyday world.

Whitman revised *Leaves of Grass* repeatedly over his career, adding new poems and editing existing ones, culminating in the authoritative deathbed edition that appeared in 1892. Whitman's poems gradually became more serious, reflecting his deep sadness about the Civil War and the assassination of Abraham Lincoln. His heartbreaking elegy to Lincoln, "When Lilacs Last in the Dooryard Bloom'd" (written 1865–1866), ranks among his finest poems.

Edgar Degas

Edgar Degas (1834–1917) is one of the best-known artists associated with the impressionist movement. Painter, draftsman, sculptor, photographer, and collector, he became especially famous for his representations of ballerinas.

Born into a wealthy Parisian banking family, Degas initially intended to study law. However, after making copies of paintings in the Louvre, he decided to become an artist and began studying in 1854. Two years later, Degas moved to Italy for several years, where he copied Old Master paintings and laid the foundations of his later career. Drawn initially to classical subjects, Degas nevertheless modeled his figures on real bodies. His early work *Young Spartans Exercising* (1860) places an ancient theme in a contemporary setting.

Like many artists of his generation, Degas was deeply affected by the invention of photography. He experimented with the camera and often used it to make preparatory studies for his paintings. He was likewise influenced by Japanese prints, notable for their lack of symmetry and centralized compositions. Inspired by the realist painters Gustave Courbet and Édouard Manet, whom he met in 1861, he began painting the everyday life of Paris.

Between 1865 and 1874, Degas developed his own personal style, one that tried to capture subjects with dispassionate objectivity. In *Interior* (or *The Rape*), painted in 1868–70, Degas made the viewer feel as if he or she were intruding on a private moment. Degas submitted works to seven of the impressionists' exhibitions. Although he supported the movement from its inception, he disliked the term *impressionism* and referred to himself as a realist or naturalist.

Degas reached the height of his powers between 1880 and 1893. Experimenting with various media, he combined pastel with tempera or gouache to achieve more fluid effects. Influenced by the Socialist views of the famous author Émile Zola, he painted sympathetic portraits of laborers, as can be seen in *Women Ironing* of 1884. After the final impressionist exhibition of 1886, Degas stopped displaying his work in group shows and worked instead with private dealers. In his later years, he tended to work in brighter, less natural colors. Depressed by his failing eyesight, Degas stopped painting in 1912, five years before his death.

The most critical assessment of Degas's work came from the artist himself, who once wrote in a letter: "I was, or I seemed, hard toward all the world, because of a kind of attraction toward brutality that came from my doubt and bad temper."

ADDITIONAL FACTS

1. In October of 1872, Degas left Paris for a five-month stay in New Orleans, birthplace of his mother. In 1873, he painted New Orleans Cotton Office.

2. Degas also wrote poetry, mostly in the form of sonnets.

Sleep

It seems strange that human beings evolved to spend about one-third of their lives lying unconscious, completely vulnerable to predators. But sleep is as crucial to our survival as food, water, and shelter. After one night without sleep, we become tired and cranky. After two nights, we suffer from memory loss and diminished concentration. After three nights, delirium sets in. Although a healthy human being can survive without eating for more than a month, humans die without sleep in less than two weeks.

So what is so important about sleep? Although no one is sure, it seems clear that sleep restores our muscles and organs, organizes our thoughts, and builds memories. According to electroencephalograph (EEG) studies that measure the activity of electrical waves in the brain, sleep occurs in stages. Normally when we are awake and not thinking of anything in particular, the brain generates alpha waves that oscillate at about ten cycles per second. When we concentrate deeply, we exhibit beta waves, which are twice as fast.

As we enter the first stage of sleep, the alpha waves become random, their rhythm coming and going. In this stage of light dozing, we can be easily awakened. As time passes, brain waves become longer and slower. After about forty minutes, we generate delta waves that oscillate less than 3.5 times per second. In this stage of deep sleep, the muscles of the body regenerate themselves, and it is very hard to wake up. Brain waves begin to quicken again, climbing back to alpha levels in another forty minutes or so. But instead of waking up, the body enters a stage called rapid eye movement (REM) sleep. The eyes twitch back and forth, as if they are looking at a moving object. It is during this stage of sleep that we dream. The average young adult experiences four or five periods of REM sleep per night.

ADDITIONAL FACTS

1. Depriving a person of REM sleep will quickly lead to delirium.

2. Babies spend more than half the night in REM sleep.

3. Cows can sleep standing up, but they can only dream lying down.

4. Whales and dolphins have to swim and breathe as they sleep, so only one-half of their brains fall asleep at a time.

Felix Mendelssohn

Born to a wealthy Jewish banker and a mother with great artistic talents, Felix Mendelssohn (1809–1847) excelled in both music and the visual arts. In fact, some of his finest works, such as *A Midsummer Night's Dream* (1826) and *Scotch Symphony* (1830–1842) can be described as the musical equivalent of impressionist paintings—full of ripe symbolism and imitations of both natural and fantastical sounds.

As a young man, Mendelssohn studied with Karl Zelter, a prominent German music teacher and a devotee of Bach. Mendelssohn studied fugue form intensively, and in his early twenties he conducted a performance of Bach's *St. Matthew Passion* that was so well-received, it is said to have touched off a continental revival of Bach's works. During the subsequent tour, Mendelssohn visited Scotland, which inspired him to write several works including his famous *Scotch Symphony*. At age twenty-seven, Mendelssohn married and became the director of the Leipzig Gewandhaus Orchestra.

Much of Mendelssohn's music has magical themes, evident in the "faerie dances" of his *Octet for Strings* (1825) and his incidental music for the play *A Midsummer Night's Dream*. He was also a very strict classical formalist, with very little of the romantic fire that drove most of his colleagues. He was widely praised as a master musical craftsman.

For several years, Mendelssohn maintained a harrowing schedule of concerts and teaching. By 1846, when his oratorio *Elijah* premiered in London, Mendelssohn had worn himself ragged. He retreated to Frankfurt to rest. Once there, he learned that his beloved sister Fanny had died, and he immediately had a fit that resulted in a broken blood vessel in his head. He emerged from the incident morose and creatively lifeless and wrote few pieces until he died, in a deep depression, the following year.

ADDITIONAL FACTS

1. As a young boy, Mendelssohn's father Abraham converted the whole family to Protestant Christianity because he thought that widespread German anti-Semitism would inhibit his son's artistic career. The new family surname was Mendelssohn-Bartholdy.

2. Mendelssohn's first teacher, Zelter, was a personal friend of the poet Goethe, who came to adore Mendelssohn's music and often invited the twelve-year-old to play for him.

3. The composer's grandfather, Moses Mendelssohn, was a renowned philosopher.

4. Mendelssohn wrote the famous "Wedding March" that has since accompanied thousands of bridal parties out of chapels.

David Hume

Born in Scotland, David Hume (1711–1776) broke with the Calvinism of his youth and developed controversial views on morality and religion. His reputation as a radical prevented him from finding work at a university. Instead, Hume was employed as, among other things, a clerk, a librarian, and later a diplomat. He spent time in the salons of Paris, where he met Jean-Jacques Rousseau and Denis Diderot. Hume died in 1776; he had arranged for his most controversial work, *Dialogues Concerning Natural Religion*, to be published after his death.

Hume's philosophy is notable for its empiricism and skepticism. Hume believed that all of our knowledge and ideas begin with experience. He demanded that some experience justify every philosophical concept. And he exhibited a remarkable willingness to discredit not merely articles of religious faith, but widespread philosophical assumptions. Most famously and influentially, Hume attacked the idea that we can rely on inductive reasoning (induction) to lead us toward true beliefs.

In the realm of moral philosophy, Hume held that only desires, not beliefs, motivate human beings to act. But he observed that moral principles do drive our behavior. Therefore he concluded those principles must appeal not to our beliefs, but to our desires. In other words, Hume argued moral judgments do not express objective features of the world, but simply record our preferences. He believed all of us have a natural moral sentiment, which makes us dislike certain acts and approve of others. When we make moral judgments, we are simply expressing our approval or disapproval and nothing more lofty than that.

ADDITIONAL FACTS

1. *In the posthumously published* Dialogues on Natural Religion *Hume criticized various articles of traditional religious faith, especially the argument that God designed the world.*

2. *To express his view that desires cannot be evaluated rationally, Hume wrote, "It is not contrary to reason to prefer the destruction of the whole world to the scratching of my finger."*

Muhammad

Muhammad was the final prophet of God on earth, according to followers of Islam. Like all Arabs, Muhammad's lineage can be traced back to Ishmael, the first son of Abraham. Muslims believe that Muhammad's revelations followed those of other prophets such as Moses and Jesus Christ.

Muhammad was born in Mecca circa 570 CE. At the time, Mecca was a thriving city, centered around a temple called the Kaaba where idolatry was practiced. Muhammad's father died before he was born, and as a young boy, Muhammad traveled around Arabia with his merchant uncle, later following in that trade.

Around the age of forty, Muhammad, who was known to be reflective and contemplative, went to the cave of al-Hira, near Mecca, where he had a vision. In this vision, the angel Gabriel spoke to him and commanded him to memorize and recite verses, which later made up the Quran. Gabriel visited Muhammad throughout his remaining twenty-three years, and Muhammad began to preach Gabriel's teachings. Throughout his whole life, however, Muhammad was illiterate, meaning that all of his revelations had to be passed along by the spoken word.

A central tenet of Muhammad's teachings was monotheism. This concept greatly angered the powerful leaders of Mecca as their town thrived on the idol-based Kaaba. Eventually, Muhammad was forced to flee with his followers to Medina. In Medina, Islam quickly became the majority. However, rather than banish non-Muslims, Muhammad allowed them to pay a tax in order to continue their religious practices.

As Medina's power increased, the city of Mecca became wary. Tensions increased, and eventually the two cities waged war. Muhammad and Medina, despite being outnumbered, emerged victorious. Muhammad then unified all of Arabia through further conquests.

Muhammad died in Medina in 632 at age sixty-three. According to oral tradition, at the time of Muhammad's death, the angel Gabriel once again appeared before him. Gabriel took Muhammad on his horse from Mecca to Jerusalem. There Muhammad met Abraham, Moses, and Jesus, before riding the angel's horse into heaven, thus ascending to his final resting place. This final ascension occurred from the Temple Mount, now the third holiest site in Islam (after Mecca and Medina).

The question of who Muhammad chose as his successor is a subject of debate and led to the schism between Shiite and Sunni Muslims. According to Suuni Islam, Abu Bakr was chosen as the next caliph. Shiite, on the other hand, claim that Muhammad appointed Ali, his son-in-law, as the next caliph, and that Abu Bakr rose to power only by overthrowing him.

Colonialism

Spanish colonization of the Americas began with the voyage of Christopher Columbus in 1492. British traders and religious refugees arrived in the New World a century later. But the era of European colonization did not end in the seventeenth century and did not stop with America. British merchants and colonizers in the age of exploration roamed across the globe, founding new settlements in India, China, and the islands of the Pacific Ocean.

In the late 1800s, the major European powers—France, Britain, and Germany—"discovered" Africa. In the span of a few decades, leading European nations divided up Africa and subjugated its indigenous population to colonial control. France took big chunks of western Africa. Britain wrested control of South Africa and much of the east coast of the continent. Germany, Portugal, and Belgium staked claims on smaller portions of Africa.

Insatiable greed coupled with a desire to spread Western civilization fired the imagination of the European colonial powers. Armed with new technologies such as the railroad, which made it easier to tame the vast spaces of Africa, the West set out to harness the resources of the continent. In the infamous words of British poet Rudyard Kipling, the European empires had selflessly assumed the "white man's burden" of spreading civilization—and earning a tidy profit.

For the inhabitants of Africa, the coming of the Europeans was a disaster. Many Europeans considered black Africans barely human, and they exterminated huge parts of the African population. In his famous 1902 novel, *Heart of Darkness*, author Joseph Conrad illustrated how colonialism turned allegedly civilized Europeans into monsters, exploiting and killing African natives. In some territories, millions died. In the Belgian Congo, it has been estimated that ten million were worked to death; a whole population was targeted for extermination in German Southwest Africa after rebelling against colonial rule. Europeans did not abandon their hold on Africa until after World War II, leaving a shattered and impoverished continent.

ADDITIONAL FACTS

1. *Just before the outbreak of World War I, only two small parts of Africa remained free and independent: Ethiopia and Liberia, a small nation in West Africa that had been founded by freed American slaves in 1847.*

2. *Most European powers let go of their African colonies peacefully after World War II, but France tenaciously tried to hold Algeria, a country on the Mediterranean coast. In a bloody war that lasted from the mid-1950s until 1962, hundreds of thousands of Algerians were killed before the country finally won independence. The revolt was portrayed in the famous 1966 movie* Battle of Algiers.

3. *During the mid-nineteenth century, British explorer David Livingstone traveled Africa looking for the source of the Nile river. His expedition lost contact with the outside world for six years, until journalist Henry Morton Stanley located him in Tanzania in 1871, famously greeting the explorer with the words, "Dr. Livingstone, I presume?"*

Charles Dickens

Few novelists have even come close to matching the productivity and celebrity of Charles Dickens (1812–1870). His enormous body of work consists of more than fifteen major novels—many of them huge tomes—and innumerable journalistic and editorial pieces. Although detractors ridiculed Dickens's work as unliterary, he ignored such criticism and found fulfillment as a socially conscious storyteller. In return, an adoring public held Dickens up as one of the most beloved figures of the Victorian era.

Dickens spent his childhood in Chatham and London, where his father clerked in the public service. When his parents' overzealous spending landed them in debtors' prison, the twelve-year-old Dickens was forced to drop out of school and take a job in a boot-blacking factory—an experience that gave him the lifelong empathy for the poor that is evident throughout his writings. Once Dickens was able to leave the factory, he finished his brief education and worked as a law clerk and, later, a journalist.

Dickens's first published novel, *The Pickwick Papers* (1836), launched him to instant fame. Like many of his works, it was published serially in a monthly magazine, which gave him a greater financial windfall. Dickens wrote at a breakneck pace over the next five years, producing four more serialized novels, including the now-classic *Oliver Twist* (1837–1839), a tale of a young orphan living on the streets.

Each new work brought Dickens greater public acclaim, from his morality tale *A Christmas Carol* (1843) to his own "favourite child," the partly autobiographical *David Copperfield* (1849–1850). Although all of these works demonstrated concern with poverty and other social ills, these concerns grew more serious in later novels, particularly *Bleak House* (1852–1853), about the inefficiency of the English legal system, and *Hard Times* (1854), about the dark side of industrialization. Dickens's career culminated with the historical novel *A Tale of Two Cities* (1859) and the comic tale *Great Expectations* (1860–1861).

The quality of Dickens's works varies considerably, from masterful fiction to maudlin plots awash in sentimentality. The fact that Dickens published his novels serially—and that he was often paid by the word—accounts for much of this inconsistency. But Dickens always worked with the conscious aim of pleasing his readership, even if that meant quantity over quality. His works continue to please readers today.

ADDITIONAL FACT

1. *Dickens's prolificacy was not limited to his writing; he also had ten children by his wife, Catherine Hogarth.*

Paul Cézanne

Paul Cézanne (1839–1906) is considered one of the major artists of the postimpressionist movement. His landscapes and still lifes were influential on the development of Cubism and Fauvism in the early twentieth century.

Born into a wealthy French family in Aix-en-Provence, Cézanne initially studied law near his hometown. There he first met the novelist Émile Zola, with whom he became close friends. Abandoning law for painting in 1861, Cézanne moved to Paris, where he was rejected from the École des Beaux-Arts. He then began studying at the Académie Suisse, where he met Camille Pissarro, who was to become a lifelong influence on his work. In 1874, Cézanne joined the impressionists in their first independent exhibition, to which he submitted *Modern Olympia*. His entry was dismissed by one unsympathetic critic as a work of "unbridled romanticism."

Although Cézanne exhibited with the impressionists twice more, he continued to submit paintings—all of which were rejected—to the official Salon. Critical of what he considered the impressionists' neglect of form and structure, Cézanne wrote to a friend, "I want to make of impressionism something valid and lasting, like the art in the museums." He thus developed his own style, which was later categorized as postimpressionism. He simplified forms and distorted perspective to capture what he believed was a truer perception of reality. In *Fruit Bowl, Glass and Apples* (1879–1882), for example, Cézanne made the stem of the bowl slightly off center, as if it was supporting the unbalanced weight of the fruit.

In 1882, Cézanne moved back to his childhood home in Aix. In his later period, he reduced the importance of subject matter, concentrating instead on pure form. Working his way toward abstraction, Cézanne noted in a letter, "You must see in nature the cylinder, the sphere, the cone, all put in perspective, so that every side of an object, of a plane, recedes to a central point." After 1900, he painted a series of views of nearby Mont Sainte-Victoire using blocks of color and shifting points of view to capture the feeling, rather than the objective reality, of the landscape.

When Cézanne died in 1906, Pablo Picasso had already begun his cubist masterpiece, *Les Demoiselles d'Avignon*. The composition owed a great deal to Cézanne.

ADDITIONAL FACTS

1. Cézanne ended his friendship with Émile Zola in 1886 when, in the French journal Le Figaro, the novelist described the artist as an aborted great talent.

3. Picasso called Cézanne "the father of us all."

Blood

The average adult has about five liters of blood flowing through his or her veins. But what exactly is blood? It consists of four essential components that help the body survive: red blood cells, white blood cells, platelets, and plasma.

Red blood cells carry oxygen from the lungs to all the tissues in the body. Normally, these cells are shaped like donuts with the holes partially filled in, but they can change shape in order to squeeze through tiny capillaries. In addition to delivering oxygen, red blood cells pick up carbon dioxide, a waste product of cellular respiration. When red blood cells are carrying oxygen, they are bright red, giving blood its characteristic color. Deoxygenated blood is a dark maroon color, but because of the way light penetrates our skin, it appears blue in our veins.

White blood cells are a part of the immune system that fights infections, killing bacteria, viruses, and parasites. There are many types of white blood cells, but the most common types are neutrophils and lymphocytes. Neutrophils literally swallow their enemies alive. They break them down and digest them in a process called phagocytosis. Lymphocytes work in more subtle and complex ways. They refine their shape to destroy new viruses and bacteria that enter the body. Although this takes time, lymphocytes remember past encounters with old diseases. Once they learn to fight a certain germ, they always know how to defeat it again.

Platelets, the third component of blood, contain chemicals that clot wounds. When you scrape or cut yourself, platelets help form the scab that stops the bleeding. Red blood cells, white blood cells, and platelets are all formed in bone marrow from the same stem cells.

Plasma is the fluid that carries red blood cells, white blood cells, and platelets throughout the body. It is 90 percent water and 10 percent a mixture of proteins, electrolytes, glucose, vitamins, hormones, and cholesterol. Altogether, blood contains everything that keeps the body alive.

ADDITIONAL FACTS

1. On average, men have 5,200,000 red blood cells per cubic millimeter while women have 4,600,000 red blood cells per cubic millimeter.

2. Frozen blood can keep for up to ten years.

3. Jewish dietary laws do not allow blood to be consumed in any way. Traditionally, salting and pickling purges blood from meat.

4. According to Chinese folklore, nosebleeds are a sign of sexual arousal in men.

Hector Berlioz

Romantic almost to a fault, Hector Berlioz (1803–1869) was egocentric and constantly in love. His turbulent life was the perfect accompaniment to the music he wrote.

Born into a modest family outside of Grenoble, France, Berlioz's doctor father sent him to medical school in Paris. There he was swept up in the spirit of romanticism, going to concerts and hanging around musicians. Against the urgings of his pious and practical mother, Berlioz abandoned his studies and entered the Paris Conservatory.

In 1827, Berlioz attended a performance of Shakespeare's *Hamlet* that would change his life. He fell madly in love with the Irish actress Harriet Smithson, who played the leading role of Ophelia, and began a crazed courtship. When Smithson rejected Berlioz's advances, he decided to win her over with music. The result was the programmatic *Symphonie Fantastique* (1830), one of the most important pieces of the nineteenth century.

The work tells the story of a young, ambitious composer who, smitten by a beautiful maiden, tries to commit suicide by overdosing on opium. Instead of dying, he tumbles through five hectic hallucinations, which coincide with the five movements of the piece: First he meets his lover and is overcome by desire; then he sees her dancing at a ball; next is a tranquil scene in a pasture; then he murders his coveted and is executed by guillotine; finally, the composer's body is tossed around at a witches' Sabbath, where his dead lover reappears in ghoulish form, accompanied by a distortion of her theme and the medieval chant for the dead, the "Dies Irae."

Symphonie Fantastique uses the revolutionary technique of the *idée fixe*, a simple, captivating melody representing the beloved, that is repeated within new musical guises in each movement. As Berlioz was obsessed with Harriet's memory, his symphony is obsessed with this theme. Many years later, Berlioz eventually married the fickle Harriet, but their cooled, overdue love did not last long.

ADDITIONAL FACTS

1. *Jean-Francois Lesueur, Berlioz's teacher at the Paris Conservatory, told him he was a genius. Berlioz never forgot it—encouraging his Babylonian instincts to compose on a grand scale, mounting huge, expensive productions. In Paris in 1844, he conducted a massive orchestral/choral ensemble that numbered more than 1,000 musicians and required seven assistant conductors.*

2. *Beyond teaching himself guitar and flute, Berlioz lacked instrumental prowess. He was a terrible pianist and didn't play the violin or any of the other usual instruments of composers.*

3. *Constantly at odds with the demanding, conservative standards of the Paris Conservatory—Berlioz applied for a job there but was repeatedly rejected—he made most of his living writing criticism for Parisian newspapers and magazines. He was a talented writer, and many of his articles survive today.*

Induction

When we reason from the way things have been in the past to draw conclusions about the way they always are, or always will be, we are reasoning inductively. For instance, we believe that the sun will rise tomorrow, because the sun has always risen in the past. Likewise, we believe that all books have pages, because all of the books we have ever seen have pages. Most of the beliefs we have about the world are based on inductive reasoning.

Induction is not as certain as deductive reasoning. We reason deductively when, for instance, we conclude that because Socrates is a man, and all men are mortal, therefore Socrates is mortal. In this case, the facts make the conclusion true. However, when using induction, the facts about the past don't settle how the future will be. The sun might explode or in some other way fail to rise.

When employing inductive reasoning, one might argue the evidence doesn't *entail* the conclusion, but it makes the conclusion probable or likely. Still the problem remains: What justification do we have for assuming that the future will, more likely than not, be like the past?

ADDITIONAL FACTS

1. *David Hume (1711–1776) first raised the problem of induction. He concluded that there is no reason to think that inductive reasoning will guide us to the truth.*

2. *In the 1950s, philosopher Nelson Goodman (1906–1998) raised what he called the new riddle of induction: What features of things are legitimate bases for inductive reasoning, and which are not?*

Quran

The Quran is the holy book of Muslims and is believed to be God's final revelation to mankind. It was transmitted from God to the angel Gabriel to the prophet Muhammad, and finally to all Muslims.

The Quran contains 114 suras (chapters) and more than 6,200 ayat (verses). Since Muhammad was illiterate, his revelations had to be spoken aloud and written down by someone else.

The original language of the Quran was an ancient form of Arabic. Arabic is a language of consonants and no vowels; therefore the meanings of words and phrases can easily be lost and reinterpreted over time. The ancient style of the Quran is revered, and its Arabic is seen as ideal because it is the speech of God. Moreover, it is believed that in order for the Quran to be truly understood, it must always be written in Arabic. Thus, translated versions of the holy book are considered mere summaries or approximations.

Muslim scholars consider the Quran to be a genre in itself. In various suras, the Quran contains everything from prose and verse to rhyming schemes and refrains. One hundred and thirteen suras begin with the words "In the name of God, the Merciful, the Compassionate."

The content of the suras also varies greatly. They contain narrative stories, legal and ethical teachings, psychological teachings regarding the nature of humans, and cosmological teachings regarding the nature of God. The Quran was not written in chronological order, but instead it is roughly arranged by the size of the sura, with the longest suras first. Furthermore, the Quran can be divided into those revelations Muhammad had in Mecca and those he had in Medina. While the Mecca sura tend to be shorter, the Medina sura tend to be longer and about legal issues.

Uthman ibn Affan, the third of the Four Righteously Guided Caliphs according to Sunni Islam, set out to codify the Quran. Because it was mostly told orally, many versions of the written Quran had been created. In order to form an official Quran, Uthman gathered many scholars, compiled multiple texts into one standard version, sent this version to the extremities of the Arabic empire, and had all other versions destroyed.

ADDITIONAL FACTS

1. *Several contradictions arise in the Quran, but Muslim scholars claim that these "errors" were merely attempts by God to reveal the path that Muhammad and all Muslims should take at a moderate pace.*

2. *People who have memorized the Quran are known as Hafiz (singular) or Haffuz (plural), meaning "Guardians."*

Andrew Jackson

Andrew Jackson (1767–1845) was the seventh president of the United States, holding office from 1829 to 1837. He was, in his time, certainly the most unusual man to win the American presidency. Born in South Carolina, Jackson joined the Continental Army to fight the British when he was only thirteen. He worked as a lawyer and politician in Tennessee in the years following American independence, then rejoined the state militia and led American forces to a surprise victory over the British at the Battle of New Orleans in the War of 1812. Jackson's military exploits made him a national hero. But his uncouth biography—Jackson killed several legal adversaries in duels in Tennessee and married a divorced woman—made him an unlikely candidate for the presidency, which had up to 1829 been occupied by well-bred members of the Massachusetts and Virginia elite.

Partly because of Jackson's background, he lost his first race for the presidency in the controversial election of 1824 to John Quincy Adams, the grandee of a Massachusetts political family and the son of President John Adams. At the time, the American presidential election system was less democratic than it is today. Many states did not give voters any say at all. Instead, state legislators appointed electors who, in turn, voted for president at the Electoral College. In the states that permitted a popular vote in 1824, Jackson defeated Adams handily. But when the House of Representatives eventually decided the winner, it chose Adams instead.

Enraged, Jackson spent the next four years campaigning to make the electoral system more democratic. He founded a new political party to advance his cause, the Democrats, and in the election of 1828 he defeated Adams easily. Jackson's election heralded a shift in the American political system. No longer would wealthy aristocrats have exclusive hold on the White House. As president, Jackson pushed to expel Native Americans from Georgia and abolish the Bank of the United States, causes popular among the newly enfranchised voters who had made him the nation's first democratic president.

ADDITIONAL FACTS

1. Since 1928—the 100th anniversary of his election—Jackson's face has graced the twenty-dollar bill. It is an ironic honor given Jackson's fierce opposition to the Bank of the United States, an early predecessor of the Federal Reserve.

2. Jackson claimed to follow the example of Thomas Jefferson, but the stately Virginian was no fan of the violent-tempered Tennessean. "His passions are terrible," Jefferson wrote of Jackson. "He is a dangerous man."

3. As president, Jackson argued that no state could override federal laws or secede from the union. This doctrine of the inviolability of the union helped shape the thinking of many Americans, including Abraham Lincoln.

Henry James

In the late nineteenth century, as the United States established itself as a world power to rival Europe, authors on both sides of the Atlantic began to chronicle the inevitable collision between the Old World and the New. The most insightful of these observers was Henry James (1843–1916).

As a native-born American but later a naturalized British citizen, James embodied the expatriate experience. He was born in New York City to a scholarly family: his father, Henry, was a prominent theorist and theologian, and his elder brother, William, would go on to become a renowned philosopher. James benefited from an extraordinarily cosmopolitan upbringing, living in London, Paris, and Geneva at various points until his family settled in Newport, Rhode Island. While studying at Harvard Law School, James penned stories and book reviews before devoting himself to writing full time. James continued to travel extensively throughout Europe during his twenties and thirties, believing it would improve his writing.

James's first major novel, *The American* (1877), explores the conflict that would pervade many of his works: New World brashness and naïveté versus Old World urbanity and corruption. In the novel, a new-money American businessman gets in over his head amid the backstabbing and hauteur of the French aristocracy, leading inevitably to disaster. Likewise, in *Daisy Miller* (1879), a willful young American woman scorns the conventions of expatriate high society, bringing herself only tragedy. And in *A Portrait of a Lady* (1881), an American heiress falls victim to predatory expatriates in Europe.

Beyond his keen eye for the habits of the international set, James had great skills as a prose stylist. His preference for long, twisting sentences was evident throughout his career but particularly in his later novels, such as *The Ambassadors* (1903). All of James's works demonstrate intense attention to detail. He paid special attention to the psychological motivations of his characters and the power dynamics of interpersonal relationships. In this regard, though James's novels fall solidly in the nineteenth century tradition of realism, he is seen as an early forerunner of the psychological novels of the twentieth century.

ADDITIONAL FACTS

1. James published several collections of nonfiction travel writings, including A Little Tour in France *(1884),* English Hours *(1905), and* Italian Hours *(1909).*

2. After decades of living in Europe, James finally decided to become a British citizen in 1915. He died in London the following year.

3. The film company Merchant Ivory Productions made several successful adaptations of James's novels, including The Europeans *(1979),* The Bostonians *(1984), and* The Golden Bowl *(2000).*

∽∾∾

Auguste Rodin

Auguste Rodin (1840–1917) is considered by many to be the last great sculptor of realistic human figures. Best known for such monumental works as *The Thinker*, Rodin emulated the flow and size of Michelangelo's massive unfinished masterpieces.

Rodin received his earliest training at the Petite École in Paris, where he studied drawing between 1854 to 1857. Rejected by the Academy, Rodin was forced to earn his living as a craftsman, ceramic painter, and jeweler during much of his early career. In 1864, he entered the studio of Albert-Ernest Carrier-Belleuse. That same year he completed *The Man with the Broken Nose*, a work that revealed his interest in naturalism, but it was rejected by the official Salon as unfinished. In 1870, he followed Carrier-Belleuse to Brussels, where he eventually formed an independent workshop and struggled to become a recognized sculptor.

In 1875, a trip to Italy exposed Rodin to the sculptures of Michelangelo, Donatello, and classical antiquity. In response, he created *The Age of Bronze* (1875), a work so life-like that some believed it was made from the cast of a real man.

In 1880, Rodin received a commission from the French government for the bronze doors of the Musée des Arts Decoratifs. Inspired by Lorenzo Ghiberti's famous *Gates of Paradise* on the Baptistery in Florence, Rodin cast more than 180 figures for his *Gates of Hell*, left unfinished at the time of his death.

In 1884, the citizens of Calais asked Rodin to create a monument honoring six men who had sacrificed their lives to end the English siege of their city in 1347. The result, *The Burghers of Calais*, was criticized for depicting the men as victims rather than heroes. In 1891, when Rodin received a commission for a portrait of Balzac, he spent seven years collecting daguerreotypes of the man, consulted his tailor, and even studied the topography around his home to get a feel for the author's personality. Like *The Burghers of Calais*, however, the work was deemed too unconventional. Rodin responded by proclaiming, "My principle is to imitate not only form, but life." Despite his critics, Rodin continued to receive important commissions from the French government.

By 1895, Rodin had bought the Villa des Brillants, where he lived as a European celebrity and received honorary degrees from foreign universities. In 1908, he moved into the Hôtel Biron in Paris, a building that was designated as the future Musée Rodin in 1916, a year before the artist's death. Converted into a museum in 1919, it continues to house the largest collection of Rodin's work in the world.

ADDITIONAL FACT

1. German poet Rainer Maria Rilke served as Rodin's secretary from 1905 to 1906 and later wrote a book about him.

Batteries

Batteries are essentially storehouses for electrochemicals, substances that react with each other to produce electrons, tiny negatively charged subatomic particles. The flow of electrons from one source to another creates the electrical currents that power our lamps, televisions, cars, cameras, satellites, and computers. Electrons flow through conductive paths called circuits. The wires in your house are examples of circuits.

Most batteries have four parts: a negatively charged anode, a positively charged cathode, electrochemicals, and electrolytes. The reaction of electrochemicals pushes electrons to one side of the battery, creating the anode (usually marked with a minus sign). The lack of electrons on the other side of the battery creates the cathode (usually marked with a positive sign). Normally, the electrons would flow straight from the anode to the cathode to balance out

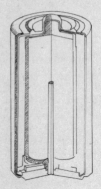

the charge, but electrolytes in the middle of the battery act like a blockade. They prevent electrons from flowing from one side to another. Instead, the electrons must travel through a circuit connecting the anode and the cathode.

If the anode and the cathode are connected to each other directly, the electrochemicals will produce electrons as fast as possible, and the battery will lose its charge quickly. But most batteries are connected to an electrical load—a lamp, a TV, a radio—which allows the electrons to flow gradually. However, eventually the electrochemicals will stop producing electrons. In rechargeable batteries, an outside power source reverses the flow of electrons, causing the electrochemicals to work in reverse and restoring the balance of electrons in the anode and the cathode. This is what happens to the battery in your cell phone when you plug it into the charger at night.

ADDITIONAL FACTS

1. There is evidence that there may have been primitive batteries in Baghdad as early as 250 BC.

2. The first modern battery was invented by Alessandro Volta in 1800. The words voltage and volt are derived from his name.

3. A new type of battery called power paper is currently being perfected. It is a thin, flexible battery in the form of ink cells that can be printed on most surfaces and produce power.

4. Worldwide, the battery industry generates forty-eight billion dollars in sales each year.

⌒∞⌒

Robert and Clara Schumann

Robert Schumann's (1810–1856) life was marked by his creative genius and also by the suffering that accompanied his mental instability. Married to Clara Wieck Schumann (1819–1896), herself a famous pianist, he composed expressive songs and chamber music in between bouts of illness, insanity, and incarceration in mental institutions.

Robert and Clara met when she was nine years old and he was studying piano with her father, Friedrich Wieck, in Leipzig. Robert had given up a career in law to pursue music, and at the time he was editing the *New Journal of Music*, a German magazine that attacked "musical philistines" and championed Berlioz, Chopin, and later, Brahms.

In 1840, Robert and Clara were married against her father's wishes. Wieck doubted Robert's stability as the young man had suffered frequent mental breakdowns—probably a result of syphilis—and had attempted suicide in 1833. In the first year of their marriage, Robert composed 140 lieder, or romantic songs, in honor of their love. Clara was a virtuoso concert pianist in her own right, and she trained some of the era's best soloists. She also wrote several pieces of her own.

But their marriage soon became tense and trying. At Clara's urging, Robert wrote two symphonies in 1841—the first highly acclaimed and the second not so well-received. Clara also encouraged Robert to become a conductor, but he had little talent and often got lost in the score while standing before an orchestra. To make matters worse, his breakdowns were becoming more frequent. When he was invited by his friend Felix Mendelssohn to teach at the newly formed Leipzig Conservatory, he performed terribly—his lectures were vague and incomprehensible—and he had to quit.

In 1844, Clara accompanied Robert on an extended European tour where he had a crippling breakdown that convinced them to move to Düsseldorf for five years. Between 1853 and 1855, Robert started going quietly insane, hearing voices in his head and sitting alone at cafés at night, whistling to himself in the corner. In 1854 he tried to kill himself by jumping in the Rhine and was committed to an asylum, where he died two years later.

ADDITIONAL FACTS

1. *One legend is that Robert Schumann had to stop playing piano as a young man because he paralyzed one of his fingers, supposedly by using a finger-strengthening device. It is more likely that the paralysis was the result of the mercury used to treat syphilis.*

2. *Robert Schumann created two characters to express the two sides of his nature: Eusebius (contemplative, dreamy) and Florestan (impetuous, lively).*

Causation

A man throws a brick at a window, and the window breaks. The brick *caused* the window to break. We think of the world in terms of things causing other things to happen. But what does it truly mean for one thing to cause another to happen?

One answer is to say: X causes Y when events like X are usually followed by events like Y. This is called a regularity theory of causation. However, this theory is flawed. Every day, bakers wake up before the sun rises in order to bake bread. But bakers getting out of bed do not cause the sun to rise. The fact that events of a certain kind often follow each other does not mean they cause each other.

Another theory: X causes Y when if X did not happen, Y would not happen. This is called a counterfactual theory of causation, and it is also flawed. Imagine a man throws a brick at a window, and a second later you throw a brick at the same window. If the man's brick hits the window first, his brick causes the window to shatter. But even if he never threw a brick, the window would still have shattered, because of your brick.

As you can see, it is very hard to say what causation is. This has led some philosophers to deny that there are causes in the world at all.

ADDITIONAL FACTS

1. *"Pre-established harmony" is the view that when God created the world, he created things so that they would change their own states in such a way that it would appear as though they were causally interacting. Gottfried Wilhelm Leibniz is the most famous philosopher to endorse pre-established harmony.*

2. *"Occasionalists" disagree with Leibniz and claim that God is the only cause in the world; things created by God don't even have the ability to influence themselves. The laws of nature are just the laws God has freely chosen to obey in changing the world. The most famous Occasionalist was Nicolas de Malebranche (1638–1715).*

Five Pillars

The Five Pillars of Islam are the five rites that every Muslim must perform.

The first is Shahadah, or faith in God. The creed of Islam is that, "There is no god but Allah and Muhammad is His prophet." This is the foundation of Islam, and it is believed that the only true evil in the world is disagreement with this statement.

The second Pillar is Salah, or daily prayer. Muslims are required to pray five times per day: at sunrise, midday, midafternoon, sunset, and night. They must ritually wash themselves first, including their hands, heads, feet, and ankles. Then they pray while facing toward Mecca. Although praying can occur anywhere, men often congregate in mosques to do so. Women, on the other hand, are either barred from mosques or forced to use a segregated space. On Fridays, men are required to gather at the mosque to hear the imam give a sermon. The prayers are memorized and must be spoken in Arabic.

The third Pillar is Zakat, or alms giving. In exchange for a later reward, Muslims are required to give a portion of their income to charity in order to further strengthen the religion or help the poor. This typically is 2.5 percent of their income, but some Muslims voluntarily give more to gain additional divine praise.

The fourth Pillar is Siyyam [saum], or fasting. During Ramadan, the ninth month of Islam's lunar calendar, Muslims are forbidden to eat, drink, smoke, or have sex between sunrise and sunset. This was the month during which Muhammad had his first revelation. During the month, Muslims pray and read the Quran more often than usual.

The fifth and final Pillar is Hajj, or pilgrimage to Mecca. Each Muslim is required to go to Mecca once in his or her lifetime. When Muslims make the pilgrimage, they wear simple clothing, thereby eliminating any indication of class or culture. This pilgrimage symbolizes Muhammad's return to Mecca after defeating the city and destroying the idol temple Kaaba. Today, the Kaaba is the center of the Hajj ceremony.

ADDITIONAL FACTS

1. *Muslims living in non-Muslim cultures often find these practices difficult to comply with, especially the Salah, which requires stopping five times a day (twice during the work day) to pray.*

2. *These requirements have the effect of constantly forcing Muslims to reconfirm their faith through small practices. Not only does this remind them of their commitment to God, but it also helps them to identify themselves as Muslims.*

3. *There are some exemptions to these rules. For instance, people without proper means do not have to participate in Zakat or the Hajj. And people who are sick, young, elderly, or pregnant do not have to participate in the Siyyam.*

Commodore Matthew Perry and Japan

When Commodore Matthew Perry's (1794–1858) squadron of four warships dropped anchor in Tokyo Bay in 1853, he found a mysterious land almost beyond his comprehension. The Japan encountered by Perry's American expedition had forcibly secluded itself from the outside world. While Europe and the United States industrialized rapidly throughout the early nineteenth century, Japan remained an island apart, for Westerners, an unexplored region of the world. Ruled by a shogun and a feudal system of samurai warriors, the Japanese allowed only limited contact with foreigners before Perry arrived.

President Millard Fillmore, eager to expand the reach of American commerce, had dispatched Perry to Japan to intimidate the shogun into allowing trade with the United States. Faced with the long guns of the American warships, the shogun had little choice. The treaty was signed, and similar agreements with other Western powers soon followed.

Despite the shogun's initial reluctance, Japan took on modernization with zeal. Within fifty years, the medieval island had transformed itself into a major industrial power. In an unprecedented leap forward, Japan caught up with and eventually surpassed many major Western powers in military might and economic firepower. By the early twentieth century, Japan was able to fight—and win—a war against a major European power, the Russian empire.

Perry was a veteran of the War of 1812, and in his long naval career he battled pirates and slave traders before completing the mission that made him famous. His legacy remains controversial. Perry's expedition triggered a chain of events that turned Japan into one of the most powerful and prosperous nations in the world, but many Japanese resent the humiliating way the West forced Japan to change its way of life.

ADDITIONAL FACTS

1. *Perry was from Newport, Rhode Island. Every year the city celebrates his voyage with a Black Ships Festival, after the name the Japanese used to describe the American ships.*

2. *The American flag from Perry's expedition was saved and flown over the USS Missouri when Japan surrendered aboard the battleship at the end of World War II.*

3. *Perry's older brother, Oliver Hazard Perry, was also a naval hero who commanded a warship in the War of 1812 against the British. He is famous for exclaiming after a victory, "We have met the enemy and they are ours."*

The Waste Land

T. S. Eliot's *The Waste Land* (1922) is the great nightmare landmark of twentieth-century poetry—a single work that encapsulates all the fear, alienation, and disillusionment that arose in the West after World War I. Full of allusions to Buddhist and Hindu myth, Ovid, the Bible, St. Augustine, Arthurian legend, Dante, Shakespeare, and a host of other sources, it represents a fascinating intersection of ancient belief and ritual with the existential crises of the modern world.

Like many works of the modernist period, *The Waste Land* is largely a response to World War I. The pointless loss of millions of lives left Europe reeling, as did the awareness that much of this brutality had been wreaked by manmade technology and machinery. To many, the world had suddenly become inhuman and spiritually barren, with civilization seemingly collapsing in on itself.

In *The Waste Land*, Eliot asked how redemption and renewal can be found in a landscape of such desolation. From its opening lines, the poem is filled with images of drought and sterility, countered by attempts by both nature and humankind to generate rebirth:

> *April is the cruelest month, breeding*
> *Lilacs out of the dead land, mixing*
> *Memory and desire, stirring*
> *Dull roots with spring rain.*

The poem's narration jumps abruptly between different voices, disorienting the reader as if he or she has been dropped into a crowd of strangers or marooned in an unfamiliar place. Though these ominous voices are often aimed directly at the reader, the speakers' identities remain unknown:

> *I will show you something different from either*
> *Your shadow at morning striding behind you*
> *Or your shadow at evening rising to meet you;*
> *I will show you fear in a handful of dust.*

The Waste Land draws heavily from Arthurian legend and its references to the Fisher King, a once-powerful leader who has been wounded or disabled, leaving his domain a barren wasteland. Only when the knight Perceval completes a series of tasks can the Fisher King be healed and his kingdom regenerated. Eliot spends much of *The Waste Land* trying to discern how the modern world can find similar renewal. Ultimately, a glimmer of hope returns, seemingly at random, but it is a fragile hope at best—one to which the poem's final speaker, like all of humankind, can cling only with a sense of resignation.

The Thinker

Auguste Rodin's monumental sculpture *The Thinker* (1880) is one of the best known works of art in the world. It has become an icon of the genius-creator or anyone lost in thought.

The figure was designed for the *Gates of Hell*, the portal commissioned by the French government in 1880 for the new Musée des Arts Decoratifs. It was supposed to represent Dante, the medieval Italian poet whose *Divine Comedy* served as the source for the entire project.

The original sculpture was only twenty-seven inches tall. Rodin used a muscular man of about forty for his model—his own age at the time he commenced the *Gates*. *The Thinker* rests his chin on the back of his open right hand. His shoulders have literally sunken beneath the weight of his thoughts. His body is tense, as is evident from the fact that his feet are gripping the base. Since the figure was destined for the exact center of the upper tier of the portals, he is pitched forward, with his head, hands, and knees projecting beyond his feet.

In 1902, a much larger (seventy-nine-inch tall), free-standing version of the sculpture was cast by Henri Lebossé under Rodin's supervision for the Louisiana Purchase Exposition in Saint Louis, Missouri. Rodin, however, rejected the copy. Another cast was exhibited to mixed reviews at the Salon of 1904. The installation of the statue in a public site finally took place in April 1906. During a political crisis several years later, the statue was adopted as a Socialist symbol. It was consequently moved to the garden of the Musée Rodin in 1922 on the pretext that it was an obstacle during public ceremonies. Today, many casts of *The Thinker* can be seen all over the world, nearly all of them, like the original, located out of doors.

ADDITIONAL FACTS

1. *In creating* The Thinker, *Rodin clearly had Michelangelo in mind, especially his* Moses *in S. Pietro in Vincoli (Rome) and* Lorenzo de' Medici *in S. Lorenzo (Florence).*

2. *A cast of* The Thinker *was placed on Rodin's tomb in Meudon.*

Friction

Friction is the force that opposes a moving object when the surface of the object rubs against another. For example, when you roll a ball on the grass, it is friction that causes the ball to slow down and stop.

According to Sir Issac Newton's first law of motion, an object in motion stays in motion unless acted upon by an outside force. If you were to throw a ball in the vacuum of space, the ball would keep moving forever because there is no friction in a vacuum. But on earth, there is no such thing as a frictionless surface. There is always something to get in the way. Even if you throw a ball into the air, the air will rub against the ball, creating heat and slowing the ball down.

Friction is caused by very complex molecular interactions on the surface of objects. In general, rough surfaces cause more friction—for example, sandpaper on jagged wood. Smooth surfaces minimize friction, like a hockey puck gliding across ice. But there are exceptions to this rule. If you make two metal surfaces extremely flat and smooth, their surfaces will actually fuse together in what is called a cold weld. In this case, the frictional resistance to motion is actually quite great.

There are many types of friction, but on a daily basis, we regularly encounter static friction and kinetic friction. Static friction is the friction of two objects that are not moving in relation to each other, like when a couch is simply resting on the ground. Kinetic friction is the friction of two objects that are in a relative motion and rubbing against each other, for example someone pushing a couch across the floor. In general, static friction is greater than kinetic friction. This explains why when you are moving furniture, the initial shove always requires more effort than continuing to push the object once it is in motion.

ADDITIONAL FACTS

1. When you rub your hands together, friction causes them to get warm.

2. Lubricants such as oil are substances that reduce the friction between surfaces. The study of lubricants and friction is called tribology.

3. Brakes on cars and bicycles work by magnifying friction.

4. The treads on sneakers increase their friction on the pavement, making it easier for you to push off the ground.

Frédéric Chopin

The collected works of Frédéric Chopin (1810–1849) are required music for any aspiring pianist. His compositions, which lacked the virtuosic bombast of his contemporaries, had no shortage of subtlety, beauty, and taste. In short, Chopin was the beloved composer for the salon, rather than the concert hall, and during his lifetime, no one could surpass him in that role.

Born in 1810 to a French father and a Polish mother outside of Warsaw, Poland, Chopin grew up around the boys of an aristocratic boarding school run by his father. He adopted many of their attitudes, and as a young man gained a reputation for being prim, snobbish, obsessed with style, and rather effeminate. Chopin began composing short pieces called mazurkas and polonaises, both based on Polish folk dances, when he was a teenager, and he became the toast of Warsaw playing them in the drawing rooms of the aristocracy. In 1830, he left Warsaw for Vienna and eventually Paris, where he would make his name.

In Paris, Chopin tried his hand at large public concerts, but his writing style—with delicate, nuanced uses of volume, harmony, and dissonance—didn't go over well. After 1835, he hardly ever performed outside of the salons of the rich and sophisticated, who adored his playing style and his dandy poseur personality.

While in Paris, Chopin made friends with various artists and intellectuals, including his nemesis Franz Liszt. Most important, he became involved in a torrid love affair with the eccentric cross-dressing novelist George Sand. She vacationed with Chopin in Majorca in 1838–1839. While there, Chopin became ill with tuberculosis, but he had enough energy to write his twenty-four *Prèludes*. After they returned to Sand's French country house, Chopin's condition worsened. Tired of her lover's neurotic and sickly ways, Sand left Chopin in 1846.

Chopin died in Paris in 1849, leaving behind one of the most important bodies of piano literature of any composer.

ADDITIONAL FACTS

1. *When Chopin left Warsaw, he took a silver urn full of Polish soil. He would never return to his homeland, but the urn was buried with him in a staunch expression of nationalism.*

2. *Nationalism was a big theme in Chopin's career, and he expressed his love of his homeland mostly through the music he wrote. His use of Polish folk and court dances, and in particular his* Military Polonaise No. 3 in A Major, *which commemorates a failed Polish uprising against the Czar in 1831, demonstrates his devotion to Poland.*

3. *Chopin wrote a cello concerto and a handful of short pieces for other instruments, but everything else he wrote—dozens of nocturnes, scherzos, ballades, preludes, mazurkas, polonaises, and etudes—was all for solo piano.*

Problem of Evil

Consider the following four claims:

God is all powerful. (Anything possible is within his power.)

God is all knowing.

God is perfectly good.

There is evil in the world.

Traditionally, theists—people who believe in God—have accepted these four claims, but many philosophers have argued that they are incompatible. If God is all powerful, he could have made a world without evil. And since a world without evil is better than a world with evil, how could a perfectly benevolent God knowingly create a world in which there is evil?

One solution is to deny that God bears responsibility for the evil in the world. Supporters of this view argue God created the world, but mankind created the evil. Mankind has free will, and the only way God could have prevented evil is by not giving us free will. But, the argument goes, a world in which we do not have free will would be even worse than the actual world. Therefore, God made the best possible choice: He created mankind with free will, which led to there being evil.

Of course, this theory does not resolve the problem of natural evil—hurricanes, earthquakes, and tsunamis that cause death and suffering. God could have created a natural world with fewer disasters that kill innocent people. So why didn't he?

Gottfried Willhelm Leibniz (1646–1716) responded to this question by famously claiming that this is the best of all possible worlds. Admittedly, there are features of this world that are bad. For instance, the existence of deadly hurricanes. However, argued Leibniz, a world without deadly hurricanes would be worse than this world. For instance, it would lack the elegant natural laws that govern the behavior of weather.

ADDITIONAL FACTS

1. The problem of reconciling God's perfect goodness with the evil in the world is called theodicy.

2. Some philosophers believe that there is no best possible world for God to choose and that he chooses among various lesser alternatives. They argue that if God must choose the best world, this conflicts with his freedom of choice.

Sharia

In Islam, Sharia, or the law, is of fundamental importance, inextricably connected to the practice of the faith.

The scholar Seyyed Hossein Nasr proposes the following analogy. Imagine a great circle. The entire circumference of the circle is the Sharia. It is at the circumference that each Muslim must begin his or her journey along the radius of the circle—which is Tariqat, or the Path—to the center of the circle—which is Haqiqa, or the Truth. Although a Muslim may still be considered a Muslim without obeying the Sharia, he or she cannot achieve Haqiqa without beginning there.

There are no realms of society that fall outside Sharia. It can be divided into two areas: ibadat, or the law pertaining to worship, and muamalat, the law pertaining to transactions. Muamalat covers all social, political, and economic relationships.

The five categories of rules in Sharia are:

> **REQUIRED:** e.g., daily prayers
> **SUGGESTED:** e.g., charity
> **INDIFFERENT:** e.g., the vegetables in one's diet
> **REPREHENSIBLE:** e.g., divorce
> **FORBIDDEN:** e.g., murder, eating pork, and consuming alcohol

As time passed, various legal scholars diverged from each other, and within Sunni Islam four individual schools of thought emerged. Still, for the most part, and for all of the basic rites of Islam, all five schools—four Sunni, one Shiite—agree.

An important distinction between Shiites and Sunnis revolves around the concept of ijtihad, or the basic sources of Sharia. Sunnis believe that since the tenth century, the ijtihad texts have been closed to reinterpretation. Shiites, however, believe it is their duty to periodically reinvestigate the ijtihad to see if any laws should be adapted to modernity.

ADDITIONAL FACTS

1. *Sharia is believed to be God's immutable law, and while Shiites believe in interpretation, they are careful not to create new laws.*

2. *Muslims are not allowed to eat pork or any meat that wasn't killed in the name of God. They are also forbidden to eat monkeys, dogs, cats, and most carnivores.*

John Brown

John Brown (1800–1859) was a militant antislavery activist executed in 1859 by the state of Virginia for attempting to spark a slave rebellion. In military terms, Brown was a complete failure, but as a social movement his uprising illustrated the commitment of abolitionists to end slavery. With a handful of followers Brown seized a federal armory in Harper's Ferry, Virginia, in the naive belief that slaves in the area would flee their masters and join him. The revolt never materialized, and he was captured within days and hanged shortly thereafter.

Brown belonged to the violent fringe of the abolitionist movement, which had grown steadily since the early 1800s. By 1859, most Northerners opposed slavery, but few embraced Brown's extreme tactics. Many moderate Northerners, including Abraham Lincoln, hoped to end the spread of slavery but stopped short of demanding immediate abolition. Radicals like Brown and William Lloyd Garrison, a leading abolitionist writer from Boston, wanted immediate abolition of what they saw as an unacceptable moral evil. Garrison, attacking the moderates, sarcastically suggested they "tell a man whose house is on fire to give a moderate alarm."

Southerners, meanwhile, regarded both camps of abolitionists as Northern liberal busybodies. Slavery, according to many Southerners, was ordained by the Bible and, moreover, crucial to the agrarian economy of the South. John C. Calhoun, an eminent South Carolina politician who served in the Senate and as vice president, called slavery not evil at all but "a positive good." In the South, the news of Brown's raid provoked widespread panic and disbelief. Brown's revolt failed militarily, but politically he was successful. Terrified, many Southerners concluded that separating from the North was the only way to preserve slavery. When Abraham Lincoln won the 1860 election with the support of Northern abolitionists, the Southern states seceded, sparking the Civil War that eventually did end slavery.

Brown's antislavery crusade remains controversial to this day. By the modern definition, Brown was unquestionably a terrorist. In a skirmish in Kansas a few years before Harper's Ferry, Brown and his sons used broadswords to hack a family that supported slavery to death. Yet Brown's terrorism aided what nearly everyone today regards as a just cause.

ADDITIONAL FACTS

1. *Brown was raised in Connecticut and Ohio by a strict Christian father, and he explicitly based his opposition to slavery on religion. On the gallows in Virginia, Brown said, "I, John Brown, am now quite certain that the crimes of this guilty land will never be purged away but with blood. I had, as I now think, vainly flattered myself that without very much bloodshed it might be done."*

2. *During the Civil War, Union soldiers sang a marching song called "John Brown's Body." A Boston abolitionist, Julia Ward Howe, heard the song and composed new lyrics. Her song, "The Battle Hymn of the Republic," remains one of America's most beloved patriotic songs.*

Marcel Proust

French novelist Marcel Proust (1871–1922) is remembered almost entirely for just one work, but that one work has been enough to cement his reputation. His mammoth novel *À la Recherche du Temps Perdu*—translated into English as either *In Search of Lost Time* or *Remembrance of Things Past*—remains one of the great literary works of the twentieth century.

Proust benefited from a wealthy upbringing in Paris and received a thorough education in both literature and law. He moved in heady social circles from a young age, active in the *belle époque* salons of the Parisian elite. After publishing his first short story collection in 1896, Proust worked on an autobiographical novel, *Jean Santeuil*, that would serve as the foundation for his later masterpiece.

Amid deteriorating health and lingering grief over the death of his parents, Proust began work on *À la Recherche* in 1909. The novel is truly gigantic, more than 3,000 pages long and featuring a cast of more than 2,000 characters. Published in seven volumes from 1913 to 1927, it was unlike any novel the world had ever seen; indeed, several publishers rejected its first installments, unsure what to make of it.

À la Recherche is essentially autobiographical, following the development of a young man as he searches for what has made him who he is, recaptures and relives memories from his youth, and ultimately prepares to write a novel. It is as much a philosophical and psychological work as a literary one: Along the way, the narrator muses on love, identity, sexual ambiguity, aesthetics, art, and other topics. Although most people see the narrator as a stand-in for Proust, he leaves the question of whether the reader should indeed view the author and narrator as one and the same ambiguous.

As its title indicates, the novel is deeply concerned with time and memory. Proust conceives of time as a flowing, amorphous whole rather than an ordered, linear progression of moments. Often, previously lost memories come rushing back to the narrator as the result of some sensory cue. In one famous passage, the narrator vividly remembers experiences from his childhood upon tasting a madeleine, which he used to eat dipped in tea. This experimentation lived on long after Proust's death, as countless other modernist authors built on his explorations of memory and time in their own landmark works.

ADDITIONAL FACTS

1. *Proust published the first volume of À la Recherche at his own expense, using money he inherited from his parents.*

2. *During the infamous Dreyfus affair of 1897–1899, Proust spent considerable time and money organizing petitions on behalf of French-Jewish army officer Alfred Dreyfus, who had been unjustly imprisoned for treason.*

Claude Monet

Claude Monet (1840–1926) was one of the central figures of the impressionist movement. He is known for his many paintings of water lilies in his garden at Giverny, France.

Born in Paris, Monet moved at the age of five to Le Havre on the Normandy Coast. His early exposure to nature and the sea profoundly influenced his artistic career. Monet soon acquired something of a local reputation for caricature, attracting the attention of the plein-air landscape painter, Eugéne Bodin. In 1862, after two years of military service in Algeria, Monet received parental permission to pursue a career as a painter and moved to Paris. There he studied in the studio of Charles Gleyre, where he met future impressionists Auguste Renoir and Alfred Sisley, as well as the Dutch landscape painter Johann Barthold.

In 1865, 1866, and 1868, Monet exhibited works at the official Salon. By the late 1860s, however, he was exploring new techniques that would eventually lead to impressionism. In 1869, for example, he and Renoir painted together at La Grenouillère, a popular boating spot. As they worked side by side, both artists used fragmented brushwork to capture the ephemeral quality of light and color in the reflection of the water.

In 1870, Monet married his mistress Camille Doncieux and moved to London in order to escape the Franco-Prussian War. During the nine months he spent there, he made numerous paintings of the River Thames and met his future dealer, Paul Durand-Ruel. In 1872, Monet returned to Argenteuil, near Paris, where he lived for the next six years. Two years later, he was a major force behind the first impressionist show, to which he submitted the painting *Impression: Sunrise* that gave the movement its name.

In 1883, Monet moved to Giverny, northwest of Paris, where he designed his own gardens, made famous by the many paintings he did of them in the last twenty-five years of his life.

Monet continued to travel extensively from Giverny—to London, Venice, and Rouen. In the 1890s Monet began working on several series of paintings that depicted an identical subject—a haystack, a cathedral, a view of poplars—as it appeared at different times of day. While engaged in a series, Monet would work on up to eight paintings at a time, devoting less than one hour to each.

In the years since his death, Monet's influence and popularity have increased enormously. In 2004, one of his paintings of the Parliament Houses in London sold for more than $20 million. Thousands of tourists flock annually to his house and gardens at Giverny. Monet's works hang in major museums throughout the world, most notably at the Orangerie and the Musée Marmottan in Paris.

ADDITIONAL FACT

1. Monet once noted that he wished he had been born blind, then suddenly gotten sight so that he could see without preconceived notions.

The Sun and Nuclear Fusion

The sun does not burn the way that wood burns in a fire. Instead, it acts like a giant nuclear reactor. The energy from the sun comes from nuclear fusion—the process of combining two small atomic nuclei into one larger nucleus. The sun mostly fuses hydrogen atoms into helium atoms to create energy. It also fuses helium into beryllium, and beryllium into lithium.

Because of the sun's immense mass and gravity, the core of the sun is an environment of intense pressure and heat. These qualities are what allow fusion to take place. Under normal circumstances, the protons in the nucleus of hydrogen atoms repel each other because they are all positively charged. But the pressure at the center of the sun squeezes them together, overcoming the electromagnetic force. When the two hydrogen atoms combine into helium, a tiny amount of the hydrogen atoms' mass is converted into a large amount of energy. The conversion follows Einstein's famous formula $E=mc^2$. The energy released is equal to the mass lost times the speed of light squared. Because fusion generates such fantastic amounts of energy from such small quantities of fuel, scientists have been trying for decades to create controlled nuclear fusion reactions on earth. But cold fusion still remains more science fiction than fact.

Over the past 4.5 billion years, the sun has used up about half of its hydrogen supply. When it runs out of hydrogen, the sun's core will contract due to gravity, heating up and expanding its outer layers. The sun will grow into a red giant, enveloping and vaporizing the earth.

ADDITIONAL FACTS

1. The sun converts about 600 million tons of hydrogen nuclei into helium each second.

2. In the process, the sun loses roughly four million tons of its mass, which is all converted into energy.

3. Energy from the sun is carried to earth in the form of photons. Each photon must interact with many gas molecules on its way from the sun's core to its surface. This takes approximately 100,000 to 200,000 years.

4. It takes about eight minutes for a photon to reach earth from the surface of the sun.

Romantic-Era Virtuosos:
Frantz Liszt and Niccol Paganini

The romantic sense of excess, decadence, and genius-worship is illustrated vividly in the careers of two early-romantic virtuosos, Niccol Paganini (1782–1840) and Franz Liszt (1811–1886).

Paganini, a gaunt-looking Italian master violinist, was so good at playing the violin—particularly long, complicated technical passages—that he was often accused of having made a pact with the devil in return for his marvelous skills. Paganini's fame began at a Paris recital in 1828, where he charmed the women in the audience and wowed the critics. However, Paganini died in Nice without, however, leaving a repertoire of great compositions. Like other virtuosos, most of his work was meant to showcase his skills with breakneck-paced fast solo sections and minimal, if any, accompaniment. He wrote six violin concertos, only two of which are regularly played.

Franz Liszt
1886

When Franz Liszt, a tremendously talented Hungarian pianist, got to Paris in 1824, he was so impressed with Paganini's playing that he vowed to become "the Paganini of the piano," locking himself up for two years to practice his technique. When Liszt finally achieved his goal and began performing, it became clear he was a born showman. He would often fake hysterical fits at the end of his performances to heighten the notion that he was completely lost in the transcendental experience of the music. Liszt's act worked on the ladies. Liszt had many lovers among the swooning upper-crust of Paris, including the Countess Marie d'Agoult and the Russian princess Caroline de Sayn-Wittgenstein, whom he later married, and who converted him to quiet Catholic piety.

These two composers and soloists, more than anything, shifted the focus of romantic music to performance, rather than composition, and in doing so pulled it further away from the classical aesthetic than ever.

ADDITIONAL FACTS

1. Paganini's most famous trick was to play so furiously that he broke three of his strings, but still continued playing using only one.

2. When Paganini was a boy, he mutilated his hands to increase the reach of his fingers.

3. Later in life, Liszt confessed his philandering sins to the pope himself, who cut the composer off halfway through his confession and said, "Enough, Liszt. Tell your sins to your piano."

Freedom of the Will

In order to be morally responsible for some action, you must take that action freely. For example, if you see someone drowning in a lake, but you are tied to a stake in the ground and cannot free yourself, then you are not morally to blame for not rescuing the drowning swimmer. Likewise, if you are somehow brainwashed and ordered to commit a crime, you are arguably not responsible for committing the crime, because your freedom was impaired.

According to some scientific theories, the world is deterministic. Given the way the world has been in the past and the physical laws that govern it, there is only one way the future can be. Consider that this applies to your actions as well. At the moment just before you perform some action, given the way the world has been in the past and given the physical laws of the universe, there is only one possible outcome. Right now it is physically determined what you will do at every moment in the future.

Does determinism of this sort erase moral responsibility? If you commit some morally bad action, could you plead that the physical laws and past history of the universe were so configured that there was no alternative?

If you believe that free will and determinism are incompatible, you must deny determinism or deny moral responsibility. If you deny determinism, you have to believe that there is genuine causal indeterminism in the world, introduced by free agents like us; the future history of the world is left indeterminate by the natural laws, and we determine it through our actions. If you deny moral responsibility, you must hold that the world is deterministic and that therefore we lack free will.

ADDITIONAL FACTS

1. *Philosophers who think that free will and determinism are compatible are called compatibilists. Philosophers who deny it are called incompatibilists.*

2. *Gottfried Wilhelm Leibniz was a famous compatibilist; he believed that all of our actions are causally determined, but that we are nevertheless free.*

Shiites and Sunnis

The major split in Islam, between Shiite Islam and Sunni Islam occurred in the wake of Muhammad's death. When Islam's prophet passed away at the age of sixty-three in 632 CE, he left no clear successor. The dispute over who—Ali or Abu Bakr—should take Muhammad's place, led to the split.

Shiites claim that Muhammad gave a speech at Ghadir al-Khumm in which he frequently referenced and praised Ali, his cousin and son-in-law. They interpret Muhammad's praise as calling for Ali to lead all of Islam. Thus, Shiites believe that Ali was the first leader, or imam of Islam. Shiites believe that they alone have remained faithful to Muhammad's initial teachings and that the Sunnis have strayed. They also claim that all future imams must be descendents of Muhammad, through his son Ali and Ali's wife, Fatima.

Sunnis, on the other hand, claim that while Muhammad did speak and praise Ali at Gadir Khorn, this did not mean that Ali was to become Islam's next leader. Instead, after some infighting, they believe that Abu Bakr emerged as the first caliph. Abu Bakr was a close confidant of Muhammad, as well as Muhammad's father-in-law. When Muhammad initially fled Mecca for Medina, Abu Bakr was his only companion. Additionally, when Muhammad was absent, Abu Bakr sometimes led prayers, which lead Sunnis to believe he was favored as a successor by Muhammad.

As the two sects have grown apart over the centuries, the schism between them has widened. Although the split essentially began as a political issue between two groups with one belief system, this is no longer the case. Having been separated for so long, their sets of beliefs, laws, and practices have also changed in various ways. A major source of these differences arises from Hadith, or oral traditions that record and narrate the teachings of the prophet and his companions. Shiites accept only Hadith as authentic when it can be traced back to Muhammad and Ali, and not those which arise from other sources. Thus, Shiites disregard many traditions that Sunnis treasure as sacred.

ADDITIONAL FACTS

1. *Although Sunnis do not believe that Ali was the first caliph, they do believe he was the fourth of the Four Righteously Guided Caliphs, succeeding Abu Bakr, Umar, and Uthman.*

2. *Today, Sunni Islam is the largest sect, comprising nearly 90 percent of Islam, with Shiite making up the second largest sect at about 9 percent. However, these statistics are suspect because Shiites are oppressed in many areas, and it is not believed that these numbers fully reflect their total population.*

3. *The Hajj, or holy pilgrimage to Mecca, is one of the few events that cause the normally separate populations of Sunnis and Shiites to congregate together. During the Hajj, however, all Muslims wear the plain clothing of a pilgrim, thus hiding ethnic and social differences.*

Abraham Lincoln

Acclaimed as the greatest president in American history, Abraham Lincoln (1809–1865) lead the nation through the Civil War that preserved the Union and resulted in the end of slavery. Born in Kentucky, Lincoln was elected to the White House from Illinois in 1860. He was tragically assassinated at a theater by a crazed Southern sympathizer in 1865, only a few days after the Confederate Army under General Robert E. Lee surrendered at Appomattox Courthouse. Under Lincoln's leadership, the United States won the war, but Lincoln did not live to see the peace.

Lincoln was a gangly, unattractive man with a penchant for melancholy. Modern scholarship has suggested that he may have suffered from depression. Before becoming president, Lincoln's political experience amounted to a few local offices, one term in Congress in 1847–49, and a failed run for the Senate in 1855.

But despite his less than auspicious start, Lincoln turned out to be one of the most determined and certainly the most eloquent men ever to win the presidency. Lincoln believed preserving the Union was necessary at all costs. Without the United States, Lincoln felt, the republican ideals it embodied would "perish from the earth." Long before the days of presidential speechwriters, Lincoln crafted moving speeches that convinced Americans to endure the hardships of the war. He was reelected to the White House in 1864 against a candidate who promised to end the war, a victory that reflected Lincoln's ability to keep Americans united around the cause of the Union despite terrible losses.

Lincoln had little military experience himself, but he did not hesitate to overrule his generals. Only with General Ulysses S. Grant did Lincoln find a leader he trusted to lead the Union effort, despite rumors that Grant was an alcoholic. "Tell me the brand of whiskey that Grant drinks," Lincoln reportedly quipped. "I would like to send a barrel of it to my other generals."

Before Lincoln's death, he planned to let the Southern states rejoin the Union on generous terms, without punishing the leaders of the rebellion. His assassination left President Andrew Johnson in charge. Lincoln "would have proven the best friend the South could have had," Grant wrote. "I knew his goodness of heart, his generosity, his yielding disposition, his desire to have everybody happy, and above all his desire to see all the people of the United States enter again upon the full privileges of citizenship with equality among all."

ADDITIONAL FACT

1. *Lincoln's assassin was John Wilkes Booth, a well-known Shakespearean actor and a distant relative of current British prime minister Tony Blair. After the shooting, Booth fled to Maryland, where he was cornered by Union soldiers and killed after refusing to surrender.*

Invisible Man

One of the rarest birds in literature is the novel that manages
to combine penetrating social criticism with groundbreaking
literary technique. Ralph Ellison's *Invisible Man* (1952)
delivers on both counts. It is an unsettling investigation
of twentieth-century African-American life and also an
innovative melding of the English language and the rhythms of jazz music. It
accomplished the uncommon feat of shocking white and black readers equally:
Whites were shaken by the narrator's anger, while blacks were stung by Ellison's
readiness to criticize blacks as much as he had whites. Not surprisingly, *Invisible
Man* became a controversial bestseller and won the National Book Award.

Born in Oklahoma in 1914, Ellison aspired to become a jazz musician, attending the Tuskegee
Institute in Alabama for formal training. After leaving college, though, he took a job with the
Federal Writers' Project, a Great Depression–era government literary initiative. He moved to
New York City in 1936, becoming friends with the poet Langston Hughes, novelist Richard
Wright, and other black luminaries.

The nameless protagonist of *Invisible Man* is a gifted black student from the South. After
enduring public humiliation from a local white group in order to receive a college scholarship,
he finds that the black president of the college is just as insidious and scheming as any overtly
racist white man. The narrator leaves for Harlem, where he becomes involved in a political
organization that prizes his abilities as an orator. But this experience likewise ends in
disillusionment, as the narrator comes under attack from both blacks and whites in the group
who resent his influence and see him as a threat to their own power.

Though stinging in its depiction of white racism, *Invisible Man* is just as brazen in its criticism
of the African-American community. The narrator encounters countless examples of self-
interested blacks who backstab and undermine one another, concerned more with politicking
than with the civil rights cause. Ultimately, the narrator realizes that he is "invisible": Everyone
he meets, blinded by either racism or self-interest, sees him as either a negative stereotype
or a tool to meet their own ends. Frustrated by this denial of his individuality, the narrator
retreats underground, where he writes his life story—the only thing he can do to make his
voice heard.

ADDITIONAL FACTS

1. Invisible Man *was the only novel Ellison wrote. The other works he published were the essay collections*
Shadow and Act *(1964) and* Going to the Territory *(1986).*

2. Several characters in Invisible Man *are modeled on real black political leaders, including Booker T.
Washington and Marcus Garvey.*

⌒∞⌒

Auguste Renoir

One of the most important painters of the impressionist movement, Auguste Renoir (1841–1919) is most famous for his scenes of leisure and his sensual portraits of women and children.

Renoir, the son of a tailor, began his artistic career at the age of thirteen when he took a job decorating fans and painting flowers on porcelain. He improved his skills by making copies at the Louvre Museum and then, in 1861, enrolled in the École des Beaux-Arts. One year later, Renoir entered the studio of the Swiss academic painter, Charles Gleyre, where he met future impressionists Claude Monet, Alfred Sisley, and Frédéric Bazille. Although Renoir contributed several works to the official Salon in the 1860s, he joined the impressionists in their first rebellious exhibition of 1874.

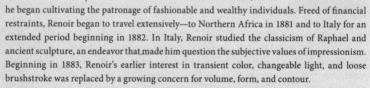

In the following decade, the principles of impressionism had a profound impact on Renoir's style. In *Le Moulin de la Galette* (1876), the composition is arbitrarily cut off, making the painting appear to be a continuation of the world outside it.

Renoir submitted *Le Moulin de la Galette* to the third impressionist exhibition in 1877. By 1878, he had returned to the official Salon, where he began cultivating the patronage of fashionable and wealthy individuals. Freed of financial restraints, Renoir began to travel extensively—to Northern Africa in 1881 and to Italy for an extended period beginning in 1882. In Italy, Renoir studied the classicism of Raphael and ancient sculpture, an endeavor that made him question the subjective values of impressionism. Beginning in 1883, Renoir's earlier interest in transient color, changeable light, and loose brushstroke was replaced by a growing concern for volume, form, and contour.

In 1900, Renoir received the Légion d'Honneur, evidence of his distinguished reputation in official circles. Soon afterward, his health began to decline. Following an attack of rheumatoid arthritis in 1894, Renoir gradually lost control of his limbs. By 1910 he could paint only by binding his brush to his hand. To make matters worse, he was plagued by family problems. In 1915, his son Jean, who later became a famous filmmaker, was seriously wounded in World War I. Soon afterward, Renoir's wife died after visiting her son in the hospital. Renoir continued working despite his hardships. At the age of seventy, he began to experiment with sculpture, instructing his assistant, Richard Guino, to cast the figures that he conceived.

Renoir's intentions as an artist were best summarized by his own words: "The earth as the paradise of the gods: That is what I want to paint."

ADDITIONAL FACTS

1. *In Italy, Renoir discovered and was deeply influenced by the* The Treatise on Painting *by Cennino Cennini, a fifteenth century Florentine artist.*

2. *Georges Charpentier, a fashionable book publisher, introduced Renoir to wealthy socialites from whom he received many commissions for portraits.*

∽∞∾

Rainbows

Rainbows are the result of sunlight bending through raindrops. This bending, called refraction, occurs when light passes through the water in the air.

Water droplets refract light, dispersing it into its component colors, which travel at different frequencies. Although you may have been taught that there are seven colors of the rainbow— red, orange, yellow, green, blue, indigo, and violet—there are actually as many colors as there are raindrops reflecting light in the sky. The rainbow possesses a full spectrum of colors, each observed at a different angle.

Primary rainbows occur between 40 and 42 degrees above the horizon, with the center of the arch directly opposite the sun. At sunset, the angle of sunlight allows an observer on the ground to see a full semicircle, whereas at noon, it is impossible to see a rainbow because the sun is directly overhead. From an airplane, it is possible to see a full circle of a rainbow because there are raindrops above and below the observer.

Secondary rainbows, or double rainbows, occur when light is reflected inside a rainbow twice. The second rainbow is fainter, and because of the double reflection, the colors appear in the reverse order. Secondary rainbows appear about 10 degrees higher in the sky than primary rainbows.

ADDITIONAL FACTS

1. Third and fourth order rainbows have been observed, and thirteenth order rainbows exist in theory.

2. Moonlight is sometimes bright enough to create a rainbow. Lunar rainbows usually appear as a faint white arc.

3. It is physically impossible to walk under a rainbow. They literally exist only in the eyes of the observer.

4. In Greek mythology, Iris, goddess of the rainbow, sent messages from heaven to earth.

Johannes Brahms

One of the last great symphonic masters to work within the conventions of traditional form, Johannes Brahms (1833–1897) was part classicist and part romantic. He was a master of the symphonic language of the nineteenth century, but he also tipped his hat to the masters of old. Brahms's music was suited to his personality—sensitive, conservative, but by no means dry—and his death would mark the death of the romantic era.

Born to a poor family in Hamburg, Germany, Brahms was taught piano at an early age, and when he was twenty, embarked on a European tour with Eduard Remény, a fine young Hungarian violinist. While traveling Brahms met Franz Liszt and Richard Wagner, but his greatest friend and the longtime champion of his music was Robert Schumann. The older composer wrote articles promoting Brahms as a genius in the pages of his *New Journal of Music*, and Brahms became almost a part of the dysfunctional Schumann family. During the last two years of Schumann's life, when his madness was grating on his wife, Clara, Brahms comforted her, and eventually fell madly in love. However, his love was reportedly never consummated.

Brahms was an itinerant conductor and soloist, traveling constantly between European capitals. He wrote his *Piano Concerto No. 1 in D Minor* (1859) for the Schumanns, dedicating its second movement to Clara and evoking Robert's first failed suicide attempt—jumping into the Rhine—in the first. He wrote his first, hugely successful symphony in 1876 and by 1888 had written three more.

Brahms's symphonies, as well as his Hungarian dances and other pieces of absolute—as in, nonprogrammatic, or appealing in only musical terms—orchestral music, are what made him famous. Brahms was a devoted student of Bach's and Palestrina's counterpoint and classical symphonic form, but he never lost his flair for writing lush, romantic-style melodies.

ADDITIONAL FACTS

1. *As a young man, Brahms played piano in Hamburg's seaside brothels, where he developed a lifelong affection for prostitutes.*

2. *Clara Schumann, to whom Brahms once wrote, "I love you more than anything on earth," was Brahms's most trusted critic. He even changed the key of his* Piano Quartet in C-sharp Minor *to C-minor at her suggestion.*

3. *Brahms lost favor with Liszt by falling asleep at one of his concerts.*

Immanuel Kant

"Two things fill the mind with ever-increasing wonder and awe, the more often and the more intensely the mind of thought is drawn to them: the starry heavens above me and the moral law within me."

—*Critique of Practical Reason*

Immanuel Kant (1724–1804) was born in Königsberg, at that time a part of Prussia. He lived his entire life there, never venturing far from the city of his birth. The son of a harness-maker, he rose to become a professor at the University of Königsberg and was eventually recognized as the greatest philosopher in Germany.

By mid-life, Kant had not accomplished anything of note. Then, at the relatively advanced age of fifty-seven, he published his single most famous work, the *Critique of Pure Reason* (1781). In the first critique, as it is known, Kant argued that metaphysics can only be scientific if it describes not the way the world is in itself, but how we experience the world. How the world is in itself, he argued, we can never know. Space and time, for example, are not objective features of the world as it is in itself, but forms of our experience.

In the *Critique of Practical Reason* (1788), or second Critique, Kant argued that there is a universal moral law that applies to everyone and tells us what we ought to do, regardless of what we want. This law reveals to us that we have free will, and it gives us reason to believe that there is a benevolent God, and that there is an afterlife. Of course, the first critique had demonstrated we can never know that we are free, that there is a God, or that there is an afterlife. Thus, in Kant's words, "I had to suspend knowledge, in order to make room for faith."

Kant's other works include the *Critique of Judgment* (1790) and a number of smaller works and essays on moral and political philosophy, religion, aesthetics, history, and natural science. The "critical" system, as he called it, aims to rationally justify natural science, morality, and religion, while putting limits on what human beings can truly be sure of.

ADDITIONAL FACTS

1. Although Kant is best known as a philosopher, he lectured on almost every topic—pedagogy, logic, mathematics, natural science, and geography—and published several significant works in physics and natural science.

2. Allegedly, Kant's habits were so orderly that the citizens of Königsberg could set their watches by his walks.

Sufism

Sufism was a reaction against traditional Islam's heavy emphasis on the words of the Quran. Instead, people who would later be known as Sufi, called for devotion to the spirit of the Holy Book.

Sufis believe that there are two parts of Islam. One is external, such as doing good deeds. The other is internal. Surfis believe that Islam is, at its core, a personal faith. Emphasis is placed on having good intentions, rather than simply good behavior.

The ideal Sufi was Muhammad, who lived a pious and virtuous life. While all Sufis attempt to emulate Muhammad as much as possible, some believe their goal is even higher—to reach the same state of inner peace that allowed Muhammad to receive God's revelations.

The first Sufi orders began after Muhammad's death, when leaders began to tell stories of his life and his everyday interaction with family and friends. These stories inspired others, and the people who told them created a following.

Many of these orders practiced ritual chanting of the Quran, which is still seen today. Others, such as the whirling dervishes, practiced a devotional spinning. Each of these orders is led by a spiritual master, or shaykh. Their varied practices represent the many paths to God, but all orders have a similar goal: to love God without external motivation.

Sufis tell the story of Rabia, an eighth century female slave whose devotion was so strong it inspired her owners to free her. She is said to have told God that if she loves God because she fears hell, then she should burn in hell, and if she loves God because she desires to reach heaven, then she should be denied heaven. Sufis seek a pure communion with the divine.

ADDITIONAL FACTS

1. *The word* Sufi, *comes from* Suf *meaning wool, signifying the simple wool clothes that many Sufis chose to wear.*

2. *Some Sufis believed that Jesus Christ was an excellent example of a Sufi because he preached the gospel of love.*

3. *Sufism often clashed with religious authorities because it deemphasized the text of the Quran as well as many of those who held power. One example of a clash between Sufis and non-Sufis is the story of Hasan al-Hallaj who proclaimed "I am the truth," or perhaps more correctly, "I see the truth." Unfortunately, the word for truth is also a name for God. Hasan al-Hallaj was believed to have said, "I am God," and he was executed for this alleged blasphemy.*

4. *Abd al-Qadir al-Gilani, a founder of one of the largest Sufi orders, was a child in a caravan that was being robbed. The thieves demanded money from all who were present, but ignored the small boy. However, his mother had sewn money into his shirt. He called out to thieves to tell them that there was more money, and, being awed by his honesty, the thieves converted to Islam on the spot.*

Appomattox Court House— Ulysses S. Grant and Robert E. Lee

On the afternoon of April 9, 1865, the commander of the United States Army, Ulysses S. Grant, rode his horse, Cincinnati, to a small farmhouse in the Virginia town of Appomattox Court House. Waiting for him inside, was his rival Robert E. Lee, the commander of the Confederate forces. After four years of fighting, Lee had concluded that his battered army was finished. Surrounded on all sides by the Northerners, the Confederates were trapped. After a courteous handshake, Lee signed an agreement surrendering his rebel army. The war was over.

The Civil War, which erupted in 1861, remains the bloodiest conflict in American history. More than 550,000 soldiers were killed, and hundreds of thousands more wounded. Lee and Grant, the two generals who led the rival armies, came to personify the great heroism and tragedy on both sides of the war.

Grant, the son of a tanner, was born in Ohio and graduated near the bottom of his class at the American military academy at West Point. Before the Civil War propelled Grant to greatness, even his father considered him a disappointment. He left the army after fighting in the Mexican War and failed at a number of business ventures before returning to work for his father's leather shop in the 1850s. The outbreak of hostilities gave Grant the chance to return to the only thing he was ever good at: war. An alcoholic, Grant's steadfast devotion to victory at any cost won him the confidence of Abraham Lincoln, who put him in charge of all Union forces in 1864.

Lee, in contrast, came from a wealthy and respected Virginia family. He graduated second in his class at West Point, where he was famously never given a demerit for discipline. Lee obeyed the code of honor that many men in the South professed but few actually lived. He had a successful career in the army and served with Grant in the Mexican War. Lee opposed Southern secession, but when his home state of Virginia left the Union, he felt honor-bound to serve the new Confederacy.

Recalling that fateful afternoon at Appomattox, Grant later wrote in his memoirs: "I felt like anything rather than rejoicing at the downfall of a foe who had fought so long and valiantly, and had suffered so much for a cause, though that cause was, I believe, one of the worst for which a people ever fought."

ADDITIONAL FACT
1. An extremely popular figure in the North, Grant was elected president of the United States in 1868, but historians judge him as one of the country's worst presidents.

"Howl"

America tends to look back on the 1950s nostalgically, whitewashing the whole decade as a utopia of postwar prosperity and *Leave It to Beaver* living. But even during this seemingly tranquil time, an undercurrent of rebellion and dissatisfaction existed in the United States. In literature, this rebelliousness coalesced into the Beat generation, one of the figureheads of which was Allen Ginsberg (1926–1997). Ginsberg's poem "Howl," a ranting but moving attack on the American status quo, is one of the most concentrated expressions of the Beat sensibility.

Ginsberg was a true New Yorker to the core: Born and raised in northern New Jersey, he attended Columbia University and lived in Manhattan for most of his life. At Columbia, he became fast friends with Jack Kerouac and William S. Burroughs, who would themselves become major authors of the Beat generation. After college, Ginsberg traveled extensively, blending his Jewish roots with Zen Buddhism, leftist politics, jazz music, and rather alarming drug habits.

"Howl" (1956), Ginsberg's first significant published work, is a lengthy, raving, nakedly emotional diatribe that upends the seemingly picture-perfect American social landscape of the 1950s:

> *I saw the best minds of my generation destroyed by madness, starving hysterical naked,*
> > *dragging themselves through the negro streets at dawn looking for an angry fix,*
> *angelheaded hipsters burning for the ancient heavenly connection to the starry dynamo*
> > *in the machinery of night,*
> *who poverty and tatters and hollow-eyed and high sat up smoking in the supernatural*
> > *darkness of cold-water flats floating across the tops of cities contemplating jazz,*
> *who bared their brains to Heaven under the El and saw Mohammedan angels staggering*
> > *on tenement roofs illuminated . . .*

The poem primarily targets the materialism of American life, although it also spins into discussions of drug addiction, censorship, homosexuality, and spirituality. The work was banned almost immediately on charges of obscenity, but after a high-profile legal battle in which the American Civil Liberties Union came to Ginsberg's aid, a California judge ruled that "Howl" had "redeeming social importance" and should remain in print.

Formally, "Howl" shows the influence of two earlier American poets, Walt Whitman and William Carlos Williams. With its long lines of free verse and realistic, strong language, the poem comes across as a spontaneous, uncontrollable outpouring of sentiment. Indeed, its tone of anger and despair was an accurate harbinger of the social upheaval that would shake the United States during the Vietnam era.

Mary Cassatt

Mary Cassatt (1844–1926), an American painter who exhibited with the French impressionists, is best known for her paintings of women and children and for her role in introducing impressionism to the American public.

Born to a wealthy family in Allegheny City, today part of Pittsburgh, Cassatt spent several years of her childhood in Germany. At the age of sixteen, she began studying painting at the Pennsylvania Academy of Fine Arts in Philadephia. In 1866, she sailed to Europe, where she remained for most of her life. After spending time in Italy, Cassatt chose Paris as her permanent home. Until 1878, she specialized in paintings of women, often set in Parisian interiors, which she exhibited in the States and at the Salons of 1870, and 1872 to 1876.

Impressed by the innovative works of Edgar Degas and Gustave Courbet, Cassatt began to modify her style. After Degas invited her to join the impressionists in 1879, she showed with them until their final exhibition in 1886. Degas even touched up one of her paintings, *The Little Girl in a Blue Armchair* in 1878. In 1877, Cassatt's mother and sister moved to Paris. Thereafter, the painter gave up her independent, Bohemian lifestyle to live in a more family-oriented household. This did not, however, dampen her professional aspirations. After 1886, Cassatt began placing greater emphasis on draftsmanship. Inspired by Japanese ukiyo-e prints, she produced a series of eighteen colored prints in the 1890s. Her famous painting of the *Bath* (1892) demonstrates her ability to combine the abstract linear designs of Oriental art with Western themes. The mother and child are formally bound by the use of coordinated colors and a strong centralized shape. Degas humorously called the work "Little Jesus with his English Nurse."

Cassatt helped promote women's rights throughout her career. In 1892, she was asked to paint a mural of the modern woman for the women's pavilion at the Columbian Exposition in Chicago. In 1915, she contributed eighteen works to an exhibition at the Knoedler Gallery in New York that was organized to draw attention to women's suffrage.

Cassatt also helped influence the reception of impressionism in the United States. She encouraged wealthy patrons to buy the works of her fellow artists, assisting them in their selections. She acted as a personal consultant to Henry and Louisine Havemeyer, whose collection of impressionist masters now hangs at the Metropolitan Museum of Art in New York City.

A successful artist in her own right, Cassatt purchased the Chateau de Beaufresne outside Paris. In her later career, she increasingly focused on the theme of mother and child. By 1900, she began suffering from cataracts, but she continued painting for another fifteen years

ADDITIONAL FACT

1. In 1878, Cassatt went to Spain, where she studied the works of Diego Velázquez and Bartolomé Murillo and painted a number of works with Spanish themes.

Sound Waves

Sound is a vibration that moves in a longitudinal pressure wave through matter. Sound has all the classic characteristics of waves—frequency, wavelength, velocity, and amplitude. Unlike electromagnetic waves such as radio waves, microwaves, and visible light, however, sound cannot travel through the vacuum of space. It requires a medium—gas, liquid, or solid—in order to move.

Sound begins when an object vibrates, moving the particles around it, which in turn move the particles around them. Thus begins a chain reaction of compression and decompression with each vibration. The waves of pressure move in a line parallel to the initial vibration, like waves through a slinky scrunching together and pulling apart. This is called longitudinal motion. The number of pressure oscillations per second is call the frequency, and the distance between points of maximal pressure is called the wavelength. We perceive higher frequencies to have a higher pitch and lower frequencies to have a lower pitch.

The velocity of a sound wave is the distance per unit of time that it travels in a given direction. The velocity of sound depends a great deal on the medium through which it is traveling. In general, the particles in solid matter have stronger interactions than the particles in liquids and gases, which allows sound to move more quickly through solids. This is why people put their ears to the tracks to hear if a train is coming. The vibrations of the train travel more quickly through the metal tracks than through the air.

The amplitude of sound refers to the amount of pressure that it creates. The more energy put into the initial vibration, the greater the amplitude. We perceive amplitude as loudness. As a sound wave travels over a distance, it loses amplitude. It becomes fainter and fainter until it can be heard no more.

ADDITIONAL FACTS

1. *The typical unit for frequency is a hertz (Hz). One hertz is equal to one vibration per second. The human ear can hear frequencies ranging between approximately 20 and 20,000 Hz.*

2. *Dogs and dolphins are particularly good at hearing the high pitches produced by high frequencies. Dogs can hear frequencies up to 45,000 Hz, and dolphins can hear up to 200,000 Hz.*

3. *Elephants are tuned to lower frequencies. They can hear sounds as low as 5 Hz.*

4. *Our ability to perceive amplitude declines with age. This is why elderly people often require hearing aids.*

Giuseppe Verdi

Giuseppe Verdi (1813–1901) represents one of the two schools of opera: German and Italian. In contrast to the German school, Verdi captures a style and an overall sensibility—soulful, personality-driven, and nationalistic—that is the perfect embodiment of the Italian operatic tradition.

Born to an illiterate innkeeper in Parma, Italy, Verdi had early success. When he was twenty-six, his first opera, *Oberto*, was performed at La Scala, Milan's most famous theater, and the Holy Grail for Italian singers and composers. After a flop or two, he re-won the hearts of Milan with *Nabucco* (1842), a monumental tale about Nebuchadrezzar's invasion of Jerusalem. Over the eight years that followed, Verdi wrote thirteen operas and earned a massive fortune. In the following decade, he slowed his pace, but he wrote some of his most famous operas: *Rigoletto* (1853), *Il Trovatore* (1853), and *La Traviata* (1853).

Until Verdi came along, Gioacchino Rossini had been the most lauded composer of Italian opera. Rossini's works were mostly light-hearted caprices with lots of passages that highlighted the solo voice. In addition to Verdi, the Italian canon was rounded out by Vincenzo Bellini, Gaetano Donizetti, and other composers of the bel canto—beautiful singing—style, which flourished in the 1830s.

Verdi wrote operas full of soulful melodies and character-driven plots that dealt with love, loss, and tragedy, but which remained lighter than the German operas. Where Richard Wagner and his imitators in the German school dealt in abstractions and wallowed in huge, audacious productions, Verdi focused on very direct, realistic emotional expression and lifelike characters singing their hearts out.

ADDITIONAL FACTS

1. Verdi was initially rejected from the Milan Conservatory for "lacking musical talent." He had to take private lessons instead.

2. During the struggle for Italian independence from Austria, vandals scribbled "Viva Verdi!" in public places, using the composer's name as an acronym for Vittorio Emanuele, Rey d'Italia *("Long live Vittorio Emanuele, king of Italy!"), a reference to the man who would become the first king of unified Italy.*

3. One of the Italian opera master's greatest contributions is the Verdian baritone, a tradition of writing the most expressive arias for the sonorous baritone part, rather than the tenor, which traditionally served that purpose.

Categorical Imperative

Compare the two commands: "Wear a coat if you want to stay warm!" and "Do not murder!" The first command gives you a reason to obey it; it tells you what you ought to do if you want to stay warm. If you do not have the desire to stay warm, you have no reason to follow that instruction. In contrast, whether or not you want to kill, most people believe the imperative "Do not murder!" still applies to them.

Immanuel Kant used the term *categorical imperative* to describe the relationship between human beings and commands like "Do not kill" and other moral laws. Kant believed there is an *unconditional* moral law—a law that says what it is permissible to do and that applies to us regardless of our desires. Therefore, the moral law is expressed by an imperative—a command to do something, again, regardless of our desires.

Kant described several ways of identifying the moral law, the most famous of which is called the formula of universal law. Kant explained, "act only according to a maxim that you could at the same time will to be a universal law." The maxim of your action is the reason, or guiding principle of your behavior. For example, if you borrow money from your friend and promise to repay it, having no intention of doing so, your maxim would be: Make a false promise in order to get money. The formula of universal law says that if you cannot desire that everyone act according to this maxim, then the act violates the moral law. If everyone made lying promises to get money, then no one would lend money on the basis of promises. Therefore, when you make a lying promise, you have to desire that not everyone else who makes such promises is lying, or your trick wouldn't work. Therefore, your lying promise violates the moral law.

ADDITIONAL FACTS

1. *Another way Kant formulates the categorical imperative is called the formula of humanity: "Act in such a way that you treat humanity, whether in your own person or in the person of another, always at the same time as an end and never simply as a means."*

2. *Kant first articulated his theory of the categorical imperative in his 1785 book* Groundwork of the Metaphysics of Morals.

3. *Kant believed that suicide violates the categorical imperative—masturbation too!*

Four Righteously Guided Caliphs

According to Sunni tradition, the Four Righteously Guided Caliphs were the first four leaders of Islam. They were seen as closely following Muhammad's path.

The first of these four caliphs was Abu Bakr. Despite the objection of Shiits who supported Ali, Abu Bakr seized the caliphate shortly after Muhammad died. He was Muhammad's close ally and father-in-law and often led prayer in Muhammad's absence. Abur Bakr was the caliph from 632–634 AD. His caliphate was brief, but given the conflict with Ali and his followers, significant for centuries to come.

Shortly before Abu Bakr died—some say he was poisoned—he suggested his successor should be Umar ibn al-Khattab. Umar became Islam's second caliph in 634 and reigned until 644. As he was chosen, Shiits still claimed, to no avail, that the true caliph should be Ali. Thus, Shiits view Umar as another usurper. Sunnis, however, look upon Umar as a great leader. They praise him for resisting the establishment of a dynasty by refusing to allow his son to succeed him. Instead, Umar appointed six men, including Ali, to choose a caliph from among themselves.

When Umar was assassinated by a man who held a personal grudge against him, this group chose Uthman ibn Affan, who reigned from 644–656. Uthman is perhaps best known for standardizing the Quran. He also greatly expanded the Islamic empire and began the practice of appointing family members to rule his vast lands. This practice caused unrest throughout the kingdom of Islam, but especially in North Africa. Soldiers eventually led masses of angry Muslims to storm the caliph's home and kill him.

After Uthman's death, Ali, who was also know as Ali ibn Abi Talib, finally became the caliph of Islam. By this time, however, the Islamic territories had descended into chaos. In order to avoid the many sunnis who opposed his rule, Ali moved his capital to what is now Iraq. Ali ruled until 661 when he, too, was assassinated by dissidents.

Ali's death marked the end of the period of the four righteously guided caliphs. His successor, Muawiyah I, began a hereditary dynasty.

ADDITIONAL FACTS

1. *All three assassinated caliphs, Umar, Uthman, and Ali, are said to have been killed while performing holy rites. Umar was leading prayer in a mosque, Uthman was reading the Quran, and Ali was performing his morning prayer.*

2. *The caliphs lasted until the twentieth century and World War I. The last caliph, Abdülmecid II, died in Paris in 1944.*

Transcontinental Railroad

Before 1869, traveling from New York City to San Francisco was a long and dangerous trip. Between the east and west coasts of the United States lay an inhospitable prairie. The four- to six-month trip was so difficult that many travelers instead opted to make the voyage by sea around the tip of South America.

The opening of the transcontinental railroad in the spring of 1869 revolutionized the American economy by connecting the two halves of the United States and making it possible to move goods and people easily across the West. Railroads, which had been invented only some forty years earlier, knitted America together and lead to a huge increase in commerce. They also brought new waves of white settlers to the West and subsequently caused the decline of the American Indian tribes in the region.

Although it was built by two private companies, the Union Pacific and Central Pacific railroads, the transcontinental railroad was, from the start, a government project. During the Civil War, President Abraham Lincoln decided the country needed a better connection to California, which had just recently become a state in 1850. Gold had been discovered there in 1849, sparking the Gold Rush of prospectors rushing west. The government offered the two companies huge incentives to complete their work quickly.

Laying two bands of steel across the entire American continent was a daunting task. The route crossed desolate plains, great rivers, and the snow-capped Rocky Mountains. Teams of Chinese and Irish immigrants built as much as ten miles of track in a single day. When the transcontinental route was done, after seven years of construction, the once-arduous trip between east and west took only six days.

ADDITIONAL FACTS

1. *One of the executives at Central Pacific was Leland Stanford, who later in life used his railroad fortune to start Stanford University in California.*

2. *The two railroads celebrated the completion of the route on May 10, 1869, at Promontory Summit, Utah, by driving a golden stake into the final length of track. The modern-day Union Pacific no longer serves the town, however, and the historic tracks were torn up in 1942 and melted down to aid the war effort.*

3. *Pay for Chinese workers on the Central Pacific began at $27 a month and was then increased to $30 a month. Irish workers earned $35 per month, with free board included.*

4. *Difficult terrain in the West often forced the railroad to build tracks over obstacles instead of around them. In Utah, for instance, the route crossed the Weber River thirty-one times!*

Tennessee Williams

If Eugene O'Neill was the great tragedian of American drama and Arthur Miller its great social conscience, Tennessee Williams (1911–1983) was the great lyrical and thematic innovator, the one who pushed the boundaries of language and content the furthest. His works also rank with the novels of William Faulkner as the finest representatives of southern American literature.

The heavily autobiographical *The Glass Menagerie* (1944), about the dysfunctional Wingfield family, gave Williams his first major success. In the play, a delusional mother's overbearing tendencies alienate both her jaded son and her disabled daughter, who has withdrawn from reality into a fantasy life amid her collection of glass animal figurines. When the work opened in Chicago, ecstatic theater critics practically begged the public to go see it, and initially small audiences soon swelled to full houses.

Productions of Williams's next major work, *A Streetcar Named Desire* (1947), demonstrated that his stories worked just as effectively on film as onstage. The play's protagonist, the haughty Southern belle Blanche DuBois, is ruined by both her own indiscretions and her run-ins with her loutish brother-in-law, Stanley Kowalski. A Pulitzer Prize for the work solidified Williams's reputation. Williams followed with *Cat on a Hot Tin Roof* (1955), a searing disclosure of the mendacity underlying the sexual and familial relationships in a seemingly prosperous southern clan. This play won Williams another Pulitzer.

The themes that Williams explored in his works—violence, sexual frustration, mental illness, incest, alcoholism, and homosexuality—were scandalous for their time and shocked audiences. Williams's language, meanwhile, was among the most innovative to grace the American stage. His characters speak in a strange, eloquent vernacular that brings mythic weight to their struggles—a world away from the acutely realistic dialogue that many of Williams's contemporaries employed.

ADDITIONAL FACTS

1. *Williams, born Thomas Lanier Williams, acquired the nickname "Tennessee" from college friends in reference to his paternal family's long history in that state.*

2. *Williams disliked the 1958 film adaptation of* Cat on a Hot Tin Roof *(starring Paul Newman and Elizabeth Taylor) because studio censors removed all references to the male lead's homosexuality, which was central to the original play.*

3. *At the shoe factory where his father forced him to take a job, Williams worked with a man named Stanley Kowalski, who became the inspiration for the now iconic character in* A Streetcar Named Desire.

Postimpressionism

The term *Postimpressionist* was coined by the art critic Roger Fry for a London exhibition ("Manet and the Postimpressionists") he organized in 1910. Fry meant it as a catch-all designation for modern artists following the impressionists. Included in the exhibition were works by Henrí Matisse, Pablo Picasso, and Georges Braque.

Today, postimpressionism carries a more specific meaning. It is used to describe art created between roughly 1886 and 1905 by painters such as Paul Gaugin and Paul Cézanne. These artists felt the impressionists had focused too much on the external appearance of things and not their meaning. They also believed the impressionists had been preoccupied with light and color. The postimpressionists consciously rejected naturalism and representational art. They wished to reinstate the value of contour, structure, and composition. Postimpressionist painters were more concerned with the emotional value of art. They viewed it as a means of self-expression.

Postimpressionism was a bridge to much of the art that would come later in the twentieth century. Cézanne's reduction of objects to geometric forms, evident in his paintings of Mount Sainte-Victoire and his many late still lifes, was crucial to the development of cubism. Gauguin's creative use of intense color and his interest in primitive culture was influential on the Fauves. Vincent van Gogh's spirituality and subjective approach to subject matter was championed by the symbolists. Although there is little unity in the style of all three artists, they were bound by their desire to express feeling with visual forms.

ADDITIONAL FACTS

1. *Compared to the gregarious impressionists, postimpressionists tended to be independent and solitary, and often, like Gauguin and van Gogh, suffered from acute depression.*

2. *Because postimpressionists were concerned with structure and composition rather than fleeting impressions of the physical world, they were more likely to work deliberately, often making many preliminary sketches for their finished paintings.*

cℛↈ

X-Rays

In 1895, a German physicist named Wilhelm Roentgen was experimenting with beams of electrons in a vacuum tube. The tube was surrounded by thick black cardboard, which should have blocked any light coming from the beams of electrons. But strangely, a fluorescent screen across the room started to glow every time Roentgen unleashed the electron beams. He had discovered, quite accidentally, a previously unknown form of radiation. It could pass through certain materials easily, but it was blocked by others. When Roentgen passed his hand in front the tube, the radiation passed through his skin but was absorbed by his bones, leaving a clear image of his skeleton on the fluorescent screen. He called the radiation "x-ray" because it was so mysterious. The name stuck.

X-rays are a form of electromagnetic radiation, just like visible light. Both x-rays and visible light are carried in tiny energy packets called photons that are produced by the movement of electrons, which are negatively charged subatomic particles. Electrons move about the center of an atom in circular paths called orbitals. When an electron drops from a higher orbital to a lower orbital, it releases energy in the form of photons. The difference between visible light and x-rays is that x-rays have more photons, and hence more energy.

The soft tissue of our skin is made of small atoms that readily absorb low-energy, visible light. High-energy x-rays pass right through it. However, the calcium in our bones, like other metallic substances, blocks and absorbs x-rays. Lead is a large atom that absorbs x-rays completely. This is why scientists who work with x-rays use lead shields to protect themselves from x-ray radiation, which can be cancerous after prolonged exposure.

ADDITIONAL FACTS

1. X-ray machines cannot be used to see through people's clothes, but legislators in the early 1900s were so scared they might be, they tried to have them outlawed.

2. Throughout medical and scientific communities, x-rays are often referred to as Roentgen rays, after their discoverer.

3. Stars, supernovas, and black holes emit x-rays, but scientists have to use telescopes in outer space to see them because they cannot penetrate the earth's atmosphere.

4. X-rays are actually faintly visible to the human eye when it is adjusted to the dark. X-rays glow a dim blue-gray.

Verdi's *La Traviata* and *Aida*

Part of a series of three early-1850s operas that established Giuseppe Verdi as an Italian master of the genre, *La Traviata* (1853) is the story of a "fallen woman," named Violetta who falls in love with a rich man, Alfredo. Alfredo's father, Germont, disapproves of their union and forbids their marriage. In the end, the courtesan Violetta, who has tuberculosis, dies a long, tragic death singing an extended aria. The piece, whose libretto was written by Francesco Maria Piavo, is full of expressive arias and contains some of the staple solo pieces for every operatic soprano. It is still performed widely to this day.

Aida (1870) is probably Verdi's second most famous opera. It was commissioned by the Khedive of Egypt in 1869 to coincide with the opening of the Suez Canal and the building of a new opera house. Verdi, a perfectionist, actually missed his deadline and *Rigoletto* was performed instead. A year later, he delivered on his promise and produced an opera about an Ethiopian slave girl, Aida, who falls in love with an Egyptian army captain, Radames. It is, like *La Traviata*, an inter-class love story, fraught with passion and tragedy. Its catchy and memorable "Triumphal March" is one of Verdi's most familiar tunes.

For the premiere, the Egyptians spent a fortune buying French-made costumes and hiring a cast of more than 300. Radames's helmet and sword were made of solid silver. Verdi, who did not actually attend the premiere, was apparently displeased with what he heard about it. He felt that such a display reduced his work to mere entertainment, rather than art, and he retired to his country house for several years, giving up opera in favor of gardening and tending to his animals. However, in 1874, he returned with his famous *Requiem* and wrote two more operas before he died in 1901.

ADDITIONAL FACTS

1. The libretto to La Traviata *is based on the play* La dame aux camélias *by Alexander Dumas, who based his story on the real-life dancer Lola Montez, who was a lover of Franz Liszt.*

2. In the premiere of La Traviata, *the diva who played Violetta, a character dying of tuberculosis, was fat. In the final scene, when she collapsed to the ground, a cloud of dust rose from the floor, obscuring the stage.*

3. At the premiere of Aida, *Khedive Ismail's harem was so big that it filled three entire loges.*

Utilitarianism

Utilitarianism is a theory about how we ought to behave. According to utilitarians, we should always do whatever produces the greatest overall pleasure in the world. Utilitarianism was first proposed by the English economist and philosopher Jeremy Bentham (1748–1832) and later elaborated by John Stuart Mill (1806–1873).

Contemporary philosophers think of utilitarianism as a form of consequentialism. Consequentialism is an answer to the question: Which acts are morally right to perform? Consequentialism's answer is: Whichever acts produce the best outcome. This outlook requires that we know what state of the world is objectively *better* than others. Some philosophers deny that this is possible.

Utilitarians are consequentialists who have a hedonistic idea of what is good. They think the only objective good is pleasure. Other consequentialists believe good includes not only pleasure, but things like respect and equality.

Some utilitarians rank the different kinds of pleasure. Bentham famously argued that "Prejudice apart, the game of push-pin is of equal value with the arts and sciences of music and poetry." He believed pleasure should be measured in quantity not quality. In contrast, Mill believed the fulfillment of intellectual desires is better than the fulfillment of merely sensual desires. He wrote, "Better to be a Socrates unsatisfied, than a pig satisfied."

ADDITIONAL FACTS

1. *Bentham designed a prison he called the panopticon wherein the wardens could observe all of the prisoners, but the prisoners could not see the wardens. Bentham tried, but failed, to have the panopticon built.*

2. *Mill was the product of an educational experiment by his father and Bentham to produce the perfect utilitarian. He began learning Latin at age three, and Greek at eight. Later, he would blame his intense education for his depression and emotional problems.*

Muhammad's Wives and Daughter

Muhammad remained single until the age of twenty-five, when he met Khadijah, who was forty and twice a widow. Khadijah married Muhammad in Mecca and became the first female convert to Islam. She was very supportive of Muhammad as he began to receive frequent revelations from Gabriel and to spread the religion of Islam.

Khadijah bore Mohammed six children. The sixth, a daughter named Fatima, would later go on to marry Ali, the fourth caliph (according to Sunnis) or the first imam (according to Shiites). Fatima died shortly after Muhammad passed away in 632 AD.

Throughout Muhammad's time in Mecca, he remained a monogamous man. However, after fleeing Mecca for Medina in order to avoid critics of his teachings, his followers became more concentrated and outspoken. They looked upon Muhammad as a leader and expected him to take many wives. After Khadijah died, he chose to oblige his followers. Many of the wives he subsequently took are often considered politically motivated. The most significant of these wives was Aisha, daughter of Abu Bakr, who, according to Sunnis, later became first caliph of Islam.

Sunnis believe that Aisha was Muhammad's favorite wife, recounting that he died with his head in her lap. Aisha then supported the next three caliphs, Abu Bakr (her father), Umar, and Uthman. When Ali rose to power, however, she opposed his rule and led an army against him in present-day Iraq. Ali easily defeated her army, but let her return to Medina to live out the rest of her life.

Native Americans

At first, the Nez Percé, a Native American tribe that had lived in the Pacific Northwest for thousands of years, had an amicable relationship with the whites who began to settle in the area in the nineteenth century. But in 1863, the US government decided to impose a new treaty on the tribe that forced them onto a tiny reservation. Washington wanted to make room for more settlers in the tribe's homeland.

Outraged by the betrayal, the Nez Percé revolted in 1877. The United States Army sent William Tecumseh Sherman, the infamous general who had wreaked havoc in the South during the Civil War, to quell the rebellion. Cornered after a few months of fighting, the chief of the Nez Percé assembled his weary fighters to announce that he would surrender to the Americans: "Hear me, my chiefs!" Chief Joseph said. "I am tired. My heart is sick and sad. From where the sun now stands I will fight no more forever."

Chief Joseph's eloquent surrender speech, which was widely circulated at the time, was seen as a eulogy not just for his tribe but for an entire defeated civilization that had once existed in the American West. By the end of the century, all organized resistance had been crushed. The massacre of the Sioux tribe at Wounded Knee in South Dakota in 1890 was the last armed confrontation between whites and natives.

Placed onto reservations, Native Americans remain some of the nation's most impoverished US citizens. A third of Native Americans live below the poverty line. The Pine Ridge Sioux reservation, the site of the Wounded Knee massacre in 1890, is the most impoverished place in the United States. The US government evicted Indians from their land in the name of progress, but Native American communities in the West are still recovering from the devastation.

ADDITIONAL FACTS

1. *The great Apache warrior Geronimo was one of the last chiefs to resist whites in the Southwest. Defeated but world-famous, he appeared in President Teddy Roosevelt's inaugural parade in 1905.*

2. *The ancestors of Native Americans are believed to have crossed into Alaska from Siberia, in present-day Russia, about 15,000 years ago.*

William Shakespeare

Few would dispute that William Shakespeare (1564–1616) was the world's greatest playwright in any language. His impact on Western culture over the past four hundred years cannot be overstated.

Despite exhaustive research, little is known about Shakespeare's personal life. He was born in Stratford-upon-Avon, England, where he probably had a short formal education. After marrying a woman named Anne Hathaway, he embarked on a career as a playwright, moving to London and working as an actor and director at the Globe Theatre, which he co-owned with other shareholders in his company. Shakespeare's brilliance was widely acknowledged during his lifetime, and his works were immensely popular with both aristocratic and common audiences.

Shakespeare is most famous for his thirty-eight plays, which scholars traditionally group into several categories. Histories, such as *Richard II and Henry V*, portray real historical figures—typically kings of England—and explore ideas of leadership and personal integrity or villainy. Tragedies, such as *Hamlet*, *Macbeth*, and *King Lear*, explore the monumental ramifications of individuals' flawed actions and decisions. Comedies, such as *A Midsummer Night's Dream* and *Much Ado About Nothing*, present alternately lighthearted and probing takes on romance, fueled by cases of mistaken identity and typically culminating in marriage. Others, such as *Measure for Measure* and *The Tempest*, are more difficult to categorize, combining elements of different genres. Over the centuries, these thirty-eight diverse scenarios have proved to be timeless, fruitful ground for reinterpretation by directors and actors, who use them as lenses through which to explore contemporary concerns.

Shakespeare also wrote significant poetry, including 154 sonnets about love, art, beauty, and other topics. Beyond the stylistic and formal influence of these poems, the English words and expressions that Shakespeare coined are virtually without number. They range from now-commonplace vocabulary, such as "lackluster" and "sanctimonious," to more poetic turns of phrase, such as "one fell swoop" and "pomp and circumstance." England recognized this literary and linguistic influence immediately and, upon Shakespeare's death, knew it had lost one of its greatest minds. Indeed, to borrow a phrase from *Hamlet*, it is probable that the world "shall not look upon his like again."

ADDITIONAL FACTS

1. *Although Shakespeare's authorship of some of his plays and poems has been contested, scholars have found little more than circumstantial evidence to support this argument.*

2. *In Shakespeare's day, all dramatic roles, including those of female characters, were played by male actors. This convention added an additional layer of complexity to some of his comedies—such as* As You Like It—*that feature female characters who cross-dress to hide their identity.*

Paul Gauguin

Paul Gauguin (1848–1903) was a major figure of the postimpressionist movement. He is remembered today for his paintings of Tahiti, his relationship with Vincent van Gogh, and his influence on twentieth century art.

Gauguin, the son of a left-wing journalist, was born in Paris in 1848. His maternal grandmother had been the daughter of a Peruvian nobleman. When his father had to leave Paris for political reasons, the family moved to Lima, Peru, where Gauguin spent four years of his childhood.

Gauguin began studying art relatively late in life. He initially joined the merchant marines and then became a stockbroker in Paris. At first, he merely collected art, but soon he began painting in his spare time. In 1876, he exhibited his works at the official Salon. By 1879, he had joined the impressionists.

When the stock market crashed in 1882, Gauguin moved to Copenhagen to work as a salesman for a canvas manufacturer. Shortly thereafter, he devoted himself to art full-time. Restless and impatient by nature, Gauguin moved from place to place seeking a quiet, noncommercial haven. In 1886, he stayed in Pont Aven, a provincial town in Brittany, for six months. Next he traveled to Rouen, Copenhagen, Panama, and Martinique. Upon his return to Pont Aven in 1888, he painted *The Vision after the Sermon (Jacob Wrestling with the Angel)*. With distorted perspective and symbolic rather than realistic imagery, Guaguin tried to capture the impact of a sermon on the listeners' minds. The hard contours and vivid colors of the canvas reveal his fascination with Japanese prints and medieval stained glass.

In 1888, Vincent van Gogh invited Gauguin to join him in Arles, where he hoped to establish an artists' colony. Incompatible in temperament, the two ended up quarrelling. For the next few years, Gauguin shuttled between Brittany and Paris. Longing for a more primitive lifestyle, he set sail for Tahiti in 1891, where he was disappointed by the lack of indigenous artifacts. Inspired all the same by Javanese carvings and pre-Columbian pottery, Gauguin began painting scenes of the island and its traditions.

In 1893, Gauguin sailed back to Paris, where he wrote *Noa Noa*, a romanticized account of his experiences in the South Seas, which he illustrated with deliberately crude woodcuts. He remained in France for two years, during which time he managed to alienate many of his friends with his ostentatious exoticism. Frustrated by the poor reception of his work, he sold off his possessions and moved permanently to the South Seas in 1895.

Three years later, he attempted suicide after painting his bleak masterpiece *Where Do We Come From, What Are We, Where Are We Going?* In 1901, after he began receiving a steady stipend from his dealer in Paris, he moved to a remote island in the Marquesas where he lived until his death in 1903.

The Atom

An atom is the tiniest unit of an element that has all the chemical properties of that element. The concept of the atom dates all the way back to 530 BC, when the Greek philosopher Democritus defined the atom as a particle of matter so minute that it could not be divided into smaller parts. The modern concept of the atom has subcomponents—notably electrons, protons, and neutrons—but the idea is the same. It is the basic building block of all matter.

Modern atomic theory states that all elements are made of atoms, and all atoms of any element are the same. Elements such as hydrogen, carbon, oxygen, sodium, potassium, gold, and uranium combine with each other through chemical reactions to form compounds. For example, hydrogen and oxygen combine to form water, and sodium and potassium combine to form table salt.

The basic structure of an atom is a nucleus surrounded by electrons, although the vast majority of an atom consists of empty space. The nucleus is a dense core made of neutrons and protons. Neutrons have no charge and weigh slightly more than protons, which have a positive charge. The number of protons in the atom determines what type of element it is. Hydrogen has one proton, while uranium has ninety-two. Elements gain and lose protons through fusion and fission, but not through chemical reactions.

Electrons are negatively charged particles with an almost negligible mass. The movement of electrons around the nucleus continues to be one of the most debated topics in chemistry and physics. Early models of the atom depicted electrons orbiting the nucleus much in the same way the earth orbits the sun. Now developments in quantum mechanics have lead scientists to believe that electrons move in complex waves called orbitals, encircling the nucleus at distinct energy levels.

ADDITIONAL FACTS

1. *Current theories of the universe's formation suggest that, after the Big Bang, the universe was too hot for atoms to form. The creation of atoms presumably did not happen until 379,000 years after the Big Bang, when temperatures fell to 3,000 K.*

2. *In the early universe, it is thought that hydrogen made up 75 percent of the atoms, helium made up 24 percent, and the other elements made up the remaining 1 percent.*

3. *Protons and electrons are made of still smaller particles called quarks, and electrons may be made of smaller particles called leptons.*

4. *It was believed that ninety-two elements occur naturally on earth, but recently scientists discovered that plutonium, which has ninety-four protons, also exists naturally on earth.*

Richard Wagner

Richard Wagner's (1813–1883) massive contribution to opera would earn him a place near the top of any list of the most influential men of the nineteenth century. But more important, perhaps, is his contribution to art overall, embodied by his concept of *Gesamtkunstwerk*—the idea of a total art work that unites music, art, movement, theater, poetry, and philosophy. There were several generations of thinkers, artists, and musicians—including T. S. Eliot, Arnold Schoenberg, Ernest Hemingway, and Pablo Picasso—who followed Wagner and were strongly influenced by his thought.

A ruthlessly competitive egomaniac, Wagner was born in Leipzig, where he attended university. In 1833, his brother got him a job as chorus master at Würzberg, one of the few successes of his frustrating early career. While at Würzberg, he wrote *Rienzi* (1842) and *The Flying Dutchman* (1843), both moderate successes, but he lived extravagantly and even spent some time in debtors' prison. Wagner moved on to the Saxon court at Dresden, where he reached maturity with *Tannhäuser* (1844) and *Lohengrin* (1848). In 1849, he supported a revolutionary political movement and a warrant was subsequently issued for his arrest. Wagner fled to Weimar, where Franz Liszt helped him gain amnesty.

In the following years, Wagner composed his famous *Ring Cycle* of four operas, as well as *Tristan and Isolde* (1859), *Die Meistersinger* (1861), and *Parsifal* (1882). Wagner saw himself as embodying the spirit of German music. He was a socialist, and along with Liszt, he formed the idea of the "Music of the Future," a theory that touted the superiority of German music and pioneered revolutionary methods in harmony, structure, and composition.

Wagner inspired conflict in listeners like no other composer before him. Some people loved his music for its revolutionary genius but hated his loathsome character, but many other contemporaries were indifferent to the defects of his character but disliked the scale and complexity of his music. In Wagner's final act of narcissism, he established a festival in 1872 in the Bavarian town of Bayreuth devoted entirely to his music. Wagner died in 1883 of a heart attack in Venice.

ADDITIONAL FACTS

1. Wagner was virulently anti-Semitic. His Judaism in Music, *published in 1850, attacked his Jewish contemporaries, even some like the composer Giacomo Meyerbeer, who had once been his friend.*

2. Wagner seduced and married Cosima Liszt von Bülow, then the wife of one of Wagner's best friends and the daughter of Franz Liszt. Afterwards, Liszt refused to speak to Wagner for many years. On the other hand, Herr von Bülow remained on good terms with Wagner, conducting his operas and conceding that Wagner, as the greater genius, had a right to Cosima.

George Wilhelm Friedrich Hegel

G. W. F. Hegel (1770–1831) was born in Stuttgart, Germany. Hegel hoped to find an academic job at the University of Jena, then the philosophical center of Germany, but his plans were cut short by the invasion of Napoleon Bonaparte. Hegel fled and worked for many years as, among other things, a newspaper editor and high school principal, before becoming a professor in Heidelberg, and then Berlin. By the time of his death in 1831, Hegel was the most famous philosopher in Germany, with students flocking to hear his lectures.

Hegel's philosophical system is bewilderingly complex. However, a few general features can be noted.

First, Hegel grants great importance to history. For Hegel, history was the process by which spirit—in German, *geist*—comes to recognize itself as spirit. It is hard to say what Hegel means by this. On one reading, spirit is the totality of norms by which human beings live. A norm is a rule that says what we ought to do, or what we are allowed to do—our social mores. To say that "spirit comes to recognize itself as spirit" is to say that through the course of history, human beings collectively realize that they themselves are the authors of the norms that govern their lives, that these norms have arisen for determinate reasons throughout history, and have been refined and changed for reasons.

Hegel had a very interesting theory about how systems of norms, which he sometimes called "forms of consciousness," change through history. He argued that they undermine themselves. A system of norms undermines itself when it starts to appear unjustified, or unreasonable, according to its own standards. When this happens, argued Hegel, a new system of norms arises, which resolves precisely the problems of the previous form of consciousness. Thus, when we examine the systems of norms that have governed human life throughout history—political, ethical, religious, aesthetic, or philosophical—we find a succession of forms of consciousness, where the transition from each form to the next appears reasonable. Thus, when we examine our world, we see our norms are the product of a historical process governed by reason.

ADDITIONAL FACTS

1. *Hegel believed his own philosophical system was the final form of consciousness, the final system of norms that would never be overcome. Therefore, he believed "history," as he understood it, had ended.*

2. *Hegel called the process by which forms of consciousness undermine themselves, giving way to new forms of consciousness, "dialectic."*

3. *Hegel once described Napoleon Bonaparte as "world history on horseback."*

Muawiyah I

Muawiyah ibn Abu Sufyan, who ruled under the name Muawiyah I, succeeded Ali and was the first leader of Islam after the four righteously guided caliphs.

Muawiyah was born in Mecca circa 602 AD. His father strongly disagreed with Muhammad's teachings and when Muawiyah became a Muslim, he had to hide his faith from his own family. After Muhammad conquered Mecca and eliminated idolatry, Muawiyah became a scribe. Eventually, as the Islamic empire expanded, Muhammad sent Muawiyah and his brother to Syria, where they lead the Islamic army against the Byzantines.

Under Caliph Umar, Muawiyah was named the governor of Syria. As governor, he raised a Syrian army that was strong enough to hold off Byzantine advances, and also to capture Cyprus and Rhodes.

Muawiyah's goals changed drastically when Ali, the fourth and final righteously guided caliph, was installed. Ali chose not to punish the murderers of Uthman, the third caliph, and Muawiyah saw this as a sign that Ali was involved with the murder himself. Muawiyah began to raise an anti-Ali following in Syria. In order to stop this uprising, Ali led his armies against Muawiyah in the Battle of Siffin. Although Muawiyah was losing the battle, he convinced Ali's soldiers to stop fighting and hold a religious arbitration to decide the victor. During this arbitration, Muawiyah convinced many of Ali's soldiers to turn against their leader. This distraction allowed Muawiyah time to send a large number of his followers to Egypt.

When Ali died, Muawiyah, holding both Syria and Egypt, was the most powerful Muslim and the logical choice to replace him. He ruled from 661–680 AD.

Unlike his predecessors, Muawiyah appointed his son, Yazid I, to replace him. In order to both establish the dynasty and continue the old traditions, Muawiyah installed a group of loyalist nobles who would vote for the next caliph. However, these nobles were in the caliph's pocket, rubber-stamping his heir. So began a series of hereditary dynasties, the first of which was the Umayyad, which ruled from 661–750 AD.

ADDITIONAL FACTS

1. *The first three caliphs ruled from the Arabian Peninsula. Ali moved his capital to Iraq, and Muawiyah ruled from Damascus, Syria.*

2. *According to tradition, Muawiyah convinced Ali's troops to submit to arbitration by placing Qurans on his army's lances. Ali's soldiers, unwilling to harm the holy book, stopped fighting.*

Otto von Bismarck

Otto von Bismarck (1815–1898) was a nineteenth-century politician and diplomat who is considered the founder of the modern nation of Germany. Prior to the mid-1800s, Germany was a patchwork of tiny, quarrelling states. The fragmentation of Germany had been a legacy of the Holy Roman Empire, which had gradually dissolved into dozens of pieces before finally disappearing in 1806. Working on behalf of Kaiser Wilhelm I, Bismarck was able to consolidate these states into one unified country.

Bismarck himself was born in Prussia, one of the more powerful German states, as the son of a military officer. He entered politics in his thirties as a conservative. Despite his initial apprehension, he embraced the cause of German unification wholeheartedly.

Appointed the Prussian chancellor, or prime minister, Bismarck used diplomacy and the threat of force to overcome opposition to unification. He also encouraged the growing sense of German nationalism. In 1870, Bismarck shrewdly provoked a war with France, which convinced many other German states to unify with Prussia. A united German empire emerged after Prussia's quick victory over France in 1871.

Bismarck then had the total trust of the Kaiser, and he largely ran the new German empire. Bismarck was not a liberal, but he did undertake a number of reforms to strengthen the German state. He developed a common currency, enacted many administrative reforms, and established a single set of laws for the whole country in an effort to solidify the country's unity.

The German empire Bismarck founded was short-lived, however. After Wilhelm's death, Wilhelm II, his successor, forced Bismarck to resign shortly after coming to the throne. Without Bismarck's steady hand, German foreign affairs took a turn for the worse. Wilhelm II made the fateful choice to drag Germany into World War I, a decision that ended the empire. And the forces of nationalism that Bismarck exploited to unify Germans in the nineteenth century had disastrous consequences in the twentieth century.

ADDITIONAL FACTS

1. Bismarck was nicknamed the "Iron Chancellor" for his reputation for toughness and determination.

2. Bismarck twice survived assassination attempts, first by a student in 1849 and again in 1874 by a barrel-maker.

3. A gigantic German battleship named after Bismarck was sunk by the British in 1941 in a pivotal World War II naval battle.

4. The capital of the US state of North Dakota, which is heavily German-American, is named after Bismarck.

Fyodor Dostoyevsky

Fyodor Dostoyevsky (1821–1881) was the undisputed master of the psychological novel. During a literary career spanning four decades, he displayed unprecedented—and arguably still unmatched—understanding of human nature, especially the torturous emotional states of guilt, despair, and preoccupation with death.

The hardship and tragedy that Dostoyevsky faced in his life probably only enriched his fiction. Born in Moscow to a rigidly Russian Orthodox family, he was stunned by the sudden death of his father in 1839. Although Dostoyevsky followed his father's urging and was educated as an engineer, he disliked the work and decided to become a writer. His first novel, *Poor Folk* (1846), won him great praise with critics, but his career was derailed when he was arrested in 1849 for taking part in a radically leftist publishing operation. After being subjected to a mock execution with a last-minute "reprieve," he spent four years at a labor camp in Siberia. This traumatic experience left an indelible mark on the tone and content of Dostoyevsky's works.

In the 1860s, Dostoyevsky hit his literary stride, penning the novella *Notes from Underground* (1864), about a bitter, neurotic recluse who is unable to function socially in the outside world, and his early masterpiece *Crime and Punishment* (1866), which dissects the guilt and misery of a young man who has killed an elderly woman. The latter work is particularly notable for its psychological depth and its conclusion that a criminal's internal self-recrimination after a crime is far worse than any punishment society can levy.

As Dostoyevsky grew older, he rejected the atheist politics of his youth and returned to the Russian Orthodoxy of his ancestral roots. His novel *The Idiot* (1868–1869) depicts a tragic Christ figure, and the great masterpiece of his later career, *The Brothers Karamazov* (1879–1880), has been called the most significant Christian novel ever written, infused as it is with Russian Orthodox morality. In this giant novel, three sons of a murdered father tackle problems of good and evil and Christian faith in very different ways.

Though detractors criticized Dostoyevsky's dense and often humorless style, the penetrating detail of his character studies is unquestioned—especially in his explorations of the minds of criminals, the mentally unstable, and others on the margins of society. Beyond their literary legacy, these characterizations influenced the nihilistic and existential philosophers of the twentieth century, from Friedrich Nietzsche to Albert Camus.

ADDITIONAL FACT
1. *Throughout his life, Dostoyevsky suffered from epilepsy, which worsened significantly during his years at the Siberian labor camp.*

Vincent van Gogh

Vincent van Gogh (1853–1890), one of Holland's greatest artists, has become the symbol of the tormented, misunderstood genius. Although he sold only one painting in his lifetime, his works are now worth a fortune.

The son of a Protestant minister, van Gogh was born in Zundert, Holland, in 1853. By 1869, he was representing the art dealers Goupil & Company, first in the Hague, then in London. Unsuccessful in business, he left the company in 1875 to train for the ministry. He worked a brief stint preaching to miners in southwestern Belgium, but he was dismissed from the clergy after he gave away all his possessions. His superiors were concerned he was adhering to Christian principles too literally. Van Gogh was active as an artist for only ten years, between 1880 and 1890. He taught himself to paint from copying prints and reading books. He was influenced by realist painters, as is clear in his *Potato Eaters* (1885), a work that owes a great deal to Jean-François Millet in terms of subject matter and technique.

In 1886, van Gogh left Holland for Paris, where he shared quarters with his brother Theo, an art dealer who supported him through most of his life. It was through Theo that van Gogh met Claude Monet, Paul Gauguin, Camille Pissarro, and Georges Seurat. Like many modern artists of his time, he also developed an interest in Japanese prints. After two years of intense artistic activity, van Gogh moved to Arles in the south of France, to realize his ambition of painting peasants. In October 1888, he invited Gauguin to join him. On Christmas Eve that same year, the two artists quarreled and van Gogh cut off his own ear. According to a newspaper report, he presented it to a prostitute. The incident was the first sign of his mental illness, probably a form of epilepsy.

By May 1889, van Gogh committed himself to a psychiatric hospital in Saint Rémy. It was there that he painted possibly his most famous work, *Starry Night*. Twelve months later, he moved into the home of the homeopathic doctor, Paul-Ferdinand Gachet, near Paris. Severely depressed, van Gogh shot himself in the chest in July 1890 and died two days later. After his death, van Gogh's reputation escalated rapidly. An exhibit of his works in 1901 featured seventy-one of his paintings. In 1987, his *Irises* sold for £47. Three years later his *Portrait of Doctor Gachet* was bought for a record-breaking $82.5 million. Today van Gogh's 1,250 paintings and 1,000 sketches are spread throughout the world, the largest single collection being the Van Gogh Museum in Amsterdam.

ADDITIONAL FACTS

1. Purportedly, van Gogh's final words were, "Sadness will last forever."

2. Some scholars believe van Gogh suffered from bipolar disorder while others have claimed that his mental illness stemmed from his excessive absinthe consumption. Still other scholars say van Gogh tasted too many of his own paints.

Elements: Metals, Nonmetals, and Metalloids

An element is a substance that cannot be changed into another substance through chemical reactions. All elements are made of atoms with a distinct number of protons, positively charged subatomic particles. For example, all carbon atoms have six protons, and all gold atoms have seventy-nine protons. Ninety-three elements exist naturally on earth, and an additional twenty can be made artificially. There are three basic classifications of elements: metals, non metals, and metalloids. Three-quarters of elements are metals, although nonmetals are more commonly found in nature.

Metals are characterized by the ease with which they share and give up electrons, tiny negatively charged subatomic particles. When a metal atom yields an electron, it becomes a positively charged ion called a cation. Metals are often thought of as cations swimming in a sea of electrons. The free-floating electrons keep metal atoms bound yet flexible, giving metals their district properties: They are ductile (capable of being drawn into wire) and malleable (capable of being pounded into a sheet). For the same reason, metals also conduct heat and electricity well and readily form compounds with other elements. They tend to be lustrous solids at room temperature.

Nonmetals often gain electrons and form rigid chemical bonds. They are brittle and break easily. Nonmetals usually do not reflect light, and they do not conduct electricity or heat very well. However, they make excellent insulators. Although there are only thirteen known nonmetals, almost all life on earth is made out of six of them: hydrogen, carbon, nitrogen, oxygen, phosphorus, and sulfur. The other nonmetals are mostly inert gases, which rarely interact with other elements.

Metalloids have some characteristics of metals and some of nonmetals. For example, silicon and germanium are semiconductors, which means they conduct an electrical current under specific conditions. This is why they are so useful in computers and calculators.

ADDITIONAL FACTS

1. Mercury is the only metal that is liquid at room temperature.

2. Oxides of metals are basic, while oxides of nonmetals are acidic.

3. Most metals react quickly with oxygen in the air, which, for example, is what causes iron to rust. Pure sodium explodes when it is exposed to oxygen. Palladium, platinum, and gold are rare metals that do not react with oxygen, which is why they make for such beautiful and expensive jewelry.

Wagner's *Ring Cycle*

Richard Wagner's masterpiece is the gargantuan *Der Ring des Nibelung* (1874), also known as the *Ring Cycle*. The four-part opera, consisting of *Das Rheingold* (*The Rhinegold*), *Die Walküre* (*The Valkyries*), *Siegfried*, and *Götterdämmerung* (*The Twilight of the Gods*), lasts almost seventeen hours and is meant to be watched on four successive nights. It is considered by some to be the greatest operatic work of all time.

Wagner began working on the piece in 1848, his idea being to create a monumental work that could recapture the magic of Greek Tragedian Theater—to unite art, music, theater, poetry, and philosophy in one giant *Gesamtkunstwerk*, or "total work of art."

Wagner wrote all four librettos, basing them on the legend of the German-Norse mythical hero Siegfried. In the story, Wotan, king of the gods, has built a fortress, Valhalla, with the help of a race of giants. In order to pay his debt to them, Wotan steals a powerful ring from the dwarf Alberich. Alberich curses the ring, but that does not deter Wotan from continuing to pursue it. Most of the story revolves around the adventures of Wotan's son Siegmund and grandson Siegfried as various powers try to retrieve the ring, which is guarded by a dragon. Also playing a major role is Wotan's daughter, the Valkyrie Brünnhilde. In the end, the curse destroys everyone in its wake, Valhalla is consumed by fire, and a new era of the world is ushered in.

The music is incredibly lavish and complex, based on the idea of a leitmotif—a short, beautiful melody that represents a character, a feeling, an object, or an emotion. Each leitmotif is re-contextualized to fit new scenes. No opera house would take on the challenge of performing the cycle, so Wagner staged it at his own Bayreuth festival for the first time in 1874.

ADDITIONAL FACTS

1. *The Valkyrie character in the* Ring Cycle *is the origin of the famous opera caricature of a fat soprano wearing a Viking helmet and a brass brassiere.*

2. *The "Ride of the Valkyries" from* Die Walküre *is the famous music accompanying the helicopter drop scene in Francis Ford Coppola's* Apocalypse Now.

3. *The Norse mythology that inspired the* Ring Cycle *is also the source of J. R. R. Tolkien's* Lord of the Rings *and the subsequent blockbuster movies.*

Karl Marx

"The philosophers have only interpreted the world, in various ways; the point, however, is to change it."

—Karl Marx, *Theses on Feuerbach* (1845)

Karl Marx (1818–1883), the intellectual father of communism, had more impact on the twentieth century than any other philosopher. Born in 1818 in Trier, Germany, to an ethnically Jewish family that had converted to Christianity, Marx initially sought an academic career, but he was rebuffed due to his radical political leanings. Marx worked as a journalist for several years before he took part in the 1848 revolution in Germany. When that revolution failed, he fled to London, where he lived for the rest of his life.

In Marx's theory of history, the means of economic production explain historical and political change. At any given time, a society has certain means of producing economic goods such as food and forms of shelter. The means of production determine a particular economic arrangement. For instance, agriculture required a large number of people to till the land and a few people to oversee this work. The economic arrangement, in turn, determines the political system. In the case of agriculture, the farmers worked for the lord, who owned the land and protected them from other nobles in exchange for a portion of their crops. Revolutions occur when the economic arrangement and political system become obstacles to the productive forces of the economy

In each economic system, there is a division of labor, so there is a division of people into classes. Marx saw capitalism—which he characterized as the economic system in which goods are created not to be used but to be exchanged—as the product of a long historical development. In capitalism, the class division is exaggerated to the breaking point. A vast number of workers—the proletariat—toil in squalor, while a tiny minority of people who own the means of production—the bourgeoisie—are made wealthy. Marx predicted that capitalism would bring about its own demise. As capitalism thrives, he argued, it will create a larger and larger proletariat living in ever worsening conditions. Eventually, the workers will revolt and establish a different, cooperative, economic system—one in which each gives according to his abilities and takes according to his needs.

ADDITIONAL FACTS

1. Marx coauthored many of his works with Friedrich Engels, the son of a German industrialist. Their collaborations include the multi-volume Capital, *which Marx regarded as his masterwork.*

2. Marx described the state that would follow the collapse of capitalism and herald true communism as the "dictatorship of the proletariat."

al-Ghazali

Abu Hamid Muhammad ibn Muhammad al-Tusi al-Ghazali (1058–1111), or simply al-Ghazali, was one of the most influential Islamic theologians and philosophers. He was born in 1058 in Tus, part of what is today Iran.

Al-Ghazali studied and taught Shafi law, one of four legal schools within Sunni Islam. By the age of thirty-three, al-Ghazali had established himself as one of the field's leaders and was appointed head of the Nizamiyyah College in Baghdad. He served in this role for four years and remained very popular throughout his tenure.

One of al-Ghazali's foremost works is "The Incoherence of Philosophers." In this work, al-Ghazali claimed that events in the world are determined by God's present whim. This essentially eliminates all other sources of causality in nature and puts everything in God's immediate hands.

In the work, al-Ghazali criticized ancient philosophers such as Plato and Aristotle and Muslims who follow in their line of thinking. He claims that these philosophers were wrong to apply reason when answering religious questions. Al-Ghazali said that if reason could be used to prove absolute truths about religion, such as the existence of God, then everyone would agree to these truths. Instead, al-Ghazali believed rational thought could not be the source of religious answers.

In 1095, al-Ghazali underwent a spiritual change. He left the college and traveled throughout Arabia. He went to Damascus, Jerusalem, Mecca, Medina, Egypt, back to Baghdad, and finally to his hometown, Tus. It was during this time that al-Ghazali began to follow one of the many Sufi orders.

Al-Ghazali had long been a believer in the Asharite school of thought, which holds that the true nature of God is unknowable. This school credits al-Ghazali's own "The Incoherence of Philosophers" as its most important work. So it was no great leap that during his travels, al-Ghazali finally determined the mysticism of Sufism offered the best way of connecting with God. Given his immense popularity, al-Ghazali's alignment with the then emerging Sufi orders is credited with establishing Sufism's credibility in mainstream society.

ADDITIONAL FACTS

1. *Philosophically, al-Ghazali's work amounts to philosophical skepticism, similar to the British school of thought arising from George Berkeley and David Hume, but appearing 700 years earlier.*

2. *Al-Ghazali's major critic was Averroës, also known as Ibn Rushd, whose major work of criticism was called "Incoherence of The Incoherence."*

Elizabeth Cady Stanton and the Suffrage Movement

"The history of mankind is a history of repeated injuries and usurpations on the part of man toward woman."

—*Elizabeth Cady Stanton, "The Declaration of Sentiments,"*

Seneca Falls Conference, 1848

Elizabeth Cady Stanton (1815–1902) was an abolitionist, temperance advocate, and tireless promoter of women's rights in nineteenth century America. Born in 1815 in upstate New York, Stanton spent her entire career campaigning for women's suffrage, a goal that remained elusive during her lifetime. Stanton died in 1902, seventeen years before women finally got the right to vote in the United States.

In 1848, the year the American suffrage movement began in earnest, the idea of women casting ballots seemed preposterous to many. Only the tiny Pitcairn Island in the Pacific Ocean allowed female suffrage. Few colleges in the United States educated women, and women's property rights were sharply limited. But in that year, Stanton and a few other women organized a convention in Seneca Falls, New York, to plot a course for women's rights.

At the Seneca Falls convention, Stanton, along with Lucretia Mott, authored a Declaration of Sentiments signed by the delegates. The document, self-consciously modeled on Thomas Jefferson's Declaration of Independence, argued "that all men *and women* are created equal." For the next fifty years, Stanton worked to convince other Americans of that proposition.

The suffragists took their cause seriously, at a time when society deemed women's involvement with politics unladylike. When Stanton married, she insisted on dropping the word "obey" from her wedding oath. Like later progressives, the early feminists endured the shallow mockery of reactionaries. Many American men and women regarded the suffragists, like the abolitionists, as only the latest in a procession of insufferable Northern liberals bent on upending society and tradition.

Stanton did not live to see the ratification of the nineteenth amendment to the US Constitution granting women the right to vote in 1920, but her colleagues were careful to pay homage to the woman who had set the movement in motion at Seneca Falls. Her fellow agitator, Susan B. Anthony, said, "I want you to understand that I never could have done the work I have if I had not had this woman at my right hand."

ADDITIONAL FACTS

1. *The first US state to permanently grant women the right to vote was Wyoming, which was admitted to the Union in 1890.*

2. *Many of the early suffragists, including Anthony, were Quakers, a small, pacifistic Christian sect in Britain and the United States whose members were also leaders in the abolition and temperance movements.*

3. *A handful of countries still do not permit women to vote: Bhutan, Brunei, and Saudi Arabia.*

Lolita

Vladimir Nabokov's *Lolita* (1955) was among the most brilliant and controversial novels of the twentieth century. The novel's notoriety initially overshadowed its literary merit, but as the din subsided, readers and critics realized that *Lolita* broke new ground not only by virtue of its content but also with its narrative voice and technique.

Born in 1899 in Russia, Nabokov was educated in England, where he started a writing career. After publishing several novels, he moved to the United States to become a professor. Along the way, he developed a stylized, self-consciously intellectual voice that readers tended either to love or hate.

Lolita portrays the tortured sexual obsession of a middle-aged professor, Humbert Humbert, for a twelve-year-old girl. Originally from Paris, Humbert moves to the United States and takes a room at a widow's house after seeing her young daughter, Dolores, sunbathing in the garden. He goes so far as to marry the widow in order to stay close to Dolores, or "Lolita," but the widow soon dies. Although Humbert and Lolita indeed consummate their relationship, the capricious girl loses interest. Eventually Humbert realizes that, for once, his lust has actually transformed into real love; Lolita, however, rejects his advances.

As a narrator, Humbert is skillful and expressive yet delusional and wholly unreliable, twisting the facts with graceful, poetic language that disguises the truly disturbing nature of his obsession with young girls. By his account, it is Lolita who seduces him, and his preoccupation with "nymphets" is merely a byproduct of his tragic childhood romance. Humbert's famous opening lines set the novel's playful but unsettling tone:

> *Lolita, light of my life, fire of my loins. My sin, my soul. Lo-lee-ta: the tip of the tongue taking a trip of three steps down the palate to tap, at three, on the teeth. Lo. Lee. Ta.*

Upon finishing *Lolita* in 1955, Nabokov could not find a willing publisher in the United States; the work was published in France, where critics found it either brilliant or utterly obscene. The novel was widely banned and did not appear in the United States until 1958, when it became a bestseller. Today, it is prized as a perceptive literary investigation of sexuality and repression, as well as a prime example of the unreliable narration that was a hallmark of postmodern literature.

ADDITIONAL FACT

1. *From his youth, Nabokov was fluent in Russian, English, and French; his early works are primarily in Russian, his later ones, including* Lolita, *in English.*

Starry Night

Starry Night (Cypress and Village) is one of Vincent van Gogh's best-known paintings. It depicts a simple subject—the Provence landscape beneath a star-studded sky—but it is often interpreted as a deeply spiritual work.

Van Gogh painted *Starry Night* on the evening of June 19, 1889 while residing at the asylum in Saint Rémy. The painting (twenty-nine by thirty-six inches) is dominated by a vast expanse of sky with swirling clouds, stars, and a moon. At its base appears a small village, overshadowed by a church, the steeple of which pierces the sky. The village is nestled amid rolling blue hills. To the left, an outline of a fiery cypress towers into the sky.

According to some scholars, *Starry Night* reveals van Gogh's admiration for the American poet Walt Whitman. Commenting on Whitman's work, van Gogh wrote of the "great starlit vault of heaven, a something which, after all, one can only call God and eternity in its place above the world."

In this particular case, van Gogh did not work directly from nature but from several preparatory sketches. In the final version, he modified the shape of the actual San Rémy church by adding a steeple, an architectural feature more typical of his native Holland.

Various meanings have been read into the painting. Some scholars believe that the dark windows and door of the church imply that inspiration is not to be found in organized religion but in nature, here symbolized by the magnificent cypress. Others have claimed that the twisted cypress and dynamic sky represent van Gogh's tormented soul. Some have even claimed that the painting is not symbolic at all, but represents the actual constellations as they appeared on that evening in 1889. Observations from the Hubble Space Telescope suggest that van Gogh may have been looking at V838 Monocerotis, one of the most mysterious stars in the Milky Way.

ADDITIONAL FACTS

1. Today the painting is on permanent view in the Museum of Modern Art in New York City.

2. The swirling brushstrokes of paint make the trees and sky resemble elemental forces, such as fire and water.

3. Van Gogh's use of thick paint swirls to suggest powerful emotion anticipated the expressionist movement of the early twentieth century.

Chemical Bonds

Chemical bonds join together two or more atoms to form compounds such as water, salt, and oil. Atoms combine in order to form more stable structures of electrons, tiny negatively charged particles that encircle the center of atoms. In a stable compound, the total energy of the compound is lower than the energy of the individual atoms. There are three basic types of chemical bonds: covalent bonds, ionic bonds, and metallic bonds.

In covalent bonds, atoms share one or more pairs of electrons. There are single bonds, sharing only one pair of electrons, double bonds sharing two pairs, triple bonds, and rarely quadruple bonds, but these tend to be explosively unstable. In general, covalent bonds tend to be the strongest and most stable chemical bonds, especially covalent bonds between nonmetals. There are two types of covalent bonds: nonpolar bonds and polar bonds. In nonpolar bonds, electrons are distributed evenly across the molecule, but in polar bonds, electrons tend to gather on one end of the molecule. This creates negative and positive poles on the molecule. The oppositely charged ends become attracted to each other, structurally binding molecules together, as in ice and water.

In ionic bonds, atoms donate their electrons to other atoms. Often ionic bonds form between metals, which lose electrons easily, and nonmetals, which gain electrons easily. When a metal atom loses an electron, it becomes a positively charged ion called a cation. When a nonmetal atom gains an electron, it becomes a negatively charged ion called an anion. Anions and cations join in ionic bonds. Ordinary table salt, sodium chloride, is an example of a metal, sodium, joining with a nonmetal, chlorine, through an ionic bond.

Metals tend to share metallic bonds. Since metals readily lose electrons, they are often thought of as cations floating in a sea of electrons. Even when different metals combine in alloys, they still share free-floating electrons, giving metals their strong yet flexible properties.

ADDITIONAL FACTS

1. Technically, pure ionic bonds don't exist. They all have a degree of covalent or metallic bonding as well.

2. Covalent bonds were first described by Gilbert N. Lewis in 1917.

3. Quintuple covalent bonds exist in some chromium compounds.

Nineteenth-Century Nationalism

For more than a century, Vienna was the global center of art music. But in the 1840s, revolutions in Austria, Hungary, Germany, Italy, and France helped spur nationalist movements that rose against imperial powers in a struggle that would grow as the nineteenth century progressed. In the musical world, composers expressed their support of nationalist movements by hearkening back to the folk music of their homelands. Their nationalism would eventually give way to the cosmopolitan internationalism of the modernists, but for a time it was the dominant inspiration for many composers.

In Paris, Frédéric Chopin (1810–1849) wrote polonaises and mazurkas to honor his native Poland and in 1831 he wrote a piece commemorating the doomed Polish uprising against the Czar. Czech nationalism was expressed by three composers: Bedrich Smetana (1824–1884), Antonan Dvorák (1841–1904), and Leoš Janácek (1854–1928). Dvorák's *Slavonic Dances* (1878) and *Symphonies No. 4* (1874) and *No. 6* (1880) used Czech folk themes and rhythmic patterns.

Richard Wagner (1813–1883) and Richard Strauss (1864–1949) thought that German music was the most advanced and pure music, a notion that would find a welcome home in the politics of the twentieth century. And, Piotr Ilyich Tchaikovsky (1840–1893) and Nikolai Rimsky-Korsakov (1844–1908) drew on Russian traditional music in service of the Czar's interests.

The most famous piece of nationalist music is probably Tchaikovsky's *1812 Overture* (1888), a piece commissioned by the Russian government to commemorate the Russian victory over Napoleon. Tchaikovsky reportedly wrote it against his better judgment, but the result is one of the most popular pieces of classical music ever written. Tchaikovsky composed the piece using music from the Russian national anthem and several Orthodox hymns, scoring it for orchestra with live artillery cannons.

ADDITIONAL FACTS

1. In 1933, Richard Strauss became the president of the Reichmusikkammer, *the Nazi party's ministry of music.*

2. Nationalism often re-emerged in the twentieth century in the compositions of Aaron Copland and Dmitri Shostakovich.

3. The height of nationalist music coincided with two important events: the unification of Germany and the establishment of an independent Italy.

Friedrich Nietzsche

Probably no philosopher has been so often, or so wildly, misinterpreted as Friedrich Nietzsche (1844–1900). Born in the German town of Röcken bei Lützen, Nietzsche became a celebrated young scholar of classical philology, achieving a professorship at the University of Basel, in Switzerland at the age of twenty-four. Nietzsche abandoned his teaching duties due to ailing health and collapsed in 1889, an invalid, both mentally and physically. He died insane in 1900, cared for by his sister.

One central theme in Nietzsche's philosophy is what he called the "re-evaluation of all values," in which he encouraged people to question their moral, scientific, and aesthetic values. Nietzsche believed many of the values that form the basis of European culture—especially Christian morality—needlessly inhibit life and joy. According to Nietzsche, many of these values were invented by the weak and resentful as a tool to gain power over the strong. He believed that Christianity, with its celebration of the meek and humble, is the victory of the sick against the healthy. For every system of values, and every philosophical system, Nietzsche asked, what kind of life does it serve?

Another important Nietzschean idea is that of the "eternal recurrence"—the notion that the world will repeat itself exactly as it was, forever. Because of the eternal recurrence, we will all live our lives, exactly as we have, down to the minutest details, again and again. Nietzsche offers this as a test: What kind of person would be willing to repeat all of the moments of his or her life, even the pettiest and most humiliating ones, for all eternity?

ADDITIONAL FACTS

1. *Many experts believe Nietzsche had syphilis, contracted from a prostitute or when he was a medical orderly in the Franco-Prussian war.*

2. *Nietzsche's sister, Elizabeth Förster-Nietzsche, was a proto-Nazi who tried to twist her brother's philosophy for her own political ends. He himself was a withering critic of both German nationalism and anti-Semitism.*

3. *Nietzsche's concept of the "Superman" (Übermensch) is a term the Nazis used to describe the ideal Aryan hero. Nietzsche did not say exactly what the Superman would be like, but it was clear that he would not be warlike or violent.*

4. *Nietzsche had a close friendship with the composer Richard Wagner. Eventually, the friendship was broken, after which Nietzsche was savagely critical of Wagner in his writings. Some evidence suggests that the cause of the break in their friendship was that Wagner had inappropriately suggested to Nietzsche's doctor the cause of the young man's vision problems—excessive masturbation!*

☙

Mahdi

Muslims believe Muhammad taught that before the end of time, a man will emerge from Islam known as the Mahdi. This man will be a member of Muhammad's Ahl al-Bayt, or lineage, and will turn the world into a pure and peaceful place. There are many beliefs about the nature of the Mahdi, and, as is common, Shiite and Sunni Muslims differ greatly.

According to Sunni Islam, the Mahdi has not been born yet. When he is born, he will be born in Medina, where Muhammad died, and his parents will be named Abdullah and Aamina, the same as Muhammad's. Sunnis also believe that the Mahdi will emerge at the age of forty, the same age at which Muhammad had his first revelation, and that both the Mahdi and a returning Jesus will inhabit the earth for many years.

Shiites, on the other hand, take a radically different view. They believe that since the death of the prophet Muhammad, Islam has been lead by a series of imams, beginning with Ali. The twelfth and final of these Imams was born in 868. However, he is not yet dead.

When the twelfth imam was five, his father, the eleventh imam, passed away. The boy's uncle was about to give the prayer service when the five-year-old Mahdi declared that only an imam could perform the honor and proceeded to do it himself. After this, he went into occultation, or disappearance, where he remains. Shiites believe that he is still alive today, named Muhammad al-Mahdi, and will eventually reemerge.

ADDITIONAL FACTS

1. *Muhammad claimed that even if the day of judgment arrived, and the Mahdi had not appeared, then that day would continue forever until the Mahdi arose.*

2. *In Frank Herbert's* Dune, *the main character is said to be the Mahdi.*

Andrew Carnegie

Andrew Carnegie (1835–1919) was a Scottish immigrant to the United States who amassed one of the greatest fortunes of the nineteenth century. Carnegie retired in 1901 as the richest man in the world—and then spent the rest of his life giving money away. By the time of his death in 1919, Carnegie had donated more than $350 million to charity, an unheard of sum at the time. To this day, many towns across America are home to a Carnegie Library built with money donated by the immigrant philanthropist.

Carnegie owed his fortune to nineteenth century America's insatiable appetite for steel. After emigrating from Scotland with his family at age thirteen in 1848, Carnegie went to work at a cotton mill. But he realized that steel presented an enormous opportunity. In 1865, at age thirty, he started the Carnegie Steel Company in Pittsburgh to produce metal for the railroads and bridges crisscrossing the rapidly industrializing North American continent. Carnegie was famous for holding down costs, and his company eventually acquired many of its competitors.

At the age of sixty-five, Carnegie sold the company and retired. He had cultivated an image of himself as a friend to the working class with humble roots, and in his book *The Gospel of Wealth* Carnegie argued that the rich should give their wealth away to the less fortunate. In retirement, that is exactly what Carnegie did. His donations funded the construction of 2,500 libraries in the English-speaking world, including more than 1,600 in the United States. He also sponsored museums, scientific expeditions, and the famous New York musical hall named in his honor.

In the United States, Carnegie's rags-to-riches life story suggested that anyone could pursue the American dream and become rich. His name endures as a symbol of American opportunity and also for the responsibilities of the wealthy.

ADDITIONAL FACTS

1. *Among his many other philanthropic pursuits, Carnegie paid for the installation of more than 7,000 church organs across the United States, some of which still remain in use.*

2. *Carnegie often returned to Scotland after earning his fortune and purchased Skibo Castle in the Scottish Highlands as a summer house. The castle remained the property of his family for many years, but it is now an exclusive vacation resort. Madonna and Guy Ritchie married there in 2000.*

3. *Carnegie was an ardent supporter of the Union cause during the Civil War. He served as superintendent of military railways and telegraphs, coordinating the transportation of troops to the battlefield.*

4. *A gigantic dinosaur—the* diplodocus carnegii *—is named in honor of Carnegie, who financed the expedition that first unearthed the creature.*

The Adventures of Huckleberry Finn

Mark Twain's *The Adventures of Huckleberry Finn* (1884) remains one of the most widely read pieces of nineteenth-century American literature. Though much has been made of its history as a banned book, it is an entertaining, moving story that appeals to younger and older readers alike.

Huck Finn is a young boy from the town of St. Petersburg, Missouri. Because Huck's father, Pap, is a violent drunk and often absent, Huck lives in the care of an old widow, whose attempts to "sivilize" Huck cause the boy much consternation.

When Pap returns to town, he kidnaps the boy to a remote cabin, beating him viciously. To escape, Huck fakes his own death and ventures onto an island in the middle of the Mississippi River, where he encounters Jim, a runaway slave owned by the sister of Huck's caretaker.

Huck and Jim set off down the river in the raft, encountering a rogues' gallery of criminals, slave hunters, con men, and other examples of the worst society has to offer. After myriad misadventures, Jim is captured but eventually rescued by Huck and his friend Tom Sawyer. Ultimately, all are returned to safety, and at the end of the novel, Huck decides that he wants to go off and explore the still untamed American West.

The novel centers on Huck's development and his struggles to reconcile the dictates of society with his own feelings and instincts, especially regarding his relationship with Jim. Growing up in the South, Huck has long been taught that it is wrong to help an escaped slave. But Jim—by far the most caring and decent character in the novel—quickly becomes the object of Huck's trust and almost a father figure. In the end, Huck comes to understand that society's rules are not always correct and that his own sense of right and wrong is often the more valuable guide.

ADDITIONAL FACTS

1. *To this day, Huck Finn is banned in many US school districts because of its frequent use of the word "nigger"—even though Twain's usage only adds realism to a story that preaches tolerance and decries the stupidity of racism.*

2. *Twain coined the now common term for the period in US history between Reconstruction and World War I—the "Gilded Age"—in an eponymous novel published in 1873.*

3. *In Twain's earlier novel* The Adventures of Tom Sawyer *(1876), Tom and Huck discover a criminal's stash of gold—the same money that Pap tries to get his hands on in* The Adventures of Huckleberry Finn.

La Grande Jatte

Sunday Afternoon on the Island of La Grande Jatte by (1884–1886) Georges Seurat (1859–1891) is one of the best-known works of postimpressionism. The painting, executed in Seurat's famous pointilist or divisionist technique, captures a tranquil scene of people walking, sitting, fishing, and sailing along the banks of the Seine River near Paris.

In the years leading up to *La Grande Jatte*, Seurat had been studying and experimenting with optics. Influenced by Ogden Rood's treatise on color, *Théorie scientifique des couleurs* (1881), he came up with a scientific system for translating natural luminosity and color with thickly applied and superimposed dots or dashes of paint. His *Bathers at Asnières* of 1883 demonstrates his earlier application of this technique to a large, outdoor scene.

Seurat began working on the 82-by-121-inch canvas of *La Grande Jatte* in 1884, completing it in time for an exhibition in 1885 that was subsequently cancelled. Thereafter he reworked many sections of the painting in a technique he called chromo-luminarism before submitting it to the eighth and last impressionist group show. From the moment that he conceived the painting until its completion, Seurat made fifty-nine preparatory sketches on paper, panel, and canvas. These provide a fascinating insight into his creative process.

The painting is set on the northwest shore of the island of La Grande Jatte, which faces the town of Courbevoie across the Seine. The scene includes forty-eight people, eight boats, three dogs, and a monkey. A standing couple on the right dominates the composition. The woman carries two leashes, apparently for the dog and monkey at her feet. To her left is a group of three men, one of whom is casually dressed and smoking a pipe while sprawled out on the lawn. Nearby—in contrast to the lounging man—is an elegantly attired man, sitting stiffly upright. A child wearing a shimmering white garment in the center of the painting is the only figure looking out at the viewer. Receding into the distance are more people set in groups or by themselves. The scene is alternately relaxed and formal. The figures appear somewhat flat as if cut from cardboard and arranged carefully in the landscape.

According to his own testimony, Seurat intended the painting to be a monumental record of contemporary life, worthy of comparison to such venerable ancient masterpieces as the frieze on the Parthenon. In 1924 Frederick Clay Bartlett purchased *La Grande Jatte* for the Art Institute of Chicago, where it can be seen today. A recent musical by Stephen Sondheim, *Sunday in the Park with George*, brought the canvas to life on stage.

The States of Matter

The three states of matter—solid, liquid, and gas—are defined by the shape and volume of the substance in question. Solids have a finite volume and shape. Liquids have a finite volume, but their shape is determined by whatever is holding them. Gases have no definite shape or volume and will expand infinitely if nothing contains them.

Matter is made of molecules, and molecules are made of atoms. It is the nature of atoms and molecules that determine the state of matter. All molecules have kinetic energy; they move. The more they move, the more likely

SOLID   LIQUID   GAS

they are to move apart from each other. But molecules, especially molecules of the same type, tend to be attracted to each other. The tension between kinetic energy and molecular attraction results in the different phases of matter. This tension is greatly influenced by temperature and pressure. Increases in temperature make molecules move faster, raising kinetic energy, while increases in pressure bring molecules closer together, heightening molecular attractions.

In solids, molecules move very slowly, vibrating or rotating, and the attraction between molecules is very strong. They can arrange themselves in rigid structures called crystals or amorphous structures like glass. Depending on temperature and pressure, the same type of molecule can be arranged into many different structures. For example, solid carbon can form graphite or diamonds. The different structures are called phases.

In liquids, the kinetic energy is high enough and the molecular attraction is low enough so that molecules slide by each other easily. Most substances have only one liquid phase, but other substances have more than one, for instance there are two phases of liquid helium. In gases, the molecules are barely attracted to each other and move freely. If molecules gain enough kinetic energy and have almost no pressure, their electrons—tiny negative subatomic particles—will detach themselves from the rest of their atoms. This phase, called plasma, occurs in stars.

ADDITIONAL FACTS

1. *Ice—solid water—has eight different phases.*

2. *One phase of liquid helium is extremely strange. If poured into a container, it will settle at the bottom, crawl up the inside, crawl over the rim, and then crawl down the outside.*

3. *At extremely low temperatures, molecules barely move at all. This allows for bizarre phases of matter called superfluids, supersolids, and Bose-Einstein condensates.*

Piotr Ilyich Tchaikovsky

Disparaged by critics in his own day, there are multiple views of what Piotr Ilyich Tchaikovsky (1840–1893) contributed to the classical music canon. He was either a bombastic, overly-sentimental hack who had little grasp of form, or he was a nationalist who composed straight from the heart and was bold enough to follow his instincts. Whatever the case, Tchaikovsky's orchestral works have claimed a place in history, and they are at least an accessible introduction to the world of art music.

Born in a mining town 900 kilometers east of Moscow, Tchaikovsky was a fragile, sickly child. He was sent to a boarding school and later a conservatory in Saint Petersburg. He became a professor of harmony at the Moscow Conservatory in 1866 and joined a small circle of nationalist composers. In Moscow, he wrote his *Symphony No. 2 "Little Russian"* (1872) and several other works utilizing Russian themes.

At first Tchaikovsky was not fully appreciated in his home country. When his *Piano Concerto No. 1* (1875) was played for the great Russian master Rubinstein, it was deemed "worthless and unplayable." It premiered in Boston to wide acclaim, however. Tchaikovsky did find acceptance in Russia later in his career, beginning with works like his *Symphony No. 4* (1878).

Tchaikovsky's most famous works are the *1812 Overture* (1888) and the music for the ballets *Swan Lake* (1875) and the perennially-performed *Nutcracker* (1892).

ADDITIONAL FACTS

1. *Tchaikovsky first conducted at Carnegie Hall in 1891. He later wrote that he was more popular in American than he had ever been in Europe.*

2. *Tchaikovsky died one of two ways: either from cholera he got drinking unboiled water or suicide by poison as a penalty in a gentlemen's dispute.*

3. *Tchaikovsky was a homosexual, but to give the appearance that he wasn't, he married an adoring fan named Antonina Milyukova in 1877. The marriage fell apart after a few weeks.*

Modality

You could have been a little taller, or a little shorter. You could have had more siblings, or fewer. All of these things are possible, but not actual. Aspects of the world that could have been different are described by philosophers as contingent. However, there are ways the world could not have been different. For instance, 2+2 could not have added up to anything other than 4. Aspects of the world such as 2+2=4 are necessarily true.

The problem of modality is the problem of identifying which features of the world are contingent, which are necessary, and how to tell the difference. The question of modality is a question that would remain even if we knew every truth about the world. We could still ask: Which of these truths are necessary, and which are contingent?

Almost all philosophers agree that logic is necessarily true: if Socrates is a man, and all men are mortal, then it follows necessarily that Socrates is mortal. It is impossible for the first two to be true, and the third false. Likewise, almost all philosophers agree that mathematics is necessary: it is impossible that 2+2 not equal 4. However, philosophers disagree about other issues, such as whether the physical laws of the universe are necessary. They also disagree about whether there are necessary truths about individual things. For instance, is it necessary, or only contingent, that you are a human being? Could you have existed without being a human being—say, as a cat or a groundhog? Or, a religious example: If there is a God, does he exist necessarily?

Philosophers also ask what about the world determines that some things are possible, while others are impossible. While some philosophers have argued that this question cannot be answered, others have argued that something is possible whenever there is a "possible world" in which it is true.

ADDITIONAL FACTS

1. *Baruch Spinoza (1632–1677) believed that everything is necessary and that there is no contingency in the world.*

2. *René Descartes (1596–1650) believed that God decides what will be necessary and what contingent. If God had chosen otherwise, it would have been false, for instance, that 2+2=4.*

Jihad

The Arabic word *jihad* has controversial connotations. Although it is frequently translated and understood as "Holy War," it also means "exertion in the path of God."

The exertion that jihad describes is the effort that one must undertake as one struggles with Islam. This effort may involve the inner struggle to become a better Muslim or the struggle against evil through writing, sermons, and scholarship.

Much emphasis has been placed on the Holy War aspect of jihad, not only because of recent events, but also due to Islam's history. After fleeing to Medina, Muhammad raised a following and then attacked and overthrew Mecca. From there, he proceeded to spread Islam throughout Arabia. Traditionally, Muslims divided the world into two parts: Dar al-Islam and Dar al-Harb. Dar al-Islam was the land of Islam, where Islam was already prevalent. Dar al-Harb, on the other hand, was the land of war, or the land that Islam had yet to reach.

Some claim this suggests that until the world is comprised solely of Muslims, Muslims will be forced to wage war. However, this is not necessarily the case. As the Muslim empire spread throughout the Arabian Peninsula, and into Africa, Asia, and Europe, Muslims encountered more people who were already monotheists. They also suffered military defeats. Thus, the Muslim expansion slowed and became less violent. Many Muslim leaders began to espouse a vision of peaceful coexistence.

ADDITIONAL FACTS

1. *Among Muslim mystics a distinction is made between lesser jihad and greater jihad. Holy War was seen as lesser jihad while struggling with one's soul was seen as greater jihad.*

2. *Muhammad is often remembered as a great warrior, thus strengthening the argument for a militant Islam. However, it should be noted that only during the last ten years of his life did he wage war. For his first fifty-three years, he was a merchant and then a priest.*

Vladimir Lenin

At the start of the twentieth century, an autocratic monarchy struggled to maintain control over Russia. From his giant Winter Palace in Saint Petersburg, the last czar, Nicholas II, ruled over a vast and troubled kingdom of wealthy landowners, impoverished peasants, and starving factory workers. Protesters demanded more political freedoms, but the czar's army repeatedly suppressed the growing clamor for reform, hanging dissidents or sending them to prison in Siberia. For the Russian people, World War I was the last straw. Horrified by the carnage—1.7 million Russian soldiers died in the name of European power politics—the Russian people finally toppled the czar in 1917.

Initially, Russian reformers hoped to replace the monarchy with a liberal democracy akin to France and Great Britain. But a middle-aged political activist from the Russian town of Simbirsk had different ideas. Within a year of the czar's abdication, Vladimir Ilyich Lenin (1870–1924) and his communist supporters had seized power across Russia. They rejected liberal democracy and sought to build a new kind of government organized around Marxist political philosophy. Out of the shards of the old czarist empire, Lenin and the communists created a new nation: the Union of Soviet Socialist Republics (USSR).

Under the czar, Lenin spent many years in exile or in prison for his subversive activities. During this time, he honed a set of ideas that would come to be known as Leninism. Leninism attempted to translate the philosophy of Karl Marx into a blueprint for actually governing a communist state. In practice, Leninism in the Soviet Union led to huge suffering for the Russian people. Before his death in 1924, Lenin's government had outlawed private enterprise, executed thousands, and triggered a famine that killed millions of Soviet citizens. Still, by the measure of industrial production, Lenin's revolution was a success. By the end of World War II, the Soviet Union was a military superpower. Joseph Stalin took power in the Soviet Union after Lenin's death in 1924, consolidating the grip of the communist party during his ruthless thirty-year reign.

ADDITIONAL FACTS

1. *After Lenin's death, his body was embalmed and placed in a mausoleum in the center of Moscow, where it remains today.*

2. *Lenin is the inspiration for the character of Old Major in the famous book* Animal Farm *by George Orwell.*

3. *The deposed czar and his family were murdered by the Soviets in 1918.*

Madame Bovary

Gustave Flaubert's *Madame Bovary* (1857) was one of the first great works of nineteenth-century realism. Although the novel's story may seem clichéd today, its realistic depiction of an unfulfilled woman pursuing adultery was revolutionary at the time. In fact, the plotline caused public outrage, leading to an obscenity trial for Flaubert and his publisher.

Born in 1821, Flaubert lived during a time of great social change in France. After the French Revolution of 1789, the fading aristocracy gave way to a rising middle class of businessmen and merchants. Flaubert, who had been groomed for the intellectual elite, detested the crass, materialistic values of the nouveau-riche. This venom is evident throughout his works, particularly *Madame Bovary*.

Young Emma Bovary grows up in the countryside, educated by nuns. After she weds a bourgeois doctor of only average wealth and minimal competence, the dull realities of marriage simply do not meet her idealized expectations. Even motherhood fails to lift her spirits; she longs for something like romantic love, but her aspirations remain aimless and fickle. Emma embarks on two adulterous affairs, one of which ends in heartbreak, the other in boredom. Although her husband remains entirely oblivious, Emma becomes indiscreet and careless with money, accumulating massive debts and ultimately resorting to attempted prostitution. In a fit of despondency, she kills herself with poison.

Madame Bovary's status as a literary classic stems from both its subject matter and its groundbreaking stylistic approach. Whereas novelists and poets of the romantic movement had maintained their optimism about the human spirit, the much more pessimistic Flaubert was analytic and detached in his approach to Emma's situation. He also manipulated prose in innovative ways, subtly altering his language in different parts of the narrative to correspond with changes in the mood of the story. After Flaubert's death, other masters of realism, from Leo Tolstoy to Thomas Hardy, created masterpieces that are greatly in his debt.

ADDITIONAL FACTS

1. *Flaubert was renowned for laboring endlessly over individual word choices, believing that he had to find* le seul mot juste—*"the unique precise word"—for every description and situation.*

2. Madame Bovary *took Flaubert more than five years to write. Friends urged him to put the project aside, but he devoted himself exclusively to it until he finished.*

3. *Flaubert's subtitle for* Madame Bovary *was* Moeurs de province, *or "Provincial Customs"—a snide articulation of his distaste for the bourgeoisie.*

Expressionism

The expressionist movement was initiated by artists who deliberately rejected naturalism in art. Rather than attempt to capture the visible world objectively, expressionists transformed it to meet their needs. Although they did not share a unified style, they gravitated toward the use of dissonant colors, unbalanced composition, and crude, childlike, or primitive techniques. Turning their backs on the refined classicism of Renaissance and Academic painters, they sought inspiration in the emotionally charged paintings of sixteenth century German masters, such as Albrecht Dürer and Matthias Grünewald.

Although Vincent van Gogh and Paul Gauguin contributed much to the development of expressionism, the beginning of the movement is usually dated to 1905, the year in which a group of artists under the leadership of Henri Matisse first exhibited their works in Paris. These men came to be known fauves, or "wild beasts," due to their use of shockingly bright colors and distorted figures.

While the fauves were stirring controversy in Paris, German Expressionism was taking root in Dresden. It was here that Ernst Kirchner inaugurated the association known as *Die Brücke*, (the Bridge), by which he meant the bridge between the old and new worlds. Inspired by postimpressionists, the fauves, and African wood carvings, members of the Bridge developed a harsh and jagged style to depict subjects such as urban street scenes. One of the most important members of the group was Emil Nolde, whose painting *Maskenstilleben III* typified their artistic priorities. After 1905, expressionism sprung up simultaneously all over Europe. Major representatives of the movement include Oskar Kokoschka and Egon Schiele in Austria, Chaim Soutine and Georges Rouault in France, Edvard Munch in Norway, and James Ensor in Belgium. In 1911, Vasily Kandinsky and Franz Marc founded *Der Blaue Reiter* (*The Blue Rider*) a short-lived association of artists based in Munich, who fused expressionist, symbolist and cubist principles, and led the way to abstraction.

Expressionism is sometimes used as a catch-all term for all the movements (e.g., cubism, futurism, Dada, and surrealism) that rejected classicism in the first half of the twentieth century. Expressionism declined in the mid-1930s when Nazi authorities proclaimed it decadent. At that point, many of its representatives sought refuge in the United States and other safe havens.

ADDITIONAL FACTS

1. Although fauvists are often seen as the first expressionists, they tended to evoke positive emotions, while their counterparts in other countries were more inclined to depict fear, anger, frustration, and misery.

2. Expressionists often worked in woodcut, a medium they appreciated because it resulted in rough outlines and harsh contrasts of black and white.

⊸⊛⊸

Photochemistry

All light comes to the earth in packets of energy called photons. Visible light is just a small sliver of light's full range, called the electromagnetic spectrum, which encompasses radio waves, microwaves, infrared light, ultraviolet light, x-rays, and gamma rays. Each type of light has a characteristic wavelength, frequency, and energy level. For example, radio waves are so long and low in energy that they pass straight through most types of matter without affecting them. Ultraviolet light, on the other hand, has just enough energy to set off chemical reactions that burn your skin. Light also triggers chemical reactions that allow us to capture images on film.

Black and white film is made of a thin protective plastic layer, an emulsion of gelatin and grains of silver salt crystals, also known as silver halides. Silver halides are sensitive to the exact wavelength, frequency, and energy level of visible light. Upon exposure, they absorb light and change into silver. The more light, the darker the silver salt crystals become. That is why negatives are darkest in the places that are the lightest in real life. When light is shone through the negative onto photographic paper, which is also coated in an emulsion of silver halides, the dark places on the negative let the least light through. The light places on the negative let the most light through. In this way, the image on the photographic paper turns into the opposite of the negative.

In color film, the emulsion is made up of layers sensitive to the separate frequencies of red, green, and blue light. When the film is developed, the layering of colors creates the full range of color that we see in everyday life.

ADDITIONAL FACTS

1. *The gelatin used in emulsion is a purified form of the gelatin found in JELL-O.*

2. *The first picture was taken by Joseph Niepce in 1827. He exposed to the sun a metal plate coated with a photochemical called bitumen. Eight hours later, he had a permanent image.*

3. *Daguerreotypes were the first commercially successful type of photograph. They were developed in poisonous mercury vapors, which led to an untimely end for many careless photographers.*

4. *The most expensive photograph in history sold for $400,000. It is a portrait of painter Georgia O'Keeffe's hands.*

Antonín Dvorák

The finest Czech musical export, Antonín Dvorák (1841–1904) was born in Bohemia and played viola in the Prague National Orchestra. In 1874, Dvorák's *Symphony No. 3* won him a national prize in Vienna, as well as the attention of Johannes Brahms, who was an adoring fan. In 1891, Dvorák was given a post as a professor of composition at the University of Prague, where he stayed only a year. He then accepted a post as director of the National Conservatory of Music in New York at a huge salary of $15,000.

After a five-month farewell tour of Bohemia, Dvorák embarked on his trip to America. His stay there would prove to be one of the most unhappy, yet productive periods of his life. He wrote his *Symphony No. 9, "The New World Symphony"* (1893) as well as his *Concerto for Violin* (1893).

The *New World Symphony* was composed while Dvorák was taking a vacation to the small Czech-speaking town of Spillvale, Iowa. On the train ride across the prairie, he was inspired by the landscape to compose his own interpretation of America. The resulting symphony suggests both the energy and the great spaces of America. As it turns out, the American folk tunes and rhythms that Dvorák incorporated into this work suggest to some listeners the homesickness of a wanderer for his own native land.

In this symphony, like most of Dvorák's orchestral works, we see a composer who has a basic romantic sensibility, but is nonetheless grounded in a classical grasp of form. What sets Dvorák apart from others is his devotion to folk melodies. *Symphony No. 5* (1875) has Bohemian-sounding melodies and *Symphony No. 6* (1880) utilizes a type of Czech dance called a furiant. Later in his career, Dvorák's work was informed by the lyrical, loosely-formed genre of the tone poem.

ADDITIONAL FACTS

1. Dvorák is also famous for his dazzling string quartets.

2. After almost three years in America, Dvorák returned to Prague and lived contentedly composing operas and tone poems.

3. Dvorák read a Czech translation of Longfellow's poem "Hiawatha" while he wrote the New World Symphony.

Pragmatism

Pragmatism is a philosophical tradition that originated in the United States with the work of Charles Sanders Peirce (1839–1914), William James (1842–1910), and John Dewey (1859–1952). Many regard pragmatism as America's most original contribution to philosophy.

Peirce, James, and Dewey differed in their specific beliefs, but they shared a general approach to philosophy. Before the pragmatists, many philosophers believed in the correspondence theory of truth. According to that theory, the truth of some belief or sentence depends on whether it matches some abstract reality independent of the mind and of language. Those who believe in that theory say it is possible that all of our best evidence is incorrect, that all our beliefs about the world, supported by the best possible experimentation, might turn out to be wrong. The pragmatists were united in their rejection of that outlook. All three of them understood truth to be a much easier proposition. They all maintained that, in some sense, what is true is simply what we have the best evidence to believe.

The pragmatists also believed that sentences and beliefs should be evaluated in terms of what role they play in facing life's practical problems. For the pragmatists, the term *practical* included moral, religious, and political life as well. Metaphysics was fine, as long as it helped us navigate our way through the world.

Both William James and John Dewey made significant contributions outside the realm of philosophy as well. James was an early pioneer of empirical psychology in America and author of the highly influential *Principles of Psychology*. Dewey wrote extensively on education, arguing that schools should be more flexible and take into account the creativity and individuality of children. He saw his pragmatism as closely connected to progressive politics, of which he was a dogged and famous champion in the early twentieth century.

ADDITIONAL FACTS

1. Dewey preferred to call his theory "instrumentalist."

2. Peirce was an early pioneer of semiotics, the study of signs.

3. William James was the brother of Henry James, the great American novelist. Their father, Henry James Sr., was a famous philosopher in his own day. The Jameses' father raised his children with the explicit goal of making them geniuses.

Gabriel

The angel Gabriel plays important roles in Islam, Christianity, and Judaism, often called on to relay important messages from God.

Gabriel is the single most important angel in the Islamic tradition. According to Islam, Gabriel appeared before Muhammad while he was meditating in a cave. Gabriel then recited the Quran, verse by verse, commanding Muhammad to memorize each line and spread it to others. The Quran is believed to be a series of quotes directly from God to Gabriel and onto Muhammad. Great attention is paid to the actual sound of the words as they resounded in the cave. This explains the Muslim emphasis on the actual spoken word of the Quran and why all prayers must be said in the original Arabic.

In Christianity, Gabriel is believed to be one of God's archangels. Some writings say there were three such higher-ranking angels, including Michael and Raphael. Others say there were seven. Gabriel makes several appearances in Christian tradition to relay God's messages. Gabriel appears before Zacharias and tells him that John the Baptist, a predecessor of Christ, will be born to Elizabeth. Gabriel also appears before Mary to tell her that she will give birth to Jesus. This interaction with Mary is known as the Annunciation.

In Judaism, Gabriel interacts twice with Daniel. The first time, after Daniel has seen a vision from God that he cannot understand, God sends Gabriel to help him interpret. The second time, Gabriel appears before Daniel and predicts the end of the Jews's exile in Babylon.

ADDITIONAL FACTS

1. Gabriel's name means "man of God."

2. Mormons believe that Gabriel and the Noah who built the Ark are actually the same person.

3. Various religious traditions have attributed several titles and properties to Gabriel: the color blue, the element water, the direction west, and the moon. He is also known in places as the angel of death, angel of vengeance, angel of resurrection, angel of revelation, angel of mercy, and angel of annunciation.

Treaty of Versailles

The Treaty of Versailles officially ended World War I. Signed in Paris in 1919 after months of negotiations, the treaty rearranged the map of the world. On the losing side, Germany lost much of its territory in Europe and its entire colonial empire. Germany was forced to accept responsibility for starting the war and agreed to pay financial reparations to the victorious Allies. The victors, France and Great Britain, occupied the former Ottoman territories in the Middle East.

Even at the time, many critics decried the treaty as a giant missed opportunity. The American President, Woodrow Wilson, had sailed to Paris with an idealistic plan to end imperialism and encourage international cooperation through a new League of Nations. But Britain, and especially France, had little interest in idealism. After losing millions of soldiers in the war, they wanted retribution. The result was a treaty that humiliated the Germans.

In the four years it lasted, from 1914 to 1918, the war had created unprecedented turmoil in the Old World. Four great empires—the German Reich, the Austro-Hungarian Empire, the Russian monarchy, and the Ottoman sultanate—disappeared from history.

At a time when the world was in such upheaval, the Versailles Treaty was unable to build a lasting peace. In the end, the United States never ratified the treaty because the Senate, dominated by isolationist Republicans, wanted no part of Wilson's League of Nations. Wilson entered the war promising to make the world "safe for democracy," but the world order that emerged at Versailles was neither democratic nor safe. Indeed, many historians believe that the humiliation of Germany lead to the popular resentment against the Western powers that Adolf Hitler would exploit in the 1930s to seize power.

ADDITIONAL FACTS

1. The treaty was signed in the famous Hall of Mirrors, which had been built by Louis XIV at the Palace of Versailles outside Paris. The choice was highly symbolic: It was the same room in which the French had capitulated to Germany at the end of the Franco-Prussian war in 1871.

2. Chemical weapons were used for the first time in World War I, first by the Germans in 1915 and then by the allies. Horrified by the slow death caused by gas, European nations agreed in 1925 to ban the use of chemical weapons on the battlefield in future wars.

3. Woodrow Wilson won the Nobel Peace Price in 1920 for founding the League of Nations. Two other US presidents—Teddy Roosevelt in 1906 and Jimmy Carter in 2002—have won the award.

4. The treaty carved the old Austro-Hungarian empire up into several new countries, in an effort to bring stability to central Europe. It didn't work out. Two of the new countries—Czechoslovakia and Yugoslavia—would not endure the twentieth century.

Waiting for Godot

En attendant Godot (1952)—in English, *Waiting for Godot*—is the best known work of Irish-French author and playwright Samuel Beckett. As one of the first pieces of absurdist theater, the play ushered in a new era of possibility for drama. It divided critics sharply: Some considered it a brilliant articulation of the monotony and meaninglessness of modern life, while others dismissed it as tedious garbage. The former view certainly won out, as Beckett's 1969 Nobel Prize cited *Waiting for Godot* as one of his greatest achievements.

Beckett was born in 1906 near Dublin. After studying Romance languages at college, he traveled widely through Europe and settled in Paris. As a writer, he dabbled in various genres, trying his hand at novels, short stories, poetry, and essays. But it is for his plays that Beckett is most renowned—and among these, *Waiting for Godot* is undoubtedly the most famous.

Little occurs during the play. One evening, two men, Vladimir and Estragon, talk and argue by the side of a road, waiting for someone named Godot. Before long, a man passes by, leading his slave on a rope. The slave does a dance and delivers a bizarre impromptu lecture. Later, a boy appears, telling the men that Godot is delayed but that he will arrive the next day. Vladimir and Estragon return the next evening and encounter the slave owner again; now inexplicably blind, he has no recollection of having seen them the previous day. Later, the same boy from the previous day arrives and states that Godot is not coming. Like the slave owner, the boy has no recollection of having seen Vladimir and Estragon before. The two men vow to leave and go home, but as the curtain falls, they continue to wait.

Absurdist theater, like *Godot*, blossomed in Europe during the 1950s and 1960s. Plays in this genre often seem meaningless or illogical, with vague, minimal settings and strange dialogue rife with non sequiturs. Indeed, the setting of *Waiting for Godot* is unknown, and the text never specifies who Godot is or why the two men are waiting for him. Critics have taken the play to represent the existential plight of the modern world, an exasperating stasis in which humankind is waiting for something meaningful yet has no idea when or if this thing will arrive—or even what it is.

ADDITIONAL FACTS

1. *Though* Waiting for Godot *may seem bizarre, many of Beckett's works are far more so. In* Happy Days *(1961), the female lead is buried in sand up to her waist and later her neck. His two* Act Without Words *plays (1956) feature mimes.* Breath *(1969) is just thirty-five seconds long.*

2. *Beckett hardly ever gave interviews or appeared publicly. When he won the Nobel Prize in 1969, he accepted the award remotely rather than attend the awards ceremony in Stockholm.*

The Scream

The Scream (1893), painted by the Norwegian expressionist Edvard Munch (1863–1944), has become the modern icon of existential angst.

Munch painted *The Scream* for a larger series entitled *The Frieze of Life*—"a poem of life, love and death." The work was meant to demonstrate contemporary theories of synaesthesia—the idea that light and color impulses can produce the impression of sound, and vice versa. Munch's first version of the painting actually included an inscribed account of the experience that had inspired the startling image: "I was out walking with two friends—the sun began to set—suddenly the sky turned blood red—I paused, feeling exhausted, and leaned on the fence—there was blood and tongues of fire above the blue-black fjord and the city—my friends walked on, and I stood there trembling with anxiety—and I sensed an infinite scream passing through nature."

The central figure, therefore, is Munch himself. The man is not screaming but shielding his ears from the noise. Behind him is the Oslofjord, as viewed from the hill of Ekeberg. The distorted perspective and lurid, swirling lines give visual form to the inescapable sound of the scream.

Although Munch painted more than fifty versions of the painting, two are particularly noteworthy. The first, done in gouache on cardboard, was stolen from the Munch Museum in Oslo in 2004. The second, done in oil, tempera, and pastel, is in the National Museum in Oslo. Munch also produced a lithograph of the image in 1895.

ADDITIONAL FACT
1. *A meteorological study conducted in 2003 suggested the source of Munch's inspiration was an unusually intense sunset caused by the eruption of Krakatoa in 1883.*

Sir Isaac Newton

Perhaps no person has contributed more to the fields of mathematics, physics, and astronomy than Sir Isaac Newton (1642–1727). Regarded as the reigning genius of his day, Newton was the first scientist ever to be knighted. His theories on motion and gravity were unsurpassed for hundreds of years.

But Sir Isaac Newton's beginnings were not promising. Born on an English manor January 4, 1643, three months before the death of his father, Newton was so premature and small that his mother joked she could fit him inside a quart pot. Newton miraculously survived infancy only to have his mother leave him at the age of two. Raised by grandparents who never loved him, Newton performed poorly in grammar school. His teachers described him as "idle" and "inattentive." But since he showed no interest in the family business of farming, his grandfather sent him to university.

At Cambridge, Newton studied Descartes, Boyle, Galileo, Kepler, Copernicus, and Euclid. When the school closed in 1665 because of the plague, Newton returned home with an educated, inspired mind. In the next two years, he began to revolutionize math and science. He invented calculus concurrently with Gottfried Wilhelm Leibnitz. Newton made advances in optics, proposing that white light is actually a combination of all the different colors of visible light. And perhaps most important, during this time Newton began to develop his three laws of motion: an object in motion stays in motion until acted upon by an outside force, the force acting on a body is directly proportional to its acceleration, and for every action there is an equal but opposite reaction.

Newton's laws of motion were not made public until 1687, when he published the *Principia*, which also included the law of universal gravitation: Every object in the universe attracts every other object with a force proportional to the product of the masses and inversely proportional to the square of the distance between them.

ADDITIONAL FACTS

1. Newton's law of gravity held up until Albert Einstein developed his theory of general relativity in 1905.

2. Newton once threatened to burn down the house of his mother and stepfather. He apologized for it later.

3. Newton and Leibnitz feuded for decades over who had really developed calculus first.

4. Newton's later years were marred by mental instability. After his death, large amounts of mercury were found in his body, probably due to his many fruitless experiments in alchemy. The mercury may have accounted for his strange behavior.

Gustav Mahler

It wasn't until forty years after he died that the status of Gustav Mahler (1860–1911) as a major composer was reestablished. Only after the destructiveness of World War II did his work seem to matter to the general and critical public.

Mahler was born into a broken home in Bohemia, the second of fourteen children. His father was an abusive distiller, and even as a young boy, Mahler sought solace in nature, taking long walks in the hills and fields around his home. At fifteen, he was accepted into the Vienna Conservatory, where he became fixated on the work of Ludwig van Beethoven and Richard Wagner. Mahler adopted some of Wagner's life theories, including the practice of vegetarianism. Sadly, for the rest of his life, some accused him of being a second-rank imitator of Wagner and others.

Some critics saw Mahler's compositions as a strange patchwork of various forms—strong symphonic movements à la Brahms or Beethoven, ringing choral works, and precious, inconsequential-sounding folk songs, all within the same works, as in his *Symphony No. 9* (1909). Mahler's compositional techniques were controversial while he was alive. He was also accused of using cheap orchestral tricks to overwhelm the listener.

Mahler was, however, one of the first real superstar conductors, and his high status was instrumental in developing the tradition of bestowing honor and respect on orchestra directors. In 1907, he was made director of the New York Metropolitan Opera and the next year started conducting the New York Philharmonic. Mahler's compositions were neglected after his death, and they only came to be popular again after years of support from other famous conductors including Bruno Walter, Otto Klemperer, and Leonard Bernstein.

ADDITIONAL FACTS

1. *Mahler married Alma Schindler, who was probably the most fashionable celebrity wife of the early twentieth century. After Mahler died, she wed the architect Walter Gropius and then the writer Franz Werfel.*

2. *Mahler was superstitious about composers dying after their ninth symphony, as Beethoven did. To avoid the curse, he composed* The Song of the Earth, *a song cycle for tenor, soprano, and orchestra, immediately after his eighth symphony, and a year later he wrote his actual ninth symphony. It didn't work. Mahler died of a throat infection shortly thereafter.*

3. *It seemed that every orchestra directed by Mahler, including the Vienna Opera and the New York Philharmonic, gained world-class status after just a few years under his direction.*

Phenomenology

Phenomenology is a school of philosophy founded by the German philosopher Edmund Husserl (1859–1938). Husserl wanted to explore our conscious experiences. (He put aside the question of what, if anything, existed beyond them.) He understood phenomenology as the attempt to describe our conscious experiences in a systematic way and believed that effort should form the basis of philosophy.

One of Husserl's main aims was to study the *intentionality* of experience—in other words, the fact that experiences are about things other than themselves. For example, if one has the experience of being pursued by a lion—either because one is having a nightmare of being pursued by a lion, or one is really being pursued by a lion—one's experience is *about* a lion. By contrast, most things besides experiences—for example, tables, rocks, or for that matter, lions themselves—are not *about* anything else. Husserl took the intentionality of experiences to be the main subject of phenomenology.

Husserl believed the goal of phenomenology was not merely a very detailed description of some particular experience. He wished to define the necessary structures and interrelations among different kinds of conscious experience. Thus, phenomenology is distinct from psychology, which, according to Husserl, merely describes how we think.

Many later philosophers were heavily influenced by phenomenology. For instance, Husserl's student Martin Heidegger (1889–1976) incorporated many phenomenological ideas into his philosophy. The French philosophers Jean-Paul Sartre (1905–1980) and Maurice Merleau-Ponty (1908–1961) were also influenced by Husserl's phenomenology.

ADDITIONAL FACTS

1. Through its influence on Heidegger and Sartre, phenomenology played an important role in the development of existentialism.

2. Husserl's term for a conscious experience that is intentionally directed at an object is noesis. *He calls the content of the act its "noema."*

3. The term phenomenology *comes from the Greek word for "to appear." In contemporary philosophy, the term* phenomenology *is often used to describe how something feels, or what an experience is like.*

Buddha/Gautama

Buddha, meaning the "enlightened one," was born in the sixth century BC as Prince Siddhartha Gautama. His father was the chief of the Shakya tribe of warriors in India.

According to some accounts, before Gautama was born, a seer appeared and declared that Gautama would either be a great king or a great religious leader. Gautama's father hoped that he would be a king and therefore attempted to shelter him from religion and the suffering of the world. At around the age of twenty-nine, however, Gautama ventured outside his father's protective walls and witnessed the Four Sights, which forever changed his life. He saw an old man, a sick man, a corpse, and a holy man or ascetic. After realizing that such suffering existed in the world, as well as such faith, Gautama renounced his way of life and retreated to Northeast India where he became a monk.

After meditating with the monks and trying several methods, such as fasting, to achieve inner peace, Gautama was unsatisfied. It was then that he discovered the "middle way" or "middle path" between self-indulgence, on the one hand, and self-mortification, on the other. After Gautama began to meditate in this fashion, he saw the truth.

Gautama believed that there were Four Noble Truths. First, there is suffering in the world. Second, there is a cause of this suffering and that is desire. Third, there is a state in which there is no suffering, called nirvana. And lastly, there is a path to reach this state.

At first, Gautama was unsure if he should teach this revelation to others. However, a spirit arrived and told him to do so. Gautama then began to preach throughout the Ganges region in India. He claimed to be only one in a line of Buddhas, whose job it was to teach others the path to enlightenment.

Gautama continued to preach the truth to others until his death, generally believed to be at the age of eighty.

ADDITIONAL FACTS

1. Many sources believe Gautama died from eating a batch of poisonous mushrooms.

2. Besides Buddha, Gautama is also known as "Shakyamuni," or "Sage of the Shakya Tribe" and "Thus-Come-One."

3. Though Buddhism originated in India, by the thirteenth century it had disappeared from the country almost completely after several foreign conquests. By this time, however, it had already spread to East Asia, Southeast Asia, and the Himalayan region, where it remains today.

Winston Churchill

Winston Churchill (1874–1965) was a British politician who led his country to victory during World War II. Prior to the war, Churchill was widely considered a failure. His career had been practically finished after he was blamed for British missteps during World War I. He had served in the Cabinet in the 1920s, but by the time Hitler took power in Germany, Churchill was warming a seat on the backbenches, his warnings about Hitler's rise ignored by colleagues who thought Churchill was an alarmist crank.

Britain turned to Churchill at one of the country's darkest hours. At the beginning of the war, Neville Chamberlain, the leader of the Conservative Party, was the prime minister. He resigned in 1940 when it became clear that he was not up to the job of leading his country in a desperate war for survival. Churchill replaced him at 10 Downing Street, the traditional residence of the British prime minister.

The first months of World War II had been a disaster for the Allies. In 1939 and early 1940, the German army invaded Poland, Denmark, Norway, Belgium, the Netherlands, Luxembourg, and France. British forces sent to help defend France were cornered by the Nazis and forced to evacuate the continent in 1940. With the United States and Soviet Union neutral, Great Britain was the only major military power left standing to oppose the onslaught of Nazi Germany.

As prime minister, however, Churchill achieved the impossible. For eighteen months, Britain withstood the Nazis virtually by itself. The Soviet Union also joined the war in 1941 after Hitler invaded Russia. In countless eloquent speeches, Churchill rallied Britons and the citizens of occupied Europe to fight the Nazis. The Allies stopped the Germans, and by D-Day in 1944 the tide had turned decisively against the Nazi juggernaut.

ADDITIONAL FACTS

1. *In addition to his political pursuits, Churchill was an accomplished journalist and historian. After World War II, he wrote a massive history of the conflict,* The Second World War, *which helped him win the Nobel Prize in Literature in 1953.*

2. *Churchill was a successful war leader, but the domestic policies of his Conservative Party were unpopular with voters. A few months after the defeat of the Nazis in 1945, voters elected Clement Attlee, the leader of the opposition Labor Party, to replace him.*

3. *In recognition of his wartime leadership, Churchill was made the first-ever honorary citizen of the United States in 1963.*

Oscar Wilde

Irish playwright and essayist Oscar Wilde (1854–1900) was one of Western literature's sharpest wits and certainly one of its most flamboyant personalities. Though best known for mercilessly exposing the hypocrisies of Victorian society, he also made significant contributions to the philosophy of art and aesthetics. His colorful personal life, meanwhile, was just as fascinating as his works, and his eccentricities made him a celebrity during his day.

Born in Dublin to well-educated parents, Wilde studied at Trinity College and at Oxford, specializing in classics and poetry. At school, he quickly made a name for himself as a writer and also adopted the affected demeanor and showy dress that would become his trademark. From his earliest college days, Wilde was fascinated by the concept of art itself: what it is, why it is important, and what its role should be in life and society. Wilde came to identify with the Aesthetic movement that swept Europe in the late 1800s, believing strongly in the concept of "art for art's sake"—the idea that art needed no justification or concrete purpose whatsoever.

Wilde wrote most of his major works during a burst of productivity in the 1890s. The first among these was a novel, *The Picture of Dorian Gray* (1890), in which the portrait of a vain young man transforms over time to reflect the man's corruption and advancing age. More famous are Wilde's plays—drawing-room comedies whose barbed wit eviscerates the attitudes and habits of affluent British society. *Lady Windermere's Fan* (1892) concerns a woman who blackmails her son-in-law; *An Ideal Husband* (1895) portrays a similar blackmail of a public official.

Wilde's masterpiece is undoubtedly *The Importance of Being Earnest* (1895), a mistaken-identity caper involving two slippery young men, two young women, and a hilariously condescending noblewoman. Typical of Wilde's work, the play is riddled with secrets and misunderstandings and skewers its targets with smart satire rather than open mockery or insult. Its characters are prodigiously quotable, uttering a near-constant stream of epigrams that are both witty and substantive.

Wilde's meteoric rise to success during the 1890s was followed by just as precipitous a crash. Though Wilde was married and had children, he was openly homosexual and in 1895 was put on trial for having an "indecent" relationship with a nobleman's son. After serving a sentence of two years' hard labor, which weakened his health considerably, Wilde died, virtually penniless, in 1900.

ADDITIONAL FACTS

1. After a much-publicized lecture tour through the United States in 1882, Wilde concluded that, "America is the only country that went from barbarism to decadence without civilization in between."

2. Upon arriving in New York for the start of this lecture tour, Wilde told US customs officials that he had nothing to declare, "only my genius."

Henri Matisse

Henri Matisse (1869–1954) was one of the founding fathers of fauvism, a movement that opposed naturalism and celebrated the beauty and psychological power of color. He is particularly known for his murals of dancing figures and for the huge paper cutouts that he did at the end of his career.

Matisse was born in Picardy, France, in 1869. The child of comfortable, middle-class parents, he earned a law degree in 1889. Having had no prior experience in art, Matisse discovered his talent for drawing while recovering from an attack of appendicitis. Determined to pursue a career in painting, he moved to Paris and enrolled at the Académie Julian where he studied under the academic painter William-Adolphe Bouguereau. The following year, Matisse was invited to join the studio of the symbolist Gustave Moreau and also entered the École des Beaux-Arts, where he learned to paint by copying old masters.

After a brief stay in Corsica in the late 1890s, Matisse returned to Paris where he led of a group of younger artists who wished to break with older traditions. In 1905, the group caused a great stir with their radically different paintings at the Salon d'Automne. A critic who objected to their use of bright colors and childlike compositions called them fauves, or savage beasts. A painting typical of this period in Matisse's career is Le Bonheur de vivre (1906), which depicts female nudes dancing and playing music in a simple landscape. Explaining his objective, Matisse declared, "Composition is the art of arranging in a decorative manner the various elements at a painter's disposal for the expression of his feeling." In many respects Matisse's goal was identical to that of the expressionists, but he disapproved of their tendency to dwell on negative emotions. He wanted his art to induce pleasure and be "something like a good armchair in which to rest from physical fatigue."

In the 1920s, Matisse moved to Nice on the Riviera, where he spent most of the rest of his life. In 1930, he sailed to Tahiti via the United States, where he received a commission from the Barnes Foundation in Pennsylvania for the mural Dance. In the 1930s Matisse devoted himself to book illustration, supplying etchings for editions of Stéphane Mallarmé's Poésies and James Joyce's Ulysses. In 1944, Matisse was asked to produce an illustrated album with his reflections on jazz, He decorated it with paper cutouts that he made by "drawing with scissors."

After an operation for an eye tumor in 1941, Matisse turned increasingly to drawing and paper cutouts. He continued to work until 1951. Among his last works were the windows, murals, and other decorations for the Chapelle du Rosaire in the southern French town of Vence. The huge paper cutouts he did in the early 1950s demonstrate that he remained a revolutionary artist even in his old age.

ADDITIONAL FACT
1. *In 1920, Matisse designed the costumes and settings for Sergey Diaghilev's production of Igor Stravinsky's opera,* Le Chant de Rossignol.

The Real Numbers

The real numbers are the numbers that you are likely to encounter in day-to-day life. The set of real numbers consists of all the numbers that can be represented on the number line. It encompasses natural numbers, whole numbers, integers, rational numbers, and irrational numbers.

Natural numbers are the counting numbers, starting with the number 1. They are the oldest numbers known to man. One can imagine a caveman discovering the natural numbers on his fingers (1, 2, 3, 4, 5 . . .). Many cultures in the early history of man also invented the concept of zero. Zero is not a natural number, but rather a whole number. The set of whole numbers begins (0, 1, 2, 3, 4, 5 . . .).

As maths became more sophisticated, people began to ask what would happen if you subtracted a large number from a small number. The idea of negative numbers came into being, but for many years mathematicians were unwilling to accept negative numbers as solutions to equations. Still, without negative numbers, it would be impossible to figure out debt. The set of all the whole negative and whole positive numbers is called the integer set.

After integers comes the concept of fractions, or rational numbers. All rational numbers can be written as ratios of integers such as 5/3 or 1/8 or −5/3. All integers are rational numbers, too.

The Pythagoreans, an ancient Greek cult that worshiped numbers, were shocked and horrified to discover some numbers that could not be expressed as the ratios of integers, such as π and $\sqrt{2}$. But these numbers definitely exist, and they can be used to solve problems like finding the circumference of a circle and the length of a triangle's hypotenuse. They are called irrational numbers. Decimal representations of irrational numbers will go on forever without repeating in a pattern.

ADDITIONAL FACTS

1. Negative numbers were invented by Indian mathematicians around 600 AD, but they were not adopted in Europe until the 1600s.

2. The Egyptians started using fractions around 1000 BC.

Impressionists Claude Debussy and Maurice Ravel

The impressionists of the visual arts tried to depict not an object or scene but to give a mere *suggestion* of representation. The music of Claude Debussy (1862–1918) and Maurice Ravel (1875–1938) was similarly different from the tradition of "programmatic" music that goes back to the baroque. Rather than directly represent a scene or idea, their music strove to evoke it more indirectly. In addition, Debussy and, to a lesser extent, Ravel, avoided the formal structures that had marked much German music up to this time.

Claude Debussy was born outside of Paris and entered the conservatory there when he was eleven. After winning a scholarship to study in Rome, Debussy returned to his hometown and indulged in an utterly Bohemian lifestyle centered in the fashionable neighborhood of Montmartre. He socialized with artists, writers, and other musicians, eventually attending the meetings of a group known as the symbolists, which included the poets Charles Baudelaire, Paul Verlaine, Arthur Rimbaud, and Stéphane Mallarmé. Their theory of poetry involved the suggestion of an object or an idea using words that allude to it, rather than the name of the thing itself.

Debussy translated this idea into music, and he sometimes even used symbolist texts. His works are almost always described with words like lush, rich, and intoxicating. Even though Debussy used new, revolutionary harmonies in works like *Claire de Lune* (1890) and *Prelude to the Afternoon of a Faun* (1894), his beautiful music has always been more accessible to listeners than revolutionary music often is.

The other great impressionist was Maurice Ravel, who, like Debussy, studied at the Paris Conservatory and lived among hipsters in Paris. His group was called "The Apaches," which comes from a French word for "street thug." Ravel's most famous works include the evocative *Rhapsodie Espagnole* (1908) and his miniature ballet piece *Bolero* (1928), an entrancing composition that is basically one long, slow crescendo over a repeated rhythm motive.

ADDITIONAL FACTS

1. *Debussy's teacher Ernest Guirand once told him, "I'm not saying that what you do isn't beautiful, but it's theoretically absurd."*

2. *Ravel studied at conservatory with the famed composer Gabriel Fauré.*

3. *Debussy accused Ravel of plagiarism many times, suggesting that the younger composer's string quartet was too imitative of his own work. These accusations would permanently sour their relationship.*

Martin Heidegger

Born in Messkirch, Germany, Martin Heidegger (1889–1976) originally planned to become a Catholic priest. He became a philosopher instead, eventually leaving the church entirely. While a student at the University of Freiburg, he began following Edmund Husserl (1859–1938), the founder of phenomenology.

From 1933 to 1934, Heidegger was elected rector of the University of Freiburg, and he joined the Nazi party. Although Husserl and many of Heidegger's other colleagues were Jewish, Heidegger never apologized for his involvements with Nazism. The relationship between his philosophy and Nazism has been controversial ever since.

Heidegger's thinking evolved over his life, but his central focus always remained what he called the "question of being"—What is being? What is it to be? According to Heidegger, this was the fundamental question of metaphysics that had been forgotten. Philosophers, argued Heidegger, have confused being with "beings," like humans or even God. Against, this tendency, Heidegger emphasized the difference between *being*—what it is to be— and *beings*—particular entities that are.

Heidegger first discussed this view in his most famous work, *Being and Time* (1927). In it, Heidegger investigated the question of being by investigating the one being that understands being—humans. In later works, Heidegger tended to de-emphasize the analysis of human existence and consider being directly. He also became increasingly interested in what he called "technology." He did not mean computers and machines, but rather a way of understanding the world in which we consider it a resource for our own disposal. Heidegger was highly critical of this attitude.

ADDITIONAL FACTS

1. *In his later writings, Heidegger described what he was doing as "thinking" rather than philosophy. He described thinking as more closely related to poetry.*

2. *Heidegger's writings on "technology" were an early influence on the environmental movement.*

3. *Despite being married, Heidegger had a love affair with a young Hanah Arendt (1906-1975), at the time a student of his, but who eventually became an important philosopher in her own right. Arendt was Jewish, and she was particularly disappointed by Heidegger's involvement with Nazism in the 1930s.*

Four Noble Truths and Eightfold Path

At the heart of Buddha's enlightenment were the Four Noble Truths. These were the first teachings that he spoke of to his fellow monks after his enlightenment.

The first truth was that, contrary to his sheltered childhood, there was suffering in the world. The second truth was that this suffering had a cause and that this cause was desire. The third truth was that a state of being existed called nirvana, in which there was no suffering. Additionally, the way to achieve this state was to eliminate desire. The fourth and final truth was that a path exists that can lead away from desire and to nirvana, and this path is the Eightfold Path.

The Eightfold Path is the following set of rules that one must follow in order to achieve nirvana and enlightenment:

Right view calls for knowledge of the Four Noble Truths and to remain free of prejudice and delusion

Right thought means to avoid ill will.

Right speech tells us not to lie.

Right action asks that we be peaceful and not, for example, steal or kill.

Right livelihood means to earn a living in an honest way.

Right effort says that we should continuously strive to overcome the ignorance of others and our own desires.

Right mindfulness asks that we remain aware of our feelings and mental state.

Right concentration suggests that we focus on the "Buddhahood" in all beings.

The Four Noble Truths and the Eightfold Path are the core of Bhuddism's teachings. The truths can be viewed as the basic belief system, and the path as a guide to practicing the faith.

ADDITIONAL FACTS

1. *After becoming disillusioned with what the Hindu gods and goddesses failed to provide for the suffering of humanity, Buddha turned to this deity-free doctrine and discipline.*

2. *Although Jesus Christ is often credited with being the first to emphasize proper thoughts—in the Sermon on the Mount he claimed that thinking of murder was just as bad as committing it—Buddha made similar claims with his concept of right thought, 500 years earlier.*

The Spanish Civil War

The Spanish Civil War was a bloody conflict that lasted from 1936 until 1939, killing hundreds of thousands of soldiers and civilians. Both sides in the war—left-wing socialists loyal to the government and the eventually victorious nationalist rebels under the command of General Francisco Franco—committed acts of terrible brutality. Estimates of the death toll range as high as one million.

In its ferocity, the Spanish Civil War was a grim preview of World War II. Fascist Italy and Nazi Germany both sided with Franco, and both Axis powers used Spain as a laboratory to test the weapons and tactics they would soon inflict on the rest of Europe. In 1937, the German air force bombed the Spanish town of Guernica, killing hundreds of civilians and inspiring Pablo Picasso's famous antiwar painting *Guernica*.

While Germany and Italy aided Franco's rebels, the Soviet Union supplied arms to the loyalists. Preserving the elected Spanish government became a romantic cause celebre among communists and left-leaning Western intellectuals. Many Americans and Europeans volunteered for the loyalist army. Famous writers, including George Orwell and Ernest Hemingway, flocked to Spain.

After his troops finally captured Madrid from the loyalists in March, 1939, General Franco ruled Spain as a fascist dictator until his death in 1975.

In the West—especially among intellectuals—the atrocities of the Spanish Civil War hardened opposition to fascism, weakened isolationism, and lead many to conclude that the West would eventually have to confront the Axis militarily. At the same time, many left-wing writers became disillusioned with the Soviet Union after witnessing its self-interested and ultimately ineffective support for loyalist Spain.

ADDITIONAL FACTS

1. *Ernest Hemingway's novel* For Whom the Bell Tolls, *about an American volunteer for loyalist Spain, was based on his experience in Spain during the war.*

2. *Rick Blaine, Humphrey Bogart's cynical character in the movie* Casablanca, *had illegally supplied arms to loyalist Spain before moving to Africa.*

3. *Despite the crucial help he received from Hitler and Mussolini in the Civil War, Franco decided to remain neutral during World War II.*

Metafiction

Writers in both academia and popular culture throw around the word *meta* with alarming frequency. Either standing alone or used as a prefix, it has become the intellectual word du jour and has thus entered the realm of reckless overuse. But the term's recent trendiness belies the fact that the literary genre of metafiction is concrete and well established—and arguably one of the most fascinating and fruitful arenas of twentieth-century literature.

From the Greek prefix *meta*, meaning "after" or "beyond," metafiction refers to fiction that is about fiction itself—its creation, devices, and outcomes. Many works of metafiction revisit previous fictional works from new perspectives, introducing new themes and shedding new light on existing material. Others focus on the process of writing, illuminating the relationship between the author and the text that he or she creates. As a result, metafiction tends by its nature to be self-referential and ironic, calling attention to its own artifice and unreality.

James Joyce's novel *Ulysses* (1922), arguably the first major work of twentieth-century metafiction, recasts the hero of Homer's Odyssey in the guise of an ad salesman in 1904 Dublin. In doing so, the novel investigates the definition of heroism in the modern world. Meanwhile, by tinkering with genres and language in the novel's various chapters, Joyce also explores the authorial process and the relationship between form and content.

Many postmodern authors followed Joyce's lead in reimagining older works. Jean Rhys's *Wide Sargasso Sea* (1966) tells the backstory of Bertha Mason, the Creole madwoman locked in the attic in Charlotte Brontë's *Jane Eyre*. John Gardner's *Grendel* (1971) retells the Anglo-Saxon epic *Beowulf* from the perspective of the monster, recasting Grendel as a lonely, philosophical creature who is arguably more human than Beowulf. Tom Stoppard's *Rosencrantz and Guildenstern Are Dead* (1967) delves into the lives of two minor characters in Shakespeare's *Hamlet*.

Other works of metafiction focus on the processes of writing and reading fiction. Milan Kundera's *Immortality* (1990) inserts the author as a character in his own work, commenting on his creation. Michael Cunningham's *The Hours* (1998) explores Virginia Woolf's *Mrs. Dalloway* through three different stories, depicting Woolf herself writing the novel in 1923, a housewife reading the novel in 1949 Los Angeles, and a woman unwittingly reliving the events of the novel in New York in the late 1990s.

ADDITIONAL FACT

1. *Metafiction arguably began as early as Miguel de Cervantes's* Don Quixote, *in which the main characters are aware of both Cervantes's account of their adventures and a fake sequel that another author published.*

Guggenheim Museum

New York's Guggenheim Museum is one of the most revolutionary structures of the twentieth century. Conceived as a huge, enclosed spiral ramp, it broke completely with earlier museum designs.

The museum was built by American architect Frank Lloyd Wright (1867–1959) to house the modern art collection of the Solomon R. Guggenheim foundation. In 1943, Guggenheim, who had already established a Museum for Non-Objective Painting, commissioned a permanent home for his art. He left the choice of architect to his artistic consultant, the Baroness Hilla von Rebay. She, in turn, turned to Wright, who had already earned fame for his many innovative structures, most notably "Fallingwater," a house built over a waterfall in Bear Run, Pennsylvania. In her letter to Wright, von Rebay proclaimed, "I need a fighter, a lover of space, an agitator, a tester, and a wise man . . . I want a temple of spirit, a monument!"

In 1951, the foundation bought a large lot on Fifth Avenue between Eighty-eighth and Eighty-ninth streets in New York City. The museum was completed in 1959. A ten-story tower was added in 1991 to accommodate the expanding collection.

In the Guggenheim, Wright fused the geometry of modern architecture with natural organic forms. The structure has been compared to a nautilus shell and to an inverted ziggurat—a Mesopotamian spiral-shaped temple. The concrete, spiral ramp that wraps around the ninety-foot tall atrium dominates the interior. Although the main exhibition space lies alongside the ramp, separate galleries branch off from the main artery on each floor. Sunlight filters in through the glass ceiling. Viewers generally take an elevator to the top floor and view the artworks on their descent.

When the building opened to the public in 1959, it received both great praise and sharp criticism. Some people felt that Wright had wasted the view of Central Park across the street by designing an enclosed spiral. Others felt that the ramp made it difficult to look at large pictures from a distance, and that its slope created a sense of instability. Although Wright claimed that the natural light from the glass dome would be sufficient to illuminate the interior, the museum proved to be too dark for comfortable viewing and artificial lighting had to be installed.

Despite the museum's problems as an exhibition space, it continues to be one of the most popular tourist attractions in New York, welcoming thousands of visitors every week.

ADDITIONAL FACTS

1. *The Guggenheim Museum is located on the Upper East Side of New York City, on what is known as "Museum Mile." There are five museums between 82nd Street and 105th Street on Fifth Avenue.*

2. *Branches of the Guggenheim Museum now exist in Venice, Bilbao, Berlin, and Las Vegas. Plans for an additional Guggenheim in New York (designed by Frank Gehry) and new ones in Rio de Janeiro and Tokyo are in the works.*

Prime Numbers

A prime number is a whole number greater than one that can only be evenly divided by one and itself.

Two is the smallest prime number, and the only even prime number. Three, five, and seven are also prime numbers, but so are 89; 2,521; and 1,299,007. The fundamental theorem of arithmetic states that every whole number greater than one can be written as a product of prime numbers. In this way, prime numbers are the building blocks of all positive numbers. For example, 209,328 can also be written as a product of its prime factors: $209,328 = 2^4 \times 3 \times 7^2 \times 89$. All numbers that are the product of two or more prime numbers are called composite numbers. Six is a composite number (2×3) and so is 209,328.

There are infinitely many prime numbers. Euclid of Alexandria first proved this fact in the third century BC. His proof is simple and elegant. He asked us to suppose the opposite: that there is a finite set of prime numbers. Multiply all of those numbers together: $2 \times 3 \times 5 \times 7 \ldots \times$ the largest number in the set, and add one. If you divide the new number by any prime number, you will always have a remainder of one. Adding one created a new prime number. Thus, there are always more prime numbers to be found.

The search for patterns in prime numbers is one of greatest challenges in mathematics today. Mathematicians still have not devised one all-encompassing formula that can generate all the prime numbers, although they are finding larger and larger prime numbers all the time.

ADDITIONAL FACTS

1. The largest known prime as of December 2005 is $2^{30402457} - 1$. It is 9,152,052 digits long.

2. There are many questions about primes that remain open. For example, are there an infinite number of twin primes, prime numbers with a difference of two, such as 3 and 5, 101 and 103, and 2141 and 2143? No one knows.

3. In the movie Contact, *the aliens that contact Jodi Foster's character transmit a list of prime numbers, indicating their intelligence and understanding of mathematics as the universal language.*

Tonality and Atonality

All music from the seventeenth to the early twentieth centuries generally falls into the category of tonal music. Tonal music is based on the idea that in each piece of music, one of the twelve tones of Western music (C-C#-D-D#-E-F-F#-G-G#-A-A#-B) is given more importance than the rest and is used as a reference point. This one special tone is called the tonal center, or the tonic note, and it is audible in most music as the "center" of a piece.

This concept is reflected in the names of classical works. If a piece is called *Symphony in G-minor*, it is probably based on the G-minor scale, with G as its tonal center.

Richard Wagner was one composer who began to change music with the extensive use of chromaticism. He composed pieces that made use of tones in between the set pitches of a scale. For example, if writing in C-major, which is based on the C-major scale of C-D-E-F-G-A-B-C, Wagner might use the tones C#, D#, F#, G#, and A# extensively.

After Wagner, composers began to push the envelope of tonality even further. The result is atonality, in which each of the twelve pitches is given equal weight, and music is not based on a tonal center. Not all melodies have to move toward any certain tonal center. Atonal composers say that the elimination of the tonic opens up new doors of expression the same way abstract expressionism opened up new worlds of possibility for the visual arts.

This may all seem technical, but tonality encompasses most music that is familiar and pleasing to the human ear. Almost all pop and folk music falls within the limits of tonal music. When this convention is challenged, be it in classical, jazz, or pop music, the result sounds harsh and unfamiliar to most people's ears. Even today, nearly a hundred years after its inception, atonal music sounds startling and "modern."

ADDITIONAL FACTS

1. *A notable piece of early atonal music was Arnold Schoenberg's* Pierrot Lunaire *(1914).*

2. *Many composers, such as Charles Ives and Igor Stravinsky, experimented with polytonality, or the practice of having more than one tonal center simultaneously in a piece of music.*

3. *The rejection of tonality in music philosophically and chronologically coincided with the rejection of a tangible subject in abstract art.*

Aesthetics

Aesthetics is the philosophy of art.

The first important question is: What is art? An ordinary kitchen table is presumably not a work of art, but the *Mona Lisa* is. Philosophers call this the problem of the ontology of art—What it is about an object that makes it art?

One possible answer is that art is beautiful. But not all beautiful things are art. Sunsets, landscapes, and certain people are beautiful, but are not works of art. Another possible answer is that art represents something, or conveys a message. However, the footage from a security camera represents something—namely, the people it records—but that footage is not art. Likewise, sentences of English convey a message, but that does not mean that all sentences of English are artworks, though some may be.

Another important question in philosophical aesthetics is: What are we saying when we evaluate art? If we say of some painting "This is beautiful," or "This is good art," are we just saying that we like the painting, or that it pleases us? If so, one observer may say a painting is beautiful, while another says it is ugly without disagreeing. All the first statement means is that the painting pleased the first observer, while all the second statement means is that it did not please the second observer. Neither statement alleges any general truth about the painting. The difficulty with this approach is that it appears to leave no room for arguing, or reasoning, about the value of art. It also leaves no room for the concept of taste, the idea that some people are better able than others to determine what is good art, and why.

Other questions in aesthetics include: What is a genre? What makes something a novel, rather than a long poem? Aestheticians also consider: What is the purpose of art? What is valuable about art, and why should we care about it?

ADDITIONAL FACTS

1. *The word* aesthetics *was coined by the little-known German philosopher Alexander Gottlieb Baumgarten (1714–1762). It comes from the Greek, meaning perception, or sensation.*

2. *Plato (429–347 BC) believed that artists were twice-removed from reality because they produced imitations of ordinary objects such as tables and beds, which were merely imitations of the ideal forms.*

Zen

Zen Buddhism, which has been known as a religion, a philosophy, a way of life, and an art form, began with a man named Bodhidharma in 520 AD. According to believers, Bodhidharma traveled from India to the Chinese kingdom of Luoyang. In Luoyang, Bodhidharma went before the Emperor Wu and declared that self-interest was worthless. He then proceeded to a monastery where he sat and meditated before a wall for nine years before accepting students.

Zen, meaning meditation, emphasizes the importance of meditating in order to calm or free one's mind so that one can eventually achieve nirvana. The most common type of Zen is Zazen, or sitting meditation, often done while posed in the lotus position. Zen Buddhists especially advocate group meditation.

An offshoot of Buddhism, Zen has been greatly influenced by both Taoism and Confucianism in China. What makes it most distinct from other forms of Buddhism, however, is its treatment of texts and its teachers. Zen deemphasizes the study of ancient Buddhist texts believing the practice of meditation to be far more important than study.

Further, Zen places an enormous emphasis on the lineage of its teachers. Beginning with Bodhidharma and his disciples, a direct line of wisdom was established. Tracing an instructor's teaching heritage is essential to his level of prestige.

After its arrival in China, Zen Buddhism spread to Japan, Korea, and Vietnam. However, over the past 1,500 years, each branch has broken off so that Japanese Zen, is no longer the same as its Chinese ancestor nor its Korean and Vietnamese cousins.

ADDITIONAL FACTS

1. Another type of meditation called Kinhin, or walking Zazen, calls for a group of people to meditate while walking around a room clockwise, their right shoulders always facing the center.

2. The original Sanskrit word for meditation was transliterated in China as "Chan." "Chan" later became "Zen" in Japan, "Seon" in Korea, and "Thien" in Vietnam.

∽∞∾

Adolf Hitler

Adolf Hitler (1889–1945) was the dictator of Germany, whose 1939 invasion of Poland sparked the beginning of World War II. The war eventually spread to almost every corner of the globe, leading to fifty million deaths along with untold destruction and human misery. Despite help from Hitler's axis partners, Japan and Italy, the tide turned against Germany by 1943. In 1945, Hitler committed suicide with a bullet to the head as victorious Allied troops approached his underground bunker in downtown Berlin.

Unlike many dictators, Hitler had enjoyed widespread public support during his reign. In fact, his Nazi Party fared well in Germany's last democratic elections in the early 1930s. Hitler was a mesmerizing speaker, and his charisma convinced many Germans that the Nazis could reverse the nation's decline after its humiliating defeat in World War I. After Germany's surrender, however, most of Hitler's countrymen quickly disavowed the führer who had led their country to ruin.

Hitler was born in Austria, then a German-speaking province of the Austro-Hungarian Empire. He aspired to be a painter, but art schools in Vienna turned him away. He moved to Germany and fought in World War I, suffering minor injuries. Prior to the war, Hitler had no strong political beliefs. But after Germany's defeat, he embraced the popular theory that a Jewish conspiracy was somehow secretly responsible for the nation's humiliation. He joined a then-obscure anti-Semitic political party, the National Socialists, and soon became its leader.

Though anti-Semitism was widespread in Germany before and after World War I, it was the personality of Hitler himself that attracted many Germans to the Nazi Party. Albert Speer, an architect who became the head of wartime Germany's arms factories, described feeling a "wave of enthusiasm which . . . One could almost feel" the first time he heard Hitler speak. ". . . it swept away any skepticism, any reservations."

ADDITIONAL FACTS

1. *After his suicide, invading Soviet forces seized Hitler's corpse. His skull remains in a government building in Moscow.*

2. *The Nazis attracted many supporters, even in the Western countries that would oppose Germany in World War II. Before the war, Hitler's admirers in the United States included famed pilot Charles Lindbergh and automaker Henry Ford.*

3. *Hitler hoped to prove his theory of German racial superiority at the 1936 Olympics, which were held in Berlin. But a black American sprinter, Jesse Owens, dashed those hopes by winning four gold medals, one of the most famous triumphs in Olympic history.*

"This Is My Letter to the World"

This is my letter to the World
That never wrote to Me—
The simple News that Nature told—
With tender Majesty

Her Message is committed
To Hands I cannot see—
For love of Her—Sweet—countrymen—
Judge tenderly—of Me

Though she remained a virtual unknown during her lifetime, since her death, Emily Dickinson (1830–1886) has been acknowledged as one of America's greatest poets. Her short, epigrammatic poems, revolutionary in both style and technique, illuminate a vast inner life.

Dickinson was born and raised in her family's hometown of Amherst, Massachusetts. After finishing her secondary education in the late 1840s, she made her first forays into writing poetry. Her early works are more conventional, utilizing meter from ballads, hymns, and other traditional forms. By the 1860s, however, Dickinson had begun to twist these established forms, experimenting boldly with rhythm, rhyme, word choice, and punctuation. The result was a body of poems that create tension between the familiar and the unexpected and that have an unmistakable look on the printed page.

"This Is My Letter to the World" (c. 1862) typifies Dickinson's style, form, and voice. Like all of her poems, it is untitled, known simply by its first line. Composed of two four-line stanzas, or quatrains, it is written in rhymed iambic tetrameter and trimeter lines, alternating with each other—a standard ballad form in which each line consists of six or eight syllables in an unstressed-stressed pattern. But Dickinson played with this standard form: In the first line, she begas not with an iambic foot but with its opposite, a trochaic foot (stressed-unstressed), which emphasizes the word "This." Typical of her style, she interspersed the poem with dashes that break up the flow of the lines and lend prominence to certain words.

The poem exemplifies the introspective themes of Dickinson's work—in this case, artistic creativity. She revealed her insecurity about releasing the product of her creative energies out into the world, the gamble inherent in committing the "Message" of her works to "Hands [she] cannot see." In the last line, "Judge tenderly—of Me," she encapsulated the anxiety of probably every artist or writer who has ever walked the earth.

ADDITIONAL FACTS

1. Of the more than 1,700 poems that Dickinson wrote, only seven were published during her lifetime.

2. Dickinson was also a prolific writer of letters, producing hundreds that have largely survived preserved. Scholars value this correspondence highly, for its language is often just as rich as in Dickinson's poetry.

3. During the last two decades of her life, Dickinson never left the boundaries of her family's property in Amherst.

Cubism

Cubism was perhaps the most important art movement of the early twentieth century. It reduced the shapes of people and things to basic geometric forms and rejected the rules of mathematical perspective. In doing so, it challenged the way a spectator understood space and volume on a two-dimensional surface.

The origins of cubism can be traced to the later works of Paul Cézanne, who gave hard, angular contours to natural forms and depicted them from different viewpoints simultaneously. In 1907, Pablo Picasso expanded on Cézanne's approach in *Les Demoiselles d'Avignon*, a painting of four prostitutes in a brothel addressing a male viewer outside the picture. The women have geometricized bodies that complement the sharp angles in the background behind them. The shadows fall arbitrarily, and the women's bodies do not diminish regularly in the distance. By making the foreground collapse into background, Picasso makes the viewer fully conscious of the picture's flatness.

Joined by fellow artist Georges Braque, Picasso developed the principles of cubism further. The name of the movement was coined by Henri Matisse, who told art critic Louis Vauxcelles that Braque created art "with little cubes." Vauxcelles, in turn, referred to Braque's works as *bizarreries cubiques*, "cubic oddities."

The first phase of cubism, from around 1908 to 1912, is called analytical cubism. At this stage, the two artists were concerned primarily with breaking down forms by playing with the rules of perspective, painting arbitrary shadows and eliminating nearly all color. Although the images seem abstract, they still relate to something in nature, generally a human figure or a still life. A typical composition of this period is Braque's *The Portuguese* (1911).

Circa 1912, Braque began gluing bits of newsprint and wallpaper onto his canvases. Thus a second phase of the movement—synthetic cubism—evolved, in which synthetic materials were added to paintings. For example, in Picasso's *Still Life with Chair Caning* (1911–12), a piece of oilcloth imprinted with the pattern of chair caning serves as the ground of the painting, and a real rope frames the entire composition.

By the beginning of World War I, the cubism movement was essentially over, but its radical rejection of traditional principles of painting was an inspiration to all subsequent modern artists.

ADDITIONAL FACTS

1. Later forms of cubism include cubo-futurism, purism, orphism, and precisionism.

2. American artists Stuart Davis and Aaron Douglas were both strongly influenced by cubism.

3. Braque and Picasso painted the same motifs over and over again during their cubist period. Most common among them were musical instruments, bottles, pitchers, glasses, newspapers, and block letters.

☙

Pi

The diameter of a circle is the distance from one side of the circle to the other, going straight through the middle. The circumference of a circle is the distance all the way around the outside edge of the circle. The relationship between the diameter and the circumference never changes. No matter what the size of the circle—whether it is a poker chip or the equator of the earth—the diameter fits into the circumference 3.14 times. But 3.14 is just an approximation. The real number is called π, or pi.

Pi is an extremely useful number. If you know the distance across a circle, or even half the distance (the radius, r), you can use pi to determine the circumference without measuring the distance all the way around. It can also help you find the area of a circle (area = πr^2) and solve most geometric problems involving circles, spheres, and arcs. But pi is also useful outside of geometry. It factors into Werner Heinsenberg's uncertainty principle, Albert Einstein's field equation of general relativity, Charles-Augustin de Coulomb's law for the electric force, and many other facets of physics, statistics, and number theory.

Pi is also fascinating because even though it is a very simple concept, no one can calculate it exactly. Pi is sometimes written 3.14159265 ... because there is no end to pi. The numbers after the decimal point will go on forever without repeating. It is called an irrational number, a number that cannot be expressed as the ratio of two integers. The ancient Babylonians and Egyptians were aware of pi and tried to approximate it, which is precisely what we are still trying to do. They calculated it to be 3.125 (Babylonians) and 3.16 (Egyptians), which aren't bad estimates. Today's supercomputers, which can carry out 2 trillion operations per second, have accurately ascertained the first 1,241,100,000,000 digits of pi.

ADDITIONAL FACTS

1. Archimedes of Syracuse (287–212 BC) used an early form of calculus to obtain a very accurate estimation of pi. He said that it was between 223/71 and 22/7. An average of his two bounds is 3.1418, a close estimate.

2. German mathematician Ludolph van Ceulen (circa 1600) accurately calculated the first thirty-five digits of pi. He was so proud, he had them engraved on his tombstone.

3. Piphilology is a field of study devoted to creating mnemonic devices to remember the digits of pi.

4. On July 2, 2005, a fifty-nine-year-old Japanese mental health counselor successfully recited the first 83,431 decimals of pi.

The Second Viennese School

Modernist composer Arnold Schoenberg (1874–1951) and his two pupils Alban Berg (1885–1935) and Anton Webern (1883–1945) are referred to as the Second Viennese School because their composing lives centered on Vienna, as did the Classical Viennese masters of the eighteenth century: Franz Joseph Haydn, Wolfgang Amadeus Mozart, and Ludwig van Beethoven. They introduced concerts of atonal and twelve-tone serial works to the musical world, sending it into uproar and disarray.

Schoenberg was raised an Orthodox Jew in anti-Semitic Austria, struggling to get by as a music transcriber when his father died. He became a professor of composition at the Stern Conservatory in Berlin in 1901, and in 1904 he took on Berg and Webern as students. Schoenberg's early music imitates the chromaticism of Richard Wagner, but it slowly drifted away from tonal systems between 1905 and 1907. Two works written in 1912, *Pierrot Lunaire* and *Five Pieces for Orchestra*, shocked the world awake with their embrace of atonality, and a new era of composition was born. Both pieces were initially criticized for their apparent lack of logical organization, and in response Schoenberg articulated a rational system for atonality: twelve-tone serialism.

Berg and Webern developed their master's technique. Webern applied serialism to dynamic changes and rhythm as well as pitches, creating something called total serialism. Webern was also known for uniting modernism and romanticism by cramming huge bursts of emotional expression into tiny, mathematical, efficient spaces. Berg used atonality to write some of the most passionate string pieces of the century, including his *Violin Concerto* (1935) as well as the opera *Wozzeck*.

All three wrote music that was jagged, passionate, and alarming, and which reflected the artistic and political thought of the time. Despite their close relationships, when Schoenberg fled the Nazis in 1933, Webern, a Nazi sympathizer, stayed behind. He was accidentally shot by an American soldier in 1945. Berg died from complications stemming from a bug bite at age fifty, and Schoenberg, who came to teach at the University of Southern California, outlived them both.

ADDITIONAL FACTS

1. *Schoenberg hated the term* atonal *because he felt it implied "without tone." Instead, he suggested* pantonal, *emphasizing the all-inclusiveness of his style.*

2. *With Berg and Webern, Schoenberg founded the Society for Private Musical Performances in Vienna in 1916. Only members were allowed to come to a series of premieres by avant-garde composers, and no applause was allowed. The series isolated the three from the public eye, but it encouraged free dialogue among the artists involved.*

3. *Webern wrote only thirty-one catalogued pieces, many of them less than ten minutes long.*

Existentialism

Existentialism is a term coined to describe the thinking of certain twentieth century French philosophers such as Jean-Paul Sartre (1905–1980) and Albert Camus (1913–1960). There is no single existentialist view on any given topic. What binds the existentialists together is an emphasis on human freedom, authenticity, and experiences like dread and anxiety.

The existentialists of the twentieth century had many influences, including the Danish thinker Soren Kierkegaard (1813–1855). Kierkegaard wrote in defense of religious faith. He argued that faith requires a voluntary, irrational leap into the absurd. But he believed religious faith was the only antidote to despair, a spiritual condition he described in his book *The Sickness unto Death* (1849).

Sartre and Camus wrote both fiction and philosophy. In his novel *Nausea* (1938), Sartre described the sickening feeling that the world is absurd and devoid of meaning. In his more straight-forwardly philosophical works, like *Being and Nothingness* (1943), Sartre argued that man is free to choose his own destiny and that the only thing we cannot do is fail to choose. However, he believed we often try to escape our freedom by clinging to some unquestionable fact, like a system of religious belief. He called this tendency "bad faith."

Camus is best known for his novels, especially *The Stranger* (1942) and *The Plague* (1947). In *The Stranger*, the main character, Mersault, kills an Arab youth for no apparent reason and is sentenced to death. As his execution approaches, Mersault reflects on his life and his responsibility for the murder. Existentialist themes of authenticity, responsibility for one's life, and freedom of choice run through Camus's books.

ADDITIONAL FACTS

1. Kierkegaard wrote many of his works under a variety of pseudonyms.

2. In Sartre's play No Exit, three strangers find themselves in an ominous hotel room, which they cannot leave. Slowly, as they grow to hate one another, they realize they are in hell. The play contains the famous declaration, "Hell is other people."

3. Friedrich Nietzsche (1844–1900) was another important influence on existentialism.

Karma

Karma is the cycle of moral cause and effect that is central to the Hindu faith.

The traditions of Hinduism can be traced back as far as 3000 BC, and the faith has no known founder. Hindus believe in a cycle of birth, life, death, and reincarnation. During life, one's good or bad deeds affect one's karma. This concept is often expressed by the notion, "As we sow, so shall we reap." Good deeds lead to a good future; bad deeds lead to a bad future. As a guide to doing good deeds or acts, Hindus follow the dharma, or "what is right" according to ancient Hindu scriptures.

There are three aspects of karma. The first is prarabadha. Prarabadha is out of our control. It describes the fundamental setup of our lives such as who our parents are, which caste of society we are born into, where our house is. Such conditions cannot be changed and are determined by our behavior in our previous life.

The second aspect of karma is samchita. It describes how all our deeds in former lives lead to our individual interests, tendencies, and persona. Samchita karma explains why two children born into the same environment may nevertheless have very different inclinations. Samchita karma can be changed during our current lives with hard work and reflection. The bad habits we are born with can be improved. On the other hand, good habits can deteriorate.

Finally, the third aspect of karma, agami, consists of the actions and deeds that we do in our current lives, which will affect us in our current lives. For instance, treating a neighbor well or poorly might determine how we are someday treated. It is agami karma over which we have the most control.

Although the notion of karma also exists in Buddhism, Hindu karma is significantly different in that it accounts for the intervention of a god. Hindus believe that when someone dies, a supernatural being, known as Brahman, weighs the good and evil done by that person and assigns them their next place of reincarnation. Moreover, if a few bad deeds are followed by many good deeds, it is believed that Brahman can mitigate the negative effect of those early mistakes. Buddhists, on the hand, view karma as an absolute natural law.

ADDITIONAL FACT
1. *Karma is a means of explaining why evil exists in a world with God. The evil deeds of people create negative karma which yields more evil in lives to come.*

Holocaust

Near the end of World War II, the 45th Infantry Division of the US Army received orders to capture a small city in Southern Germany. Lieutenant Colonel Felix Sparks, the division's commander, entered the town, sending a detachment of his battle-hardened troops to a nearby Nazi concentration camp alongside the railway. The name of the camp, and the town, was Dachau.

What Sparks witnessed that morning in Dachau would soon haunt the conscience of the world. In the pleasant Bavarian forest, thousands of innocent people lay dead or dying. The remaining German soldiers around Dachau put up little resistance. As the horrified men of the 45th division entered the camp, the smell of human flesh hung in the forest air. "The scene near the entrance to the confinement area numbed my senses," Sparks later told historians. "Dante's Inferno seemed pale compared to the real hell of Dachau."

Dachau had been a gruesome prototype: The first concentration camp Adolf Hitler opened shortly after taking power in Germany in 1933. At first, the camp housed opponents of the Nazi regime, but during the war the Nazis imprisoned German citizens simply for being Jewish. More than 30,000 prisoners had been systematically murdered at Dachau—a horrifying total but a mere fraction of the six million Jews killed across Europe during the Nazi Holocaust. The gas chambers at Auschwitz, a concentration camp in Nazi-occupied Poland, accounted for more than one million of the deaths.

Only as the British, Soviet, and American armies began to liberate Nazi concentration camps in the spring of 1945 did the full extent of German brutality begin to emerge. In the name of ethnic purity, Hitler and his henchmen had ordered the extermination of the entire Jewish population in Germany and Nazi-occupied Europe. The Nazi camps also murdered untold thousands of Gypsies, Poles, gays, and political opponents. After the war, the Allies captured and executed a number of German officials held responsible for the massive genocide in Europe.

ADDITIONAL FACTS

1. *A handful of Sparks's soldiers were so outraged that within minutes of entering Dachau, they began summarily executing the camp's SS guards. The American soldiers were court-martialed, but General George S. Patton ordered the prosecutions to stop.*

2. *The architect and logistical planner of the Holocaust, Adolf Eichmann, managed to escape from Europe in the chaos of postwar Germany and was not captured until 1960 in Argentina. He was tried for crimes against humanity in Israel, convicted, and hanged in 1962.*

3. *Despite the efforts of the Allies, most participants in the Holocaust were never punished. For instance, of the 7,000 SS troops that served at Auschwitz, only 800 were put on trial, according to one estimate.*

Romanticism

Romanticism was a wide-ranging intellectual and artistic movement that swept Europe and the United States during the first half of the nineteenth century. It was a direct reaction against the rationalism, precision, and restraint that had dominated Western intellectual thought during the Enlightenment period of the 1700s. Once romanticism took root, it found its place in many arenas, from literature to art to music.

Whereas Enlightenment thinkers valued empirical and rational thought, romantics held that human emotion and passion were truer guides than reason or the intellect. Romantic literature thus celebrates creativity, the imagination, the senses, and the rejection of convention in favor of one's own individual vision—a perspective that English romantic poet William Blake encapsulated in his famous declaration, "I must create a system or be enslaved by another man's." Not surprisingly, many works of romantic literature exhibit a fascination with anomalous or misunderstood characters, such as geniuses or madmen. These figures may be grotesque, such as the monster in Mary Shelley's *Frankenstein* (1818), or merely marginalized from society, such as the wrongly imprisoned Edmond Dantès in Alexandre Dumas's *The Count of Monte Cristo* (1844–1845).

The start of the romantic period in literature is often identified as 1798, when English poets William Wordsworth and Samuel Taylor Coleridge published a joint collection of poems entitled *Lyrical Ballads*. In 1800, Wordsworth added a highly influential forward to *Lyrical Ballads* that defined poetry as a "spontaneous overflow of powerful feelings." This blatant rejection of reason became a call to arms for the romantic movement.

The early figureheads of romantic literature were its English poets: Blake, Wordsworth, and Coleridge, along with John Keats, Percy Bysshe Shelley, and Lord Byron. Before long, romanticism infiltrated prose and spread to other parts of Europe, influencing such novels as Victor Hugo's *The Hunchback of Notre-Dame* (1831). It later crossed the Atlantic, where American transcendentalist writers built upon the romantics' appreciation of nature. In fact, most of the major figures of mid-nineteenth-century American literature—Edgar Allan Poe, Nathaniel Hawthorne, Herman Melville, and others—fall solidly in the romantic tradition.

By the late 1800s, romanticism subsided in favor of realism, which was ushered in by works such as Gustave Flaubert's *Madame Bovary* (1857). Its influence has remained significant, however, and the works of romantic poets and novelists remain among the most popular of the Western canon.

ADDITIONAL FACT

1. *With its roots in the passionate, emotional works of Ludwig van Beethoven, romanticism flourished in music throughout the nineteenth century. Major composers included Frédéric Chopin, Richard Wagner, and Piotr Ilych Tchaikovsky.*

Pablo Picasso

Pablo Picasso (1881–1973) was one of the most famous and influential artists of the twentieth century. He founded and mastered such an enormous range of styles throughout his eighty-year career that he may well be considered the most prolific and versatile painter of all time.

Born in Málaga, Spain, Picasso was a child prodigy. His father, an art teacher, recognized and fostered the young boy's talent. At the turn of the twentieth century, Picasso went to Paris, the center of the avant-garde art scene at the time. Following his best friend's suicide in 1901, Picasso entered what has since become known as his Blue Period; he painted compositions in various shades of blue in order to convey the sadness and poverty of his subjects. By 1904, Picasso had switched to warmer tones and entered his Rose Period, when he began focusing on images of circus performers and harlequins.

In 1907, Picasso painted his first cubist picture, *Les Demoiselles d'Avignon*. Departing from western canons of female beauty, he used Polynesian, Iberian, and African sculptures as models for the figures. By rejecting the rules of one-point perspective—the dominant technique since the Renaissance—Picasso and fellow cubist Georges Braques changed the course of art forever.

Picasso constantly revised his styles and approach to painting. In 1917, for example, he began restoring color to his monochromatic cubist paintings. Later, in *Three Musicians* (1921), he combined cubist elements with vivid colors and lively patterns to capture the dynamic rhythm of the figures. In the late 1920s Picasso became involved in the surrealist movement. Intrigued by the concept of metamorphosis, he produced paintings of half-human, half-bestial creatures throughout the 1930s. During this phase, Picasso also wrote poetry and a surrealist play entitled *Desire Caught by the Tail* (1941).

Picasso's work became more political in the mid-1930s after the onset of the Spanish Civil War. His best-known painting of this type, *Guernica* (1937), depicts the annihilation of a small Basque town by German bombers commanded by the Fascist general, Francisco Franco. Throughout World War II Picasso lived in Nazi-occupied Paris, where fame protected him from persecution. Picasso's creative energy did not weaken with age. He continued to produce paintings, lithographs, and drawings until his death. When Picasso died without leaving a will in 1973, the French government appropriated much of his estate to found the Musée Picasso in Paris.

ADDITIONAL FACTS

1. *In addition to the Musée Picasso in Paris, there are major collections of Picasso's works in the Museo Picasso in Málaga and the Museu Picasso in Barcelona as well as in both the Museum of Modern Art and the Metropolitan Museum of Art in New York City.*

2. *Picasso's early painting* Garçon à la Pipe *sold for $104 million in 2004, a world record for a painting.*

The Pythagorean Theorem

Pythagoras was a Greek philosopher of the sixth century BC and the leader of a cult that worshiped numbers. His cult prayed to the *tetraktys*, the first four digits. *One* represented reason, *two* represented argument, *three* harmony, and *four* justice. Out of their religion of mathematics sprang some of the most elegant geometric proofs in the history of mankind, including the proof that bares

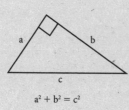

$$a^2 + b^2 = c^2$$

Pythagoras's name, the Pythagorean theorem. It simply states that for all right triangles (triangles with a 90 degree angle), $a^2 + b^2 = c^2$, where a and b are the short sides of the triangle and c is the longest side, the hypotenuse. According to legend, Pythagoras was so excited when he proved the theorem that he sacrificed a bull.

Of course, many cultures knew about the theorem before Pythagoras proved it. The Babylonians knew that $a^2 + b^2 = c^2$ at least 1,000 years before the time of Pythagoras, and the ancient Egyptians probably used the formula to build the pyramids circa 2550 BC. By 600 BC, it was known in China, India, and most of Mesopotamia. Pythagoras is simply given credit for being the first one to prove it in Western culture. Hundreds of proofs of the Pythagorean theorem exist today. But here is just one of them.

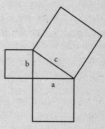

ADDITIONAL FACTS

1. *A Pythagorean triple is a set of three whole numbers* a, b, *and* c, *such that* $a^2 + b^2 = c^2$. *Two well-known examples are (3, 4, 5) and (5, 12, 13).*

2. *President James Garfield wrote his own proof of the Pythagorean theorem in 1876.*

3. *In China, the theorem is called the Gougu theorem, and it originally appeared in a mathematical treatise dated between 500 BC and 200 AD.*

Schoenberg's *Pierrot Lunaire*

This piece, whose title means "Moonstruck Pierrot," opened the floodgates for atonality and avant-garde composition in the twentieth century. It is a series of twenty-one miniature pieces for soprano and a small chamber group. The text, from the poetry of Belgian symbolist Albert Giraud, describes in sickly, often frightening episodes, the protagonist's love for the moon, "feverishly swollen" in the black night sky, as well as other disturbing images, including madness and decapitation.

Pierrot Lunaire premiered in Berlin in 1912, to a huge public uproar, but a wildly positive critical response. Many critics see it as the most important piece of the expressionist movement. Expressionism, in both visual art and music, was an introspective sensibility that coincided with the world's embrace of Freudian psychology. Expressionist painters such as Oskar Kokoschka sought to explore the nether regions of their minds, bringing to light their Freudian dream-states and unconscious desires.

Arnold Schoenberg's work sought to do the same. It was one of the first pieces of music to use the technique of *sprechstimme*, a method of vocalization that fell halfway between speech and song. The composer notated approximate pitches with an X on the staff paper. A written manuscript that accompanied *Pierrot* indicated that the performer was to strike the note for only a moment, then drop away, avoiding any sustained pitches. It is one of the most challenging vocal pieces ever written, but it is more important for its theoretical innovations.

After *Pierrot*, it became clear to the musical world that melody and tonality no longer had a grip on composers' aspirations. Later composers, including Schoenberg's student John Cage, eliminated more and more vestiges of tonal music, but in 1912, *Pierrot Lunaire* sent a clear message. It can be seen as a definitive breaking point in Western music.

ADDITIONAL FACTS

1. Igor Stravinsky, who was at the premiere as a young man, later described seeing Pierrot *as a life-changing experience.*

2. The character of Pierrot comes from the Italian theater genre of commedia dell'arte, *and in that tradition was a clumsy, comic harlequin. For some performances of* Pierrot Lunaire, *the soloist dresses in harlequin costume.*

3. Schoenberg was also an expressionist painter, and he understood the links that visual art had in common with modernist musical compositions.

∽∞∾

Analytic Philosophy

Analytic philosophy is a tradition that dominates academic philosophy in the English-speaking world and Scandinavia. What binds analytic philosophers together is a shared intellectual heritage, some broad agreement on the nature of philosophical problems, and an emphasis on clarity of expression and rigorous argument.

Analytic philosophy first arose in England in the early twentieth century. G. E. Moore (1873–1958) and Bertrand Russell (1872–1970) were heavily influenced by recent advances in logic, especially in the foundations of mathematics. This gave their philosophy a strong emphasis on logic and on language. In fact, they approached many philosophical problems through the logical analysis of language. Russell's student Ludwig Wittgenstein (1889–1951) developed these ideas in his book *Tractatus Logico-Philosophicus*, in which he described the logical structure of language and the world.

Another important influence on analytic philosophy was logical positivism, developed by the Vienna Circle, a group of philosophers and scientists who lived in Vienna in the 1920s. The positivists saw no role for philosophy other than in analyzing the logical structure of scientific theories. The British philosopher A. J. Ayer (1910–1989), who was not a member of the Vienna circle, popularized many positivist ideas in Britain and the United States in his book *Language Truth and Logic*.

Analytic philosophy is often contrasted with continental philosophy, which is practiced in Europe. Continental philosophy tends to focus more on the history of philosophy and its role within culture and history.

ADDITIONAL FACTS

1. *Russell pointed out a contradiction in fellow philosopher Gottlob Frege's logical system and Frege was plunged into despair over the failure of his life's work.*

2. *Late in his life, A. J. Ayer purportedly encountered Mike Tyson at New York party. Ayer thought that Tyson was behaving inappropriately and said as much. Tyson responded, "Do you have any idea who I am? I'm the heavyweight champion of the world!" Ayer replied, "Yes, and I am the former Wykeham professor of logic at Oxford. We are both preeminent in our field. Let us discuss this as reasonable men."*

Hindu Epics

In the Hindu tradition, there are two important epics—the Mahabharata and the Ramayana.

The Mahabharata, which means "Great Epic of the Bharata Dynasty," is the second longest epic known to exist, containing more than 100,000 verses. Its origins can be traced back as far as 3000 BC, but its current form was most likely compiled around 300–400 AD.

The Mahabharata tells of an ancient battle waged thousands of years ago between two related clans. The two clans were the Pandavas and the Dhartarashtas. Originally they shared a kingdom, but after losing a game of dice, the Pandavas were banished for twelve years. When they attempted return after the banishment, the Dhartarashtas refused to relinquish half of the land. Thus, a horrible war ensued, in which relatives and friends were forced to fight against each other, and eventually the Pandavas emerged victorius.

Within the overall plot, many minor stories highlight Hindu ideals and lessons. One such episode is the Bhagavad Gita, a sermon delivered by the god Krishna to Arjuna when Arjuna hesitated on the battlefield. The teachings of the Bhagavad Gita lay out many of the Hindu faith's central tenets.

Krishna told Arjuna that, despite his fears, he should not shy away from battle. The only way for someone to achieve salvation was by facing one's duties in life. Krishna taught that this material world was an illusion and that the soul was eternal. By going through this world and remaining devoted to God, one could actually be removed from the endless cycle of death and rebirth and become one with God. Thus, Krishna told Arjuna to be unafraid of death on the battlefield because shedding one's body can actually lead to oneness with God.

The other major Hindu epic, the Ramayana, is much shorter than the Mahabharata at 24,000 verses. This epic tells the tale of Rama, who was banished with his wife, Sita, after failing to succeed his father to the throne. In exile, Sita is captured by another king, and Rama tries at length to save her. Eventually he does, but he worries about her sexual purity after living in another man's house. Rama tests Sita by placing her in a fire. When she survives, he believes she is pure again. However, rumors of her infidelity continue, and Rama is forced to expel Sita. Sita then gives birth to Rama's two sons who proceed to tell Rama's story, the Ramayana, wherever they go. This epic contains important lessons regarding devotion, family loyalty, and respect for one's elders.

ADDITIONAL FACT

1. *It is said of the Mahabharata: "What is found herein may also be found in other sources. What is not found herein does not matter."*

The Battle of Midway

The Battle of Midway, a giant naval clash between the United States and Japan, marked the turning point of World War II in the Pacific. During the battle, the Japanese lost four of the ten aircraft carriers in their entire fleet, a crippling blow to their naval strength. The United States lost one carrier, the USS *Yorktown*. The consequence of the American victory at Midway proved enormous. Six months after the surprise Japanese attack on Pearl Harbor, the United States had rebounded to gain the upper hand in the Pacific.

Japan and the United States had drifted toward war throughout the late 1930s and early 1940s. From a reclusive island kingdom in the nineteenth century, Japan had transformed itself into a major industrial power. Japan's defeat of Russia in the Russo-Japanese War in 1904–1905 signaled its arrival as a significant military force. Shortly thereafter, Japan began invading and pillaging its neighbors. By 1910, Korea and the island of Taiwan belonged to Japan. In the 1930s, Imperial Japanese forces invaded mainland China, triggering a war that killed tens of millions of Chinese. Japan's military strategists saw the United States as the main obstacle to total domination of the Asian Pacific area.

The United States, the only power that could check Japan's expansion, had little interest in the 1930s. After the horrors of World War I, the isolationist American public wanted no part in foreign entanglements. When Hitler declared war on Great Britain, the United States was widely sympathetic to its traditional British ally but remained officially neutral. Only the bombing of Pearl Harbor on December 7, 1941, forced President Franklin D. Roosevelt to ask for a congressional declaration of war against Japan.

ADDITIONAL FACTS

1. *The battle took its name from Midway Atoll, a tiny group of uninhabited Pacific islands discovered by an American sea captain in 1859 and turned into a military base during the war. The islands, which remain US property, are now home to a National Wildlife Refuge.*

2. *As a diversion, the Japanese sent forces to take the Aleutian Islands in Alaska, hoping that the Americans would waste resources trying to defend them. The gambit didn't work, but the Aleutians were the only piece of any of the current fifty US states that the Japanese conquered during the war.*

"Sonnet 18"

Shall I compare thee to a summer's day?
Thou art more lovely and more temperate:
Rough winds do shake the darling buds of May,
And summer's lease hath all too short a date;
Sometime too hot the eye of heaven shines,
And often is his gold complexion dimmed;
And every fair from fair sometime declines,
By chance or nature's changing course untrimmed.
But thy eternal summer shall not fade,
Nor lose possession of that fair thou ow'st;
Nor shall death brag thou wander'st in his shade,
When in eternal lines to time thou grow'st:
So long as men can breathe or eyes can see,
So long lives this, and this gives life to thee.

William Shakespeare's towering plays often overshadow the fact that he also wrote 154 sonnets, many of which are great achievements of English literature. First published as a collection in 1609, these sonnets are a profound collective meditation on love, poetry, and death. Among the set, the eighteenth sonnet is the best known and most frequently quoted.

Readers often assume that "Sonnet 18" is addressed to a young woman, an object of the speaker's romantic love. But though the sonnet is indeed a love poem, it is actually an expression of love for a male friend—the same nameless young gentleman to whom the first 126 of Shakespeare's sonnets are addressed. The early sonnets in the set are reserved, advising the young man on lessons of life and marriage. But the later sonnets grow increasingly passionate in emotion, demonstrating joy, disappointment, and jealousy with an intensity more typical of a romantic relationship than a friendship. Though scholars have long debated the identity of the young man and the nature of his relationship to the narrator, the matter is clouded by uncertainty. It is unclear even whether Shakespeare is narrating.

"Sonnet 18" meditates on beauty, transience, and the enduring power of art. The speaker notes that the beauty of nature, and even of the sun itself, fades with time and the passage of the seasons. But because the young man's beauty is recorded in the form of this sonnet, his "eternal summer shall not fade." Even death itself is impotent against the endurance of the sonnet, for the poem, through its "eternal lines," effectively "gives life" to the young man "so long as men can breathe or eyes can see."

The sonnet form that Shakespeare popularized originally emerged in Italy in the 1300s, pioneered by Dante Alighieri and Petrarch. In most Italian sonnets, the opening eight lines, or octave, pose a question or dilemma that is then answered or commented upon in the final six lines, or sestet. The form changed slightly on its way to England: rather than divide between octave and sestet, most English sonneteers used three four-line quatrains, followed by a final couplet that brings an unexpected twist or development. It is this form that Shakespeare employed.

~∞~

Guernica

Pablo Picasso's *Guernica*—a shocking and powerful image of modern warfare—depicts the chaos wrought by German bombers on a small town during the Spanish Civil War.

In January of 1937, the Republican government of Spain commissioned a painting from Picasso, the most renowned Spanish painter of the period, for their pavilion at the International Exposition in Paris.

On April 26, German bombers, commanded by fascist authorities, destroyed the Basque town of Guernica in northern Spain. This, in fact, was the first aerial assault on a strictly civilian target in human history. Picasso, dismayed at the event and sympathetic to the Republicans, made the attack the subject of a huge (eleven by twenty-five feet) mural, hoping to draw international attention to the horrific war. Dora Maar, Picasso's mistress at the time, documented his progress in a series of photographs.

The composition of *Guernica* consists of a central triangle flanked by two rectangles. At the apex of the triangle, the starkly illuminated head of an injured horse conveys the suffering of all the innocent victims. To its left is a bull that, according to Picasso, represents brutality and darkness. Below the bull, a lamenting woman holds her dead child in a pose evocative of Christian images of the Virgin holding her crucified son. Sprawled at the foot of the picture is a fallen townsman, clutching a broken sword with which he had hoped to combat the fighter planes. On the right are three more figures in agony. The painting is done in a style reminiscent of synthetic cubism. Although Picasso did not use collage, some of the figures look as though they were cut out of newsprint and pasted onto the canvas.

After the work was exhibited at the Parisian Exposition, it was sent to Scandinavia, then to London. When the fascists triumphed in Spain, Picasso requested that *Guernica* be sent to the Museum of Modern Art in New York. He specified that the painting should be returned to Spain only when the country had been liberated from fascism. After Generalissimo Franco's death in 1981, the painting was sent to Madrid, where it can be seen today in the Museo Reina Sofia.

ADDITIONAL FACTS

1. A tapestry copy of Guernica *was commissioned by Nelson Rockefeller for the United Nations.*

2. Basque nationalists have petitioned to have the painting sent to the new Guggenheim Museum in Bilbao, thirty miles west of Guernica.

The Golden Ratio

The arms of a starfish, the spiral of a conch, and the petals of a rose have something in common with the Parthenon in Athens and the Pyramids of Giza. They are all structured around a number known as the Golden Ratio. It is also called phi after the Greek sculptor Phidias, who used it artfully in his works. In mathematical notation, it is written φ. Phi is approximately equal to 1.618, but it is an irrational number, which means the decimals go on forever without ever repeating in a pattern.

$$\phi = \frac{1+\sqrt{5}}{2} \approx 1.618033988...$$

Here is how we find phi. Two line segments are said to be in Golden proportion if the ratio of the shorter line (S) to the longer line (L) is equal to the ratio of the longer line to the sum of both lines.

$$\frac{S}{L} = \frac{L}{L+S}$$

If we solve for L using the quadratic equation, we find that

$$L = \left(\frac{1+\sqrt{5}}{2}\right)S = \phi S \approx 1.618S$$

Objects constructed in a golden ratio are visually pleasing to the human eye. They show up again and again in art and nature. Examine the three common shapes below.

In the regular pentagram, all five sides are equal in length. This causes the sides to be in Golden proportion to the five diagonals connecting the points. The ancient Greek philosopher Pythagoras was so impressed by the regular pentagram that he chose it as the secret symbol for his religious sect, which worshiped numbers.

The cross is a common graveyard cross that was first examined by a German psychologist named Gustav Fechner. He noticed that the upper and lower portions of the main stem are in a perfect golden ratio.

In the triangle, the long sides are in golden proportion to the short side.

ADDITIONAL FACTS:

1. The length and width of the Mona Lisa's face are in golden proportion.

2. The human body is riddled with golden ratios.

3. Michelangelo arranged his painting The Holy Family in a regular pentagram.

Twelve-Tone Serialism

With works like *Pierrot Lunaire*, Arnold Schoenberg was challenging the world's ears, but his new system of atonality was still "free atonality," the grammar of this new musical language having not yet been formally developed. The solution was Schoenberg's codification, in his theoretical writings and his later compositions, of a system called twelve-tone serialism.

Twelve-tone serialism is a way of making sure each of the twelve chromatic tones in Western music (C-C#-D-D#-E-F-F#-G-G#-A-A#-B) is given equal importance. It garnered Schoenberg the most criticism of his career. He was accused of making music too technical and dry by mixing it up with mathematics. And, in the end, the modernists' assault on tonality and other conventions was probably more important to music than the twelve-tone system. Few contemporary composers still use it as a guide.

Serialism works as follows: Schoenberg took the twelve pitches and arranged them into a series, which he called a row. The row serves as the melodic guide for the piece, with the basic rule being that no note can be repeated until the entire row has been played. In addition, the composer may manipulate the row by writing it backward (retrograde), by turning it upside down (inversion), by transposing it, or by any combination of these techniques.

In his writing, Schoenberg avoided intervals that he saw as tonal, or pleasing harmonies such as octaves and thirds, that suggested a tonal center. Despite its dryness and harsh sound, twelve-tone music remained the central style for "serious" composers from around the end of World War II until the 1970s, when it gave way to electronic music, minimalism, the new tonality, and other new musical styles.

ADDITIONAL FACTS

1. Schoenberg's pupil Alban Berg developed his own style whereby he incorporated tonal intervals and other elements, but he remained loyal to serialist techniques.

2. Anton Webern wrote cellular compositions in the twelve-tone tradition. Within each row, he created repeating rhythmic, harmonic, and intervallic patterns.

Truth

In ordinary use, we say that many things are true: There are true friends, true ideas, and true wisdom. However, philosophy concentrates on truth as it applies to sentences. Some sentences are true, while some are false. What exactly is the difference? This is the philosophical problem of truth.

According to one popular philosophical view, truth consists in a correspondence between a sentence and the world; a true sentence is a sentence that corresponds to a fact. Philosophers who accept this view have to explain what this correspondence relation is, and under what conditions it exists. They also have to define facts. The notable feature of this theory is the claim that truth is a relationship between language (sentences) and parts of the world (facts) that are not themselves parts of language. Thus, truth is a relation between sentences and objective, language-independent reality.

Other philosophers think that the truth of a sentence depends on its coherence with another set of sentences. According to this theory, to say a sentence is true is to say it fits well with other things we hold true. Coherence theories have to explain what the relation of coherence is, and under what conditions it exists, and which group of sentences we should judge the truth of other sentences against. This theory contends we could not turn out to be wrong about *everything*. We might be wrong about some of our beliefs but the set of privileged sentences we judge others against is, by definition, true (provided it is consistent).

A third view is the deflationary theory of truth. According to this approach, saying that a sentence is true is just a convenient way to endorse that sentence. For instance, imagine Jane and Bill are in a long meeting, and Jane says, "We're all tired. We should take a break." Bill would also like to take a break, and so instead of repeating Jane's words, he simply says, "That's true." According to the deflationary theory of truth, saying that some sentence is true is just another way of saying that sentence. On this view, there is no property of truth that all true sentence share.

ADDITIONAL FACTS

1. *Some philosophers have taken the correspondence theory of truth to be so obvious as not to require argument.*

2. *Consider the following sentence: This sentence is false. If this sentence is true, then it is false. But if it is false, then it is true. This is called the paradox of the liar.*

Caste System

The Indian caste system is a structure of social segregation that is deeply ingrained in both Indian political history and the religion of Hinduism.

According to Hindu tradition, the god Brahma created a man from clay, and four castes arose from his body parts. Brahmans (priests) arose from his mouth, Kshatriyas (rulers and warriors) arose from his arms, Vaishyas (landowners and merchants) arose from his thighs, and Sudras (artisans and servants) arose from his feet. Years later, a fifth caste, known as Dalit, or "downtrodden," emerged who were charged with, among other things, cleaning human waste.

Membership in the castes is determined by birth and is based on the concept of karma. If one does good deeds during this life, he or she will be reincarnated in a higher caste. On the other hand, bad deeds lead to lower castes. Once in a caste, a member cannot change, and the hardships that must be endured are seen as divinely ordained.

There is also a loose correlation between caste and skin color. Traditionally, lighter skinned Indians were believed to be of higher caste than those with darker skin. However, this is less true today. In addition to these five overarching castes, there are hundreds of sub-castes throughout India. These are broken down based on more specific occupation, physical location, and genealogy. Although many castes live in the same cities and are economically dependent on one another for survival, some of the more remotely located castes are roughly equivalent to isolated ethnic groups. Regardless of the distinctions, intermarriage between castes is traditionally rare, although in recent years there has been some increase.

Castes have a number of other social and religious implications. While the first four castes are considered clean, the Dalit are unclean. This has led to such rules as forcing the Dalit to ring a bell wherever they go, warning others of their approach.

Higher castes—the Brahmins, Kshatriyas, and Vaishyas—are seen as twice-born. Between the ages of eight and twelve, depending on caste, members come of age and are considered to have a rebirth. This rebirth allows them to fully practice the Hindu faith.

In order to compensate for past inequalities, the Indian government has instituted a program known as reservations. This is somewhat similar to affirmative action, but it is much more explicitly codified. Jobs that have been reserved, require a certain quota of each caste to fill the open positions.

ADDITIONAL FACTS

1. Nepal, the only country whose state religion is Hinduism, also has a caste system. This system originated in 1854 with the authorizing document Muluki Ain.

2. The fifth caste, Dalit, are more commonly known in the West as untouchables. However, this term is considered to be derogatory in India today.

D-Day

On June 6, 1944—D-Day—Allied forces invaded Nazi-controlled Europe. The scale of the invasion was without precedent. In a single day, more than 150,000 American, British, and Canadian troops crossed the English Channel and landed on the coast of France. More than 5,000 ships and 11,000 airplanes from a dozen countries participated in the invasion, which had been planned practically since the French surrender in 1940. With D-Day, the Allied liberation of Europe finally began. Germany's collapse was swift. Less than a year later, Hitler was dead, Germany was in ruins, and the war in Europe was over.

The human carnage on D-Day was immense. More than 4,000 Allied troops and thousands of Germans died during the invasion. The American troops who landed at Omaha Beach in Normandy, one of the main landing sites, suffered tremendous losses. The German defenders, however, were overwhelmed by the end of the day. "For each American I see fall, there came ten hundred other ones!" a German gunner recalled years later to a historian. Hitler had known an invasion was imminent, but the Allies successfully tricked him into believing they would land in a different part of France.

The impact of D-Day is incalculable. Before the landings, General Dwight D. Eisenhower sent a message to the troops, urging them to victory. "The eyes of the world are upon you," wrote Eisenhower, the supreme Allied commander in Europe. "The hopes and prayers of liberty-loving people everywhere march with you." And indeed, the French greeted the Allies with jubilation. A few months after the invasion, Paris was liberated. Soviet troops rushed in from the east, dislodging the Nazis from Eastern Europe. Germany could not fight the war on both fronts, and by the spring of 1945, the Nazi regime was finished, allowing the Allies to focus on defeating the remaining Axis power, Japan.

ADDITIONAL FACTS

1. Contrary to widespread belief, the D in D-Day doesn't actually stand for anything. D-Day is a generic military term for the day on which something begins—in this case Operation Overlord, the code name for the Normandy invasion.

2. Even the planning for D-Day took a deadly toll on the Allies. In practice operations in April and May of 1944, the Allies lost 12,000 men—killed or injured—and 2,000 airplanes.

3. Pigeons played an important role in D-Day. Before the invasion, members of the underground French resistance spied on German troops and sent their reports to London tied around the legs of homing pigeons.

Leo Tolstoy

Though history has produced many great novelists, arguably none is held in higher esteem than Leo Tolstoy (1828–1910). The status this Russian master enjoys among readers and critics is exceeded only by his even greater veneration among writers, who have long regarded him as a virtually untouchable genius. Tolstoy wrote prolifically, but his reputation rests largely on two great works, *War and Peace* (1865–1869) and *Anna Karenina* (1875–1877), which have served as archetypes for the modern novel. These masterpieces of realism combine unprecedented depth of characterization and keenness of observation with a profound interest in the philosophical underpinnings of everyday life.

Born to a prominent family in the Russian nobility, Tolstoy began a university education but grew bored and dropped out before earning a degree. During the restless years that followed, he served in the army, opened a school, and traveled throughout Europe, unable to find direction. In 1862, Tolstoy settled down in an infamously unhappy marriage that nonetheless produced thirteen children.

During the second half of the 1860s, Tolstoy wrote his first great masterpiece, *War and Peace*. This vast novel, set during the Napoleonic Wars, culminates in France's 1812 invasion of Russia—the famously doomed assault that fell victim to the harsh Russian winter. The novel mixes fact and fiction, with a large cast of invented characters sharing the stage with Napoleon, Tsar Alexander I, and other real-life figures. Although much has been made of the work's length, it reads surprisingly quickly due to its masterful intertwining of individual stories with the wider sweep of history. Ultimately, Tolstoy concludes that the great shaping force of history is the unpredictability and irrationality of human behavior.

The intimate focus of Tolstoy's second masterpiece, *Anna Karenina*, is evident from its legendary opening: "All happy families are alike; each unhappy family is unhappy in its own way." The title character is an intelligent, beguiling woman who seeks the romantic love that her husband, a devoted but bland government official, fails to provide. After falling in love with a debonair military officer, Anna gives up her marriage and young son to pursue love, only to receive society's scorn for her adultery. Tolstoy's description of the moments before Anna's final, tragic suicide is a masterpiece of realism and considered one of the finest scenes in literature.

ADDITIONAL FACTS

1. *In his later years, Tolstoy advocated pacifism, anarchy, and devout Christianity. He ultimately renounced material possessions entirely, precipitating an irreconcilable split with his wife.*

2. *Tolstoy held the official title of count and came from a long line of Russian nobility.*

Marc Chagall

Marc Chagall (1887–1985) is best known for his stained glass windows, murals, and tapestries of biblical themes. He also made many paintings evoking the small Belarusian village where he had been born.

Moishe Zakharovich Shagalov was born in 1887 in Vitebsk, then part of the Russian Empire. He was the eldest of nine children in a Hasidic family. After studying art near home, he moved to Saint Petersburg, where he studied under Leon Bakst.

In 1911, Chagall moved to Paris, where he met the artists Amedeo Modigliani, Chaim Soutine, and Robert Delaunay. His brightly colored, geometric compositions from this period reflect the influence of both fauvism and cubism, though he never associated himself with any modernist movement. Typical of his work at this stage is *I and the Village* (1911), which depicts life in Vitebsk in a cubist style, while still evoking the spirit of Russian folktales and Jewish proverbs.

Chagall was visiting his hometown in 1914 when World War I broke out, preventing his return to Paris. In 1915, he married Bella Rosenfeld, who later became one of his favorite subjects. After the Russian Revolution, he was appointed Commissar of the Arts for the region of Vitebsk. When he was replaced by Vera Yermoyaleva in 1919, he left for Moscow, where he designed sets for Shalom Aleichem at the New State Kamerny Theater.

In 1922 to 1923, Chagall went to Berlin and from there to Paris, where he worked on illustrations for Nikolai Gogol's *Dead Souls*, La Fontaine's *Fables*, and the Bible. In 1941, Chagall sought asylum from the Nazis in the United States. Profoundly affected by his wife's death in 1944, he painted works of himself making contact with her spirit.

After World War II, in 1948, Chagall returned to Paris. Two years later, he moved to Venice, where he worked on seventeen large paintings for the Chapelle du Calvaire. Toward the end of his career, he designed stained glass windows for Metz Cathedral, the Art Institute of Chicago, the United Nations, and Hebrew University. In 1973, the Musée National du Message Biblique de Marc Chagall opened in Nice. Today his works can be seen in major museums around the world.

ADDITIONAL FACTS

1. In 2005, popular musician Tori Amos released Garlands, *an album with lyrics inspired by a series of Chagall lithographs.*

2. Chagall stated, "All colors are the friends of their neighbors and the lovers of their opposites."

Fermat's Last Theorem

In 1637, mathematician Pierre de Fermat scribbled a mysterious note in the margin of his copy of *Arithetica*. He wrote that there are no positive integers x, y, and z such that $x^n + y^n = z^n$, where n is an integer greater than two. He had a "truly marvelous proof" for this statement, but he didn't have enough space in the margin to write it down.

As far as anyone knows, Fermat never recorded his proof anywhere. Mathematicians tried and tried to recreate what it might have been for hundreds of years. Others attempted to solve the theorem themselves, doubting whether Fermat had ever proved it in the first place. Some stopped trying, believing that it was impossible. It became known as Fermat's last theorem, not because it was the last theorem he ever wrote, but because it was the only one that had never been verified.

It is well known that there are positive integers x, y, and z such that $x^2 + y^2 = z^2$. They are known as Pythagorean triples, and there are an infinite number of them.

> For example, take 3, 4, and 5.
> $3^2 + 4^2 = 5^2$
> $9 + 16 = 25$

But it is never the case that $x^3 + y^3 = z^3$ ($n = 3$) or that $x^4 + y^4 = z^4$ ($n = 4$). Although these special cases of n had been proven many times, it took 357 years for someone to prove that n could equal any number great than two.

The answer came from professor Andrew Wiles from Princeton University in 1995. Combining seemingly unrelated branches of mathematics, notably elliptic curves and modular forms, he wrote a 150-page proof, solving the problem that had been itching mathematicians' scalps for generations. Wiles used many twentieth century techniques that would have been unknown to Fermat. For this reason, Wiles believes that Fermat never proved his theorem.

ADDITIONAL FACTS

1. Wiles began to obsess over Fermat's last theorem when he was ten years old. He always believed that it was his destiny to prove it.

2. Later in his life, Fermat wrote a proof for the special case in which $n = 4$. Many mathematicians speculate that if he had really proved the general case for all n greater than two, he would never had bothered to write the special case for $n = 4$. This is taken as further evidence that Fermat never proved his theorem.

⌒◎◞

Igor Stravinsky

Inspired by Arnold Schoenberg, the rhythms of dance, Russian music idioms, and the wisdom of the classical composers, Igor Stravinsky (1882–1971) came to be the ultimate symbol of the modernist movement. He was smart, serious, and cutting-edge—a meticulous artist who took his craft seriously, and as a result he never ceased to be revolutionary.

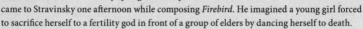

Stravinsky was born in Saint Petersburg, where he met and studied with the Russian nationalist composer Nikolai Rimsky-Korsakov. In 1909, Stravinsky met Sergey Diaghilev, Russia's main ballet impresario and director of the Paris-based *Ballets Russes* dance company. They would collaborate to produce three of the most revolutionary ballets of all time. The first was *The Firebird* (1910), a fairytale story colored by late romantic-era chromaticism. Next was *Petrushka* (1911), a rhythmically original and charming story of a puppet that drew on folk and burlesque themes. The most startling of the three ballets is *The Rite of Spring* (1913), a piece based on an idea that came to Stravinsky one afternoon while composing *Firebird*. He imagined a young girl forced to sacrifice herself to a fertility god in front of a group of elders by dancing herself to death.

The piece starts off with a haunting, visceral bassoon solo, its melody taken from an Eastern European folk song, and quickly goes into a violently dissonant, but ruthlessly precise exercise that inspires, if not the scene that Stravinsky imagined, surely a morbid, chaotic image. The insistent rhythms and repeated melodic motives of this work marked a new era. Stravinsky later worked in both neo-classical and twelve-tone styles, constantly developing his art in new ways. In 1939, Stravinsky came to America and settled in Hollywood, tired of European life and working on a commission for a *Symphony of Psalms*. His later works include the opera *The Rake's Progress* and the ballet *Agon*.

ADDITIONAL FACTS

1. At the premiere of The Rite of Spring*, hissing and booing erupted within the first minute, and after few more, a riot ensued, with audience members punching each other and screaming so loudly that the dancers could not hear the music and were forced to stop.*

2. Also present at the premiere of The Rite of Spring *were composers Claude Debussy and Maurice Ravel. While Debussy tried to calm the crowd, Ravel was shouting "Genius! Genius!" in admiration.*

3. The libretto for the late-stage opera The Rake's Progess *was written by poet W. H. Auden.*

Justice

The question of justice is one of the most important philosophical problems, and one with significant real-world applications. What is a just way to behave? What kinds of political institutions are just? And what does it even mean to be just?

Plato's *The Republic* was one of the first philosophical works to deal with this question. Plato concluded that a just society is one rigidly organized and ruled by wise kings who understand the true nature of the world.

Modern philosophers have come to very different conclusions. John Stuart Mill proposed a utilitarian theory of justice. According to Mill, a just set of institutions, or a just society, is one that maximizes the well-being of its citizens. For instance, a utilitarian defense of punishing criminals would be: Punishing criminals is just because it makes others less willing to do wrong, and thus leads to less overall wrongdoing.

John Rawls was another philosopher with a famous theory of how to measure justice. Rawls asked us to imagine a hypothetical situation in which human beings do not yet have a government and are choosing their own political system. To ensure that the system they choose is just, he argued, they should have to make their decisions from behind a veil of ignorance. What this means is that they must agree to a set of institutions and laws without knowing what share of wealth, talent, and status they will have under the new system. This procedure will ensure that the institutions will be rationally acceptable to a person who knows he or she might turn out to be the least-powerful person in the system. Rawls argued that a truly just political arrangement is one that could have been chosen by rational agents from behind this veil of ignorance.

ADDITIONAL FACT

1. *Perhaps the most famous critique of Rawls's theory of justice was by his Harvard colleague Robert Nozick. In his book* Anarchy State and Utopia, *Nozick argued that theories such as Rawls's would lead to systematic violations of individual rights.*

Taoism

Taoism is one of China's ancient spiritual traditions. Today it is viewed as both a philosophy and a religion. People who see it as a religion view taoism's most important contributor, Laozi, to be a god.

Taoism emerged during the philosophically fertile period in China known as the Hundred Schools of Thought, which lasted from approximately 700–200 BC. It gained momentum during the Han dynasty and solidified into its current form during the fifth century AD.

Laozi, taoism's founder, was said to be a contemporary of Confucius and served a Chinese emperor as the keeper of the Imperial Library. According to legend, at the end of his life, Laozi left the Chinese court and traveled west. As he reached the last gate of the Chinese Empire, he encountered a guard already familiar with his great teachings. The guard asked Laozi to record his thoughts before leaving China, and Laozi did so, writing the Tao Te Ching—the Book of *Tao and Virtue*.

Aside from Laozi, taoism also traces its roots to the Yellow Emperor, Huang-Di, and taoism is sometimes known as Huang-Lao philosophy. Taoism also considers one of Laozi's disciples, Zhuangzi, to be a very influential teacher.

The *Tao Te Ching* is a short book, comprising only 5,000 words. However, it lays out the entire taoist philosophy. Tao, or "the way," is believed to be present in everything that exists in the world. It is seen as the continuity behind life's ever-changing forces.

Taoism calls for a reunification with tao. Taoists believe that the world has become overrun with conflict and that by reuniting with tao, we can achieve harmony. Taoism advocates both self-cultivation and social transformation.

For the self, it suggests spontaneity, a healthy lifestyle including breathing exercises, and the minimization of desires. Taoists do not believe in an afterlife, emphasizing the importance of being peaceful and harmonious in this life. Socially, taoism suggests minimizing government intervention and warfare. Unlike Confucianism, which relies upon society, taoism suggests that a solitary life is a sufficient existence.

ADDITIONAL FACTS

1. *Taoism was officially suppressed during Mao Zedong's rule of communist China, and now the largest concentration of taoists live in Taiwan.*

2. *Feng shui and tai chi are both taoist practices.*

Manhattan Project

In August of 1939, the famous scientist Albert Einstein wrote a short letter to Franklin D. Roosevelt, the president of the United States, expressing his deepest fear that Nazi Germany might develop an atomic bomb out of uranium. The effects of such a bomb in the hands of the Nazis, Einstein told the president, would be unimaginable. "A single bomb of this type, carried by boat and exploded in a port," he wrote, "might very well destroy the whole port together with some of the surrounding territory." As the news from Europe turned increasingly ominous that summer on the eve of War World II, at his adopted home in leafy Princeton, New Jersey, Einstein was increasingly despondent.

Einstein's letter was meant as a warning to Roosevelt, but it had an unintended consequence. If Nazi Germany could develop such a terrifying weapon, Roosevelt decided, the United States had better get one itself first. Before the United States even entered the war in 1941, the American government had started a program to study uranium's military potential. After Pearl Harbor, this program grew into the Manhattan Project. After years of study at a remote site in New Mexico, a team of Allied scientists finally perfected an atomic weapon in 1945.

At its busiest point during the war, the Manhattan Project brought together hundreds of the world's top scientists. Such a gathering of great scientific minds has never been matched. Like Einstein, many of the scientists were themselves refugees from Nazi-occupied Europe. Altogether, the US government spent the equivalent of about $20 billion on the bomb.

The bomb's use against the Japanese cities of Hiroshima and Nagasaki in 1945 destroyed the two major industrial centers crucial to the Japanese war effort and killed 120,000 civilians. The bomb was intended to force the Japanese to surrender, and it did. Days after the bombing of Nagasaki, Japan chose to give up. The bomb's use in 1945 remains controversial. At the time, many American generals, including Dwight D. Eisenhower, felt using the bomb was unnecessary and would tarnish America's reputation. Others felt dropping the bomb would hasten the end of the war. Einstein himself, the man whose discoveries had made the bomb feasible, was horrified. After the war, he said he regretted warning FDR of the atom's terrible powers.

ADDITIONAL FACTS

1. *The first successful nuclear chain reaction took place in downtown Chicago in 1942, in a squash court under the bleachers of the football stadium at the University of Chicago.*

2. *One of the British scientists who worked on the Manhattan Project in New Mexico, Klaus Fuchs, later admitted to spying for the Soviet Union. Partially aided by details pilfered by Fuchs and other spies, the Soviets tested their first atomic weapon in 1949.*

"I, Too, Sing America"

I, too, sing America.

I am the darker brother.
They send me to eat in the kitchen
When company comes,
But I laugh,
And eat well,
And grow strong.

Tomorrow,
I'll be at the table
When company comes.
Nobody'll dare
Say to me,
"Eat in the kitchen,"
Then.

Besides,
They'll see how beautiful I am
And be ashamed—

I, too, am America.

Langston Hughes's "I, Too, Sing America" (1926) is one of the great poems of the Harlem Renaissance, the resurgence of African-American cultural awareness and artistic productivity that occurred during the 1920s. In just a few elegant lines of free verse, Hughes expresses both the sad reality of blacks' second-class status in American society and his own confident optimism for the future.

"I, Too, Sing America" is a direct response to Walt Whitman's poem "I Hear America Singing" (1881). Whitman had written about the glorious cacophony of different voices that make up America—the mechanic, the carpenter, the mother, and so on. Hughes, in his poem, contends that one major voice has been forgotten and that Whitman's song is thus incomplete.

The power of Hughes's poem stems from its minimal, direct language. The narrator begins with the bold declaration, "I, too, sing America," set into its own stanza for emphasis, followed by a proud, unadorned assertion of his identity—"I am the darker brother." He describes how he is denied a place at the American "table," an extended metaphor in which "eat[ing] in the kitchen" stands for all types of segregation and unequal opportunity.

But the narrator displays virtually no resentment or anger. Rather, he laughs off the slights against him and brims with confidence that he is strong and beautiful regardless of the denigration he has endured. Moreover, he is certain that his own strength and achievement will inevitably cause the rest of America to come to its senses. The last line brings the poem full circle, repeating the opening with a slight but important change: the narrator asserts, "I, too, am America," convinced that he will someday be considered a true part of the nation in which he lives, an equal partner in both its freedoms and its responsibilities.

ADDITIONAL FACT
1. Hughes was launched to fame in 1921, when his first major poem, *"The Negro Speaks of Rivers,"* was published in the NAACP's Crisis magazine.

American Gothic

American Gothic by Grant Wood (1891–1942) is one of the most widely known works of American art. Although the painting is often viewed as a satire of middle America, it was not intended to be so by its creator.

Wood spent the first ten years of his life on a farm in Iowa. After studying art in Minneapolis, Chicago, and Paris, he returned to his home state where he applied his talent to paint the world of his youth.

In August 1930, Wood came across a nineteenth century house in Eldon, Iowa, built in a style known as carpenter Gothic. Imagining a farmer and his daughter standing before their home, he made a rapid sketch on brown paper and took some photos.

Woods reworked the composition at home, using his sister Nan as the model for the girl, and a Cedar Rapids dentist, Dr. Byron McKeeby, for the farmer. Drawing inspiration from Victorian photographs and nineteenth century portraits, he transformed the dentist into a protective father and Nan into the old man's plain-faced, unmarried daughter. Both wear austere clothing typical of the Victorian era. Wood provided the farmer with a pitchfork in order to suggest an earlier period, when such agricultural implements were still being used. Its prongs complement the window frames of the house, and its rounded bottom repeats the oval of the two faces. The immobile, stony expressions of the characters recall those seen in early photographs, when long exposure times forced subjects to remain still for up to five minutes.

Wood finished the painting just in time to enter it in a competition at the Art Institute of Chicago. Much to his surprise, the painting won a bronze medal and a $300 prize. Today it hangs permanently at the Institute.

ADDITIONAL FACTS

1. The pitchfork has been interpreted as a symbol of masculinity, the devil, and farming.

2. The house in the painting has drawn blinds and closed windows, a detail that seems to emphasize the hostility and phobic attitude of the couple.

3. In 1934, Wood was appointed state director of the New Deal's Public Works of Art Project. He later joined the faculty at the University of Iowa.

The Prisoner's Dilemma

Two criminals are arrested for a robbery, and the police don't have enough evidence to convict them. They separate the two suspects and make them the same offer. If they both confess, they will both serve two years. If one of them confesses, but the other one stays silent, the confessor will go free and the silent partner will serve ten years in prison. However, if neither one of them says a word—if they trust each other—they will both serve only six months. Neither one knows what the other is going to do. Is it better to hold your tongue or squeal? This hypothetical situation is known as the prisoner's dilemma, and it was first proposed by mathematician Albert W. Tucker. It has important implications for game theory, economics, evolution, and psychology.

The Prisoner's Dilemma	Prisoner B Remains Silent	Prisoner B Confesses
Prisoner A Remains Silent	They both serve six months.	Prisoner B walks free; Prisoner A serves 10 years.
Prisoner A Confesses	Prisoner A walks free; Prisoner B serves 10 years.	They both serve two years.

The rational choice for prisoner A seems to be to betray his partner and confess. The outcomes are better. But, prisoner A knows that prisoner B will probably think the same way. They will both wind up serving two years. Of course, if they could only trust each other, they would only serve six months.

In 1980, political scientist Robert Axelrod performed an experiment he called the iterated prisoner's dilemma. Essentially, participants played the prisoner's dilemma over and over again, sometimes with the same partners and sometimes with different partners. Players were allowed to use information from past encounters. Some people developed greedy strategies tending toward betrayal, and some players developed altruistic strategies tending toward trust. Over long periods of time, the altruistic players faired better than the greedy players. The nice guys finished first.

ADDITIONAL FACTS

1. Two countries in an arms race are often thought to be playing out prisoner's dilemma. They can both spend a lot of time and money increasing their arsenal in order to keep pace with each other, or they can agree to disarm. But how can they know for certain that the other country isn't still bulking up in secret?

2. Males in the animal kingdom often exhibit behavior that fits the pattern of the prisoner's dilemma. Do you just strut your stuff, back down, or engage in the cock fight? The best strategies in the animal kingdom seem to encompass a little of each approach.

Aaron Copland

It's a testament to the low status of American classical music among Europeans that its premiere composer for almost forty years was not taken seriously by anyone but Americans. Born in New York City, Aaron Copland (1900–1990) traveled to Paris to study when he was twenty-one. He studied keyboard harmony and composition with the brilliant Nadia Boulanger, and four years later he returned to New York to see the premier of his *Symphony for Organ and Orchestra* (1925) at Carnegie Hall.

After his debut, Copland immediately started composing pieces heavily influenced by American jazz—the *Piano Concerto* of 1926 and the *Piano Variations* of 1930—a style that was just entering the mainstream, but still considered a bit dangerous. Copland also studied the works of Igor Stravinsky, but assimilated the Russian's neoclassical tendencies rather than his more revolutionary ideas.

Later in his career, Copland turned to the music of traditional America, including the bluegrass and Appalachian music being played by string bands. He combined these styles with the prevailing pop sensibilities of the day, as embodied by Tin Pan Alley and Broadway, and stories drawn from American folklore, to produce several charming ballets, including *Billy the Kid* (1938) and *Rodeo* (1942). His 1954 opera *The Tender Land* is a beautifully and colorfully orchestrated treatment of American folk music, and his *Appalachian Spring* is one of the most durable pieces of American classical music ever produced.

Later in Copland's life, he was drawn to twelve-tone serialism, but very few of his works became popular, save for *Connotations*, which was commissioned for the opening of Lincoln Center in 1962. He remained active as a composer, teacher, and conductor through the 1980s until he died in late 1990 in Westchester County, New York.

ADDITIONAL FACTS

1. While composing The Tender Land, *Copland was subpoenaed to appear before the House Subcommittee for Investigation and forced to testify as one of the hundreds of artists labeled purveyors of communist propaganda by Senator Joseph McCarthy.*

2. Copland was also a composer of movie scores, including Of Mice and Men *(1938),* Our Town *(1940), and* The Heiress *(1948).*

3. The "Hoe Down" from Copland's ballet Rodeo *will forever be memorialized in the "Beef: It's what's for dinner" commercials of the early 1990s.*

Philosophy of Language

The philosophy of language tries to understand how language—sounds uttered by speakers and written marks on a page—can be used to make meaningful statements about the world. It has much in common with the field of linguistics.

In contemporary philosophy, the most important problem in the philosophy of language has been the problem of reference: How do names identify objects in the world and thereby have meaning?

Consider the following two sentences:
(1) "Superman is Superman."
(2) "Clark Kent is Superman."

If the meaning of a name is merely the thing it refers to, then both sentences mean the same thing. However, we can believe the first sentence is true and not the second. Therefore, the meaning of the name Superman is not merely the thing it refers to (Superman). According to this argument, the meaning or "semantic content" of a name has two parts: a *referent*, the thing it refers to, and a *sense*, a description of the object. Therefore, the sense of "Superman" might be "superhero who can leap tall buildings" while the sense of "Clark Kent" might be "lowest-paid reporter at the *Daily Planet*." In this example, the meanings of the names "Clark Kent" and "Superman" are different because they have different *senses*. Therefore, the second sentence doesn't necessarily strike us as true.

Some philosophers disagree with this analysis. They argue that the meaning of a name cannot carry a description. For instance, consider the sentence: "It is possible that Clark Kent is not the lowest-paid reporter at the *Daily Planet*." That sentence is true, because, after all, Clark/Superman might have chosen a different job when he moved to Metropolis. However, according to our first theory, the meaning of the name "Clark Kent" is the description: "lowest-paid reporter at the *Daily Planet*." So, we've just said: "It is possible that the lowest-paid reporter at the *Daily Planet* is not the lowest-paid reporter at the *Daily Planet*." This is obviously absurd and is why the debate over the meaning of names continues.

ADDITIONAL FACT
1. The distinction between sense and reference was first made by Gottlob Frege (1848–1925), a German mathematician whose work on language and logic is highly influential in contemporary philosophy.

Confucianism

K'ung Fu Tzu, better known as Confucius, lived from 551 to 479 BC. His philosophy is such an integral part of some East Asian cultures that it is seen as a way of life, and not a deity-based religion.

Although Confucius's legacy is revered today, during his own life, few of his teachings were respected. He traveled from kingdom to kingdom seeking employment, usually unsuccessfully.

Confucius believed the tao is the underlying force of the universe. The tao gives rise to the opposite but complementary forces of yin and yang, which are the source of the endless changes that the world endures.

Confucius's goal was to create a harmonious society that could withstand this constant change. He believed that although people were inherently good, those who were unenlightened, along with disorganized societies, caused evil to exist.

Confucius believed that each person had his or her own place in the world and that by cultivating individuals, he could improve society. He believed that one must begin with filial piety. This concept, at its heart, calls for a son to honor his father and ancestors.

From filial piety, Confucius laid out five relationships, each with a superior and an inferior partner, which he believed should be the model for all of society. The first, and most important, relationship was between father and son. This was followed by ruler-subject, husband-wife, older brother-younger brother, and friend-friend. If these relationships were properly honored, that is, the subordinate always respected the superior—Confucius believed society could reach the harmonious state once achieved by the ancient kings.

Confucius's teachings are largely taken from the *Analects of Confucius*. However, much of his original teachings are unknown because the Qin dynasty (221–207 BC) waged a campaign of suppression against Confucian works. Much of the Confucianism that exists today is actually neo-Confucianism, which was influenced by both taoist and Buddhist thought.

ADDITIONAL FACTS

1. *Confucius's five relationships have historically been incorporated into the Chinese legal system. If a crime violated the sanctity of one of the relationships—i.e., a son stole from a father—punishment was increased.*

2. *Confucius taught that leaders should be chosen for their intelligence and skill. This led to the first civil service examination system in the world, implemented in China in 165 BC.*

∽∾

Chairman Mao

Mao Zedong (1893–1976) was the ruler of communist China from 1949 until his death in 1976. Mao modernized his impoverished country, but at an enormous cost in human lives. By most estimates, tens of millions of Chinese died of starvation or were executed during Mao's tumultuous rule. Contemporary Chinese leaders have repudiated most of Mao's philosophy, but he remains a venerated figure as the man who united the most populous country on earth and ended centuries of humiliation at the hands of the West.

The son of a peasant farmer in rural China, Mao embraced communism along with many other young Chinese intellectuals in the 1920s. At the time, China was under threat from Imperial Japan but was too divided to resist the invaders. Mao was a schoolteacher, but he soon devoted all his energies to politics. From the late 1920s until the outbreak of World War II, the communist Red Army battled both the Japanese and other Chinese factions. As a guerilla leader in this period, Mao formulated the radical political philosophy that would become known as Maosim.

The Red Army finally emerged victorious, and the People's Republic of China was proclaimed in 1949 with Mao as its leader. Governing presented a new set of challenges for the communists. The results were often catastrophic. Mao's bungled 1958 attempt to increase China's industrial production, for instance, lead to as many as thirty million deaths. In 1966, Mao launched the so-called Cultural Revolution to root out capitalist and religious influences, which lead to hundreds of thousands of deaths and destroyed much of China's ancient heritage. Mao himself, though—dubbed Chairman Mao, the Great Helmsman—was practically worshipped by his followers.

In the West, Mao attracted many supporters from the left, and Maoism influenced several other guerilla movements, but most people were horrified by the brutality and destruction of his rule. Only after Mao's death did China begin to discard communist practices. A capitalist country in all but name, China built on the unity forged by Mao to become a great emerging world superpower.

ADDITIONAL FACTS

1. *During the Cold War, China initially sided with its fellow communists in the Soviet Union against the United States. However, Mao eventually grew suspicious of the USSR. Seeking closer ties to the United States, Mao invited President Richard Nixon to make his famous trip to Beijing in 1972.*

2. *During the Cultural Revolution, Chinese were forced to read a collection of Mao's quotations known as the* Little Red Book. *The book was distributed worldwide. Although the vast majority of its readers read it unwillingly, the* Little Red Book *is one of the most popular books in the world.*

3. *Mao's corpse, like Vladimir Lenin's, was embalmed and put on public display after his death. His marble mausoleum on Tiananmen Square in Beijing continues to draw thousands of visitors annually.*

"The Second Coming"

Turning and turning in the widening gyre
The falcon cannot hear the falconer;
Things fall apart; the centre cannot hold;
Mere anarchy is loosed upon the world,
The blood-dimmed tide is loosed, and everywhere
The ceremony of innocence is drowned;
The best lack all convictions, while the worst
Are full of passionate intensity.

Surely some revelation is at hand;
Surely the Second Coming is at hand.
The Second Coming! Hardly are those words out
When a vast image out of Spiritus Mundi
Troubles my sight: somewhere in sands of the desert
A shape with lion body and the head of a man,
A gaze blank and pitiless as the sun,
Is moving its slow thighs, while all about it
Reel shadows of the indignant desert birds.
The darkness drops again; but now I know
That twenty centuries of stony sleep
Were vexed to nightmare by a rocking cradle,
And what rough beast, its hour come round at last,
Slouches towards Bethlehem to be born?

"The Second Coming" (1920) by William Butler Yeats contains some of the most vivid imagery found in twentieth-century poetry. The work is actually quite atypical for Yeats, who is best known for his contributions to the Celtic revival movement—an attempt to preserve the culture of his native Ireland against English influence. But whereas much of Yeats's writing is heavily influenced by Gaelic folklore and mythology, "The Second Coming" is imbued with his fascination with the occult.

Yeats had a rather unique view of history that he believed he received in revelations from spirits. He conceived of history as a series of 2,000-year cycles of ascent and decline, which he referred to as gyres. In Yeats's view, the world's last rising gyre culminated with the birth of Jesus, which meant that the corresponding declining, or antithetical, gyre was due to reach its bottom sometime in the twentieth century. Having just lived through the horrors that World War I visited upon Europe, Yeats believed in 1920 that the Christian gyre was losing its hold on the world, and the end could not be far off.

"The Second Coming" is filled with images of chaos and evil. It begins with a dizzying visual of a falcon "turning and turning" in a spiral, unable to hear the call of its handler. Ominous visions pile up before the reader, culminating with the appearance of a sphinx-like beast that arises in the desert. In a perverse reversal of Christian mythology, the beast "slouches towards Bethlehem to be born." Although Yeats's precise intent is unknown, critics generally see the beast as representing the totalitarian systems of communism and fascism that arose in Europe following World War I.

ADDITIONAL FACTS

1. The titles of Chinua Achebe's Things Fall Apart (1958) and Joan Didion's Slouching Towards Bethlehem (1968) were both lifted from Yeats's poem.

2. Several lines in the poem refer indirectly to Percy Bysshe Shelley's play Prometheus Unbound (1820), which Yeats admired greatly.

Salvador Dalí

Salvador Dalí (1904–1989) combined refined, academic technique with wild flights of surrealist fantasy to produce some of the most provocative and outrageous art of the twentieth century.

Dalí was born in Catalonia, Spain, in 1904. In 1921, he registered at the Real Academia de Bellas Artes de San Fernando in Madrid, where he met the poet García Lorca and the filmmaker Luis Buñuel. Within two years, Dalí was expelled from the academy for inciting students to rebellion and claiming that his teachers were unqualified to judge his works.

In 1929, Dalí moved to Paris, where he joined the surrealist movement. Intrigued by the creative potential of paranoia, he developed what he called the paranoiac critical method. According to surrealist philosophy, paranoia was characterized by the ability to comprehend things from multiple perspectives, and it was therefore a means of destabilizing the world. By inducing it in himself, Dalí believed he could create more powerful art.

A classic work by Dalí is *The Persistence of Memory* (1931), a stark landscape in which a pocket watch melts over a distorted head. Nearby are two other melted watches, while a third is covered with crawling ants. The eerie scene alludes to time's distortion in a dream state.

In 1929, Dalí also worked on the Surrealist film *Un chien andalou* (An Andalusian Dog), one of two he made with Buñuel. That same year, he met Gala, who became his wife and muse for more than fifty years. One year later, he and Buñuel wrote and filmed *L'age d'or* (The Golden Age).

Over the years, Dalí continued to shock and fascinate the public. He was put on the cover of *Time* magazine in 1936, and he wrote a never-produced screenplay for the Marx Brothers in 1937. In the late 1930s, he was repudiated by the surrealists for his right-wing political views and avid pursuit of commercial success. In 1940, Dalí moved to the United States, where he lived until 1955. During his American stay Dalí was invited by Walt Disney to design a cartoon for *Fantasia*. His contribution was made public only in 2003 when a revised version of the classic was released. Dalí also created a dream sequence for Hitchcock's *Spellbound* (1945). Always craving attention, he appeared twice as the mystery guest on the popular 1950s television show, *What's My Line?*

Dalí spent the last years of his life in Spain. In 1984, he was seriously burned in a mysterious fire. He died five years later, leaving all of his fortune and art to the Spanish state. Today there are several museums dedicated exclusively to his works, including one in Saint Petersburg, Florida, and three in Spain.

ADDITIONAL FACT

1. *In May 1955, Dalí painted a paranoiac-critical version of Jan Vermeer's* Lacemaker *while sitting in the rhinoceros enclosure at the Vincennes Zoo near Paris.*

Factorials!

The symbol ! in mathematics is as much fun as it looks. It is a factorial. If you write $n!$ it is pronounced n factorial. The factorial of a number is the product of all the whole numbers greater than zero that are less than or equal to the number itself. For example the factorial of six looks like this:

$$6! = 6 \times 5 \times 4 \times 3 \times 2 \times 1 = 720.$$

And twelve factorial looks like this:

$$12! = 12 \times 11 \times 10 \times 9 \times 8 \times 7 \times 6 \times 5 \times 4 \times 3 \times 2 \times 1 = 479,001,600.$$

Factorials are very important in number theory, probability, and computer science. In everyday life, they can be used to find out the number of ways a distinct group of objects can be arranged in a sequence. For example, imagine you want to figure out how many different ways you could arrange six books on a shelf. For the first slot, you would have six books to choose from. For the second slot, you would have five books to choose from. For the third slot, you would have four books to choose from. For the fourth slot, three books. For the fifth slot, two books. And for the last slot, one book. To calculate the number of ways you could arrange the books, you would multiply:

$$6 \times 5 \times 4 \times 3 \times 2 \times 1 = 6! = 720.$$

Intriguingly, zero factorial is equal to one.

$$0! = 1$$

Why? Imagine for a moment trying to arrange zero objects on a shelf. How many different ways are there to do it? The answer is one.

ADDITIONAL FACTS

1. Mathematician Christian Kemp introduced the notation n! *in 1808.*

2. Factorials can also be used to find extremely large prime numbers.

3. There are other types of factorials in mathematics. There are multifactorials, hyperfactorials, superfactorials, and superduperfactorials.

Copland's *Appalachian Spring*

Copland's best-known work comes from what some people refer to as his "American Pastoral" period—which also includes the ballets *Rodeo* (1942) and *The Tender Land* (1954). *Appalachian Spring* (1940) started as a ballet written for the preeminent choreographer of the time, Martha Graham, but it later emerged as an orchestral suite, the form in which it is most often performed today.

In 1943, Copland was in Hollywood, working on the score for the movie *North Star* (1943), which was based on a story by Lillian Hellman. While there, he received a commission from the Elizabeth Sprague Coolidge Foundation of the Library of Congress for a new ballet to be performed by Martha Graham's dance company. The piece that Copland wrote was originally for a small chamber group, but he orchestrated it as a suite for a full orchestra later on. It is suffused with the spirit of American folk music, although the only tune actually used is the Shaker hymn, "Simple Gifts." In the section based on this tune, Copland takes a melody that very aptly expresses the plain, earnest nature of the Shaker lifestyle and uses it as the basis for variation. The result is a clear, accessible style that audiences and critics alike found wholly American. It quickly became a classic, to Copland's surprise.

The original story for the ballet is about a pair of newlyweds on the frontier somewhere near western Pennsylvania. The young couple celebrates their love, and together they build their house. At the same time, a revivalist and his congregation shout in exultation, and a pioneer woman follows her dreams to the promised land. The ballet is fraught with biblical imagery and wholesome "breadbasket"-type themes.

ADDITIONAL FACTS

1. *Copland originally titled the piece "Ballet For Martha," a nondescript name he changed only a few weeks before the first performance. The name "Appalachian Spring" comes from a poem by Hart Crane.*

2. *Graham also collaborated with the other most "American" composer of the century, George Gershwin.*

3. *Though the bulk of the ballet was written in California and Mexico, Copland didn't complete it until he moved to Cambridge, Massachusetts, to start a teaching job at Harvard.*

Bertrand Russell

Bertrand Russell (1872–1970) was a founder of analytic philosophy. Born in 1872 to an aristocratic British family, he was orphaned at ten. Upon the death of his brother in 1931, he became the third Earl of Russell and is therefore sometimes referred to as Lord Russell.

Beginning in 1890, Russell was associated with Trinity College, Cambridge, first as a student, and later as a teacher. He split with the college in 1916 over his involvement in anti-World War I protests, activities that led to his imprisonment in 1918 for five months. While at Trinity, Russell did some of his most important philosophical work and also mentored both Ludwig Wittgenstein and the American poet T. S. Eliot. Russell's expulsion from Trinity effectively ended his academic career, and for the next several decades he made a living writing, which he did prolifically. Some of Russell's most famous and popular works are *Why I Am Not a Christian*, *Marriage and Morals* (a critique of the institution of marriage), *Problems of Philosophy* and *A History of Western Philosophy*.

Russell developed analytic philosophy along with G. E. Moore. Russell was an important proponent of logicism—the view that all mathematical concepts could be defined using the vocabulary of logic, and that all mathematical truths could be derived from these definitions, using the laws of logic. Russell's labors in logic and mathematics culminated in the book he coauthored with Alfred North Whitehead, *Principa Mathematica*.

Russell also made major contributions to metaphysics, philosophical analysis, the philosophy of language, epistemology, and the philosophy of science. He was awarded the Nobel Prize in Literature in 1950, one of very few philosophers ever to receive that honor.

Russell was an outspoken critic of the war in Vietnam, and he died in 1970.

ADDITIONAL FACTS

1. One of Russell's most lasting contributions in the philosophy of language is his theory of definite descriptions. A definite description is a phrase such as "the King of France" in sentences such as "The King of France is bald." In his classic paper, "On Denoting," Russell showed how to analyze proper names as definite descriptions.

2. Russell discovered a formal inconsistency in Gottlob Frege's logical system, known as Russell's paradox. Upon learning of this inconsistency, Frege felt, incorrectly, that his life's work had been for naught.

Shinto

Shinto is the indigenous religion of Japan, inextricably imbedded in that country's culture.

Shinto originated between 300 and 600 AD. It holds that the most important deity is Amaterasu, usually translated as sun goddess, whose descendents unified Japan. According to legend, this goddess's parents, Izanagi and Izanami, gave birth to the islands of Japan. All people are believed to have descended from Izanagi and Izanami, but the emperor is said to be a descendant of Amaterasu herself. It is through the sun goddess that the emperor was believed to have received his power and right to rule.

Aside from the sun goddess, followers of Shinto believe in many other gods, known as kami, who are said to reside in nature. As a result, nature and its preservation are of extreme importance to Shinto. In addition, respect for one's family and participation in various cleanliness rituals are also integral to practicing the faith.

Four denominations of Shinto have existed in Japan. The first is Shrine Shinto, the most common type still found today. In this type of Shinto, worshippers congregate and pray at shrines.

Sect Shinto describes thirteen groups who worship in meeting halls. These different sects formed during the nineteenth century and incorporate other belief systems such as mountain worship, which focuses on Mount Fuji, and Confucianism.

Folk Shinto incorporates many folk beliefs such as divination and shamanistic healing. It is far less organized than the other traditions.

Lastly, State Shinto, which no longer exists, was the official state religion of Japan before World War II. This religion demanded complete devotion to the emperor during the Meiji dynasty and also tried to eliminate Confucian and Buddhist influences.

ADDITIONAL FACTS

1. Today, most Japanese follow a combination of Zen Buddhism and Shrine Shinto.

2. State Shinto's emphasis on loyalty to the emperor led to the Japanese suicide plane attacks, known as kamikaze, during World War II.

Brown vs. Board of Education

The pivotal 1954 Supreme Court decision Brown vs. Board of Education ended racial segregation in American public schools and helped spark the civil rights movement that established full legal rights for African-Americans. Historians consider the case, which involved the school system in Topeka, Kansas, and several other cities, to be among the most important decisions ever handed down by the court.

Prior to the Brown decision, black Americans in the South and other parts of the United States were denied full equality with whites. Not only did black children attend separate schools, but blacks were expected to ride in the back of buses, eat at different lunch counters, and even use separate bathrooms. This system of official discrimination was known as Jim Crow. The Supreme Court had upheld segregation in the 1896 case of Plessy vs. Ferguson. In that decision, the court ruled that as long as the facilities reserved for blacks weren't tangibly inferior, then segregation was allowed under the constitution.

The plaintiffs in the Brown case, however, argued that separate was inherently unequal. The court sided with the black families, unanimously overturning its own 1896 ruling in Plessy. Chief Justice Earl Warren, who wrote the landmark opinion, held that "in the field of public education the doctrine of 'separate but equal' has no place."

The decision, which forced public schools across the South to integrate, met with stiff resistance from many whites. In 1957, President D. Dwight Eisenhower was forced to send the US Army into Arkansas to protect the first nine black students who attended the white high school in Little Rock.

However, the decision also galvanized support for the nascent civil rights movement. After Brown, African-American civil rights leaders such as Rosa Parks and Martin Luther King Jr. successfully campaigned to overturn remaining Jim Crow laws in the South. The civil rights movement culminated with the Civil Rights Act of 1964 and the Voting Rights Act of 1965, federal legislation signed by President Lyndon Johnson that forbade job discrimination against blacks and outlawed practices that had been used in the South for generations to prevent blacks from voting.

ADDITIONAL FACTS

1. *The head NAACP lawyer who argued the Brown case was Thurgood Marshall, who would go on to become the first African-American Supreme Court justice in 1967.*

2. *The case took its name from Oliver Brown, one of the thirteen black parents who sued the Topeka school system in 1951 because his eight-year-old daughter had been forced to attend a segregated elementary school. That school, the Monroe School, eventually closed in 1975 and was declared a National Historic Site in 1992 by President George Bush.*

3. *President Harry Truman integrated the US military in 1948—against the intense opposition of many fellow Southern Democrats—in one of the first federal efforts against segregation.*

∝

Magic Realism

Magic realism has a long tradition in both Western and non-Western literature. Still, only in the twentieth century has it come to be considered as a discrete genre. Although the term *magic realism* is often associated exclusively with Latin American literature—perhaps because it was first popularized in a literary context by Cuban novelist Alejo Carpentier—it can be found in works of authors from other regions as well.

German artist Franz Roh first used the term *magic realism* in 1925, to describe an emerging visual art movement that depicted the world realistically but had surreal or dreamlike qualities at the same time. The term has roughly the same meaning when used in reference to literature: Literary works of magic realism depict the world in detailed, authentic fashion but weave supernatural or magical events and situations seamlessly into these otherwise realistic narratives. An important characteristic of the genre is the fact that characters do not perceive these supernatural events as unusual or out of the ordinary; rather, they witness them dispassionately, without amazement or awe.

The author most responsible for bringing magic realism to worldwide notice is Colombia novelist Gabriel García Márquez. Works such as *One Hundred Years of Solitude* (1967) and *Love in the Time of Cholera* (1985) exemplify the genre, mixing vivid, carnal, and often bloody supernatural events into the characters' everyday lives. Often, these otherworldly events are steeped in elements of local folklore. Many come in the form of signs from nature, such as a torrential flood that occurs on the day of a character's funeral.

Other prominent works of Latin American magic realism include Isabel Allende's *The House of the Spirits* (1982), Laura Esquivel's *Like Water for Chocolate* (1989), and Jorge Amado's *The War of the Saints* (1988), along with Jorge Luis Borges's short stories. But many authors outside Latin America have displayed elements of magic realism in their stories and novels, from Salman Rushdie's *Midnight's Children* (1981) to Toni Morrison's *Beloved* (1987) to Haruki Murakami's *The Wind-Up Bird Chronicle* (1995).

ADDITIONAL FACTS

1. *García Márquez said that his most important task as a writer was "destroying the lines of demarcation that separate what seems real from what seems fantastic."*

2. *Magic realism is often considered to be a manifestation of postmodernism, the literary sensibility that emerged from the 1940s onward.*

3. *Magic realism is not the same as fantasy or science fiction. Works of these genres take place in alternate realities, worlds, or futures, whereas works of magic realism are set firmly in the real world.*

Jackson Pollock

Jackson Pollock (1912–1956) is best known for his "drip" paintings. He produced them by pouring, splashing, and dripping paint onto huge canvases—a method he labeled action painting. Claiming that works of art should be appreciated as independent objects in their own right rather than as representations of some extraneous subject, Pollock insisted that his paintings were about nothing; they were painting in its purest, most autonomous form.

Pollock was born in Cody, Wyoming, the fifth and youngest son of Stella May McClure and LeRoy Pollock. He spent his childhood in California and Arizona, and he was introduced to modern art while attending Manual Arts High School in Los Angeles.

In 1929, Pollock moved to New York City, where he enrolled in the Art Students League and studied with the regionalist painter Thomas Hart Benton. Pollock's early works show the influence of Albert Pinkham Ryder and the Mexican muralists José Clemente Orozco and David Alfaro Siqueiros. During the Depression, Pollock lived in poverty until 1935, when he was employed by the WPA Federal Art Project. In 1937, Pollock underwent psychiatric treatment for alcoholism. While in therapy, his drawings were analyzed by therapists, who introduced their patient to Jungian psychology. Thereafter Pollock became obsessed with dream symbolism and the unconscious.

In 1945, Pollock married the artist Lee Krasner. The couple moved to East Hampton, Long Island, where, two years later, Pollock created his first drip painting, *Full Fathom Five*. Although seemingly random, drip paintings were created with great care and deliberation. After laying an uncut canvas on the floor, Pollock splattered paint on it with sticks, turkey basters, and heavily loaded brushes. Carefully lifting the canvas, he allowed the paint to flow further, until he had achieved a balanced composition. When the paint dried, he cut the canvas and framed it.

In action painting Pollock discovered a method through which he could create pure painting with no reference to anything outside of itself. In order to clarify his intention, he began giving the works numbers instead of titles so that viewers would focus on the paint rather than on the subject. To Pollock, the physical act of painting was as important as the finished product. In this respect, he was an important forerunner of artists who engaged in performance art and the happenings of the 1950s and 1960s.

In 1951, Pollock began drinking heavily once again. As his health and stamina declined, he struggled to maintain his foothold in the art world. In the summer of 1956, Pollock drove into a tree and was killed instantly.

The Normal Curve

The normal curve describes the pattern of distribution for certain sets of statistics. For example, height and intelligence test scores often fit nicely onto a normal curve. The curve has the shape of a bell, so it is also frequently called the bell curve.

In a normal curve, the central values—the mean, median, and mode—are all the same. That means the average score (mean) equals the middle score (median) and also equals the most common score (mode). For example, in the normal distribution of height for American women, the average height is 5'5". There are just as many women who are taller than 5'5" as are shorter than 5'5". And the most common height for American women is 5'5".

Normal curves include information about variance and standard deviation, which describe how widely or closely values are dispersed around a central value. For example, say a group of children is given a test. Some of them fail; others make Ds, Cs, Bs, and As, although the average score is a C. In a second test, the children mostly make Cs, and the average score is a C. The first test is said to have high variance, while the second test has low variance.

Standard deviations are a measure of variance. On the normal curve, 68 percent of the values are within one standard deviation of the mean, 95 percent are within two standard deviations of the mean, and 99.7 percent are within three standard deviations. This is known as the empirical rule, and it is often simply stated 68-95-99.7. In IQ scores, a score of 100 is the central value—mean, median, and mode. A score of 145 is three standard deviations from the mean, and a score of 65 is also three standard deviations from the mean. This means that for every 2,000 people, 3 people would have a score higher than 145 and 3 people would have a score lower than 65.

ADDITIONAL FACTS

1. The normal curve was first conceived by Abraham de Moivre in 1733.

2. The normal curve is also often called the Gaussian curve after Carl Friedrich Gauss. He did not invent it, though he did discover many of its properties. His face was on the 10 deutschmark bill.

3. Blood pressure in adults is also distributed along the path of the bell curve.

4. The variation of light intensity from a single source is also distributed normally.

The Bridge between Classical and Pop: George Gershwin and Leonard Bernstein

The two composers responsible for the classical world's embrace of jazz and pop styles were both lifelong New Yorkers and heroes of the Broadway stage.

Brooklynite George Gershwin (1898–1937) started out as a Tin Pan Alley songwriter in the style of Irving Berlin, composing and selling comic, jazzy, pop songs. In 1924, he teamed up with his brother Ira to compose *Lady Be Good!* and thus began one of the most fruitful composing teams ever, producing *Strike Up The Band* (1927) and the opera *Porgy and Bess* (1935), among many others. Gershwin also wrote many notable orchestral works, including the jazzy and colorful piano tours de force, *Rhapsody in Blue* (1924) and *Piano Concerto in F* (1925). He died young, of brain cancer, in 1937.

Raised on a steady diet of music from his childhood in Lawrence, Massachusetts, Leonard Bernstein (1918–1990) was a disciple of the famous conductor Fritz Reiner at the prestigious Curtis Institute of Music in Philadelphia. After working for various orchestras, Bernstein became director of the New York Philharmonic in 1958, a post he held for eleven years.

Bernstein was undeniably versatile. Much of his work is intensely passionate, like the *Symphony No. 1 "Jeremiah"* (1941), inspired by his own Jewish heritage, and the solemn *Chichester Psalms* (1965), a setting of psalm verses in Hebrew written for the rededication of the war-destroyed Chichester Cathedral in England. Bernstein also succeeded with pop-inspired works like the score for *On the Waterfront* (1954), the Broadway musical *On the Town* (1944), and his brilliant adaptation of Voltaire's *Candide* (1956).

Bernstein's most famous piece is the Broadway musical *West Side Story* (1957), an adaptation of Shakespeare's *Romeo and Juliet* set in 1950s New York. The work is highly influenced by the jazz rhythms of the mambo, the rhumba, and other Latin-American dances that Bernstein heard in the barrios of New York City.

ADDITIONAL FACTS

1. *Bernstein got a job as assistant director of the New York Philharmonic after substitute-conducting for Bruno Walter on November 14, 1943. The performance happened to be broadcast nationally and thus made a lasting impression.*

2. *Gershwin never had time to write parts for his most famous work for piano and orchestra,* Rhapsody in Blue. *It was orchestrated by composer Ferde Grofé.*

3. *A fixture on the New York and national music scenes, Bernstein was an energetic promoter of the young Aaron Copland and the disregarded Gustav Mahler.*

Ludwig Wittgenstein

Ludwig Wittgenstein (1889–1951) was born in 1889 in Vienna, Austria, to a wealthy family. On the advice of Gottlob Frege (1848–1925), he went to Cambridge University, where he studied the foundations of mathematics with Bertrand Russell (1872–1970). When World War I broke out, Wittgenstein returned to Austria to serve in the army. In the trenches of the war, and later in a prisoner of war camp, Wittgenstein wrote his first book, the *Tractatus Logico-Philosophicus* (1921). After the armistice, Wittgenstein returned to England where he taught philosophy at Cambridge, composing manuscripts that became his second and final book, *Philosophical Investigations* (1953), which was published posthumously.

Wittgenstein's first book, *Tractatus Logico-Philosophicus* ("Logico-Philosophical Treatise") was a series of numbered propositions. He claimed that language has a certain logical structure, and this structure mirrors the structure of the world. Wittgenstein distinguished what a proposition says from what it shows. Propositions say that the world is a particular way, but they show us, in their organization, what the world's structure is. Logic is about the structure of propositions. It does not say anything, but it shows us what the structure of language and the world is. Wittgenstein concluded that most philosophical problems spring from the misguided attempt to say what can only be shown. He argued that philosophers encounter problems when they attempt to say the world has a certain structure, rather than just making that structure apparent through logic.

In his later work, *Philosophical Investigations*, Wittgenstein elaborated on why he believed philosophy was misguided. He believed philosophical problems arise from confusion about language. He argued difficulties arise only when we use words in nonstandard ways or we ignore the variety of ways in which they can be used. He wrote, "Philosophy is a battle against the bewitchment of our intelligence by means of language." Thus, Wittgenstein advocated a therapeutic conception of philosophy, in which the point is to clarify the meaning of language.

ADDITIONAL FACTS

1. *Wittgenstein concludes the* Tractatus *with the cryptic remark, "What we cannot speak about, we must pass over in silence."*

2. *Wittgenstein, Martin Heidegger, and Adolf Hitler were all born in 1889.*

Sikhism

Sikhism was founded in fifteenth century India by Guru Nanak, who had a revelation that there was a single, ever-mindful God, when he was thirty-eight years old. This deity was named Ek Onkar. Guru Nanak preached that people should display their love for Ek Onkar in everyday life, rather than through superstition and ritual.

At the core of the Sikh faith is a deep belief that all people are equal, a rejection of the prevailing caste system. This was exemplified by their kindness to lepers, who were believed by most to be sinners reaping divine punishment. The Sikhs, not believing that God was vindictive, set up an area where lepers could receive treatment.

Guru Nanak was succeeded by a line of nine additional gurus, each of whom spread Sikhism through parts of India and Arabia. Despite their importance, the gurus refused to be worshipped as deities, insisting they were only repeating the word of God. The last guru, Guru Gobind Singh, died in 1708. He was replaced by a text, which is now recognized as the Eternal Guru and is the scripture of Sikhism.

This scripture is called the Guru Granth Sahib. It consists of not only the teachings of the ten gurus, but also contains hymns from the Muslim and Hindu faiths. It was written in Sanskrit, Persian, Hindi, and Punjabi. During worship, the passages of this scripture are usually sung or chanted.

Sikhs believe that time is cyclical and that their souls are caught in a pattern of birth, death, and rebirth. The cycle is fueled by the self-centeredness of humans—their ego, anger, greed, attachment, and lust. If humans can rid themselves of this self-centeredness and achieve enlightenment, they can break the cycle. However, this enlightenment is believed to be given by the grace of God, and not, necessarily the result of one's own actions.

Sikhs are forbidden to consume tobacco and alcohol, commit adultery, or cut any hair on their body. They also must always wear the five symbols of Sikhism: a turban covering their hair, a comb, a steel bracelet, a short sword, and a type of knickers (usually as undergarments).

ADDITIONAL FACTS

1. There are twenty-one million Sikhs in the world today.

2. The majority of Sikh men have the surname Singh—meaning "lion"—while the majority of Sikh women have the surname Kaur—meaning "princess." This helped eliminate distinctions between classes, which, in Hindu culture, were evident from people's last names.

Nelson Mandela

"I have fought against white domination, and I have fought against black domination. I have cherished the ideal of a democratic and free society in which all persons live together in harmony and with equal opportunities. It is an ideal which I hope to live for and to achieve. But if needs be, it is an ideal for which I am prepared to die."

—*Nelson Mandela, on trial for treason in 1964*

In 1964, Nelson Mandela (1918–) was convicted of treason against his country, South Africa. Narrowly escaping the death penalty, the forty-six-year-old lawyer was instead sentenced to life in prison on an island near Cape Town. Mandela's crime had been to organize resistance against South Africa's racist laws known collectively as apartheid. Apartheid, meaning "apartness," denied black South Africans—three-fourths of the country's population—many political rights, keeping them legally inferior to the white minority.

Prison was intended to break Mandela's spirit. He was forced to do hard labor in a quarry, allowed only one visitor every year, and never allowed to turn off the light in his tiny cell. Because Mandela's political party, the African National Congress (ANC), had endorsed violence in resisting apartheid, the South African government considered Mandela a terrorist. The ruling South African whites, descendents of Dutch and British settlers who had migrated to South Africa since the seventeenth century, imposed apartheid in order to maintain their grip on power in the country.

Mandela, however, refused to bend. He continued to lead the ANC from inside the prison's walls. His steady determination won the respect of even his wardens. Outside prison, Mandela became a hero to millions of blacks in South Africa and elsewhere, focusing the world's attention on the injustices of apartheid. In 1990, under international pressure, South Africa's white-dominated government finally abolished apartheid and released Mandela from prison. He was awarded the Nobel Peace Prize in 1993 and elected president of South Africa after the country's first multiracial elections in 1994.

After Mandela's election, he invited one of his white former jailers from the island to his birthday party. The old warden told a PBS filmmaker: "I was very proud that one of my prisoners ... became my leader." One of the world's most respected statesmen, Mandela retired from the presidency in 1998.

ADDITIONAL FACTS

1. *Under apartheid, a system akin to segregation in the southern United States before the 1960s, race was the determining factor in the everyday lives of South Africans. Interracial marriage and sex were banned, and everything from beaches to hospitals were segregated.*

2. *In protest of apartheid, the International Olympic Committee banned South Africa from the games in 1964. South African athletes did not compete again until the Barcelona Olympics in 1992.*

"Ode on a Grecian Urn"

Thou still unravished bride of quietness,
Thou foster-child of silence and slow time,
Sylvan historian, who canst thus express
A flowery tale more sweetly than our rhyme:
What leaf-fringed legend haunts about thy shape
Of deities and mortals, or of both,
In Tempe or the dales of Arcady?
What men or gods are these? What maidens loth?
What mad pursuit? What struggle to escape?
What pipes and timbrels? What wild ecstasy?

O Attic shape! Fair attitude! with brede
Of marble men and maidens overwrought,
With forest branches and the trodden weed;
Thou, silent form, dost tease us out of thought
As doth eternity: Cold Pastoral!
When old age shall this generation waste,
Thou shalt remain, in midst of other woe
Than ours, a friend to man, to whom thou say'st
"Beauty is truth, truth beauty,"—that is all
Ye know on earth, and all ye need to know.

Among the English romantic poets of the early nineteenth century, John Keats (1795–1821) is an enduring favorite. His most famous poem, "Ode on a Grecian Urn" (1819), remains an object of fascination for readers and critics alike, who still dispute the subtle meanings of its key passages. In a way, this ongoing debate is a fitting fate for the poem, which itself expresses wonder about the stories frozen in time on a Greek vase.

Throughout "Ode on a Grecian Urn," the poet's words are aimed at the vase itself. This technique of addressing a concept or inanimate object directly, called apostrophe, is a staple of Keats's poetry in general and his odes in particular. The poet is captivated by the vase both as an object of aesthetic beauty and as a thought-provoking symbol, a sliver of permanence in a world of transience and change.

In the first of the poem's five stanzas (only the first and last of which are reproduced above), the poet characterizes the urn as an embodiment of the ages themselves, calling it an unspoiled "bride of quietness" and a "foster-child of silence and slow time." He marvels at the images painted on the vase, eager to know the stories behind them: "What men or gods are these? What maidens loath? / What mad pursuit? What struggle to escape?" But this mystery and uncertainty only adds to the images' appeal; as the poet says in the second stanza, "Heard melodies are sweet, but those unheard / Are sweeter." Likewise, he envies the vase's two lovers, whose images are frozen eternally on the verge of embrace: "[T]hough thou hast not thy bliss, / For ever wilt thou love, and she be fair!"

Few lines in poetry have come under as much scrutiny as the final two of "Ode on a Grecian Urn." It is clear that the vase itself addresses the poet with the words "Beauty is truth, truth beauty," which are themselves a cipher. But because of uncertainty about the punctuation in Keats's original written manuscript, it is unclear whether the last thirteen words of the poem are spoken by the urn or by the poet himself—a timeless mystery fitting for a poem about timeless mystery.

ADDITIONAL FACT

1. *Although many have wondered whether Keats's poem is based on a specific vase, scholars have generally concluded that it is not.*

Pop Art

The term *Pop art* was first used by British art critic Lawrence Alloway to describe the work of the Independent Group—an association of artists who were opposed to the pretentiousness and affectation of the art world. Creating works modeled upon popular advertisements, comic strips, cheap products, and mass media, they sought to celebrate and parody consumer culture.

Alloway defined Pop art as popular, transient, expendable, low cost, mass-produced, and oriented toward youth and big business. These terms characterize the works of Richard Hamilton, whose work, *Just what is it that makes today's home so different, so appealing?* features a muscular man carrying a giant Tootsie Pop.

The origins of the movement can be traced back to the 1920s, when a group of artists who referred to themselves as Dada derided the pomposity of high culture. Their leader, Marcel Duchamp, earned notoriety by painting Mona Lisa with a moustache and transforming a mass-produced urinal into a sculpture by inverting it.

Pop art developed independently in the United States, where it was represented by major American artists, such as Jasper Johns, Robert Rauschenberg, and Larry Rivers. Many Pop artists adopted easily recognizable styles—trademarks that granted their work a commercial quality. Roy Lichtenstein, for example, produced paintings that resembled giant comic strips, imitating the field of dots used in real comics. Claes Oldenburg created huge sculptures of mass-produced household objects such as clothespins, lipsticks, and typewriter erasers. Duane Hanson made sculptures so life-like that when placed in museums they could be mistaken for visitors. Andy Warhol mechanically mass-produced images of celebrities, such as Marilyn Monroe and Chairman Mao, and Campbell's Soup cans—thereby reducing human beings to the level of consumer products.

Whereas British Pop artists tended either to mock or glorify popular culture, their American counterparts were more inclined toward ambiguous images. Warhol's silk screens of car wrecks and the Kennedy assassination are both tragic and commercial. The ultimate aim of both groups, however, was to demonstrate that capitalism had desecrated art by transforming it into just one more object of consumption.

ADDITIONAL FACT

1. *The Pop art movement is sometimes referred to as the "new realism" or neo-Dadaism.*

Nuclear Fission

In nuclear fission, an atom's nucleus—the dense center made of protons and neutrons—splits into fragments. The fragments have less combined mass than the original atom. But the mass is not lost. It is converted into energy according to Einstein's equation $E=mc^2$, which means the energy released is equal to the "missing" mass times the speed of light squared. Even though only about one-thousandth of the mass is converted, this translates to incredible amounts of energy. The amount of energy contained in nuclear fuel is roughly one million times the amount of energy contained in a similar amount of chemical fuel, such as gasoline.

Fission can happen spontaneously, or it can happen when a free neutron hits the nucleus of a heavy atom. After the neutron hits the nucleus, it splits into two or three smaller atoms and two or three more neutrons. These neutrons can then proceed to bombard other atoms, causing a nuclear chain reaction. It only takes 1 millisecond for fission to take place. This means that if you start with one free neutron, after ten milliseconds, you can create about 10,000 neutrons and 10,000 reactions. This is called a runaway reaction, and it is the basis for nuclear bombs. Nuclear power plants control nuclear chain reactions and prevent them from running away.

Uranium-235 is the most common type of nuclear fuel. It is a rare form of uranium with 92 protons and 143 neutrons (92 + 143 = 235). Natural uranium is .72 percent U-235 and 99.27 percent U-238, a more stable form of uranium with 92 proton and 146 neutrons that will not undergo fission. Natural uranium has too little U-235 in it to be used in power plants. Even if you bombard it with neutrons, the neutrons have trouble finding the sensitive nuclei of U-235. They are too scattered. Furthermore, even if you are lucky enough to hit a few sensitive nuclei that undergo fission, there are too few neutrons released to start a chain reaction. To be used in a power plant, natural uranium has to be enriched by very complex means to 2.5–3.5 percent U-235. To be used in a bomb, uranium is enriched up to 90 percent U-235.

ADDITIONAL FACTS

1. *Power from more than 400 nuclear power plants worldwide provides 17 percent of the energy used by humans. The US has more than one hundred nuclear power plants, and France gets 75 percent of its energy from nuclear power.*

2. *In nature, uranium is found in uranium oxide. After it has been purified, it has a rich yellow color. They call it "yellowcake."*

3. *The two fission bombs the United States dropped over Japan in August 1945 were Little Boy and Fat Man.*

Twentieth Century Music

With the advent of the mid-twentieth century came a host of composers whose works challenged the very essence of Western art music. One main development was that of electronic music made through the use of tape loops, synthesizers, and computers.

Parisian Edgard Varèse (1883–1965) came to America in 1915, and within his lifetime he revolutionized modern music. A student of science and math, he is credited as being the father of electronic music. His early works show a fascination with percussion but only begin to escape the conventions of European orchestral music. Later in his career, after years of frustration, Varèse experimented with mixing and creating synthetic sound using labs provided by the Philips Company. Unfortunately, technological limitations prevented him from reaching his full potential.

John Cage (1918–1992), a student of Arnold Schoenberg, started as an experimental atonal composer and later began to blur the lines between music and conceptual art. He invented instruments such as the prepared piano—a grand piano with various percussive objects stuck between the strings. He incorporated Zen and other Eastern philosophies into his music. In the piece *Music of Changes* (1951), Cage flipped a coin to determine the types of variations he would play.

Steve Reich (1936–) is a descendant of Varèse in his fascination with percussion and electronics. His *Drumming* (1971) elaborates on a simple percussion rhythm for more than an hour. More recently, he has begun using melody and harmony, and his *Different Trains* (1988), for string quartet and tape, won a Grammy for the best new composition.

ADDITIONAL FACTS

1. Varèse's 1931 piece Ionisation *was written for thirty-seven percussion instruments and a blaring siren.*

2. Rock band Pink Floyd's 1969 album Ummagamma *supposedly contains a spoken voice saying the words, "Can you dig it Varèse?" a reference to the composer, whom they idolized.*

3. Cage once wrote a piece called "4'33," which consisted of his sitting at a piano playing "silent notes," or rather, not playing anything at all. He explained the piece saying, "If something is boring after two minutes, try it for four. If still boring, then eight. Then sixteen. Then thirty-two. Eventually one discovers that it is not boring at all."

⤜⤚

Moral Relativism

Different cultures have widely different moral standards and often contrasting views about what is morally permissible. Does this mean that there are no objective moral standards?

Moral relativism is the view that there is no objective truth concerning what is right and what is wrong. All we can do is judge if an action is right or wrong against one of various standards. The fact that there is a diversity of moral opinion does not necessarily mean moral relativism is a correct view. For instance, there may be a diversity of opinion about the world's physical characteristics, but that doesn't mean all scientific systems are equally valid. The scientific methods of some cultures may simply be inaccurate.

To defend their position, there are two strategies the moral relativist can pursue. The first is to argue that moral relativism best explains moral diversity. They might ask, given that there are different moral standards, what explains why the person with the correct moral view came to hold the correct beliefs, while the person with the false beliefs got it wrong?

The second defense of moral relativism is to argue directly that there is no such thing as an objective moral fact. Objective moral facts require objective moral properties—"goodness" and "badness." However, being good is not a physical property, because morally good acts often don't share any physical properties. Therefore, the moral relativist concludes, there aren't any objective moral properties, despite what we ordinarily think.

ADDITIONAL FACTS

1. Moral relativism has few defenders among contemporary philosophers.

2. Philosopher Gilbert Harman (1938–) is the most influential contemporary moral relativist.

Zoroastrianism

Zoroastrianism is the world's oldest monotheistic religion, founded between the eighteenth and fifteenth centuries BC. Its founder was Zoroaster, also sometimes known as Zarathustra, a wealthy man who lived in Persia, or modern-day Iran.

Zoroaster was a priest in the local polytheistic religion when, at the age of thirty, he had a revelation. He was visited by an angel who told him that there was one God, Ahura Mazda, who was responsible for good and evil. (Zoroastrianism is also sometimes known as Mazdaism, named after this deity.) Ahura Mazda was said to be nine times the size of a man. He was attempting to create a perfect world and enlisted both angels and humans in this task. He emphasized the importance of keeping the natural world—its air, water, and land—pure.

After his revelation, Zoroaster began to spread the teachings of Ahura Mazda. Zoroaster wrote five Gathas, songs and poems now considered to be a central part of Zoroastrianism's scriptures. The complete scriptures, called the Avesta, consist of the five Gathas, as well as the Hapatan Haiti, written by Zoroaster's disciples.

Although Zoroastrianism remains a world religion today, no one followed Zoroaster for the first ten years after his revelation. The practice has always attracted only a small following. Because of this, Zoroastrianism has always stressed tolerance toward other faiths, as well as an emphasis on understanding different religions.

In addition to being the first monotheistic religion, Zoroastrianism was the first religion to believe in a heaven, hell, and final judgment, during which Ahura Mazda determined each person's fate.

ADDITIONAL FACTS

1. *Today, the largest population of Zoroastrians, known as Parsees, live in India and Pakistan and number approximately 60,000. Roughly, 28,000 remain in Iran with another 37,500 in Europe and North America.*

2. *Zoroaster's description of hell is quite frightening. According to legend, there is a pit within a dark, narrow crevice. There is a horrible smell and such a feeling of loneliness that three days feels like nine thousand years.*

3. *Zoroastrians worship in fire temples. This is somewhat misleading as the fire itself is not worshipped, but it is instead seen as a symbol of purity.*

CONGRATULATIONS on completing your year-long journey through *The Know-It-All Book*. We hope that this volume has been a source of growth and refreshment. And, we hope it is only the beginning . . .

Continue to carve out a slice of each day for reading and quiet contemplation. There is no better way to stimulate the mind and invigorate the spirit.

For a variety of resources to help you maintain a daily habit of learning, please visit www.theintellectualdevotional.com.

If you are reading this in 2008, please turn over for your special bonus entry.

—David S. Kidder and Noah D. Oppenheim

Leap Year

The common year is made up of 365 days. However, the solar year, or the time in which it takes to complete one orbit around the sun is more like 365¼ days. In order to keep the seasons in unison with the calendar one day is added to February every four years. This is called a leap year.

It took time to arrive at this state of affairs. The ancient Roman calendar had only 355 days in the year, with an additional 22-day month added every so often in order to correct seasonal change. Julius Caesar recognised that a more mathematical approach was required and so in 46BC, as Pontius Maximus, he oversaw the introduction of the Julian calendar. This incorporated the leap year, the seven-day week (borrowed from the Hebrews) and the 12-month rule (an Egyptian innovation).

But Caesar hadn't entirely solved our calendar woes. The truth is that the solar year is not quite 365¼ days. It's 365.242375. That's a difference of approximately eleven minutes, which over the course of 125 years amounts to just over one day. This so alarmed Pope Gregory XIII that in 1582 he postulated that Easter and Christmas would eventually fall on the same day. And so, through divine intervention, and some rather complicated calculations (carried out by the Neopolitan doctor Aloysius Lilius), the calendar was tweaked again.

What we are left with is the Gregorian calendar, adopted by most countries today. It stipulates that a leap year is divisible by four, unless it is divisible by 100 and not by 400. Hence 1600, 2000 and 2400 are leap years but 1700, 1800 and 1900 are not. The cancelled leap year that is brought back every four centuries means that we will only run half-a-day behind in 4000 years. Even for Know-It-Alls, that's not something to think about right now.

ADDITIONAL FACTS

1. *Old English law did not recognise February 29th as a legal date. Anything occurring on February 29th would be referred to as February 28th, thus ignored or 'leaped' over.*

2. *Traditionally women can make a marriage proposal to a man on February 29th or any time during a leap year. Custom dictates that if he turns the proposal down he must give a kiss and silk gown in recompense.*

Index

Image Credits

© Bettmann/Corbis: pages 9, 13, 61, 80, 196, 219, 233

© Stefano Bianchetti/Corbis: page 139

© Burstein Collection/Corbis: page 290

© Hulton-Deutsch Collection/Corbis: page 170

© Corel: pages 17, 262

© Eclecti Collections: page 192

© The Bridgeman Art Library/Getty Images: pages 20, 36, 43, 57, 76, 93, 101,

115, 143, 157, 227, 255, 318

© Hulton Archive/Getty Images: pages 125, 130, 199, 202, 234, 332

© Photodisc/Getty Images: page 85

© Time & Life Pictures/Getty Images: pages 237, 353

© Image Club: pages 66, 73, 87, 108, 122

© David S. Kidder: pages 2, 10, 12, 75, 96, 105, 123, 124, 138, 160, 173,

188, 194, 201, 208, 214, 222, 236, 243, 256, 257, 258, 265, 272, 277, 278,

285, 292, 294, 300, 312, 319, 334, 341, 349, 356

Library of Congress/Prints and Photographs Division, Abdul-Hamid II

Collection, LC-USZ62-82161: page 31

Library of Congress/Prints and Photographs Division, Carl Van Vechten

Photographs, LC-DIG-ppmsca-10445: page 72

Library of Congress/Prints and Photographs Division, Carl Van Vechten

Photographs, LC-USZ62-116608: page 346

Library of Congress/Prints and Photographs Division, Detroit Publishing

Company Photograph Collection, LC-D416-591: page 220